D0208419

Margaret Mead

"The one I liked best is Margaret Mead."

Mead cartoon by Ed Fisher, *Saturday Review* magazine, June 7, 1958.

Margaret Mead

The Making of an American Icon

NANCY C. LUTKEHAUS

PRINCETON UNIVERSITY PRESS
PRINCETON AND OXFORD

Published by Princeton University Press, 41 William Street,
Princeton, New Jersey 08540
In the United Kingdom: Princeton University Press, 6 Oxford Street,
Woodstock, Oxfordshire OX20 1TW

Library of Congress Cataloging-in-Publication Data

Lutkehaus, Nancy C.
Margaret Mead : the making of an American icon / Nancy C. Lutkehaus.
p. cm.
Includes bibliographical references and index.
ISBN 978-0-691-00941-4 (cloth : alk. paper)
1. Mead, Margaret, 1901–1978. 2. Women anthropologists—
United States—Biography. I. Title.
GN21.M36L87 2008
301.092—dc22
[B]
2008001570

British Library Cataloging-in-Publication Data is available

This book has been composed in Sabon text with Caxton Book display

Printed on acid-free paper. ∞

press.princeton.edu

Printed in the United States of America

1 3 5 7 9 10 8 6 4 2

To Jim and James
With thanks for their patience and their love

CONTENTS

ILLUSTRATIONS

PREFACE

This book has had a long gestation. Not only did I have the idea for it over a decade ago,[1] its inception dates back even further to 1972 when, as an undergraduate at Barnard College, I went to work for Margaret Mead at the American Museum of Natural History. I had encountered her even earlier as a child when I read *People and Places*, a book she had written for children that described anthropology and what archaeologists and anthropologists do.[2] Reading about Eskimos living in the icy expanse of northern Canada and Ashanti children growing up in the tropical heat of West Africa was a welcome escape from the summer doldrums of life in 1960s Midwest America.

Eventually, I rediscovered anthropology in college. I also learned at that time that Mead employed students; I was hired to be her "administrative assistant," thereby entering the ranks of a large cadre of young women and men who have worked for her over the course of her lengthy career at the museum.[3] The job entailed organizing her daily schedule, finalizing her speaking engagements (in conjunction with a speakers' bureau), and compiling her travel itineraries. It also meant that sometimes I ended up hemming her unraveled skirt while she waited for a taxi to take her to the airport, or that I was rudely awakened by a phone call from her at 5 a.m., wondering where some piece of work that she was ready to attend to was. Sometimes I was actually able to travel with her. Not just to her talk show appearances in New York City, but also to the United Nations Conference on the Environment in Stockholm, Sweden, and American Anthropology Association meetings where I had a chance to observe professional anthropologists in action.

Mead could be unpredictable and quixotic to work for (she was also highly organized and had a remarkable mind for details). When she was in the office, which varied considerably—sometimes she was traveling for several weeks or months at a time—there was always a great flurry of activity that kept her three office assistants on the run.[4] I remember one occasion near Christmas when she had been particularly overbearing and demanding; she expected us to address her Christmas cards in time to be delivered before the holiday. (Each year her Christmas card was a different black and white photograph. One year the card was a photo of her two-year-old granddaughter Vanni Kassarjian clanging toy cymbals together; another year it was a photograph of a New Guinea infant nestled safely in a *bilum*, the knotted net bags that New Guinea women use as baby carriers and to hold their garden produce.) This year the cards had come back late from the printer and we were rushing to get the envelopes addressed and off to the post office by the end of the day. Mead stormed out of the office (she was once described by a colleague as "the stormy petrel of anthropology," and this day she certainly fit that description) and we could hear her loud footsteps echoing down the empty hall. A few minutes later the telephone rang. Mead was on the line. "Girls," she said (her assistants were usually female—friends used to jokingly refer to us as "the Meadettes"), "I just want to warn you. I've discovered some mistletoe hanging from the ceiling in the entrance to the museum. Watch out when you leave tonight!" This bit of foolishness was her way of apologizing to us for her brusque behavior.

While working for Mead I decided that I wanted to become an anthropologist myself. When I started to take graduate courses in anthropology at Columbia University—where I continued to work for her as her teaching assistant[5]—I became acutely aware of the discrepancy between how the public viewed her and how many of her fellow anthropologists regarded her.

While the public couldn't get enough of her (especially in 1972 when she had just published her memoir, *Blackberry Winter: My Earlier Years*),[6] I soon realized how much she was disparaged and her work denigrated by some of her professional colleagues. My interest in understanding the dynamics of this gap—which at the time simply made me aware that in certain circumstances it was best not to announce that I worked for Mead—became a subject worthy of investigation when I began to teach anthropology. By this time, Mead had died, the Australia-based anthropologist Derek Freeman had published his infamous book *Margaret Mead and Samoa: The Making and Unmaking of an Anthropological Myth* that criticized Mead's Samoan research, and biographies and biographical films about Mead were beginning to appear. A plethora of different images and narratives about her circulated in the press and professional journals.

Teaching courses in visual anthropology at the University of Southern California also prompted me to think more critically about the constructed nature of ethnographic and documentary films, films that purported to be representing reality.[7] I had been asked to be a consultant for two documentary films about Mead—*Margaret Mead, Taking Note*, directed by television journalist Ann Peck for PBS, and *Margaret Mead: An Observer Observed*, produced and directed by Rutgers historian Virginia Yans—and had begun to think about the constructed nature of these, and other, visual portrayals of Mead's life.[8]

The late 1980s and early 1990s were also a moment in the history of anthropology when ethnographic representations—the written descriptions of other cultures that anthropologists produced based upon their fieldwork—were coming under attack.[9] The whole notion of representation, whether visual or verbal, was the subject of intense scrutiny and debate. Thus, I became increasingly interested in analyzing the various ways that different individuals described Mead for different audiences.[10]

I have written about the paradox of the disjuncture between Mead's public acclaim and her ambivalent professional reputation—what I have called her "liminal position" within anthropology—elsewhere.[11] This book represents my analysis of Mead as a cultural icon. More specifically, it is an analysis of the role of anthropology in twentieth-century America as seen through the lens of Mead's celebrity and her role as a public intellectual. Although I do not dwell upon the theoretical or anthropological dimensions of my study of Mead and her relationship with the media in any detail, it is inherently anthropological. This is true in three regards. First, in that the study of fame, and its closely related cousin, celebrity, can be regarded as the study of a particular social practice, one that individuals endow with cultural meaning. Fame, like power, entails a social relationship, directly between individual fans and "the famous" and indirectly as mediated through agents, producers, and the mass media. Second, fame is culturally and historically specific—who becomes famous at any given time, and for what reasons, is fundamentally a cultural question. Third, the study of Mead as a cultural icon is a symbolic study of the meanings associated with her that transcend or go beyond Mead. This latter dimension of Mead's fame is of particular interest. What was her cultural significance to the American public at different points in time? And what is her significance today? Finally, what does the iconization of Mead tell us about twentieth-century American society, and anthropology's place in it?

ACKNOWLEDGMENTS

In writing this book I have been as much a historian as an anthropologist, spending more time in archives—the traditional haunt of historians—than "in the field," although the time I spent in my early twenties working for Margaret Mead in her office tower at the American Museum of Natural History was a form of participant observation. Thus the American Museum of Natural History was both a field site and an invaluable source of print and visual material about Mead. It is fitting that visits to that museum were the first and last I made with regard to archival material for this book, and I would like to thank the librarians there for their help. The bulk of my research utilized the extensive collection of material housed in the Margaret Mead Archives at the Library of Congress. I regret that I cannot celebrate the completion of this book with the late Mary Wolfskill, the archivist in the library's Manuscript Division who first catalogued the Mead collection. Mary not only generously shared her wealth of knowledge about the archive but also graciously assisted me when, eight months pregnant, I spent hours photocopying material from the archives.

I also want to thank the helpful archivists and librarians at Vassar College's Archives and Special Collections, where I consulted the Ruth Fulton Benedict Papers; the Oral History Project at Columbia University, where I read the revealing interviews with Sey Chassler, Mead's editor at *Redbook* magazine, as well as psychologists Otto Klineberg and Abram Kardiner; the British Library of Political and Economic Sciences at the London School of Economics, where I read correspondence between Margaret Mead and anthropologist Bronislaw Malinowski; the Special Collections and Manuscripts at Cambridge University and the Archives of the University of Sydney where I read correspondence between Margaret Mead and Camilla Wedgwood; and the Bentley Historical Library at the University of Michigan, where I read correspondence between Mead and anthropologists such as Leslie White, who had once written to Mead asking her advice on how to reach a larger audience with his anthropological writings. And special thanks to Jane Barnwell, archivist at the Pacific Collection, University of Hawaii, for providing me with information about Musa-shiya, the Shirtmaker.

My work on Mead has benefited from my involvement with a large circle of scholars who have written about her. I had the good fortune to meet Jane Howard, author of *Margaret Mead: A Life*, the first extensive biography of Mead, in New York while she was working on her book. Subsequently, after her untimely death, I also have benefited from the wealth of material she collected for her book that is available to scholars in the Rare Book and Manuscript Library at Columbia University. Particular thanks are due to Mead's daughter, Mary Catherine Bateson, who throughout the writing of this book has always been helpful in answering my queries. My colleague at the University of Southern California, historian Lois Banner, who has written an extensively researched study of Mead and her close circle of friends, lovers, and colleagues, generously shared her manuscript with me before it was published. I also want to thank Margaret M. Caffrey and Patricia A. Francis for sharing with me the volume of Mead's letters, *To Cherish the Life of the World*, they recently edited. I have also found the comments and work about Mead by anthropologists Ira Bashkow, Lise Dobrin, Deborah Gewertz, Maureen Molloy, Nancy McDowell, Paul Roscoe, Paul Shankman, Gerald Sullivan, Eric Silverman, Sharon Tiffany, and Kamala Visweswaran presented at the meetings of the Association for Social Anthropology in Oceania and the American Anthropological Association to be particularly helpful, and I thank Gerald Sullivan and Sharon Tiffany for inviting me to be a discussant at their session on Mead at the 2005 meetings of the Association for Social Anthropology in Oceania. I also want to thank Lois Banner and Dolores Janiewski for inviting me to contribute a chapter on Mead to *Reading Benedict, Reading Mead: Feminism, Race, and Imperial Vision*. Thanks are also due to my colleague Alexander Moore; to Chauncey Olinger, the editor of *World Apart*; to Ray McDermott who kindly shared with me his article about Mead and education before it was published; to Robert Foster for sending me his unpublished paper about Mead and *Redbook* magazine; and to Alfred Kinsey's assistant, Paul Gebhard, an anthropologist by training, who agreed to talk with me by phone.

For reading all or portions of the manuscript—as well as for their intellectual camaraderie during the years our Narrative Group met—I thank anthropologists Janet Hoskins, Cheryl Mattingly, Linda Garro, Gelya Frank, Elinor Ochs, and Candace Goodwin. I also thank anthropologists Rena Lederman and Ann Stoler for their insights and support over the years that this project has grown from a glimmer of an idea to completion.

My thanks, too, to those friends here in Los Angeles and elsewhere—especially Abigail Adler, Judith and Eileen Blumenthal, Diana Hines, Dana Polan, and Ella Taylor—who read and commented on portions of the manuscript. I also want to thank Claudia Pott and Peter Sherman, who generously opened their home to me on numerous occasions when I visited the Library of Congress in Washington, DC, as did Eileen Blumenthal, Laurel Kendall and Homer Williams, and Ann Stoler and Larry Hirschfeld when I did research in New York City. I would also like to thank photographer Ken Heyman, director Craig Gilbert, and producer Perry Wolff for allowing me to interview them while in New York.

I owe a special debt of gratitude to the School of American Research (now the School of Advanced Research) in Santa Fe, where this book first began—to Douglas Schwartz, the former director of the school, my fellow scholars-in-residence during 1997–98—especially Ross Hassig—as well as other friends and colleagues in Santa Fe, for their insightful comments on various stages of this project.

Over the years, portions of this book were presented to audiences at Vassar College, the University of New Mexico, the University of Rochester, Barnard College, the New York Academy of Sciences, the University of Southern California, and the annual meetings of the American Anthropological Association, where I benefited from the probing questions and helpful suggestions of colleagues and interested listeners.

My thanks to Erica Angert, Sarah Blake, Scott Frank, Patricia Gilson, Sadie Moore, Charley Scull, Meredith Schulte, and Jody Valentine for their research assistance, and to USC College and the Center for Visual Anthropology for research support, leave, and subvention of the book's illustrations.

I would also like to thank Mary Murrell, formerly at Princeton University Press, for having initially contacted me about this project, and Fred Appel, who, having inherited it, has shepherded the book to completion. I especially appreciated the helpful comments and suggestions made by the two anonymous readers for Princeton University Press. Finally, I would like to thank my father for the diligence and enthusiasm with which he read the manuscript. It was a delight to be able to discuss it with him.

I have dedicated this book to the two people who have lived most closely with it along side me, as they came into my life just as I began to work on the project—my husband Jim, who has endured numerous conversations about Margaret Mead and read and reread various drafts of the book, and my son James, who has never known a time in his life when his mother was not working on "the Mead book." I want to thank Jim not only for his incredible editorial skills and critical insights, but foremost for his love and faith in me. In so many ways this book is so much better because of him.

INTRODUCTION

Mead as American Icon

. . . a man has as many social selves as there are individuals who recognize him and carry an image of him in their minds.
—William James, *The Principles of Psychology*[1]

Margaret Mead was the best-known, and most controversial, anthropologist in twentieth-century America. Born in 1901, Mead died in 1978, thus her life spanned the greater part of the period Henry Luce first referred to as "the American century." It is also the century in which the science of anthropology came to maturity. By the time of her death in 1978, Mead had become a media celebrity and an iconic figure who represented a range of different ideas, values, and beliefs to a broad spectrum of the American public—critics and supporters alike. For many she also came to symbolize the discipline of anthropology, as she was the only anthropologist they had ever heard of.

Her name as well as her image—that of a short (she was only 5 feet 2 inches), stocky, gray-haired woman often dressed in a flowing cape, wearing sensible low-heeled shoes, and carrying a forked walking stick—had become recognizable to a large portion of the American public through her many appearances on television talk shows and her monthly column in *Redbook* magazine. Since her death, fellow anthropologist Derek Freeman's allegation that Mead's conclusions about Samoan culture—first published in 1928 in her best-selling book *Coming of Age in Samoa*—were completely wrong precipitated a deluge of work both defending and condemning Mead and catapulted her name into the public arena once again.[2]

Numerous books have been written about Mead, popular biographies as well as detailed analytic studies of her ethnographic work by social scientists.[3] So, why another book about her? And why focus on Mead as an icon?

One answer is because Mead was more than simply someone who "became famous for being famous" (as Daniel Boorstin once described twentieth-century celebrity)[4]—although there is no doubt that later in life many people recognized Mead's name but had little idea of what she had actually done. In many respects Mead became what Ralph Waldo Emerson once called a "representative" figure, someone who has "a pictorial or representative quality and serves us in the intellect."[5] American popular culture is rife with representative figures such as George Washington, Thomas Jefferson, and Abraham Lincoln, or more recently Martin Luther King Jr., John F. Kennedy, and movie stars such Marilyn Monroe and John Wayne. Each of these individuals represents something more in American culture than simply their own personal achievements or the roles they played, either in American history or American movies. Like the culture heroes and mythic figures of other cultures whom anthropologists have traditionally studied, public figures like Mead serve our culture's need for heroes and heroines—persons we can imbue with larger-than-life expectations and embrace as symbols of cherished or new values—or as enemies of them.[6]

This book is neither a biography nor a hagiography of Mead. It does not present a detailed chronological account of Mead's life. Instead, it shares common goals with several other recent studies of American cultural icons such as Garry Wills's study of John Wayne, Paige Baty's analysis of Marilyn Monroe, Ronald Steel's investigation of the American public's "romance" with Robert Kennedy, and Larry McMurtry's essays about Buffalo Bill, Annie Oakley, and the beginnings of superstardom in America.[7] Like these studies, as well as others that deal specifically with the notion of icondom such as Wayne Koestenbaum's personal reverie about Jacqueline Onassis and Tina Brown's *The Diana Chronicles*; Carl Rollyson and Lisa Paddock's *Susan Sontag: The Making of an Icon*; and Brenda Silver's interpretation of the British literary icon, Virginia Woolf,[8] my aim is to understand what Margaret Mead came to represent to the American public and why she was embraced by so many people, to such a great extent that when she died *Time* magazine described her as "fond grandmother to the global village."[9] In short, this book is a study of the

Figure I.1 Garry Trudeau, Doonesbury cartoon, 1973. (Courtesy Universal Press Syndicate)

different images of Margaret Mead that have circulated in American popular culture during the twentieth century and the meanings ascribed to the different "social selves" individuals have attributed to her. By image I mean both visual and verbal representations that people (journalists, writers, advertisers, photographers, painters, scholars) have created of Mead and the responses to these representations by different segments of American society.

In her youth the press characterized Margaret Mead as having studied the "flapper of the South Seas" and promoted her best-selling book *Coming of Age in Samoa* as a description of Samoan youths' carefree lives of free love under the palms trees. By middle age her name appeared in crossword puzzles and cartoons in popular newspapers and middlebrow magazines, while the mature Mead was the subject of a grassroots movement to draft her as a candidate for president in 1971 as well as a frequent guest on late night television talk shows and a character in *Hair*, Broadway's first "tribal love rock musical." Posthumously, her image has appeared on everything from sugar packets to feminist heroine trading cards, at Disney's Epcot Center (one of five famous scientists), and on a U.S. postage stamp in a series that commemorates the 1920s. Today, the American Museum of Natural History includes her as one of its treasures, the only person in a list that includes fossilized dinosaur eggs, meteorites, and rare uncut emeralds.[10]

Even after she died her name made newspaper headlines as a result of philosopher Allan Bloom's critique of her in *The Closing of the American Mind* as exemplary of the worst of American liberalism and fellow anthropologist Derek Freeman's attack on the veracity of her Samoan research in *Coming of Age in Samoa*.[11] In the mid-1990s, she was even transmogrified by Australian playwright David Williamson into the misguided antagonist in *Heretic*, a play about the Mead-Freeman controversy that received rave reviews when it opened in Sydney.[12]

Mead remains an icon to this day, aided largely by the advent of the Internet. Her name and face can be found on numerous Web sites, especially those that list pithy quotes and humorous Meadisms.[13] One phrase in particular has captured people's imagination: "Never doubt that a small group of thoughtful committed citizens can change the world; indeed, it is the only thing that ever has."[14] As we will see, because this statement expresses core values that many Americans associate with themselves and with America—such as the importance of community and of grassroots initiative, along with the idea that individuals have the freedom to shape and change their own lives—Mead too has come to symbolize these values to a range of different groups and individuals.

Finally, at the end of the millennium and for the centenary celebration of Mead's birth in 2001, pundits, journalists, and scholars reassessed Mead's contributions to anthropology and to American society. While as a result of the brouhaha Derek Freeman caused over Mead's reputation, *Time* magazine evaluated her as an equivocal icon of twentieth-century American science, other individuals such as historian Susan Ware selected Mead unequivocally as one of seven outstanding popular heroines who helped to shape "the American century."[15] These contradictory assessments of Mead are typical of the diametrically opposite reactions she engendered throughout her life. And it is exactly these differing responses that make Mead such an intriguing and important subject of study in the development of twentieth-century American intellectual and cultural history.

Mead as Public Anthropologist

Although Margaret Mead's name is most commonly associated with the study of what used to be called *primitive* people—in large part because she first became known to the public through her books about Samoa and New Guinea—her role in American society as a public intellectual was based on her ability to apply anthropological data, methods, and insights to the elucidation of problems and issues Americans faced as they adjusted to the rapid changes of the twentieth century. Because of this latter role—that of social critic and commentator on contemporary American society—Mead became a media celebrity.

By the time she died, Mead had spent more time thinking, writing, and talking about American culture—crisscrossing the United States many times over giving public lectures and professional talks—than she had spent doing fieldwork in far-off places. But her perspective on American culture was firmly grounded in a cultural relativism that her early fieldwork in South Pacific cultures had afforded her, thus giving her a unique and timely vantage point. Mead brought to her role of social commentator a compelling and provocative combination: the knowledge of non-Western societies that afforded her new perspectives on human behavior coupled with her ability to use insights derived from these cultures to offer Americans new ways to think about their own society. As we will see, Mead developed this successful formula at the beginning of her career with the publication of her first book, *Coming of Age in Samoa*, and practiced it throughout her life. Underlying this strategy was her flair at communicating her insights in easily understood and entertaining prose—both in books and when speaking before an audience.

In 2005, Catherine Besterman and Hugh Gusterson, editors of *Why America's Top Pundits Are Wrong: Anthropologists Talk Back*, dedicated their volume to Margaret Mead and Franz Boas as "pioneers of public anthropology." Furthermore, they published the book "out of the conviction that it is time for anthropologists to reclaim Margaret Mead's legacy and find our voice as public intellectuals once more."[16]

One of the goals of this book is to elucidate the nature of that legacy—how and why Mead developed into a prominent public intellectual—and to show how Mead embodied and anticipated important developments in twenty-first-century anthropology, in particular the arena of what today is referred to as *public anthropology*. Different from applied anthropology—a subfield of anthropology that emerged after World War II as a result of the wartime activities of anthropologists such as Mead who had applied anthropological methods and insights to the solution of problems facing the United States government and its allies, such as morale building, the rationing of food, and such[17]—public anthropology is broader in scope and more activist in orientation. Its aim is to apply anthropological methods not only to projects sponsored by governmental or international organizations, but also to issues of concern to a wide range of social sectors, including those initiated by the subjects of research themselves. Moreover, public anthropologists aim to make the theoretical and descriptive insights of anthropology available in more accessible forms—the Internet, popular press, video and CDs, and so forth—and see their audience not only as government officials, administrators, or other experts and professionals, but also as the broader public.[18]

Mead was in the vanguard of this contemporary orientation. As a result of her research on children in Samoa and New Guinea, Mead became an expert on the lives of non-Western children and child development, sharing her expertise with professionals in the fields of psychology, early childhood development, and pediatrics. But she also wrote popular articles for *Parents* magazine, spoke at YWCAs and parents' associations, and was interviewed widely on the radio and in the popular press, because she had things to say about contemporary American children based on her insights. She was a founding member of SIPI (Scientists' Institute for Public Information), an organization dedicated to public outreach. In her seventies she was particularly concerned with issues of air quality, urbanization, and the potentially harmful effects of nuclear energy. She educated herself on these topics and spoke about them at congressional hearings and wrote about them in her column for *Redbook* magazine. Her perspective on these issues was global. Long before other Americans thought in global terms, Mead was concerned about the impact of Western technological developments on the world as a whole.[19]

An important premise of this book is that Mead became a media celebrity—indeed, a cultural icon—because of her skill at translating anthropological insights garnered from non-Western societies into meaningful and accessible critiques of American society. Moreover, she did so at a time when the United States was poised to take on a new role as world leader and in a manner—utilizing various forms of mass media that she engaged with humor and self-assurance—that afforded her a unique opportunity to have her voice heard as a public anthropologist.

Four Iconic Images of Mead

I focus on four categories of images that recur in media representations of Mead throughout her career and interpret what the various responses to them symbolize and tell us about American society. The categories are

Mead as Modern Woman, Mead as Anthropologist, Mead as Scientist, and Mead as Public Intellectual and Celebrity. These iconic images represent roles, values, and ideas that were important to various segments of American society at different points during the course of the twentieth century.

Each of the following chapters focuses on one of these four images of Mead and the historical contexts in which they appeared. Since in reality these images are never strictly separated one from the other, each image also contributes to and is inflected by the others. By the end of the book I hope to have shown how the density of these four categories of images combined and recombined to create a sense of Mead as bigger than life. This is how icons are created. One image upon another, the repetition of certain ideas, statements, and anecdotes about a person become both tropes and identifying characteristics; they are the stuff of caricature and iconization. Nor were these images static. It is significant that unlike the relatively unchanging meanings associated with the images of John Wayne or Marilyn Monroe, for example, as Mead grew older and times changed, the images of her—and their meanings—changed as well.

Mead as Cultural Icon

When *Time* magazine identified Margaret Mead as "an American icon" in 1999, what exactly did they mean?[20] And why have I chosen to use the term *icon*, especially since it has received much criticism because of its increased use in the 1990s by academics and journalists alike? Humorist Russell Baker has bemoaned the fact that "this lovely word, with its odor of incense . . . is now reduced to a pretentious way for depraved language butchers to speak of computer cartoons and entertainers and athletes once dismissed as 'heroes' or 'stars.' "[21] At the risk of sounding clichéd, I have chosen to use the term *cultural icon* to describe Mead precisely because of its use in popular discourse. William Safire has very helpfully identified three current uses of *icon*. The simplest is "a graphic representation of an idea" (the example he gives is computer icons). The second meaning is a "symbol, a sign that represents, or a token that stands for something else." The third meaning is an "idol." By this Safire means "a living idol, a superstar," and the related subset of "media celebrity, the famous famed for being famous."[22] Both Safire's second and third definitions express the sense in which the term has been used to refer to Mead.

Aspects of Mead's status as cultural icon are also similar to those Brenda Silver has identified for Virginia Woolf. Silver suggests that Woolf's elevation to the status of a "transgressive cultural icon" in the 1960s and "the contradictory often vehement, responses provoked by it," are the result of Woolf's location on the borders between high culture and popular culture.[23] Mead also has incited a range of contradictory responses, largely because she too occupies similar multiple, often-contradictory sites in our cultural discourses: American intellectual and best-selling author/media celebrity, innovative ethnographer and popularizer of anthropology, dedicated social scientist and outspoken social critic, bourgeois liberal and staunch Episcopalian, undeclared feminist and proponent of the family, professional career woman and champion of motherhood, a woman successful in a man's world, feminine and masculine, heterosexual and homosexual.

Her iconicity is the result in part of her ability to cross boundaries that usually separate an individual known primarily for her intellectual and scholarly contributions from the world of popular or mass culture. Mead's portrait at Disney's Epcot Center—where she symbolized science (and women scientists in particular)—or in an ad for the *Wall Street Journal* certainly represent the iconization of her image. The ad's creators assumed that readers would recognize Mead as an important intellectual, who not only used a computer (or would have, had personal computers been easily available in her lifetime), but who also relied on newspapers, in particular, the *Wall Street Journal*, for information. And, if Mead did, so should others. The ad used the fact that Mead's image and name had become associated with intelligence and expertise. At the very least, the ad's creators may have figured that even if people did not recognize Mead's image or name they would nonetheless assume that she was someone famous, knowledgeable, and important.

So too does the use of a photograph of Mead by the American Museum of Natural History in its catalogue of the museum's fifty greatest treasures. The photograph shows Mead in Bali smiling intently at a Balinese baby held in her mother's arms. As we will see, pictures like this reproduce the image of the maternal Mead, an image that speaks to her focus on the anthropological study of children and parents and also to the media's portrayal of her as "mother (and later, grandmother) to the world.[24]

To speak of Mead as an icon is neither to trivialize her achievements nor to dehumanize her by reducing her to a symbol, but rather to suggest

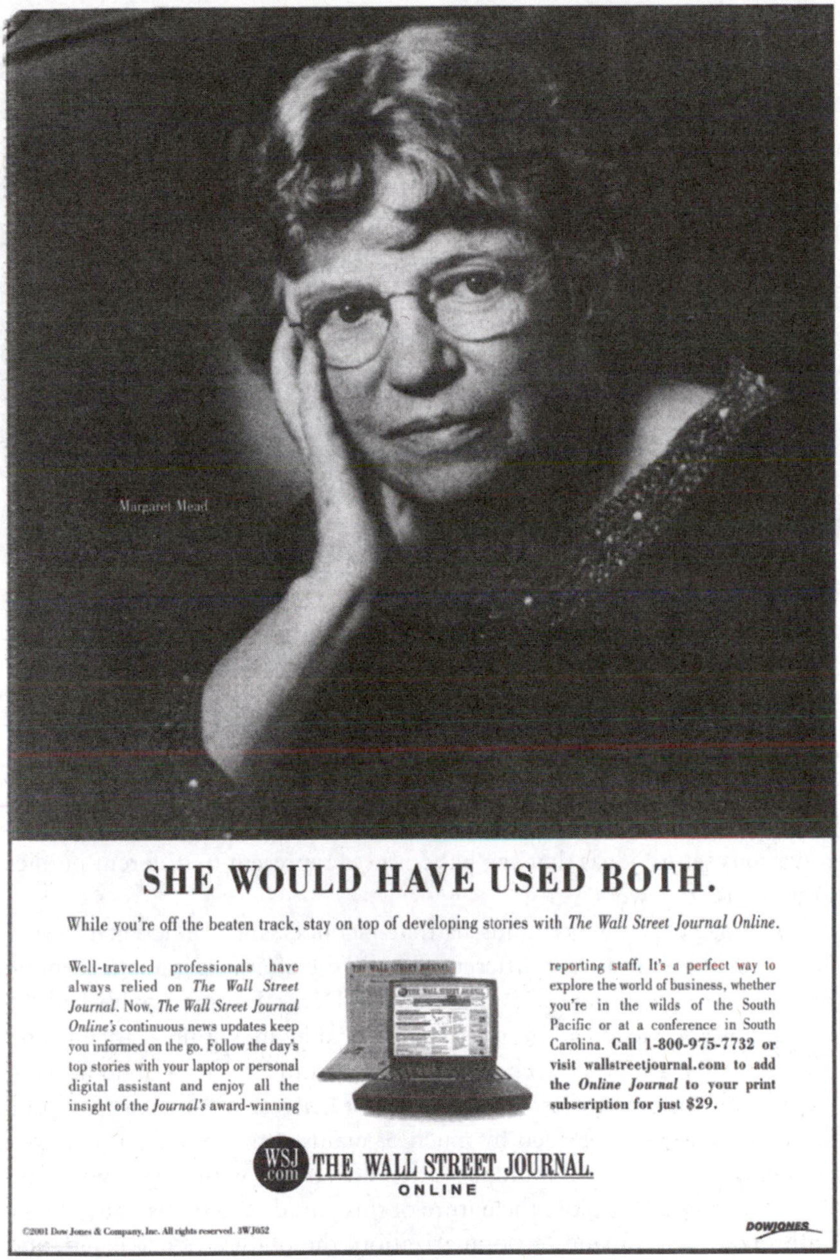

Margaret Mead

SHE WOULD HAVE USED BOTH.

While you're off the beaten track, stay on top of developing stories with *The Wall Street Journal Online*.

Well-traveled professionals have always relied on *The Wall Street Journal*. Now, *The Wall Street Journal Online's* continuous news updates keep you informed on the go. Follow the day's top stories with your laptop or personal digital assistant and enjoy all the insight of the *Journal's* award-winning

reporting staff. It's a perfect way to explore the world of business, whether you're in the wilds of the South Pacific or at a conference in South Carolina. **Call 1-800-975-7732 or visit wallstreetjournal.com to add the *Online Journal* to your print subscription for just $29.**

DOWJONES

Figure I.2 *Wall Street Journal* ad, 2001. (Courtesy Dow Jones and Company, Inc.)

Figure I.3 Frequently reproduced image of Mead peering at a Balinese baby, 1957. (Courtesy of Ken Heyman)

that she has achieved a particularly distinct role in American culture, that of a representative figure. As such over the course of her lifetime, as well as after her death, images of her have circulated in popular culture and scholarly arenas that function as referents to Mead the person and also to various sets of ideas that she has come to represent to different publics and different viewers.

Time magazine also reminds us that "iconoclasm is inherent in every icon, and heroes can wear different faces in the afterlives granted them by history and remembrance."[25] Long before Derek Freeman published his critique of her, Mead had been a controversial figure within academia and among the wider public. There was the paradox of her public acclaim versus some of her profession's dismissal of her work. Why was someone who was so highly regarded by much of mainstream American society—including presidents and pundits—often denigrated within her own or related disciplines? I explore the nature of this paradox in terms of academic anthropology's aversion to popularization, the politics of academia, and the pros and cons of Mead's main theoretical orientation, culture and personality, as well as its later manifestation, the study of national character.[26]

I also suggest that the contradictory meanings associated with Mead provide insight into the changing character of twentieth-century American society—and the role anthropology has played in it—with regard to social issues such as race, ethnic identity, and sexual variation.

Mead and the Media

Through the mass media—first newspapers and magazines, then radio and television, and finally through film and the Internet—Margaret Mead acquired a legendary, even mythic status in American culture in the twentieth and twenty-first centuries. Her books, of course, have played an important role as well. Without the books she wrote Mead would never have become as famous as she did, but fewer people ever actually read Mead's books than saw her on television, read her column in *Redbook* magazine, or heard her speak at a lecture or over the radio.

To look at the media in relationship to Mead is to acknowledge the dominant role that visual media in particular have come to play as myth-making mechanisms in American culture. Technological developments in the nineteenth century, such as the camera—first daguerreotype, then dry-plate photography, and eventually film and the motion picture camera—heralded what scholars have identified as a "pictorial turn" in Western culture.[27] What they mean by this phrase is that these and other technological innovations provided the means to easily reproduce, preserve, transmit, and rapidly disseminate images. As a result, by the twentieth century everyday life in America and Europe increasingly came to be dominated by images—first in newspapers, magazines, and on billboards, postcards, and other ephemera—and then in the second half of the twentieth century on the television screen and now over the Internet.[28] This plethora of images contributed to America's celebrity-focused culture, and to Mead's fame.

The Culture of Celebrity

It is difficult these days not to see or hear a reference to celebrities or our "culture of celebrity," or to read that everyone in America wants to be a celebrity—to have their "fifteen minutes of fame" that Andy Warhol spoke of—or to be associated with someone famous. That this is the case has much to do with the media and the creation of visual images. Thus, one result of the "pictorial turn" has been the ability to create what Daniel Boorstin has identified as "pseudo-events." Boorstin suggested that over the course of the twentieth century the "business" of modern American society became the creation of illusions and images with which we deceive ourselves. This business—the creation of pseudo-events and celebrities (the individual equivalents, according to Boorstin, of pseudo-events)—he said, feeds a desire the American public has for excitement and helps to sustain its insatiable appetite for extravagant expectations. It was enabled through the activities of public relations firms, press agents, the news media, popular magazines, advertising, gossip, and political rhetoric.[29]

Since Boorstin first articulated his ideas over forty years ago, other scholars of American culture and celebrity have delineated the intimate connections between the increasing importance of the visual image, industrial capitalism, and the culture of consumption that characterizes modern American society.[30] They have also documented the shift in American culture from a focus on the hero or heroine, once renowned for something he or she actually did, to the cult of the celebrity characterized by the commodification of personality and style over substance. Scholars such as Neil Postman and Neal Gabler, who have looked critically at the long-term effects of mass media and the entertainment industries on American culture, have shown us in great detail the degree of degradation that public discourse has suffered and the extent to which "Real Life" has been turned into entertainment (even before the onslaught of Reality TV) as a result of our insatiable appetite for the pseudo-events and celebrity stories that Boorstin first outlined.[31]

The rise of a culture of celebrity in twentieth-century America is relevant to an understanding of Margaret Mead's fame and the meaning she came to have to different groups of Americans. As Richard Schickel has said of celebrity, which he sees as the most vital, as well as the most distorting, force in contemporary American society: "[it is] the principle source of motive power in putting across ideas of every kind—social, political, aesthetic, moral. Famous people are used as symbols for these ideas, or become famous for being symbols of them."[32]

When Mead's daughter, Mary Catherine Bateson, was about twelve, she complained that it was hard to have "a 'half-famous' mother because when I assume that people know who you are, so often they don't."[33]

She said that in 1950, just before Mead became a frequent presence on television talk shows and in popular magazines such as *Life*, *Time*, *Redbook*, and the *New Yorker*, so much so that one journalist referred to her as "a household name." Although Mead subsequently became even more widely known in post–World War II America, she had already achieved a degree of fame with the publication of *Coming of Age in Samoa* that was quite unusual—especially for an anthropologist—while still in her twenties. What was different later was that she was "100 percent famous," in other words, she had become a media celebrity (so much so that she joined the American Federation of TV and Radio Artists union as the result of her increasingly frequent media appearances). She also had the ability to continually reinvent herself as an anthropologist. She came to symbolize a range of ideas and values related to the changing social and political topography of the times, as well as to her own aging body.

In addition to her symbolic value, there is a second aspect to celebrity relevant to Mead as a cultural icon: the fact that aspects of celebrities' lives are fictionalized. Although today revealing facts about a celebrity's personal life is de rigueur, while she was alive, Mead succeeded in keeping her private life private. In fact, one of the reasons Mead remains such a popular subject of contemporary scholarly investigation is that her public persona contrasted so greatly with her private life. Perhaps anticipating this interest, Mead kept voluminous files filled with her personal correspondence, much of which has only gradually become available to scholars as the individuals involved either die or time limits placed on the public circulation of the material expire.[34]

But in addition to being able to explore the contrast between Mead's public and private lives, there are also narrative fictions and frequently repeated tropes about Mead that occur again and again in newspaper articles and other popular media. These narrative devices have also created certain images of Mead and what she stands for. Mead was very media savvy, and some of these images she introduced to the media herself. For example, she often explained to an interviewer that she had acquired her skill at observing other people's behavior by the age of eight when her mother, a social scientist, had Mead record the behavior of her younger siblings in notebooks. This anecdote is repeated time and again in different accounts of Mead, as well as in her memoir. It assumes the function of an origin story, locating Mead's observational skills as an anthropologist in her childhood. It also contributes to a sense of overdetermination, that, of course, Mead would become a social scientist—and one renowned for her study of child rearing in other cultures.

Such narrative details begin to function symbolically when we come to understand the role Mead eventually played in American society as an expert on the subject of how to raise American children. For, as Ann Hulbert has demonstrated in *Raising America: Experts, Parents, and a Century of Advice about Children*, in twentieth-century America, advice from experts about how to raise children was also advice about how to raise good American citizens.[35] At a time when reliance on expert advice about child rearing was steadily increasing, Mead, like her friend and family pediatrician, Dr. Benjamin Spock, became a symbol of how to raise a healthy, happy, and well-adjusted child in modern American society.

Mead as Writer

In 1998, when the editors of *Ladies' Home Journal* included Margaret Mead as one of their choices for the one hundred most important women of the twentieth century rather than categorize her as a scientist, they included her among the journalists and writers.[36] What is interesting about the magazine's decision to include Mead as a writer rather than a scientist is that it provided a convenient way for them to circumvent the controversy over the veracity of her Samoan fieldwork that Derek Freeman's book had raised in 1983. The categorization also underscored Mead's success as a popularizer of anthropology. Mead first attracted popular attention through books such as *Coming of Age in Samoa*, and because she wrote in an engaging and non-jargon-laden prose, nonspecialist readers read her books. She also became successful because she used her anthropological insights to present new perspectives on issues that readers cared about, such as American adolescents.

I do not focus specifically on the image of Mead as a writer, except to acknowledge how frequently reviewers of her books noted her felicitous writing style. However, the fact that she was an exceptionally good writer contributed greatly to her popular acclaim. While Mead thought of herself first and foremost as an anthropologist, an early aspiration had been to be a writer. Throughout her career she experimented with different modes of writing for both professional and popular readers.[37] However, she was also aware that her ability to write engagingly for a popular audience had sometimes been a liability in terms of her reputation among her fellow anthropologists. Thus, for example, Colin Turnbull, Mead's colleague in the Department of Anthropology at the American Museum of Natural History, remembered her warning him of the possible backlash he might receive from his academic peers as his books *The Forest People* and *The Mountain People* achieved popular acclaim.[38]

With regard to Mead's celebrity, however, her skill as a writer and a public speaker elevated her status from merely that of a proficient anthropologist to that of a cultural icon. As Emerson said about the writer as a representative character, it is the writer's role to re-present to the reader his world and his self, thus allowing the reader to experience him (or herself) in a new way, from a new perspective, and with new insight into himself or the world around him.[39] This uplifting and reinvigoration, this ability to cause her readers or her audience to gain a new understanding of themselves, or of their children or their culture, was an important aspect of Mead's popular success. So too was her ability to engage her readers or viewers in a form of transference in which they vicariously experienced some of what Mead had experienced living in other cultures. Although many anthropologists have practiced cross-cultural comparison, Mead was particularly adept at using examples from other cultures as a means of elucidating aspects of her own culture, or her own experiences, to her fellow Americans.

Mead and Visual Anthropology

Along with her third husband, anthropologist Gregory Bateson, Mead was a pioneer in the use of film and photography in her ethnographic research. As the history of anthropology is intimately linked to the development of visual culture in the West, Mead symbolizes this important relationship between anthropology and visual media.[40]

Just as Mead's fame as an anthropologist was dependent upon the mass media, likewise anthropology's development as both an academic discipline and a form of popular knowledge and entertainment was closely associated with the development of new visual technologies in the nineteenth and twentieth centuries. In particular, the development of portable still and motion picture cameras has been intimately linked with the development of anthropology.[41] Still photography and motion pictures aided both travelers and professional anthropologists to record images of exotic peoples they encountered in remote parts of the world. Many of these images were quickly reproduced for new forms of popular entertainment such as the stereoscope, lantern slides, and, once the motion picture camera was developed, travelogues and adventure movies that highlighted the cultures of non-Western peoples.[42] Mead's use of photography and film in her research helped to underscore the importance of visual evidence in ethnographic research as well as the value of images in conveying cross-cultural information to the public.

Not only was Mead one of the earliest anthropologists to integrate visual methods into her research, she was also one of the first anthropologists to focus on the study of visual communication, including nonverbal communication, kinesics (the study of body motion), and proxemics (the study of territoriality and personal space), and she pioneered teaching anthropology courses on culture and communication (both verbal and visual).[43] Mead's relationship to ethnographic film (and to the American Museum of Natural History) is symbolized by the museum's use of her name and image for their annual showcase of new documentary film and video. The Margaret Mead Film Festival began in 1976 in commemoration of Mead's seventy-fifth birthday and has grown in size and importance during the past thirty years. It is now the preeminent venue for viewing nonfiction film in the country.

New York City—Cultural Hub of the World

The rise of the image and the cult of celebrity in twentieth century America were necessary but not sufficient explanations of Mead's popularity and the role she came to play in American culture. There were, of course, her skills as a writer, ethnographer, and public speaker. But other important factors also contributed to her fame, including her decision to live in New York City, her position as a curator of anthropology at the American Museum of Natural History, and the development of New York City as a center for new forms of mass media and the fields of advertising and public relations.

For Mead, New York City was the perfect counterbalance to the relatively unpopulated jungles and islands where she did her research. Personally, she loved the hustle and bustle of the city and its endless diversity; professionally, it allowed her an important perspective and rhetorical stance from which she could compare and contrast the "primitive" worlds of her fieldwork. After she arrived in there in 1920, the city remained her home until she died there in 1978. Once asked where she would prefer to live, Mead answered rather testily, "New York City, where I *do* live."[44]

New York was also home to Columbia University and Barnard College, the institutions where Mead earned her academic degrees, formed her most important professional and personal relationships, especially those with Franz Boas and Ruth Benedict, and where she taught scores of graduate and undergraduate students. At the time Mead studied there, Columbia was *the* intellectual center for the study of anthropology under the leadership of Franz Boas.

Equally significant was the fact that during the almost sixty years that Mead lived there, New York City became Capital to the World. As such, its dynamism, institutions, wealth, and cultural diversity of inhabitants all contributed to the development of Mead's fame. During World War I New York City began to replace London as the center of a developing global economy. After World War II the city not only became the business, financial, mass media, and cultural and intellectual center of the United States (and by extension, of the world), but also, with the establishment of the United Nations in New York in 1944, an important center of international politics as well.

The most important factor for Mead's public success was the concentration of all important forms of mass media: the publishing industry (books and magazines in particular, but also large-circulation newspapers), radio, and later television, as well as the ad agencies that sustained all these media, in New York City. In addition to being home to the *New Republic* and *The Nation*, two magazines that offered insightful criticism of American society for which Mead eventually wrote, two other important intellectually oriented national circulation magazines were based there, the *American Mercury* and the *New Yorker. Time* magazine was also based in New York, as was *Life*. All of these magazines at one time or another featured articles either written by Mead or about her.[45]

Moreover, since the 1880s the center of the women's magazine industry has been in New York City. In the 1920s the number of magazines for women grew as magazine postal rates declined and the number of middle-class women, in particular, who sought advice about their changing role in American society from magazines such as *Ladies' Home Journal*, *Cosmopolitan*, *McCall's*, *Parents* magazine, and later, *Redbook*, expanded. Not only did these magazines publish articles written by Mead or about her, by 1965 she had also begun to write a regular monthly column for *Redbook* magazine.

New York City also became the center for commercial radio after the major commercial networks were formed there in the 1920s, and the cultural activities and personalities in the city influenced programming for radio networks nationwide.[46] During the 1920s, as a result of then governor of New York Franklin Delano Roosevelt's habit of discussing his political decisions over the radio, broadcasting over the radio became a more important force in politics and social issues. Thus, Mead was well situated to appear on radio programs that originated in New York City that dealt with a broad range of social issues. For example, between 1941 and 1972 she appeared repeatedly on the CBS affiliate station WOR on the *Martha Deane Show*.[47]

After World War II both radio and magazines were forced to compete with television for an audience. But for Mead the advent of television simply opened a new venue and an expanded audience for her ideas. In the early days of television broadcasting, when programs still aired live, New York City was the center for most national television production. CBS even set up a production center in the American Museum of Natural History for its science series, *Adventure*, produced live at the museum between 1951 and 1957.[48] Because she was a curator of anthropology at the museum, Mead was asked to appear on several episodes of the *Adventure* series, thus launching her career as a television personality.

Mead had joined the museum at age twenty-four, before she embarked upon her first fieldwork to Samoa in 1925. At that time there were few jobs available for anthropologists. Having just completed her doctorate in anthropology, Mead was very fortunate to have received the appointment. It meant that she had a job waiting for her when she returned from the field, and she remained at the museum until her death. It also meant that the prestige of the museum and its reputation as a bastion of scientific knowledge, its masculine ethos of science, its association with adventure and expeditions, and its grand scale and labyrinthine layout, all contributed to her authority as a scientist and an expert. When writing about her, journalists who interviewed Mead in her office often referred to the building's "sacred precincts" and to her inaccessible location in the Tower Room tucked away at the top of the southwest turret of the museum.[49] The plethora of strange objects stored on shelves and stowed in nooks and crannies outside her office added to the mysterious and exotic atmosphere of the inner depths of the museum. Getting to Mead's office was an adventure that took one past museum guards, beyond the public domain of the museum, and down long, dimly lit corridors that passed by the closed doors of numerous offices and laboratories.

Clark Wissler, the curator of anthropology at the museum who had hired Mead, thought that women were well suited for curatorial work because the job was like housekeeping. But Mead's early career as a fieldworker in Samoa and New Guinea also fit into the masculine image associated with the scientist-as-explorer—represented by the museum curator Roy Chapman Andrews (said to be the prototype for Indiana Jones),[50] as well as the museum's masculine iconography expressed by the large bronze statue of Teddy Roosevelt astride his horse that stands sentry over the museum's main entrance on Central Park West and the African animals in the Carl Ackley dioramas, redolent of Hemingwayesque hunting safaris.[51]

Finally, since the museum was a public institution, curators were expected to make their research and that of others in their field accessible to the public. Mead took this mandate seriously, writing popular ethnographic books for general readers as well as more technical scientific monographs. It was the timely and serendipitous combination of these different factors—personal, structural, and institutional—that together contributed to Mead's fame. Not only was she in the right place at the right time, she was also the right person, with the right talents, attributes and choice of career.

A Quintessentially American Icon

When she died in 1978, British anthropologist Meyer Fortes noted that "a phenomenon like Margaret Mead could perhaps not have emerged in any other country than modern America"—a reference in part to Mead's

Figure I.4 Mead's turret office at the American Museum of Natural History overlooked Columbus Avenue. Having had to hike up to it, journalists frequently commented on the office's remote location and exotic decor. (Neg. No. 338668, Courtesy of the Department of Library Services, American Museum of Natural History, New York City)

rise as a media celebrity.[52] It was also a reference to her style—decidedly different from understated British academics in her bold and broad-sweeping pronouncements on a multitude of topics. Moreover, as a young woman and also as an elder statesperson Mead became a symbol of aspects of America itself, first as an exemplar of the twentieth century's New Woman and in old age as a wise, although sometimes cantankerous, sage. As in the tradition of late nineteenth- and early twentieth-century iconography that depicted the nation as a woman, Mead in her various guises also became a symbol of the nation. An example of this symbolic role is the United States Information Agency decision in 1975 to make a film about her for distribution abroad.[53] Another is the fact that the U.S. government chose to send Mead to Britain during the World War II to interpret American culture to the British, who were inundated with American troops stationed throughout their country.

Mead was chosen for this job in part because in 1942 she had published her first book about American culture, *And Keep Your Powder Dry: An Anthropologist Looks at America*.[54] Written as part of the war effort to encourage American support for the war, Mead sought to identify those characteristics of Americans she felt would be most useful in fighting against fascism—and in leading the world after the war had ended. Not surprisingly, some of the most prominent aspects of what she identified as the American "national character" apply to Mead as well.[55] Mead characterized America as a moral culture, one in which the concepts of good and bad permeated discussion and behavior.[56] Similarly, Mead was a highly moral individual, not only in that she was religious—which she was (throughout her life she was closely involved with the Episcopalian Church)—but also in that she sought justice and equality for all cultures and peoples of the world, and—always self-confident and assured—believed that she knew what was best for others. Mead also characterized Americans as perpetually in motion, with the expectation that they would not live where they grew up and, with their steadfast belief in progress, as always searching for a better way of life. In fact, not only did Mead leave her childhood home to move to New York City, throughout her life she was also constantly on the move, traversing the United States and the world in search of a better understanding of human behavior and ways to improve human societies. In this respect, she was convinced that anthropology had an important role to play in changing the world for the better. Finally, Mead identified the success ethic as a primary American value. More specifically, she said that to have succeeded in American society, Americans believed that they had to surpass their parents in achievements, be they material, intellectual, or social. It could be said that Mead succeeded with a vengeance, for she wrote that when she was a child her father had remarked to her, "It's a pity you aren't a boy," for "you'd have gone far"![57]

Mead's enduring interest in other cultures, coupled with her steadfast faith in American democracy and her admonishments to her fellow Americans that they think more globally and less ethnocentrically, was a message the U.S. government was eager to transmit abroad, especially after World War II when the idea of cultural pluralism—one which Boasian anthropologists had helped champion with their idea of cultural relativism—became increasingly important to liberal American politicians.[58] These characteristics were also the reasons why President Carter awarded Mead the Medal of Freedom, posthumously.

Although a majority of Americans have viewed Mead as patriotic and well intentioned, and hence as a positive symbol of the United States and the commendable values they believe it stands for, there have been other individuals, both to the right and to the left of center politically, who have viewed Mead and her allegiance to the United States with suspicion. On the right, J. Edgar Hoover and the Federal Bureau of Investigation kept extensive files on Mead from the 1940s into the 1970s.[59] At the same time, left-leaning anthropologists and other scholars, educated Samoans and Papua New Guineans, and political satirists such as cartoonist Garry Trudeau have seen Mead as a symbol of U.S. imperialism and anthropological paternalism, whose effects have ranged from benign neglect to overt racism.[60]

In the chapters that follow we will see how Mead became the American phenomenon that she did, as well as how she came to represent such a range of different ideas to various people at different points in time. In the process we will see how integral the discipline of anthropology has been to the development of modern twentieth-century American intellectual and political thought as well as popular culture, articulating a new concept of culture, ideas about the Primitive Other, as well as the concepts of the unity of humanity, cultural relativism, and equality among human societies. Although these were ideas that many anthropologists helped to shape through their research and writing, Mead played a dominant role in their popular dissemination in her role as public intellectual and celebrity and, indeed, as the discipline's most famous "public anthropologist."

This book is organized both thematically and chronologically. It is comprised of nine chapters, each of which deals with one or more of the four iconic images of Mead I have identified. Within each chapter the material is presented chronologically. Thus, chapter 1, "Mead as Modern Woman," covers Mead's infancy through her twenties, when she embarks on her first fieldwork to Samoa in 1925. It reveals that even before Mead published *Coming of Age in Samoa* she was a media figure, having made headlines in local papers from Honolulu to Philadelphia for her research studying "the flapper of the South Seas." Chapter 2, "The Image of the Mature Mead," looks at the married and the maternal Mead. It traces the changing image of Mead as a woman from the young, flapperesque Mead of the 1920s to the elderly Mead who upon her death was eulogized as "grandmother to the world." It also charts Mead's posthumous emergence as an icon of bi- and lesbian sexuality. Chapters 3, 4, and 5 deal with the image of Mead as anthropologist. Chapter 3, "Mead as Anthropologist: 'Sex in the South Seas,' " tracks the media's response to *Coming of Age in Samoa*, as well as the work she and her publisher performed to shape the book into an anthropological argument with popular appeal. With the book's publication we see the association among Mead, the study of "primitive" people, and sexuality set in motion by the media. Chapter 4, "Mead as Anthropologist: 'To Study Cannibals,' " focuses on Mead's second book, *Growing Up in New Guinea*, as well as her third, less well-known book, *The Changing Culture of an Indian Tribe*. Mead's second book cemented the association of Mead with the study of exotic non-Western people in the public's mind. The lack of popular success of her third book, about the Omaha Indians in Nebraska, underscores the point that much of the popular appeal of Mead's books was their descriptions of far-off places and exotic peoples. Chapter 5 discusses the publication of *Sex and Temperament in Three Primitive Societies* in 1935 and the impact of the media's response to all three of Mead's books about South Pacific cultures. Chapter 6, "Mead and the Image of the Anthropologist," argues that twentieth-century American popular understanding of anthropologists and what they did, although shaped by earlier nineteenth-century American anthropologists, was heavily influenced by media representations of Mead and her work, especially from the period 1928 to 1935, when she published her three Pacific ethnographies. Chapter 7, "Mead as Scientist," concentrates on the post–World War II period and the effect that television had on the spread of Mead's fame. It discusses the importance of film and photography in Mead's Balinese research in terms of the use she made of this and other visual material in her television appearances. During this period Mead was transformed in the public's mind from simply being an anthropologist who studied remote and primitive people into a social or behavioral scientist who was an expert on human behavior in general, including her own society. Chapter 8, "Mead as Public Intellectual and Celebrity," looks at the last two decades of Mead's life, during the 1960s and 70s, when she had become a major public figure and media celebrity whose name and face were well known in the United States and abroad. It discusses her role as a public intellectual and the reasons why an anthropologist became a celebrity in twentieth-century America. Finally, chapter 9, "The Posthumous Mead, or Mead, the Public Anthropologist," looks at the so-called Mead-Freeman controversy and considers why Derek Freeman's critique of Mead and *Coming of Age in Samoa* became an American media event. It also considers Mead's symbolic role today in American culture and anthropology and discusses how the Internet, as well as more traditional forms of mass media, have created and perpetuated Mead as a quintessentially American icon.

CHAPTER 1

Mead as Modern Woman

Margaret Mead: First of the Libbies
—*Cosmopolitan* magazine, September 1972[1]

One of the most prevalent images of Margaret Mead, whether young or old, is that of a pioneer among woman—exploring new roles and untraditional behavior, an exemplar of modernity's "New Woman," or second-wave feminism's totemic "First Libbie"—in short, as a trading card image of Mead proclaimed, a "Supersister."[2] Just as frequent as the accolades that focus on her female identity are critiques that also focus on her as a woman. Thus, for example, Betty Friedan, in her classic manifesto of mid-twentieth-century feminism, *The Feminine Mystique*, excoriated Mead for having essentialized women's role as mother in her popular book *Male and Female*.[3] And conservative scholar Allan Bloom characterized her as a "sexual adventuress," linking what he considered to be her promiscuous sexual behavior with the "closing of the American mind."[4] While others have attributed to her—both positively and negatively—the origins of the sexual revolution of the 1960s, with its mottos of Free Love and Make Love, Not War.[5]

These comments, whether celebratory or condemnatory, focus on Mead's identity as a woman—her sexuality, her unconventional behavior, or her research on women and gender—making Mead a popular icon of the modern American woman. Although the term *New Woman* originally referred to women born in the 1860s and 1870s, such as Jane Addams and the suffragists who fought for women's right to vote, it is also used to describe a later more radical cohort of women who identified themselves in the 1910s as "feminists."[6] Mead's mother, Emily Fogg Mead, fits the category of New Woman more specifically than Mead herself.[7] Born in 1872, Emily Mead supported women's suffrage and higher education for women. But unlike many New Women of the era, Emily married. She also did not advocate free love. But Margaret did. For this reason, as well as for her independent spirit and outspoken support of the ability of women to do many things traditionally done by men, Mead has long been associated in the minds of many people with feminism, women's liberation, and women's rights, all modern and predominantly twentieth-century phenomena.

Mead eschewed the label *feminist*, especially early in her career. Nonetheless, throughout her life she had much to say about women, women's roles, the relationship between men and women, and women's relationships to other women. It is also true that one of the main reasons the media were interested in Mead was that she was female. It was an adjective that Mead resented when used to describe her, as, for example, "the most famous woman anthropologist in America."[8] Nonetheless, it is true that she was newsworthy because she was a woman who was doing and saying unconventional things and because she was a woman who had made a name for herself in an arena—academia and intellectual work in general—traditionally dominated by men.

Being female was a necessary but not sufficient element in Mead's success. As author Carolyn Heilbrun wrote, "She was, with the possible exception of Eleanor Roosevelt, who came to fame through marriage, the most famous professional woman of her day. Mead made it wholly on her own, as a single gifted female."[9] Heilbrun also noted that "[for women,] to search for a tradition of past female autonomy and influence is to enter a problematic realm, full of anxiety and ambivalence. Probably no famous woman represents this anxiety and ambivalence better than Margaret Mead."[10] While Heilbrun was referring to contemporary American women's search for female role models, I think her statement applies to men's reactions to Mead as well. For they, too, reacted with anxiety and ambivalence to her, to a large degree perhaps because of her gender blending, that is, her mixing of qualities of behavior and attitude of mind associated with men while she celebrated being a woman.

The Young Mead as Popular Heroine

During the first half of the twentieth century, and especially the 1920s and 1930s, as historian Susan Ware has noted, the American public developed a seemingly insatiable desire for popular heroes and heroines.[11] Mead was just one of a range of talented women in a variety of fields—aviation, athletics, journalism, photography, the stage, the movie screen, and science—who the media helped thrust into the public's attention through stories that highlighted unique aspects of their various endeavors.[12] The print media in particular—tabloid newspapers such as the *New York Sun*, weekly periodicals such as *Time* (which began in 1923), and mass circulation women's magazines—were heavily influenced by Hollywood's development of the star system with its calculated use of publicity (often based on entirely fabricated anecdotes and events) to promote the public's awareness of a new movie actor or actress.[13] Mead shared the stage with a cohort of outstanding women who became popular American heroines and legendary figures during the 1920s and 1930s in large part because of the exposure they received in popular magazines and newspapers. Women such as Amelia Earhart and Mead "served as role models and examples of what women could accomplish in the modern world."[14] There is a link, Ware argues, between popular culture of the 1920s and 1930s and feminism in that through their very example these female heroines and independent women kept feminism alive during a period otherwise believed to be dormant. These women's individual achievements "substituted for, and also sustained, the feminist momentum."[15] Moreover, Mead was an unconventional icon—an outspoken female intellectual—in an age that increasingly valued women who were famous for being glamorous movie stars, svelte athletes, or the wives of famous men.

In this and the following chapter we will look at photographs of Mead from childhood to old age published in books and articles; they demonstrate the changing images and associated meanings of Mead as a woman that evolved over the course of her life. Mead was exceptional in that often women who were famous in their youth faded into the background of public interest as they grew older. Not Mead. Her image morphed from youthful ingenue to elderly guru, as she maintained her place in the limelight. Over time she and the media crafted new female images of her, shifting from the representation of Mead as a precocious young woman breaking new ground to that of a middle-aged woman who challenged the status quo by being both a female scientist and a mother. As Mead grew older she and the media fashioned an increasingly maternal role for her, first as mother to generations of younger women and then as grandmother, both literally and metaphorically. As Mead grew stouter and gray haired, she transformed into an elder "statesperson" and wise woman, revered by many as a valuable American resource, pundit, and sage. In looking at these photographs we will also see how certain images have become iconic representations of Mead herself and of popular notions of what it has meant to be a new kind of woman in twentieth-century America.

Mead's Mother and Grandmother

It is impossible to discuss Mead as a woman without talking about her mother, Emily Fogg Mead, and her paternal grandmother, Martha Ramsey Mead, both of whom played prominent roles in her upbringing,[16] as Mead placed great import on the role of the parent-child relationship in understanding a child's socialization and the development of an individual's adult personality.[17]

Mead liked to point out that both her mother and her grandmother had managed to combine work and family (otherwise, she would often quip, "I wouldn't be here!"). She stressed that "because both my mother and grandmother were professionally educated women, I never had to struggle with the problems of identity which bedevil most first-generation professional women. . . . Women both used their brains and married and had children. (Unless, of course, they were nuns, a career that appealed to me at ten . . . active, energetic nuns who became saints.)"[18]

Mead's mother was born in Chicago in 1872. She began her college education at Wellesley and completed her undergraduate degree at the University of Chicago, where she met Edward Mead, a graduate student studying economics.[19] In college Emily became an advocate of women's rights and the equality of men and women.[20] Influenced by the social reformist work of Jane Addams and the progressive theories of professors such as Thorstein Veblen and John Dewey, she had majored in sociology and minored in economics.[21] After marrying Edward Mead in 1900, the couple moved to Pennsylvania, where Edward became a professor at the Wharton School of Business and Emily became a graduate student in sociology at Bryn Mawr College.

Margaret was born December 16, 1901. She was the first of four children, followed two years later by her brother Richard, then her sisters Elizabeth (seven and a half years younger) and Priscilla (nine years younger).[22] At the time of Mead's birth Emily had just completed an article on the role of advertising in business, published by Veblen in the *Journal of Political Economy.*[23] With a degree of sincerity and faith in advertising that it is hard now not to view as naive, she argued that advertising would enlighten individuals with little education, especially women. She thought that advertising would make them aware of new products that could ease their workload and thus enrich their lives.[24] Like her mother, Mead developed a similar faith in the ability of new forms of mass media to educate the public and promote more equitable and democratic lives.

Mead's grandmother had also attended college. She became a teacher, and when her husband died suddenly she continued to teach until she moved in with her son and daughter-in-law when Margaret was born. Because Martha Ramsey Mead oversaw her grandchildren's education, and because the Meads, like many other middle-class educated families at that time, were able to employ cooks and nurses to tend to meals and child care, Emily Mead was able to continue her dissertation research in sociology while bearing children and raising a family.[25] Her research entailed the study of the adaptation of immigrants from Southern Italy to the Pine Barrens region of New Jersey that bordered Pennsylvania.[26]

Looking at the photograph of Mead and her mother that Mead included in her autobiography, *Blackberry Winter*, we see in the clothes they wear, in Emily's hairstyle, in the restrained, calm formality of the setting, an image of late Victorian middle-class American domesticity. Margaret was proud of her Yankee heritage—the Foggs, the Meads, and the Ramseys all traced their family lineages back to the Puritans and other early English immigrants to America—and she used her family background as her touchstone for understanding aspects of what she later called American "national character."[27]

The reserve Emily Mead displays in the photograph was not merely a matter of Victorian photographic convention; for according to Mead her mother was neither playful nor particularly emotive. What maternal intimacy she does allow herself to express in this portrait of mother and daughter is located in her hands: she holds Margaret's right hand protectively in her own. A golden-haired four-year-old Margaret with curly ringlets wears a light-colored, feminine-looking dress with a bit of petticoat showing. Mead tells us that it was her grandmother who used to brush her curly hair, while confiding to her things about her parents, such as her father's dalliance with another woman, that a young child should not have been told.[28]

Emily Mead was a practical woman who cared little about pretty clothes or fancy jewelry. Like other progressive, educated women of the era, she focused her time and energy on doing good, supporting social causes such as women's rights, and carrying out her research. She valued efficiency over aesthetics. Thinking it important that Margaret be free to do things such as climb trees, Emily wanted to dress her in bloomers, the appropriate feminine apparel for such activities. Margaret preferred petticoats.[29]

In contrast to her mother, Mead loved pageants and plays, dress-up, and make believe. The seeds of Mead's pleasure at being in the public limelight and her ability to deftly master multiple roles seem to have been sown in her childhood experiences of writing plays for neighborhood children to enact and her own public performance of poetry recitations in which her father trained her to focus on a particular individual in the audience when speaking, rather than letting her eye rove over the crowd.[30] Her inherent theatricality and her ease in front of an audience served her well in later years, helping her become a successful radio and television guest on talk shows.

At a point in time when child rearing was being approached scientifically, Emily Mead heeded the advice of the influential child-care specialist L. E. Holt, who admonished parents to feed children at regularly scheduled intervals rather than on demand and not to pick up a crying baby unless it was in pain in order to protect the infant from being smothered by an overabundance of motherly love.[31] Perhaps because of her sociological focus on observation and data collection, she recorded in minute detail—thirteen fat notebooks full—the progress of Margaret's infancy. Mead said that she learned from her mother that "being observed seemed to be an act of love." She in turn began to observe the behavior of her

Figure 1.1 Mead as a child with her mother, Emily Fogg Mead, 1905. (Courtesy of Corbis/Bettmann)

younger siblings, writing down her observations in small notebooks, and when her daughter Mary Catherine was born also made extensive observations about her.[32]

As Margaret grew older her mother included her in her research endeavors and social causes. She attended marriages and christenings among Italian immigrant families and rallies in support of women's suffrage. "Mother," Mead wrote, "was a suffragist (the anti's called them suffragettes) but grandma, a professional woman a generation earlier, shared none of her rhetoric and rancor about women being classified with the feebleminded and criminals."[33] Mead identified with her grandmother rather than her mother when it came to feminism and women's rights. "Obviously," she said, "it was necessary [for women] to get the vote. . . . But in a household which was alive to change and to the necessity for change, working for changes in the position of women seemed reasonable, necessary, but did not in anyway disturb my sense of myself."[34]

Eventually, like other young women of her generation who came of age in the early decades of the twentieth century, Mead benefited from the changes in attitudes toward women that had been enacted as a result of the actions of women like her mother. But, like the generation of young women born to mothers who had come of age during the second wave of feminism in the 1960s and 70s, she had no desire to self-identify as a feminist. For she, like them, perceived the image of a feminist to be one of angry women who hated men.[35]

Although Mead's father once said that it was a shame that she had been born a girl, Margaret benefited from being her parents' firstborn child, as well as having been born a girl. Although Mead learned from her mother and grandmother that a woman did not have to make a choice between a career or motherhood, she was aware of the sacrifices that her mother had had to make in her career in order to raise her family. She wrote that "my mother never grudged for a moment, but instead delighted in the fact that I was able to live fully the life she would like to have lived."[36] Perhaps because Mead knew as much as she did about the nature of those sacrifices, which included enduring a philandering and overbearing husband,[37] she never made similar sacrifices herself, shedding marriages that conflicted with her career and ensuring that she always had an extensive network of friends, especially female friends, to help her professionally and personally.

College Days: Mead and Katharine Rothenberger

During her freshman year at DePauw University, her father's alma mater,[38] Mead became friends with Katharine Rothenberger, a slim, attractive, red-haired upperclassman who was new to DePauw herself. In her autobiography, Mead includes a picture of Katharine and herself dressed up as king and queen for a May Day pageant that Mead had written and directed.[39] They must have been a striking pair, Katharine as king with her flame-colored hair set off by a lavender ruff wrapped around her elegant, long neck and the shorter Mead at her side with her golden brown tresses swept up on top of her head.[40]

Although Mead left DePauw the following year, disillusioned by the small-mindedness of this midwestern institution with its focus on the elitism of sororities and fraternities and its rigid Methodist orientation, she and Katharine became lifelong friends.[41] Even though there is no explicit indication that Mead and Rothenberger had been sexually intimate, their correspondence shows how fond they had been of each other and how disappointed Katharine was at Mead's departure.[42] Recently their friendship has become the subject of speculation by psychologist Hilary Lapsley and historian Lois Banner, who have studied Mead's sexuality and her intimate relationships with women for the light they might shed on understanding changes in twentieth-century women's sexual behavior. Aided by the rich documentation of correspondence between Mead and her friends and family, dreams and dream analysis, and a preliminary draft of Mead's autobiography, their scholarship has contributed a new image of Mead, one of her as an exemplar of a modern woman's sexual experimentation who was both attracted to and, as we will see later, sexually involved with women.[43]

What is clear from the archival record is that when Mead arrived at DePauw she was engaged to Luther Cressman, a seminary student she had met when she was sixteen, but that her strong emotional and physical attraction to Katharine caused her to feel confused about her sexual identity. Although she thought that she wanted to marry Cressman, and envisioned a life for herself as a pastor's wife with a brood of children,[44] her conflicting feelings of attraction to women led her to read the work of Freud and other scholars writing about the scientific study of sex, as she sought an answer to her questions about her own sexuality. Thus, to con-

Figure 1.2 Mead and Katharine Rothenberger, Queen and King of the May Day Pageant, DePauw University, 1920. (Courtesy of the Library of Congress and the Institute for Intercultural Studies)

temporary scholars of gender and sexuality, Mead's relationship with Rothenberger has come to represent her developing consciousness of her sexual attraction to women and the beginning of her questioning the innate nature of sexuality.[45]

Mead and New York City: The Roaring Twenties and the Ash Can Cats

While in Indiana, Mead yearned for the excitement and intellectual stimulation of the East Coast, epitomized by New York City. "I used to sit in the library and read the drama reviews in *The New York Times*," she wrote in *Blackberry Winter*. "Like so many other aspiring American intellectuals and artists, I developed the feeling that American small towns were essentially unfriendly to the life of the mind and the senses. I believed that the center of life was in New York City, where Mencken and George Jean Nathan were publishing *Smart Set*, where F. P. A. and Heywood Broun were writing their diatribes, and where the theater was a living world of contending ideas."[46]

Mead was absolutely right about New York City being the "center of life" for her; there is no doubt that the city played a significant role in the creation of her fame and her successful career as an anthropologist. After moving there in 1920 to attend Barnard College, it became her home for the rest of her life. She arrived in New York at the beginning of that heady period between 1919, the year after the end of World War I, and 1929, the year the stock market crashed—referred to as the Jazz Age or the Roaring Twenties. These names reflect the hedonism and excess of this period that was marked by major changes in the social, political, and economic standards and mores of postwar America.[47] It was a period defined in large part by the rebellious spirit of the young who had survived the Great War and those who had been adolescents during the years of its confusion. Disillusioned by the war, "cynical rather than revolutionary" and feeling that they had inherited a flawed world from their parents and grandparents, it was characteristic of the Jazz Age, F. Scott Fitzgerald wrote, "that it had no interest in politics at all."[48] Flaunting Prohibition—which had gone into effect in 1919—and parental authority, young women and men drank bootleg liquor from hip flasks, smoked cigarettes, listened to jazz bands, and petted in the backseats of automobiles. "America," according to Fitzgerald, "was going on the greatest, gaudiest spree in history," or so it seemed to him at the time. "Something had to be done," he said, "with all the nervous energy stored up and unexpended in the war."[49]

The "nervous energy" Fitzgerald wrote of was expended in 1920s New York City by upper- and middle-class white urban dwellers flocking to Harlem to listen to jazz and to be seduced by its unrestrained rhythms and wild sounds. White intellectuals turned their attention to what they saw as the virtues of negritude—whether in the form of black urban jazz, the folkways of Southern and Caribbean blacks, or the art of tribal Africa. Thus, New York City, with its emphasis on speed, efficiency, industrialization, and consumption, also became the locus of an intellectual and emotional fascination with modernity and urbanity's antithesis—the primitive. New York City was important to Mead not simply because of its support of the life of the mind; rather, because from the 1920s on it played an increasingly important role in the United States as the center of mass media—first monthly and weekly magazines, then radio and television—and new forms of popular culture that shaped Mead's career as a public figure.

Having convinced her father to let her transfer to Barnard, Mead enthusiastically embraced living in the city and quickly made friends there. To represent this period of her life in her autobiography, Mead included a photograph of herself seated outside on a bench along with two other Barnard classmates, the fledgling poet Léonie Adams, and Eleanor Pelham Kortheuer.[50] The caption for the photo reads: "Three Ash Can Cats." The young women are similarly dressed in dark clothing, each coifed with a fashionable short, bobbed haircut, and each holding a balloon. Bobbed hair came to symbolize the flapper, a predominant and enduring female symbol of the 1920s in America.[51] In contrast to the refined image of Victorian and prewar women with their corsets and bustles, petticoats and bloomers, long hair and long skirts, flappers were characterized as loud, fun-loving, fast-living young girls who had bobbed their hair, hiked their skirts up to their knees, rolled down their stockings, thrown away their boned corsets, and learned to dance the Charleston—a dance thought to be so physically vigorous and immoral that it was banned at some colleges.[52] The high-spirited, flirtatious flapper acted like a daring,

Figure 1.3 Mead, in the middle, and two other Ash Can Cats, Léonie Adams and Eleanor Pelham Kortheuer, Barnard College. (Courtesy of the Library of Congress and the Institute for Intercultural Studies)

sometimes naughty, tomboy. And her boyish figure, flat chested, slim hipped, and lanky, added to this tomboy effect. The flapper was a pal to men, always ready to have a good time.[53]

The emphasis was on the image of youth.[54] The younger generation scorned the older generation, rejecting many of its values and beliefs as outmoded or dysfunctional; hence, the desire to reinvent not only themselves but also the world they lived in. Women's fashion, too, reflected this change in attitude, both in its rejection of the past restrictive fashions for women and in the current emphasis on perpetual youth and the freedom—physical, emotional, and ideological—that young women associated with it.

The essence of the image of the flapper, in literature and the movies, was her development into a sexually mature woman—a woman who both enjoyed her sexuality and flaunted it.[55] Flappers were of concern to parents because "they were frank, opinionated, sexually liberated, and extremely difficult to control" and many parents and other members of the older generations could not understand the mind or the manners and mores of the flapper.[56]

In addition to the movies, other important new sources of images of male and female sexuality in the 1920s were the proliferation of tabloid newspapers, photo magazines, and the work of Freud and Havelock Ellis, which became more generally known to the American public after World War I. Other factors that gave rise to changes in men's and women's behavior included the passage of the Nineteenth Amendment in 1920 that gave women the right to vote, women's increased participation in the work force, increased accessibility of the automobile, prohibition, accelerated industrialization and urbanization, and the development of a consumption ethic. This latter was fueled by a growing advertising industry that encouraged people to buy in order to keep factories that had been built during the war producing in a postwar economy.[57]

Although Mead was by no means a flapper (her classmates at Barnard noted her "simple, Yankee style"), she had succumbed and had her luxurious long hair bobbed.[58] Mead's diminutive size and her bobbed hair were physical attributes that contributed to her public persona of girlish youthfulness, a combination that proved to be popular with the media in the 1920s and '30s.[59]

The loosely affiliated group of friends who called themselves the Ash Can Cats were of disparate backgrounds—Catholic, Jewish, Episcopalian, and atheist—but united in their common passion for literature and poetry, and for new roles for women.[60] They chose as their personal credo and anthem (as did an entire generation of American women yearning for change), Edna St. Vincent Millay's famous quatrain, "First Fig," with its image of "wild freedom edged with death":[61]

> My candle burns at both ends;
> It will not last the night;
> But ah, my foes, and oh, my friends—
> It gives a lovely light!

In a similar manner, they chose Millay herself as their personal heroine. On May Day, 1925, they rode the subway to Greenwich Village and left May baskets outside Millay's house to honor the poet whose work they felt so captured their own restless female spirits.[62]

Mead had initially thought she would become a writer but changed her mind after she got to know Léonie Adams, who as a college undergraduate had already begun to have her poetry published. Comparing herself to Adams, Mead realized that although she was a good writer, she was not an exceptional one.[63] Although she continued to write short stories and poems throughout her college years, ever pragmatic, as well as determined to be successful, Mead decided to double major in English and psychology, figuring that the social sciences offered her more opportunity for success. In a draft of her autobiography, she wrote, "I had no taste for failing gloriously or for spending my life trying to write the great American novel."[64] While an undergraduate she also took an anthropology course with Professor Franz Boas, one of the leading figures in the field at the time, where she became friendly with Boas's teaching assistant, Ruth Benedict. The friendship was to become one of the most important relationships in both their lives. After graduating from Barnard, Mead began to work on a master's degree in psychology, but eventually Benedict persuaded her to pursue a doctorate degree in anthropology.

Mead and the Ash Can Cats were too serious-minded and intellectual to be flappers themselves.[65] However, they did share the flappers' desire to push aside the conventions—especially those surrounding female sexuality—that had governed earlier generations of American women's behavior.[66] As Mead describes them, "We thought of ourselves as radicals—in terms of our sentiments rather than our adherence to any radical ideology. . . . We belonged to a generation of young women who felt extraordinarily free—free from the demand to marry unless we chose to do so, free to postpone marriage while we did other things, free from the need to bargain and hedge that burdened and restricted women of earlier generations. We laughed at the idea that a woman could be an old maid at the age of twenty-five, and we rejoiced at the new medical care that made it possible for a woman to have a child at forty."[67] Here Mead succinctly expresses the values and beliefs that characterized her and her friends, a group of privileged, intelligent, young women attending college in one of the most dynamic modern cities in the world (with Paris perhaps in close contention).

New forms of birth control and new attitudes toward sexuality and marriage, such as the notion of free love, also meant that the Ash Can Cats experimented sexually with both men and women. Although Mead was engaged to Luther Cressman while she attended Barnard, and they married in 1923, neither her engagement nor her marriage prevented her from engaging in other sexual liaisons. A proponent of the doctrine of Free Love expounded by intellectuals such as Havelock Ellis and Ellen Key, Mead wrote of herself and her fellow Ash Can Cats that

> we did not bargain with men. Almost every one of us fell in love with a much older man, someone who was an outstanding figure in one of the fields in which we were working, but none of these love affairs led to marriage. Schooled in an older ethic, the men were perplexed by us and vacillated between a willingness to take the love that was offered so generously and uncalculatingly and a feeling that to do so was to play the part of a wicked seducer. Later most of us married men who were closer to our own age and style of living, but it was a curious period in which girls who were too proud to ask for any hostage to fate confused the men they chose to love.[68]

While still at Barnard, Mead was involved in sexual liaisons with other Barnard students too.[69] For Mead and her fellow Ash Can Cats, one dimension of their newfound freedom as women involved their changing attitude toward women in general. They expressed a new respect not only for themselves as women, as expressed in their right to do as they pleased, but also a new respect for their fellow women. Mead wrote: "We learned loyalty to women, pleasure in conversation with women, and enjoyment of the way in which we complemented one another in terms of our differences in temperament, which we found as interesting as the complementarity that is produced by the difference of sex."[70]

In Mead's reflections we see the seeds of her own subsequent thinking about relationships between men and women and about the nature of masculinity and femininity. She was, for the first time, beginning to question the issue of innate characteristics and once again to see that the variation in what she called temperament, or personality, within one gender was as great as the variation between the two genders.

In her description of the Ash Can Cats we also see the development of Mead's commitment to female-centered friendship and loyalty. These and other relationships, such as her friendship (and initial romance?) with Marie Eichelberger, whom she also met at Barnard, continued to be important throughout her life. Marie, who Mead once said "took one look at me and fell in love with me," became a surrogate mother to Mead's daughter as well as manager of Mead's business and financial affairs.

The Photographs That Are Missing: Edward Sapir and Ruth Benedict

Missing from the photographs Mead included in *Blackberry Winter* are any of her with her mentor Ruth Benedict or the linguistic anthropologist Edward Sapir. Benedict and Mead, her daughter Mary Catherine Bateson revealed in 1984, were lovers during the 1920s and remained intimate (although not sexually involved) friends and colleagues until Benedict's death in 1948. Mead also had an affair with Sapir, although unlike her relationship with Benedict, her affair with Sapir was short-lived.[71]

When Mead wrote in *Blackberry Winter* that many of the Ash Can Cats had fallen in love with older men, she was referring indirectly to her own experience with Sapir, seventeen years her senior. By all accounts a brilliant man, when Mead met Sapir in 1924 she was married and he had recently lost his wife. Widowed, with three young children to raise, Sapir was attracted to the vivacious young Mead, and she was enthralled by his intelligence and the attention he lavished upon her.[72] Mead does not mention her subsequent affair with Sapir in her autobiography. In fact, as Sapir and Benedict were also colleagues and friends, years later in her biography of Benedict, *An Anthropologist at Work*, Mead made it appear as though it was Benedict who had had an affair with Sapir.[73] However, in the middle of a visit to Pennsylvania in the summer of 1925, Mead traveled back to New York City where she and Sapir spent the night together in a hotel, Mead ostensibly in the city for a job interview at the American Museum of Natural History.[74] Sapir, Mead later recorded, implored her to leave Cressman and to marry him.[75] He was so desirous of marrying Mead that it appears he suggested to Boas that Mead was too frail to go to the field alone.[76]

In retrospect we can see Mead's insinuation that Benedict was the one who had the affair with Sapir as her manipulation of her own reputation and of Benedict's. On the one hand, Mead may have been trying to create a heterosexual "cover" for the homosexual Benedict, while also not wanting the public to know that she had had an extramarital affair. While Mead's attraction to Sapir was fleeting and intense, it apparently ended when she went off to Samoa. On the other hand, Mead has written in glowing terms about the importance of Benedict to her professionally and

Figure 1.4 Ruth Benedict, 1931. (Special Collections, Vassar College Library)

Figure 1.5 Edward Sapir. (Special Collections, Vassar College Library)

personally, first in two biographies she wrote about Benedict and later in *Blackberry Winter*.[77] When asked by fellow anthropologist Jean Rouch, in a film portrait he made of Mead at the American Museum of Natural History in 1977, who was the most influential anthropologist in her life, she responded "Franz Boas *and* Ruth Benedict."[78]

Although Mead never published a photograph of herself together with Benedict (perhaps considering it too dangerous to their careers and public personae to appear together in a photo), in the documentary film *Margaret Mead: An Observer Observed*, historian Virginia Yans includes an imagined dramatic reconstruction of Mead and Benedict together on what we now know was an amorous train ride they had secretly arranged to take across the country in August of 1925 when Mead was en route to Samoa.[79]

The scene takes place in a dining car as the train moves through the night. And while the dialogue is somewhat prosaic—it focuses on the details of doing fieldwork—Benedict, with apparent envy, gushes about how extraordinary Mead is to be going off on her own to do fieldwork somewhere as far away and exotic as Samoa. Given our knowledge of the sexual relationship between Mead and Benedict, the scene takes on a more nuanced and emotionally charged significance, as it symbolizes the eventual erotic relationship between the two women.[80]

Mead, the Press, and "The Primitive Flapper"

After leaving the Grand Canyon, Mead continued by train to San Francisco, where she boarded a boat for Hawaii. She stopped in Honolulu briefly before departing for American Samoa. In the 1920s, this was common practice as the only way to the South Pacific from the United States was by sea, and Honolulu was an important port and gateway to the other islands in the Pacific Ocean. She had arranged to stay in Honolulu with Mrs. May Dillingham Frear, a friend of her mother's from Emily Mead's college days at Wellesley, so that she could consult with Professor Edward Craighill Handy, an anthropologist with extensive knowledge of Polynesia, at the Bernice Bishop Museum.[81] May's husband, Walter F. Frear, had been governor of the Hawaiian Islands from 1907 to 1913, and May Dillingham was a daughter of one of the original missionary families on the islands. One suspects that Mead's arrival in Honolulu was newsworthy in large part because of the local stature of her hosts. The following interview with her appeared in the August 15, 1925 edition of the *Honolulu Star-Bulletin.*

TO MAKE STUDY OF "FLAPPER" IN PRIMITIVE STATE
Dr. Margaret Mead Will Visit South Seas to Carry Out Her Research Plan

Can the usual character traits of the adolescent girl be attributed to heredity—or to civilization? Can the problems of her delinquency be controlled through modern methods or is the tendency so deep-rooted that it cannot easily be eradicated?

In other words, is it a hopeless task to attempt to change the social conditions under which the majority of the young girls of America are placed in order that their characters may be properly formed for a life of happy usefulness—or do her occasional lapses into unruliness come from established natural causes?

These are some of the problems which Dr. Margaret Mead, M.A., Ph.D. and a fellow in biological science of the National Research Council of America, expects to solve during her stay of a year in American Samoa.

"I intend to make a study of the adolescent girl in her native surroundings," the young woman stated a few days ago—Dr. Mead is surprisingly youthful to have become an authority on the subject—in order to discover just what phenomena of adolescence are determined by civilization and by natural heredity and environment.

"It is a popular subject just now, you know, that of the adolescent girl, or 'flapper' as she is usually called, and the various organizations for social welfare are having their problems dealing with her. If I can determine whether qualities which sometimes work for her delinquency are common to all young girls of certain ages—even in the so-called primitive communities—and can learn the reasons for conditions as they are found, I shall have gone a long way in making clear the proper method of handling them in juvenile courts, schools, churches, Y.M.C.A.s and similar organizations."

Such questions as are necessary of solution are these, Dr. Mead pointed out: "When the girl of 14 cannot get along with her parents, demands unsuitable clothes and insists on seeking the company of undesirable boys, can that condition be eradicated by proper recreation and supervision or is she 'as she is' and can no permanent change in her rebellious attitude be made?"

This article appears to be the first time in which Mead's research on adolescent girls in Samoa had been described as "a study of the flapper."[82] However, the article was reprinted verbatim a few days later in the local paper in Doylestown, Pennsylvania, where Mead had graduated from high school. Hence, the idea that Mead was studying "the flapper" in the South Seas made its way from Hawaii to the environs of Philadelphia. Mead had titled her Samoan research, which was funded by the National Research Council, "A Study in Heredity and Environment Based on an Investigation of the Phenomena of Adolescence among Primitive and Civilized Peoples." But given the cultural background of the Roaring Twenties and an older generation's concern about its youth, symbolized most graphically by the flapper, we can easily understand how when Mead commented that her upcoming research on adolescent girls in Samoa was focused on a topic of popular concern—"the flapper"—that the press easily made the connection that Mead was studying "the flapper in [her] primitive state." Already Mead demonstrated her knack at catching the press's attention with an apt image that could be easily translated into terms accessible and interesting to a general audience.

"How Musa-Shiya the Shirtmaker [and Mead] Broke into Print"

Soon after the article about Mead had appeared in the *Honolulu Star-Bulletin* the following advertisement for the tailoring services of Musa-shiya, a Japanese shirtmaker with a shop in Honolulu, appeared in the paper. The text of the ad alongside an image of a bobbed-haired flapper mentioned Mead and her impending research in Samoa, jokingly suggesting that Mead did not really need to go to Samoa to conduct her study of adolescent girls, as she could find such a "flapping girl" right there in Honolulu in Mr. Musa-shiya's household.

By the 1920s, the Hawaiian Islands had already become a popular tourist destination for Americans and Europeans, and the islands were populated with an ethnic mix of people, many of them from Japan and the Philippines, who had been brought over to work on the sugar and pineapple plantations.[83] The pseudo-Pidgin language of the Musa-shiya ad, a form of broken English, would have appeared humorous to the English-

Please observe rising daughter Musa-shiya house just now had the adolescent I think so. Because I been read inside Nippu Jiji newspaper Dr. Margaret Mead speak "why cannot 14 years flapping girl get along with parent and demands unsuited clothe etc and etc?" Shis Samoa go find it.

Rising daughter all same.

I think so Dr. Mead desired of study adolescent girl it are my house also. Maybe Samoa go no use. Before, I speak Mrs. Musa-shiya rising daughter very sassy etc and etc. She rasply speak mind business, make more shirt. All right.

Just now bery importance onnounce out of

Musa-shiya the Shirtmaker

(Also Kimono Make & Dry Good Sell)

HOISERY AND GARTER

Any kind

Garter of man, children also lady around leg kind very nice. Well, that is all for this time thank you.

HOW FINDING THIS PLACE

If you forgot to finding Musa-shiya Shap because never came to it please King Street until famous Fish Market. This one is not to paused for it. Advance until from there but little more River. When little more River this shop between this place 179 N. King Street if you are there now. All right.

(NOTE: So persistent has been demand for clippings of Musa-shiya's ads that a collection of them, with the story of How Musa-shiya the Shirtmaker Broke Into Print, have been published in booklet form. Copies may be obtained from any newsdealer at 25 cents each. An enlarged photo of Musa-shiya himself, and the handsome silver cup his advertising won at the Seattle convention last month, are being exhibited next week at Patten's Book Store.—STAR-BULLETIN.)

Figure 1.6 Musa-shiya the Shirtmaker ad, *Honolulu Star-Bulletin*, 1925. (Mead Archives, Manuscript Division, Library of Congress) speaking visitors to Hawaii, while the joke about "the flapper problem" Musa-shiya has at home and its reference to Dr. Mead would have been a bit of local knowledge recognized by regular readers of the paper. This rapid incorporation of Mead into a local advertisement demonstrates how early in her career her role as an icon began.

Perhaps Mead's youthfulness, or her research focus on adolescent girls, or the unconventionality of a young woman going off on her own to live in Samoa—or all three—caught the imagination of ad man George Mellen, who had the Musa-shiya assignment. Mellen quickly transformed news about Mead's impending research in Samoa into the text of a Musa-shiya ad.[84] In "How Musa-Shiya the Shirtmaker Broke into Print," a small publication written as a result of the popularity of the ads, Mellen wrote about the successful ad campaign for the shirtmaker and noted its popularity with tourists and American servicemen, who sent copies of the ads to family and friends around the world.[85]

The use of Mead's name in an ad for a local business is in and of itself not remarkable. However, the fact the Musa-shiya ads had become popular tourist souvenirs meant that the ad that referred to Mead may have traveled much farther afield than was typical of most ads in local papers. Due to the happenstance of her staying in Honolulu with a family of local repute and the coincidence of her visit occurring during the run of an idiosyncratic local ad campaign, Mead made the news, and was ensconced in popular culture even before she had set off for Samoa.

"Fear Felt for Philadelphia Girl Cut Off in Samoa by Hurricane"

Mead arrived in American Samoa August 31, 1925. Five months later she was in the news again when a devastating hurricane hit the Samoan Islands, cutting off communication between the United States and American Samoa. An article in the *Philadelphia Public Ledger* reported: "Professor E. S. Mead Unable to Reach His Daughter by Cable since Storm—She Is Doing Research Work on Origin of Flapper." A photograph captioned "Miss Margaret Mead" (even though she was married and had a doctorate at the time) showed an anxious-looking youthful Margaret.

PUBLIC LEDGER—PHI

Fear Felt for Philadelphia Girl Cut Off in Samoa by Hurricane

Prof. E. S. Mead Unable to Reach His Daughter by Cable Since Storm—She Is Doing Research Work on Origin of Flapper

The parents of a twenty-four year old girl of this city who is doing research work into the origin of the "flapper" in the Samoan Islands expressed fear yesterday for her safety and welfare since the hurricane which struck the islands last week destroyed means of communication.

A cablegram was received from the girl, Miss Margaret Mead, by her parents, Professor and Mrs. E. S. Mead, of 4213 Chestnut street, on Monday, but efforts to get a cable back to her proved fruitless. Miss Mead has been sending a cable to her father, who is Professor of Finance in the Wharton School of the University of Pennsylvania, each month, but it is believed by her parents that the last cable she sent was filed the day before the hurricane struck the islands.

Miss Mead is living on the island of T'au in the Manua group, being the only white person there except E. R. Holt, the U. S. government representative and his wife. The island is eight miles wide and eleven long. About a thousand natives in four villages inhabit it.

The young woman has been on the island since September, her parents said last night, and will probably stay until next August. She is doing anthropological research work, seeking to prove that the much reviled "flapper" is not a modern phenomenon but has existed in all civilizations since the world began.

MISS MARGARET MEAD

Her work is sanctioned by the American Academy of Science which awarded her a research fellowship.

Figure 1.7 Newspaper article from the *Philadelphia Public Ledger*, January 1926. (Mead Archives, Manuscript Division, Library of Congress)

The article explained that Mead was doing anthropological research "seeking to prove that the much reviled 'flapper' is not a modern phenomenon but has existed in all civilizations since the world began" and played up the inherent drama of the situation. Mead was characterized as "the only white person there except E. R. Holt, the government representative, and his wife," thus accentuating the fact that she was a young, twenty-four-year-old white American woman on her own in a remote and dangerous place. Here Mead's research has been transformed into the topic of "the origin of the flapper" (whatever that might mean exactly), while the description of her research goal seems to be at complete odds with what she was actually interested in proving: that adolescent behavior is not the result of inborn hereditary traits, but, rather the result of environmental factors, which in the case of the flapper were modernity and Western civilization.

The article represents the confluence of several factors that contributed to Mead's early fame. First, there was the serendipity of a dramatic natural disaster striking the very island in the far-off Pacific where Mead was living. Second, the fact that she was alone in the field, young and female, as well as the daughter of a member of Philadelphia's professional community. And, finally, the press's transformation of the subject matter of her research into a topic that peaked the public's curiosity: the origin of the "much reviled flapper."

A few days after the article appeared, Mead was able to cable her parents that she was fine, which was also reported in the Philadelphia papers.

Mead in the Popular Press: 1926–31

Even before Mead published *Coming of Age in Samoa*, upon her return to New York in 1926 articles about her research in Samoa began to appear in local newspapers as well as national magazines. Most of these highlighted her research on the flapper, but they also focused on her youthfulness and anthropology as adventure. For example, a 1927 article in the *New York Sun* ran the headline: "Says Scientist—Idea Archaic Survival: Has Studied the Flapper in the South Seas, Where Western Civilization Has Not Imposed Its Misconception of Flaming Youth." The article's headline referred to *Flaming Youth*, the popular novel of the period about the younger generation.[86] Visiting Mead in her office at the American Museum of Natural History, the reporter commented:

> Dr. Mead is pleasantly different from what one might expect of a person with degrees, intelligence and a position of importance. She is small, attractive, with bobbed hair, and young. Only 26 years old and she sits amid her books and papers behind a very large desk, and in addition to her regular routine of work steals away at times to delve sympathetically into the problem of our younger generation. She is vivid, interested in her work and exceedingly enthusiastic; and how much nicer it is that one her age should ring down the curtain on the flapper-sheik farce than some old person who years ago lost contact with the age about which he attempts to write.[87]

Again, Mead's youthfulness comes to the fore. In an era when the gap between the old and the young was seen as insurmountable, and youth was admired and subjected to the scrutiny of experts and the limelight of the media, to be a young researcher was not only advantageous but also imperative to the newsworthiness of her endeavor. All the more so since the subject she was investigating was adolescent behavior.

The photo that accompanied this article showed Mead posed against a background of Samoan bark cloth, emblematic of this South Seas island. She stands holding a woven skirt such as she wore when dancing as a *taupou*, or ceremonial princess, in one hand and a woven fiber fan in the other. With her bobbed hair, short skirt, and Mary Jane–style black strapped shoes—the "little girl" shoes that were de rigueur for young women in the 1920s—Mead looks like a flapper herself ready to dance. In reality, Mead was neither Samoan princess nor flapper; but the juxtaposition of the two roles, one exotic, the other ultramodern and civilized, and Mead's ability to appear to perform them both, was part of the image she and the media created to capture the public's attention.

However, it was the combination of Mead's youthfulness *and* being female that really made her noteworthy, as this 1931 article for a series, Youth Takes the Lead, that featured women who had achieved prominence in the arts, professions and business, demonstrates.[88] A headshot of Mead, hair bobbed, glasses removed, accompanied the article. Her determined young face is posed against the backdrop of a medallion decorated with lines that radiate from the center like rays of the sun, setting her off as if she were in a spotlight. This celebrity-style treatment of Mead's image attempts to reproduce the aura of a movie star in a photo magazine.

'Adolescence Not a Time of Conflict, Says Scientist—Idea Archaic Survival

Has Studied the Flapper in the South Seas, Where Western Civilization has Not Imposed Its Misconception of Flaming Youth.

IS adolescence necessarily a time of conflict? Should mother and father throw up their hands in horror when daughter reaches the age of sixteen, when she expresses her modern ideas at the breakfast table and they see nicotine stains on her fingers and resign themselves to the inevitable? Are the theories we have accepted concerning the turmoil and strife that is supposed to seethe in every young person's breast fundamentally wrong? And, after all, is there really any conflict, any struggle, or is it merely an illusion that has afforded superfluous material for novelists and scenarists? And does son really storm introspectively under his coonskin coat?

Only a Pet Theory.

Dr. Margaret Mead, assistant curator of ethnology at the American Museum of Natural History, says there is no period in the development of the normal child such as we have exaggerated and commercialized. Positively not. She says that we expect a conflict; that if there is any it is superficially demonstrative, necessitated by our present-day civilization, and is not the result of any physiological changes. And she destroys our idea, catalogues it as archaic and sets it aside in the dust among certain other pet theories that passed away with hoopskirts and good manners. And she proves her statement.

Dr. Mead is pleasantly different from what one might expect of a person with degrees, intelligence and a position of importance. She is small, attractive, with bobbed hair, and young. Only 26 years old and she sits amid her books and papers behind a very large desk, and in addition to her regular routine of work steals away at times to delve sym-

Sun Staff Photo.

Dr. Margaret Mead.

Figure 1.8 "Has Studied the Flapper in the South Seas." Mead, looking somewhat like a flapper herself, holds artifacts from Samoa. A piece of Samoan bark cloth serves as the backdrop. *New York Sun*, 1927. (Mead Archives, Manuscript Division, Library of Congress)

Another article titled "An American Princess of the South Seas: The Fascinating Experience of a Young American Girl Who Lived among the Natives of the South Seas and Was Adopted by Them and Made a Princess," employed the long-popular American trope of being adopted (or captured) by natives.[89] While another (falsely) dramatized the danger of her being a white woman alone among "primitive savages":

> When she was 23 she journeyed alone to Samoa in parts where no other white woman had ever been. . . . She learned their language and became bosom friends with these brown-skinned people in less time than a New Yorker could scrape up a speaking acquaintance with the family in the next apartment . . . being the only white woman living with South Sea natives is "old stuff" to Dr. Margaret Mead. . . . And what's more, she claims there's nothing for a white woman to be afraid of living among primitive savages—that is, if she makes friends with the women folk.[90]

Ignoring any personal inconvenience, Mead commented that,

> getting yourself killed in the jungles is very unfair to other women who might want to follow you in this work—one woman's death would ruin things for all women. You see, most governments already frown on women going where there is danger. And so I always felt an added responsibility.[91]

Here Mead conveys her awareness of her responsibility as a *female* anthropologist—because there were not many women going off to do fieldwork in remote places—and also her growing sense of herself as a role model for other women.

The Romance of Becoming the Other

In 1931 Mead wrote a chapter titled "Life as a Samoan Girl" for a book titled *All True! The Record of Actual Adventures That Have Happened to Ten Women of Today.*[92] In her piece, Mead wrote about her transformation from the modern young woman of twenty-three we see pictured at the beginning of the article into the role of a young Samoan girl eight years her junior:

> I was twenty-three, but because the Samoans are tall and well built and I am not, I was about the height and build of a fifteen year old. . . . My hair

> was bobbed, as was the hair of their girls in the teens—while the older ones used to let their hair grow. And my cue was to become a Samoan girl as nearly as possible. . . . I had to learn to walk barefoot, eat raw the rich little *tuitui* fish which taste like custard, and to dance in Samoan dress with my skin rubbed with scented coconut oil and a hibiscus flower carefully balanced behind my ear.[93]

No photographs of Mead dressed in Samoan garb accompany the article. Instead, the reader is allowed to let her imagination wander freely, transposing Mead's description of herself in Samoan dress into an image of the reader herself becoming a Samoan girl. With no actual image of Mead in Samoa, the reader can more easily imagine being in Samoa, tasting the *tuitui* fish, and walking barefoot on the beach without actually leaving the safety of her home.

Heightening the dramatic tension of her adventure for her readers, Mead writes: "I wasn't very sure of how I would succeed in this strange kind of adventure, this adventure of shedding all one's own ways of eating, sleeping, talking, laughing, just as if they were an old skin instead of the most important part of one, and putting on the attitudes of a Samoan girl, as easily as if they were only a party dress."[94] For Mead, who loved to dress up and perform in pageants and plays, being a participant observer in Samoa may have seemed simply like learning to play another role, this time that of a young Samoan girl.

The climax of Mead's story comes when she demonstrates her successful performance of her role as well as her quick-wittedness. Toward the end of her stay a Samoan chief wanted to marry her and accompany her on her trip home. She found herself caught in a web of her own creation: by transforming herself into a young Samoan woman, she had also placed herself in the position that any young Samoan woman might face, of being asked for in marriage. On the one hand, the request indicated her successful transformation; on the other hand, it also called her bluff. As she admits, "Now I wondered as I sat in that circle of dark expectant faces, if all the flimsy structure was going to collapse about my head, and end only in my insulting a Samoan chief in his native village."

Not wanting to offend the chief, but also knowing that her Samoan hosts were wondering how she would handle the situation, she offered the chief a gracious way out of a proposal that she thought no one really took seriously. She explained to the assembled crowd that when she had left America she had told people that she was going around the world by herself. "All the people laughed and said that a mere girl could not go around the world by herself. Were I to accept his lordship's most honorable invitation and were he to accompany me, all the people would laugh and say that they had been right. And I would be ashamed because I had boasted of something I could not perform." Apparently this explanation satisfied everyone; Mead said that the tension in the crowd dissipated and the crisis passed, "For I had given the courteous answer."[95]

Mead structured her article around the trope of identity transformation, suggesting that success as an anthropologist lies in the ability to lay aside one identity and assume another, for "only by losing my identity, as far as possible, had I been able to become acquainted with the Samoan girls, receive their whispered confidences and learn at the same time the answer to the scientists' questions."[96] But she also knows that some of the appeal for her readers of her experience in Samoa is *their* transformation, that is, their ability to imagine themselves in one or both of her roles: Mead the anthropologist and Mead the Samoan girl.

Mead and the Importance of Being Twenty in the 1920s

While Mead was not the first female anthropologist to be a "New" or "Modern" woman,[97] she happened to be a Modern Woman in the 1920s when women had recently gained the vote and the nation was enjoying the economic prosperity and postwar euphoria of the Roaring Twenties. The media's ability to fashion Mead into a popular heroine was the result of her youthfulness and the adventure and romance associated with her travel to far-off Samoa as an anthropologist, a profession the press glamorized and exoticized. In short, "the girl scientist and her book [*Coming of Age in Samoa*] embodied the American Dream,"[98] a dream of adventure, achievement, and self-assurance.

There has long been a tradition in America of representing the nation and the values, beliefs, and ideals that it stood for with the image of a woman, or more precisely, with a variety of different images of women. As Martha Banta has demonstrated, during the late nineteenth and early twentieth centuries:

> America was symbolized as "female, young, pretty, Protestant, and northern European. She was the heiress of America's history, as edited by the American Whigs. Her features were 'regular' and Caucasian. Her bloodline was pure and vigorous. That she might have 'nerves' and that her will was at times inconveniently strong, was, after all, to be expected of any physical or psychical type that represented the nation's own restlessness and independence of spirit. Whether too selfless or too selfish, whatever else the Girl was, her various images had power over the public imagination. She was problematic, just as the country was."[99]

In the 1920s, Mead was a comely, petite, flapperesque-looking young woman. She used her petite frame and short stature to emphasize her youthfulness—much in the way that flapper's themselves celebrated androgyny with their flat chests, short hair, and straight, loose-fitting dresses. More importantly, her petite size also accentuated the contrast between her seeming frailness and the strength of her wit, intelligence, and determination to do things that other women were not allowed to do or were thought too weak and helpless to undertake, such as traveling around the world alone or undertaking fieldwork in a remote locale.

Her features were "regular" and Caucasian, her brown hair bobbed as was then the fashion among daring young women, and, as the descendant of Anglo-Saxon forebears from New England and the Midwest, her bloodline was both "pure and vigorous." In many respects the young Margaret Mead was an apt representation of the symbolic "American woman" Banta described. Part of her appeal to the American public may have been that she came to represent a set of ideas and ideals about the nation, its culture, and what it meant to be "an American." Even Mead's unconventionality—such as her decision to keep her own last name when she married—was noteworthy and seen as evidence of her independent spirit, as was the fact that she went alone to do research in American Samoa.[100]

Thus, the process of the creation of Margaret Mead as an American icon began during the 1920s, when Mead was still in her twenties. Given this American tradition of representing the nation with the image of a woman, it was highly significant that Mead was a woman. A male anthropologist simply would not have been able to play the same symbolic role.

The association of Mead with the 1920s is perhaps best exemplified by her appearance on a 32-cent U.S. postage stamp, one in a series that

Figure 1.9 "Margaret Mead, Anthropologist," United States 32-cent stamp. (Courtesy of the United States Postal Service)

celebrates each decade of the twentieth century in America. Mead, along with Charles Lindbergh, F. Scott Fitzgerald, and Babe Ruth, is in the set commemorating the 1920s, representative of an era "known for its thrill seekers and heroes," for jazz, prohibition, women's suffrage, and radio entertainment, and for new words such as "motel," "robot," "fan mail," and "teenager."[101]

The image of Mead reproduced on the stamp is that of a young, bobbed-haired Margaret (sans glasses) set against a background of patterned Samoan *tapa* cloth. On the back of the stamp Mead is described as an anthropologist who "explored the effect of culture on the behavior and personalities of children and adults, as well as the differences between men and women."[102]

As we will see in chapter 3, Mead's Samoan research added to our understanding of adolescence in general by means of her reflection on the significance of her Samoan findings for youth in America. However, although it is true that her work on culture and its effects on personality and behavior commenced in the 1920s, the statement on the stamp more accurately summarizes the broader scope of her research and thinking about gender and sexuality that continued into the 1930s and 40s and beyond.

CHAPTER 2

Images of the Mature Mead

Sexual adventurers like Margaret Mead . . .
—Allan Bloom, *The Closing of the American Mind, 1987*

Unlike many females who became celebrities in their youth but faded quickly from popular memory, Mead was able to maintain her fame as she became middle-aged and older. This chapter considers various meanings associated with images of the mature Mead and the roles she assumed as a mature woman, including wife, mother, grandmother, older sage or guru, and, most recently, as an icon for gays, lesbians, and bisexuals.

Mead and Marriage

Just as Mead had created the illusion in Samoa that she was unmarried in order to facilitate gaining the confidence of adolescent girls, in New York she had sometimes acted as though she was not married, having extramarital affairs with men as well as women. Thus, marriage was another arena in which Mead did not hold to traditional societal attitudes or female standards of behavior, causing some people to see her as daring and liberated from bourgeois norms, while others, such as conservative scholar Allan Bloom, viewed her disparagingly as a "sexual adventurer."

Mead was married three times, first to Luther Cressman in 1923, then to New Zealand–born anthropologist Reo Fortune in 1927, and lastly, in 1937, to British anthropologist Gregory Bateson. From the very start she

Figure 2.1 Mead and Luther Cressman, Doylestown, Pennsylvania, 1918. (Courtesy of the Library of Congress and the Institute for Intercultural Studies)

kept her own name, a fact the press commented upon when she married Luther Cressman: "Miss Mead denies she is following a fad, or carrying out some 'feminist principle' in determining to retain her maiden name after marriage. 'I simply want to continue to be known as Miss Mead for my own convenience,' she said."[1]

Anthropology, Mead once quipped, was hard on marriages.[2] In her case it was also accurate to say that fame was hard on her marriages, especially to Fortune and Bateson. Even so, after her marriage to Bateson ended she entertained the fantasy of marrying British anthropologist Geoffrey Gorer,

Figure 2.2 Mead with Reo Fortune in Pere Village, Manus, 1929. (Courtesy of the Library of Congress and the Institute for Intercultural Studies)

Figure 2.3 Mead with Gregory Bateson, late 1930s. (Photograph by C. H. Waddington, Courtesy of the Library of Congress and the Institute for Intercultural Studies)

although she knew he was gay. Being married, it appears, was another role Mead liked to assume. Not only did she enjoy the companionship of men, intellectual as well as emotional (and sexual), just as much as she enjoyed the companionship of women, it was also useful in terms of a division of labor in anthropological research. Although her friendships with former female lovers were more enduring than those with men, she remained friendly with all three of her husbands after they divorced. She also established long-lasting friendships with other men, including the psychologists Lawrence Frank and Erik Erikson, social scientist Ray Birdwhistell, and photographer Paul Byers. As she grew older she also initiated intellectual collaborations with men considerably younger than herself, such as *Life* magazine photographer Ken Heyman and anthropologist Theodore Schwartz, whom she took with her on field trips to Bali and New Guinea.

Her own marriage record not withstanding, Mead was regarded as an expert on male-female relations and marriage. She cultivated this role through her books and a monthly column in *Redbook* magazine and on television talk shows and lectures, always thinking innovatively about changes that could be made to modify, yet preserve, the institution: ideas such as trial marriages, marriage insurance, and two-step marriage that generated much heated debate among audiences. In a draft of her autobiography, she acknowledged her surprise and pleasure that the American public was willing to ignore the fact that she had been divorced three times and accept her as an expert on the topic of marriage.[3]

The public may have done so in part because Mead's behavior reflected a changing marriage pattern in twentieth-century America. When her marriage to Bateson ended in 1948, Mead was middle-aged and a single mother with an adolescent daughter to raise. She insisted that divorce did not mean a failed marriage; it meant that one or both individuals had outgrown their relationship. Such changes were bound to happen over time, she observed in 1949 in a chapter titled "Can Marriage Be for Life?" in her popular book *Male and Female*.[4] Obviously, she did not believe so.

Mead had indeed kept the fact she was married a secret from the Samoans, and during her lifetime she also kept the fact that she engaged in extramarital affairs hidden from the public. As anthropologist Rhoda Metraux, her partner later in life, once said, Mead's private life was just that—"private." This type of discretion—or the discrepancy between her public persona and her private life—was not unusual during the twentieth century for high profile women such as Mead, Eleanor Roosevelt, and

Katharine Hepburn. Although societal standards for female sexual behavior were changing, they still held women, especially married women, to a standard different from men. Whereas men such Franklin D. Roosevelt and John F. Kennedy might be allowed to have affairs on the side, famous women were expected to be loyal to their spouses.[5]

Mead and Motherhood

Like marriage, motherhood was another topic Mead focused on throughout her professional life, even before she was a mother herself. Ever since she was a young girl, Mead said that she had wanted to have children, a passel of them. However, in 1926 when her gynecologist told her that she would never be able to conceive, the news did not distress her.[6] Instead, she divorced Luther Cressman, whom she had thought would make an outstanding father, and married Reo Fortune, an anthropologist whose personality she thought would be antithetical to parenthood. Later, while doing fieldwork with Fortune among the recently pacified Mundugumor people in New Guinea, for the first time Mead encountered a culture that did not value children. Repulsed by the Mundugumor's aversion to children, Mead vowed to have a child herself. After a miscarriage while in the field (provoked, it appears, by a fall she suffered when Fortune, in a fit of anger, struck her), Mead divorced Fortune and eventually married Gregory Bateson, another man whom she felt would be a good father.

We see in this narrative that Mead recounts in her autobiography yet another example of her indomitable self-confidence and willfulness. Medical prognostications to the contrary, she *was* going to have a child.[7] Finally, after marrying Gregory Bateson and enduring subsequent miscarriages and a period of confinement, on December 8, 1939, she gave birth to her first and only child, Mary Catherine Bateson. Mead was thirty-eight years old, a world-renowned expert on child development, and an experienced observer of childbirth in several Pacific cultures. Based on these experiences, she had a very clear idea of how she wanted things organized for her own child's birth—she wanted a pediatrician in the delivery room along with the obstetrician, she wanted to be able to breastfeed her baby on demand, to have access to a wet nurse if her milk did not flow sufficiently in the beginning, and to facilitate feeding on demand she wanted her baby to be able to sleep in the same room with her.[8] She also wanted to have the birth recorded on film, for she believed that in the first hour after birth an infant is "more clearly herself than she will ever be again for days or months as the environment makes an increasing mark, so that these moments were critical to record."[9] (As it turned out, the obstetrician had to delay the birth by ten minutes in order for the filmmaker to get extra lights from her car![10])

None of these things were common practice in American hospitals at the time. In order to get her way Mead had to find both an obstetrician and a hospital willing to allow a pediatrician to be in the delivery room, as well as an unconventional pediatrician.[11] Prior to her pregnancy Mead had met a young pediatrician interested in psychiatry and psychoanalysis at lectures they had both attended at the New York Psychoanalytic Institute.[12] The pediatrician, Dr. Benjamin Spock, was interested in the work Mead and Bateson had done on child development in New Guinea and Bali.

When Spock first published his popular *Baby and Child Care* book in 1943, it reflected the influence Mead had had on him. For example, he too advocated "self-demand feeding" and the benefits of breast-feeding.[13] As her daughter observed, "The innovations that Margaret made as a parent were actually greater than they now seem because so many have since been incorporated in the patterns of society."[14] Like Mead, Spock later became a regular contributor of a monthly column in *Redbook* magazine. Their ideas about children, family, and American culture often complemented each other and influenced several generations of American parents. It was only in the 1970s, when conservatives criticized both Spock and Mead for their political views—in particular, their antiwar stance—that their views on child care came under attack as well.[15]

As her mother had done when she was an infant, Mead took copious notes on Mary Catherine's behavior. The image of a maternal Mead, one of the most prevalent and enduring associated with her, was now authenticated by the fact that she was a mother herself.

Mead Mobilizes for War: Assignment—Cross-Cultural Mediator

By the time she was middle-aged, as one of her colleagues noted, Margaret Mead had become "a brand name."[16] This was largely the result of her

Figure 2.4 Mary Catherine Bateson as a baby with her father Gregory Bateson, 1940. Note the camera around Gregory Bateson's neck. (Courtesy of the Library of Congress and the Institute for Intercultural Studies)

frequent appearances at conferences, on the radio, and in the press. Images of the mature Mead often show her on a podium delivering a lecture or behind a microphone. Even when talking over the radio Mead spoke with her hands, gesticulating to emphasize a point to her invisible audience.

During the war years Mead went to Washington, DC along with Ruth Benedict, Bateson, and other anthropologists to "mobilize" anthropology in the fight to defeat fascism.[17] Initially, she participated in the Committee on National Morale, a quasi-official group of intellectuals concerned with the war in Europe. After Pearl Harbor, she became the executive secretary of the National Research Council's Committee on Food Habits.[18] This assignment offered her the opportunity to crisscross the United States to observe how different communities in different regions of the country were adapting to food rationing and changing their food habits as a result of wartime living conditions. Her observations of many different American communities, rural and urban, large and small, those newly formed in response to the war such as Oak Ridge, Tennessee,[19] or older communities

Figure 2.5 Even when talking on the radio, Mead used her hands expressively to punctuate her statements. (Date of photograph unknown. Neg. No. 33742. Courtesy of the Department of Library Services, American Museum of Natural History)

depleted of their youth as a result of wartime activities, provided her with material for her first book about American culture, *And Keep Your Powder Dry: An Anthropologist Looks at America.*[20]

Mead's experience observing American society and applying anthropological methods and insights to the solution of problems of immediate practical concern during the war marked a momentous shift in her career as well as the beginning of a new field of applied anthropology and a new methodology, the study of cultures at a distance, which Mead helped initiate.[21] It also initiated a new role for her as cultural commentator and translator of American culture to non-American audiences. In 1943, the Office of War Information asked Mead to travel to England to use her expertise on male-female relations and sexuality to analyze the dating practices of American GIs and British women.[22] Her task was to clear up a cross-cultural misunderstanding about the American idea of "a date"

Co-op Housekeeping Solves the Problem

Mr. and Mrs. Gregory Bateson and their daughter photographed before Mr. Bateson went on overseas service. Mrs. Bateson is Margaret Mead, the anthropologist. From her own experience as a "war widow," Dr. Mead has gained valuable pointers for other mothers in her position.

Figure 2.6 Mead and Gregory Bateson with their daughter, Mary Catherine, 1943. The article identified Mead as a "war widow," as Bateson was soon to depart for overseas duty. (Mead Archives, Manuscript Division, Library of Congress)

that was causing tension between American soldiers based in England and British civilians among whom they were residing. In an eight-page memorandum later published as a pamphlet for public distribution Mead explained that English girls had been raised to expect boys to do what American boys expected girls to do: impose restraints on how far a couple went sexually on a date.[23] Given this cultural misunderstanding, neither partner had been calling a halt and both parties considered the other to be immoral. Although the British Foreign Office considered the pamphlet to be "an admirable document," it also felt that it overemphasized the "boy meets girl" relationship to the detriment of other social issues. Repeating a popular stereotype about Mead, it went on to say that this emphasis was "perhaps rather natural since Miss Mead is an anthropologist of a school notable for its studies into the mating habits of certain aboriginal tribes in the SW Pacific."[24]

While in England, Mead toured the country as a guest of the British Ministry of Information speaking on topics that included The American Family, Men and Women in America, Parents and Children in America, and The Cult of Success in America; or, American Puritanism in 1943, all subjects that she had focused on in *And Keep Your Powder Dry.*[25] The

British Federation of Business and Professional Women, however, wanted Mead to talk about the implications of her South Pacific research for the role of British women because, they said, her research (in *Sex and Temperament in Three Primitive Societies*) had "startled the scientific world" with her finding that "temperament was neither male or female but human." Moreover, she had demonstrated by comparative studies "how men and women in varying cultures have developed widely different characteristics in response to social demands."

Mead's talk, titled "Science, Women, and the Problem of Power" was advertised as follows:

> Before the war many people in this country held that women could not do certain jobs because they were women, or that if they did them they would cease to be womanly.
>
> The war has proved that they were wrong . . .
>
> THE BRITISH FEDERATION OF BUSINESS AND PROFESSIONAL WOMEN which represents over 110,000 trained women, believes that in war and in peace women must make their full contribution as citizens according to their talents and not according to their sex if there is to be work stability. This means problems of re-adjustment which need straight thinking. We have asked Dr. Mead to help us evaluate and face these problems.[26]

In a letter to Mead the federation's president wrote, "I do feel that your lecture will be a land-mark in the women's movement in this country. I have felt for a long time that we needed a reorientation of thought about the part which women should play in the community, and I know that your lecture will help to clarify the minds of many of us."[27]

Just as she had become a symbol of women's rights and the equality of the sexes in the United States with the popular success of her books, talks such as this one promoted her reputation in Britain as a champion of women's rights. As a result of the time she spent there, she became even better known internationally than she had been before the war.

The Postwar Years: Mead and *Male and Female*

A mature Mead, her own marriage on the rocks, presented the Jacob Gimbel Lectures in Sex Psychology in California in 1946. She used comparative data from all seven of the South Seas societies in which she had worked to sum up her findings about sex similarities and differences. These lectures provided the basis for *Male and Female*, the last book she wrote on sex and gender in which she argued the importance of women's biological role as mothers.[28]

One of Mead's most provocative statements about parenthood in *Male and Female* was that human fatherhood is a social invention. Basing her insights on her observations of fatherhood in non-Western societies as well as her reading in the field of primatology, she came to the conclusion that, "Somewhere at the dawn of human history, some social invention was made under which males started nurturing females and their young."[29] This behavior makes humans different from their other primate relatives where males leave females and their children to fend for themselves. The result was the creation of the human family. There are many different forms of the family in different cultures, but "within the family, each new generation of young males learn the appropriate nurturing behavior and superimpose upon their biologically given maleness this learned parental role."[30]

The Maternal Mead

After the birth of her daughter, Mead and the media emphasized maternal images of herself even more than before. Photographs such as one of Mead holding a Balinese baby that Ken Heyman took for *Life* magazine in 1957 or of Mead seated with a group of college students at Columbia University gathered at her feet listening raptly to her, present images of a matronly mother figure, one with graying hair who had put on a considerable number of pounds since her slim youthful days in Samoa. Images such as these led one journalist to call Mead the "den mother to all of humanity."

The postwar American public seemed to find this maternal, somewhat dowdy-looking figure comforting. Like a scolding mother who has her children's best interests at heart, people were willing to accept Mead's sometimes-radical ideas and stinging critique of contemporary American society. Here, for example, is her assessment of the complacency and mediocrity of 1950s America:

> What we have today is a retreat into low-level goodness. Men are all working hard building barbecues, being devoted to their wives and spending time with their children. Many of us feel, "We never had it so good!" After three wars

> and a depression, we're impressed by the rising curve. All we want is it not to blow up.[31]

As well as the equally low-level expectations American parents had for their children:

> We have refused to recognize the creativity of youth. We don't want our children to write poetry or go to the stars. We want them to go steady, get married and have four children.[32]

She was a mother figure who constantly chided her wayward children, egging them on to do better for themselves, their children, and America. She was also a mother figure who had much to say about childbearing and motherhood as important female roles and activities just at a time when the United States was on the verge of the postwar baby boom.

The Feminine Mystique: Betty Friedan's Critique of *Male and Female*

In 1963, the time was ripe for Betty Friedan's incendiary book, *The Feminine Mystique*.[33] Friedan used her own life story as the basis for her diatribe against the "problem that has no name," which she then labeled "the feminine mystique." She was critical of the ways in which American society kept American women helpless and in the home. Her jeremiad struck a resounding chord among her generation of postwar, mostly white, educated, middle-class American women. As did her solution to the problem: self-actualization as a challenge to the traditional feminine roles of housewife and mother.

The Feminine Mystique appeared at a point when Friedan could assert with justification that Mead was the best-known social scientist in America:

> Her work on culture and personality—book after book, study after study—has had a profound effect on the women of my generation, the one before it, and the generation now growing up. She was, and still is, the symbol of the woman thinker in America. . . Margaret Mead is her own best popularizer—and her influence has been felt in almost every layer of American thought.[34]

Friedan, who had studied psychology until she dropped out of graduate school and got married, had more than a passing understanding of Mead's work and its place in contemporary social science.[35] In *The Feminine Mystique* she devoted an entire chapter to excoriating Mead for having turned traitor to her own sex.[36] First establishing the breadth of Mead's influence, Friedan then singled out *Male and Female* as the cornerstone of the feminine mystique: "increasingly, in her own pages, her interpretation blurs, is subtly transformed, into a glorification of women in the female role—as defined by their sexual biological function.[37]

Friedan's portrait of Mead is a complex one; she admired Mead for her earlier anthropological work and for the example she had set for other women in the independent manner in which she had lived her own life. Friedan even acknowledged that in the decade following the publication of *Male and Female*, Mead had expressed concern over the "return of the cavewoman" mentality in contemporary American women who had retreated wholeheartedly into the cosseted domesticity of their homes.[38] But rather than celebrating the plasticity of women's behavior and the variety of roles women play in different societies, Friedan opined, Mead rejected her own earlier findings and reverted to a neo-Freudian functionalist framework in which anatomy was destiny and the pinnacle of a woman's achievement was the fulfillment of her biological function as a mother. Moreover, Friedan bitterly observed, Mead seemed oblivious to the fact that through her neo-Freudian take on the importance of women as mothers and caregivers in *Male and Female*, she had been a major influence on women and their acceptance of the feminine mystique.[39]

Friedan's argument presents an image of Mead as a traitor to her sex and as a functionalist social scientist whose work had the effect of "freezing" women and men in their existing sex roles. She portrays Mead as a fallen heroine who was bold, even revolutionary, in her youth when she was an exemplar of women's potential. But over time Mead lost that vision of women and ended up glorifying the same timeworn masculine and feminine roles that her fellow functionalist social scientists were touting.

As a result of the overwhelming success of *The Feminine Mystique*, Friedan went on to play a major role in the creation of the second wave of feminism in the United States. In 1966 she helped establish NOW (National Organization for Women), and throughout the 1960s and early 1970s she was a major figure in the women's movement, albeit a controversial one. One legacy of *The Feminine Mystique* was that a younger generation of feminists such as Kate Millet, Ti-Grace Atkinson, and Robin Morgan, who spearheaded the second wave of feminist activism in the late 1960s and 70s—many of whom were much more radical in their politics than Friedan—also rejected Mead as a mentor or model for the type of activist feminists they envisioned themselves to be. They considered her to be too mainstream, too much an apologist for the status quo. (These same radical feminists soon abandoned Friedan too, for many of the same reasons.)

Later, in the late 1970s and 80s, a less radical cohort of feminists chose to claim Mead as a founding mother, anointing her with titles such as "first of the Libbies" and "Supersister" and according her a foundational role in feminist scholarship and the reshaping of academic disciplines such as the social sciences.[40] For example, comparing Mead to the nineteenth-century feminist Margaret Fuller, feminist historian Eugenia Kaledin wrote that "like Fuller, [Mead's] broad human concern about the nature of our civilization set her apart from the issue-oriented feminist thinkers of her lifetime, but the depth of her appreciation of women's dilemmas should not be minimized."[41]

According to Kaledin, "Margaret Mead, in the public eye almost as long as Eleanor Roosevelt, continued to make Americans aware that women, even old women, in other societies often had roles of significance and power. If her 1950s audience picked up the side of her message that accepted women's biological function, it was not because Mead herself ever neglected to talk about cultural conditioning as the source of women's self-images." Kaledin had in mind statements that Mead made to the press in the 1950s such as this one about American mothers: "we've made an abortive effort to turn women into people. We've sent them to school and put them in slacks. But we've focused on wifehood and reproductivity with no clue about what to do with mother after the children have left home."[42]

Mead and "Postmenopausal Zest"

The "empty-nest syndrome" that Mead was referring to above was never an issue for her. A recurring image of her throughout her life was that of being a hardworking overachiever. As Mead matured, descriptions of her conveyed what we would now label a *workaholic* personality. Depicted as constantly on the go, giving lectures, attending conferences, testifying at congressional hearings, she was "an energetic 58, working 15 hours a day" who needed only six hours of sleep a night and who got up at five in the morning "to write, answer correspondence, or read student papers.[43]

In the film *Margaret Mead: An Observer Observed*, a clip from the 1970s shows Mead with television talk show host David Frost. When he asked her how she managed to accomplish so much at her age, keeping a pace that would exhaust someone half her age, she quickly shot back: "It might have killed me too at that age! I attribute my energy to postmenopausal zest."[44]

Her retort, of course, brought down the house—and left Frost momentarily nonplussed, since in the 1970s the word menopause was seldom used in public. Her mention of postmenopausal zest on commercial television gave new life to a concept she had first introduced in a 1959 profile in *Life* magazine. There she had bemoaned the fact that "we've found no way of using the resources of women in the 25 years of postmenopausal zest."[45]

In attributing her prodigious productivity to postmenopausal zest, Mead was contradicting the prevailing stereotype of menopausal women as "over the hill" and once again putting herself forth as a role model to other women. Moreover, in her book *Woman, an Intimate Geography*, Natalie Angier recently reminded readers that "Margaret Mead famously talked in the 1960s of the 'zest' of the postmenopausal woman," helping to perpetuate this classic "Meadism."[46]

"On Being a Grandmother"

On October 9, 1969, Mead became a grandmother.[47] Her daughter had married an Armenian named Barkev Kassarjian and they had a baby girl named Sevanne (Vanni) Margaret.[48] As Mead wrote effusively in her monthly column for *Redbook* magazine, "Curious! Through no immediate act of my own, my status was altered irreversibly and for all time."[49]

The role of grandmother delighted Mead, and she and the media cultivated her grandmother image as an important dimension of her now elderly public persona. The role pleased her in part because of the fond

Figure 2.7 Mead with her granddaughter Vanni Kassarjian, 1969. (Photograph by Robert J. Levin. Courtesy of Corbis/Bettmann)

memories she had of her own grandmother, Martha Ramsey Mead. Grandparents and grandchildren, Mead observed, were allies united against the parents.[50] The symmetry of the role of grandmother also allowed Mead an artful way to conclude *Blackberry Winter*, coming full circle from her childhood to her now assuming the role her grandmother had originally occupied in relationship to her, while also emphasizing the importance of the continuity of generations to the continuity of cultures.

The role of grandparent was personally rewarding and also culturally significant to Mead. She understood that grandparents needed grandchildren "to keep the changing world alive for them." As she wrote in the *Redbook* article, through the stories grandparents told, their grandchildren not only learned about the world as it had been for the grandparent but also what their parents' childhood had been like.[51] Grandparents thus linked the past to the present, while grandchildren linked the present to the future. Mead saw the value of the link between the generations that grandchildren established as a model for mutual learning across generations, as a means whereby the gap between generations was bridged.

"Folk Heroine to Youth": Mead and the Generation Gap

Just prior to her granddaughter's birth, Mead had delivered a series of lectures on the subject of the generation gap at the American Museum of Natural History that were subsequently published in a small volume titled *Culture and Commitment*. The generation gap of the 1960s was in many ways a modern version of the crisis between youth and adults of the 1920s. And once again, what Mead had to say about adolescence caught the media's attention. As a *Cosmopolitan* magazine profile of Mead noted, "her latest vogue is as folk heroine to today's youth." Rather than criticizing the rebelliousness of American youth during the 1960s and 70s, Mead championed their cause, seeing them as avatars of the future. Speaking of the postwar baby boom generation, she said: "These children were born into a whole world. They're involved in everything at once—the bomb, space exploration, computers, pollution. Things happen every place and every place—through television—is theirs. We know this world as a second language. They know it as a mother tongue. . . What's needed is a lingua franca, a common language."[52]

Another reason Mead delighted in the role of grandmother cum folk heroine was that it afforded her a new social persona, a new role to play not only in her own family pageant, but vis-à-vis the American public. It was a role that fit well with her aging body and graying hair. As one journalist described Mead at seventy-one: "The looks are strictly American—what you might call granny-raffish or apple-pie bluestocking: gray bangs, rimless glasses, pug nose, soft pretty skin jauntily traced with smile lines." When Mead died in 1978, many television broadcasts, newspaper headlines, and magazine obituaries used the phrase "Grandmother to the Nation" or "Grandmother to the World" to describe the elderly Mead and her special relationship to the public.

The Older Mead as Prophet, Priestess, or Sage

Dressed in a pantsuit, often wearing a flowing cape and carrying her signature forked walking stick, in her later years the short, plump Mead had assumed an ageless, almost androgynous, appearance. A common image of this elderly Mead and description of her role in American society was that of a sage or prophet or, more humorously, a "Yoda-like" figure. Another mischievous writer referred to her as a "Big Bo-Peep," capturing the thumb stick's similarity to a shepherd's crook as well as Mead's short stature and portly size.

Mead acquired her walking stick in 1960 after breaking her ankle for a third time, necessitating the temporary aid of a cane. But at fifty-nine Mead was not ready to use something that symbolized old age and infirmity to her, so she chose a tall English cherrywood walking stick—called a "thumb stick" since a "Y" at the top of the stick provided a convenient place to rest the thumb—instead. She liked the thumbstick so well that even after her ankle healed she continued to use it, although she only needed it on rough ground and for stairs. It was, as biographer Jane Howard noted, "one of the most inspired decisions of her career as a public figure."[53]

While the thumb stick had a practical function, it also acquired a symbolic role. As anthropologist Robin Fox wryly observed, "Mead was left over from the time when to be an anthropologist was, by definition, eccentric, and to be a famous anthropologist demanded a striking public presence. She never let her public down."[54] Although Fox's comment conveys little respect for Mead—characterizing her as "left over" from an earlier time when the fledgling discipline still attracted marginal characters—he is absolutely right to imply that Mead's striking appearance was quite conscious.

She was aware of the religious associations the thumb stick conjured; she referred to it as her "pastoral rod." "Every society," she said, "has some symbol that goes with a staff. In Israel I look like a prophet; in Greece, like Tiresias from *Oedipus Rex*. I can fit into their myths."[55] And into our own as well, as the reference to Mead as *Yoda-like* reveals by putting a cleverly updated popular culture spin on the familiar image of the sage.[56] Remember who Yoda is. None other than the wisest and most benevolent of the Jedi Masters, the old, wizened, gnomelike creature in George Lucas's *Star Wars* movies, who, like Mead, is short in stature, wears a capelike garment and carries a long staff.

The wisdom of a Jedi master and the image of a wise creature from another galaxy reverberates with anthropologist Roy Rappaport's explanation of how Mead achieved the status of a prophet or seer in American society. Rappaport, an expert on the anthropology of religion, suggested that Mead had come to be regarded as a prophet by Americans because of her age, her appearance—complete with a staff of wisdom—and her pithy insights into American culture. Moreover, he said Americans viewed her as wise and prophetic because, like the ancient Greek heroes, she had acquired her knowledge by going on a voyage to a distant land and returning home to share her knowledge so that it might benefit others.[57]

Phyllis Grosskurth described Mead as "the female counterpart of Norman Vincent Peale . . in her flowing cape and with the forked cherrywood stick that she now carried with her everywhere, she spoke and looked like a prophet, a role she found particularly satisfying."[58] Grosskurth's reference to Norman Vincent Peale, the popular twentieth-century American minister who was also the author of the best-selling self-help book, *The Power of Positive Thinking*, not only links Mead with the religious imagery of a prophet but also with the quintessentially American "pull yourself up by your bootstraps" attitude typical of the secular self-help advice provided by various "experts."

It is noteworthy that so many individuals have used terms that allude to the possession of divine or supernatural powers, or the mediation between human and divine power, to describe Mead. Although the initial impetus for the use of these terms may have come from her appearance, especially her tall crooklike thumb stick, all these terms are used metaphorically to convey the idea that Mead is different from ordinary people because of her acute powers of perception and intelligence.

Although Allan Bloom—one of Mead's most vocal critics—noted that "the social science intellectual in the German or French mold, looked upon as a kind of sage or wise man who could tell all about life, has all but disappeared," it appears that Mead fulfilled that role for many Americans.[59] Fundamentally, these images of Mead as seer seek to convey the role people felt Mead played in twentieth-century American society: that of a wise and perceptive social commentator or cultural critic. "To a society troubled by its own shifting folkways, and hungry for guidance in coping with them," journalist David Dempsey wrote in the *New York Times*, Mead was "a global prophetess" helping Americans to maneuver the unfamiliar territory of shifting mores and relationships that were generated by modernity and its heir, postmodernity.[60]

The Posthumous Mead as the Bisexual Mead

Images of Mead as prophet or sage lack any reference to her as a sexual being. They are gender neutral, or at least androgynous, as was Jane Howard's identification of the older Mead as "elder statescreature," again emphasizing the ambiguous gender identity that often characterized descriptions of Mead late in her life.[61] The dual nature of Mead's sexual identity, her androgyny, or more accurately, her ability to combine both female and male qualities—her quality, that is, of "gender blending"—was both a strength and a weakness, for it inspired admiration in some and fear and repulsion in others.[62]

Although Mead had conformed to many American standards of feminine behavior in her clothing, manners, and body language, in more profound ways she had challenged traditional female behavior with her emphasis on her career, her bold, forthright manner of speaking, and her assertiveness. While more common today, this blending of gender roles was one of Mead's most important contributions as a woman; rather than accepting many of the limits that had traditionally been placed on what women could do or say, Mead often ignored the limits and transformed them.

If in her old age the media saw Mead as either a benevolent grandmother figure or an asexual Yoda-like guru, after her death she was resurrected in the popular mind as a gendered, indeed sexualized, individual. This transformation began in 1983 when Australian anthropologist Derek Freeman's attack on Mead's Samoan research caused people to rethink Mead's conclusions about Samoan attitudes toward adolescent sexuality and to wonder if she had imposed her own youthful ideas about sexuality onto her Samoan subjects.[63]

More recently, scholarly studies have focused on Mead's early adult life—especially her sexual relationships with Ruth Benedict and other women—and the relationship between her personal life and her scholarly research. Informed by queer theory and scholarship in the fields of gay, lesbian, bisexual, and transgender studies, these studies seek to place Mead and her quest to understand both her own sexuality and human sex roles in general in historical and intellectual context. They have inspired a new image of Mead as someone who was sexually radical in her belief in free love and her own bisexuality.[64]

Although the public did not know that Mead had been bisexual until her daughter disclosed the information in 1984, as early as 1953 the homosexual community in the United States saw in Mead a comrade-in-arms, someone whose work on the variety of sexual behavior considered to be normal in other cultures could bolster their own critique of American attitudes toward sexual difference. For example, *ONE* magazine, a publication established in the early 1950s "for the purposes of bringing about a better understanding of sexual deviation by both heterosexuals and homosexuals," chose this quote from *Coming of Age in Samoa* for its epigraph: "Realizing that our own ways are not humanly inevitable nor God-ordained, but are the fruit of a long and turbulent history, we may well examine in turn all of our institutions, thrown into strong relief against the history of other civilizations and weighing them in the balance, be not afraid to find them wanting."[65]

Similarly, in a recent collection of essays titled *Margaret Mead Made Me Gay*, lesbian anthropologist Esther Newton writes of the influence that reading *Coming of Age in Samoa* had on her personally and professionally.[66] When she read Mead's book in 1961 for an introductory anthropology course, she had no idea that Mead was bisexual. Nor did she read the book as a defense of homosexuality. Instead, the book offered her the insight that "my adolescent torments over sex, gender, and the life of the mind could have been avoided by different social arrangements."[67] Even before reading Mead's book, Newton was aware that Mead had done a great deal to popularize the concept of cultural relativity: "Her voice had reached into my teen-age hell, to whisper my comforting first mantra: 'Everything is relative; everything is relative,' meaning 'There are other worlds, possibilities than suburban California in the 1950s.' "[68] Like the editors of *ONE*, the value Newton found in *Coming of Age in Samoa* was its defense of cultural, sexual, and temperamental differences.

In an article for *Redbook* magazine titled "Bisexuality: A New Awareness," Mead suggested that an individual might experience a range of different types of love and sexual attraction over their lifetime, and that this trajectory might begin in adolescence by being in love with someone of the same sex, transform during one's "reproductive years" into a passion for someone of the opposite sex, and change in old age into love for someone of the same sex again. In hindsight, with the knowledge of Mead's multivalent sexuality and variety of sexual partners, male and female, over the course of her lifetime, we can see that this article is autobiographical with its description of Mead's experience and feelings of sexual attraction and intimacy. Mead had strong feelings of love as well as other same-sex relationships with female students at Barnard and had an affair with an older man and became involved sexually with Ruth Benedict while married to Luther Cressman. She married three times while in her twenties and thirties and bore a child. Finally, in old age she shared a household and professional partnership with anthropologist Rhoda Metraux. Like Mead, Metraux had been married and had a child, but was widowed at an early age. Their status as mothers and ex-wives offered them a gentile facade behind which to conceal what may also have been a sexual relationship.

Newton's book and the new historical scholarship about Mead have contributed to the iconization of the bisexual or queer Mead—Mead the sexual iconoclast. While this work places Mead within the radical and bohemian traditions of sexual experimentation and free love that characterized the first few decades of twentieth-century America, as we have seen, there is another politically conservative perspective, symbolized by scholar Allan Bloom, that denigrates Mead with the label of "sexual adventuress."

However, Bloom's description of Mead actually has little to do with her sexual behavior. His sexist epithet of "sexual adventuress" hides what really bothers him about Mead—her promulgation of cultural relativism, or the idea that all cultures are equally "good," rational, and to be respected. According to Bloom, cultural relativism has been the source of multicultural values within government and higher education and the decline in scholarly excellence and the pursuit of truth in American culture, all of which have led to "the closing of the American mind."[69] It is quite telling however that Bloom has chosen a sexual metaphor to describe what he sees as intellectual miscegenation.

The Iconic Mead as Modern Woman

From another perspective, Allan Bloom was absolutely right. Mead was indeed a "sexual adventuress." What we see in the correspondence, records of dreams and dream analysis, notebooks, and memos that scholars have unearthed in their archival research is the "lived experience" that Mead and her circle of intellectuals, lovers, and friends enacted that led to the creation of our present-day understanding of sexuality as an individual attribute that is far more fluid and malleable than previous generations had understood or believed imaginable. In an early draft of *Blackberry Winter*, Mead wrote about her exploration of her own sexual identity and then thought better of it, excising those portions from the published version.[70] Today's scholars can present such detailed material about Mead because of what some might call Mead's hubris, but what I think more accurately reflects her self-conscious contribution to posterity. She wanted this material to be available to others. She believed that letters, drafts of manuscripts, even scheduling folders and itineraries were historical and ethnographic data that could be of value to future scholars.[71]

Mead had the rare experience of continuing to be a role model for generations of American women well beyond her initial rise to fame in the 1920s as a young popular heroine. At the time of Mead's death her former critic Betty Friedan said, "I felt that Mead, who was born twenty years before me, had gone as far as she could with feminism and that I, in reacting to her, took it a step further and was in a way her heir."[72]

In addition to being a model of female autonomy, of women's ability to have both a career and a family, and of women's right to use both their minds and their bodies as they desire, Mead helped change twentieth-century America's understanding of human sexuality. She played a major role in changing how twentieth-century women and men conceived of themselves as gendered and sexual beings and in the creation of a new discourse about sexuality, laying the groundwork for today's concepts of gender and sexual identity.[73] She did this through her research and her observation of people in other cultures—topics we will look at in more detail in the next three chapters—but also through her reflection upon her own feelings and experiences and in her intimate relationships with others. In sum, Mead exemplified—and then became a symbol of—the modern American woman.

CHAPTER 3

Mead as Anthropologist: "Sex in the South Seas"

The Anthropologist

Sing a song of mores!
  Tell us of taboo!
Sort out sex stories!
  Watch how menfolk woo!
Study twenty slatterns
  Clad in wool and weed
Call them culture patterns
(Words by Margaret Mead)

—Howard Mumford Jones,
Saturday Review[1]

As this bit of doggerel—published in the *Saturday Review* sometime after 1935—reflects, Margaret Mead's name had become irrevocably linked in the public's imagination with anthropology—and with the study of sex. Although English professor Howard Mumford Jones was familiar enough with Mead's work to have associated it with the idea of "culture patterns," it appears that he did not think highly of her endeavors, nor, perhaps, of the discipline of anthropology.

We move now from a focus on popular images of Mead as a woman to a focus on images of Mead as an anthropologist through consideration of the media's response to her first book, *Coming of Age in Samoa*. In doing so we will see how in the late 1920s Mead and her publisher worked together to craft a particular image of her for public consumption, as well as the role various media played in shaping popular images of her as anthropologist. The period between 1928, when *Coming of Age in Samoa* was first published, and 1935, when Mead published *Sex and Temperament*, were crucial years in the shaping of Mead's reputation as an anthropologist. The enthusiastic response of the media to her books, and in particular to *Coming of Age in Samoa*, launched her career as a popularizer of anthropology and as an incipient media figure.

Mead had not always intended to become an anthropologist. Having chosen *not* to pursue a literary career after graduating from Barnard with majors in English and psychology, Mead studied for a master's degree in psychology.[2] The work of Freud and his followers had spawned much interest in the science of the mind, and psychology was developing in many new directions.[3] The social sciences, Mead had concluded, were easier disciplines in which to distinguish oneself than literature. Moreover, since both her parents were social scientists, she felt that she was already familiar with this intellectual terrain.[4]

In the spring of 1923, Ruth Benedict suggested to Mead that she switch fields from psychology to anthropology. Benedict told her that because of the rapid disappearance of primitive peoples, the need for anthropological research was urgent: "Professor Boas and I have nothing to offer but an opportunity to do work that matters."[5] For Mead, that settled it. Anthropology had to be done *now*, she thought, before it was too late. At the time of her conversation with Benedict, Mead happened to be reading a book by Katherine Routledge titled *The Mystery of Easter Island: The Story of an Expedition*.[6] Routledge, a wealthy Englishwoman trained in archaeology, had spent several years studying the huge enigmatic carved stone heads found on that remote Polynesian island. She had been fortunate to be able to talk with some of the last elderly Easter Islanders who had a distant memory of the ancient festivals held to celebrate the erection of the statues. Her written account of her adventures was a popular success both in England and the United States. Perhaps reading about Routledge's adventures and her encounters with the few remaining elderly Easter Islanders had underscored Benedict's message about the urgency of anthropological research. It may also have fed Mead's sense of drama with the realization that a scientific expedition could be an exciting adventure.

In 1924, when she attended the meetings of the British Association for the Advancement of Science in Toronto, Mead wrote that she discovered that each anthropologist had “a field of his own, each had a ‘people’ to whom he referred in his discussion.” She continued, “I had entered anthropology with the expectation of working with immigrant groups in the United States and perhaps of doing some research on American Indian groups. . . . At Toronto, I learned the delights of intellectual arguments among peers. I, too, wanted to have a ‘people’ on whom I could base my own intellectual life,”[7] a culture that she alone had studied and could discuss with authority. Mead set her mind to going to the South Pacific. She and Boas decided on American Samoa because there was regular communication between there and the United States.[8] That decision proved to be of enduring consequence to her career as it led to her best-selling book, *Coming of Age in Samoa*.

Coming of Age in Samoa (1928)

Mead's sojourn in Samoa—touted as “a study of the flapper in the South Seas”—had already received attention in the press. However, in August of 1928, when William Morrow, a relatively new publisher willing to take a chance on a young unknown author, published Mead's first book, *Coming of Age in Samoa*, neither he nor Mead had anticipated its astonishing success. A second printing of the book occurred the next month, followed by a third in December, a fourth in February 1929, and subsequent printings in 1930 and 1932. An Armed Services Edition of the book came out during World War II, and it has been translated into seven different languages. The most recent American reprint of *Coming of Age in Samoa* occurred in 2001, to mark the centennial of Mead's birth. While not the most popular book by an anthropologist in America, it is certainly the most notorious.[9]

The book's longevity is noteworthy. And it is no exaggeration to say that this book established Mead's career as an anthropologist and brought her name to public attention. It was also this book that fifty-five years later again brought Mead's name into the limelight when anthropologist Derek Freeman challenged the book's veracity.

Looking back at 1928 and the years after Mead published *Coming of Age in Samoa* allows us to see what the public at the time found of interest in the book as well as how her fellow anthropologists received it. We will also see that the disparity between the public's enthusiastic embrace of Mead and her work and her academic peers' ambivalent and often negative response to her work can be traced back to their different reactions to her very first book.

William Morrow suggested to Mead that she add the concluding chapters to *Coming of Age in Samoa* in which she discussed "what all this means to Americans."[10] As these chapters proved to be of much interest to the public, they provided a successful model of cultural commentary and comparative ethnography that Mead continued to use in her subsequent books and public speaking for the rest of her career. Indeed, such "edificatory ethnography" became a hallmark of Mead's popular writing.[11]

Initially, however, Mead's decision to follow Morrow's suggestion entailed some deliberation on her part. Thus, on January 25, 1928, she wrote to Morrow:

> I have been thinking over the possibilities of the concluding chapters of my book very carefully. I finally decided that I would be willing to incorporate in my final discussion a discussion of education which I had been working on from a different angle. This is a speculation about the education of the future and can be tied up very definitely with the problem of the conflict of adolescence. It is definitely a speculation, but one in line with what seems to be our present development. I am enclosing an abstract of this chapter as I would write it. I am couching it in as simple terms as possible and using concrete illustrations. I believe it would save both your time and mine if you were able to tell from this abstract whether such a chapter would satisfy you. In all events, I am most grateful to you for your criticism and encouragement for this conclusion now seems to me to be a great improvement upon my former short summary, and the instigation to make the improvement I owe to you.[12]

In her new conclusion Mead first delineated various differences between Samoan and American culture and then restated her point that there is nothing biologically inherent in the period of adolescence that produces the difficulties American children have. Rather, Americans should look at adolescent conflicts as something for which society is responsible and ask the question, "What can we do about them, as parents, legislators, and educators?" Her answer lay in training adolescents to meet the difficult choices that are thrust upon them.[13]

While complying with Morrow's initial request, the youthful Mead expressed a trace of discomfort in saying that "any improvement which I would be able to make in these last chapters could not lie along the lines of further speculation, which I have pushed to what seems to me to be the limit of permissibility."[14] Her discomfort at further speculation was well founded; it was exactly these new chapters that anthropologists such as fellow Boasian Robert Lowie objected to as "pedagogical sermonizing" and therefore inappropriate to an anthropological text.[15] While the general public found these chapters of much interest, many anthropologists were critical of them.

William Morrow advertised *Coming of Age in Samoa* in magazines such as *The Nation*, whose educated and socially progressive readership they felt would be interested in the book. The ad in *The Nation* carried endorsements by the pioneering British sexologist Havelock Ellis, author of a much-discussed recent series of books, Studies in the Psychology of Sex, and anthropologist Bronislaw Malinowski, whose recently published ethnography *Argonauts of the Western Pacific* had already introduced an interested readership to the Trobriand Islanders, another South Seas people with liberal attitudes toward sexuality. Clearly with this ad Morrow was targeting a specific audience, one that he thought would be intrigued by the book's combination of the scientific study of sexuality, adolescence, and the exotic. The ad in *The Nation* read: "Havelock Ellis says of this provocative comparison of adolescent folkways in Samoa and the United States: 'It is not only a fascinating book to read, but most instructive and valuable. The great master in these fields is Professor Malinowski, and I could not pay higher tribute to Miss Mead than to mention her name in connection with his.' " It continued with a statement from Malinowski: " 'An absolutely first-rate piece of descriptive anthropology, an excellent sociological comparison of primitive and modern conditions in some of the most problematic phases of human culture. Miss Mead's style is fascinating as well as exact . . . an outstanding achievement.' "[16]

Mead had not yet met Malinowski when she requested his endorsement for her book. She wrote to him in flattering, slightly unctuous terms, saying that "no student who attempts to do psychological field work should fail to acknowledge the debt that is owing you in the field which you originated, ploghed [*sic*], sowed and made fruitful for those who should try to do the same kind of work, however indifferently they may succeed." She continued self-deprecatingly, saying that, "This work is a work of

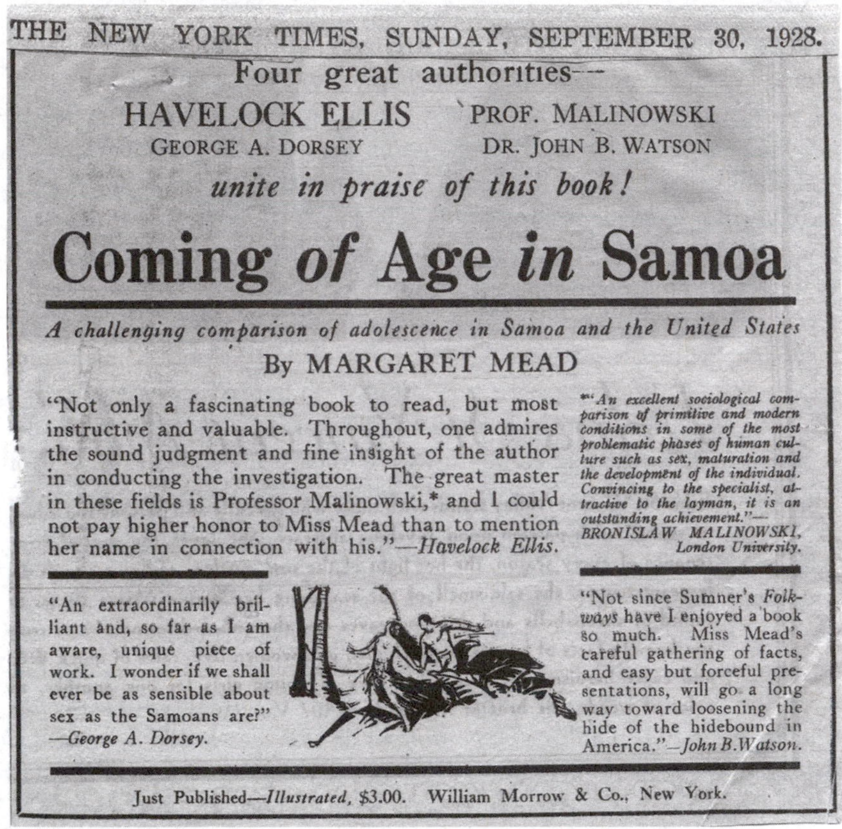

Figure 3.1 Ad for *Coming of Age in Samoa*, *New York Times*, September 30, 1928. (Mead Archives, Manuscript Division, Library of Congress)

apprenticeship, my first field work, undertaken before much of my definition of the problem was published. I hope very much that I may have the benefit of your criticism."[17]

For the young Mead to have gained endorsements from these two renowned men, both highly regarded in the United States and the United Kingdom for their intellectual achievements, added credibility as well as luster to the reputation of her book among nonanthropologists and must have caught the attention of anthropologists as well. If the endorsements did not solidify the association of the book with the currently hot topic of sexuality, the cover design for the book certainly did.[18] With its evocative image of a couple silhouetted against the moonlight holding hands

Figure 3.2 Dust jacket for the first edition of *Coming of Age in Samoa*, 1928. (Mead Archives, Manuscript Division, Library of Congress)

underneath a swaying palm tree, the cover sought to resonate with readers' romantic notions of free love in the South Seas. Mead's vivid prose, such as this paragraph that begins a description of a typical day in a Samoan village, undoubtedly added to it:

> The life of the day begins at dawn, or if the moon has shown until day-light, the shouts of the young men may be heard before dawn from the hillside. Uneasy in the night, populous with ghosts, they shout lustily to one another as they hasten with their work. As the dawn begins to fall among the soft

> brown roofs and the slender palm trees standing out against a colourless, gleaming sea, lovers slip home from trysts beneath the palm trees or in the shadow of beaching canoes, that the light may find each sleeper in his appointed place.[19]

It is a passage such as this that British anthropologist E. E. Evans-Pritchard had in mind when he sardonically described Mead's prose as exemplary of "the-wind-rustling-in-the-palm-trees" school of ethnographic writing.[20] However, in 1928 many Americans would have read this passage within the context of popular imagery of the South Seas that had been shaped by such influences as Herman Melville's nineteenth-century novels *Omoo* and *Typee*, set in the Marquesas and Tahiti; Robert Louis Stevenson's accounts of his life in Samoa; and Jack London's *Cruise of the* Snark; as well as photographs tourists brought back from Samoa.[21] Recently, W. Somerset Maugham's 1921 short story of the downfall of a self-righteous missionary stationed in Samoa had been turned into the Broadway stage production *Rain*, and two movies, *White Shadows in the South Seas*, a dramatic film based on Frederick O'Brien's romantic travelogue, and Robert Flaherty's dramatic romance *Moana*—hyped as "The Love Life of a South Sea Siren"—had appeared.[22] Both movies abounded in stereotypical images of scantily dressed Polynesian maidens living in a South Seas Eden. Not surprisingly, reviewers of *Coming of Age in Samoa* sometimes referred to these stereotypical images of life in the South Seas that were then prevalent in the popular imagination. Nor is it surprising that William Morrow would have picked up on the same motif of clandestine lovers for the cover of *Coming of Age in Samoa*.

Mead had already left New York and was headed to New Guinea to embark on fieldwork with her second husband, Reo Fortune, when *Coming of Age in Samoa* reached the public, so she had no immediate knowledge of the book's initial success. A letter from her publisher dated January 11, 1929, filled her in on the details:

> You know from Miss Phillips' [Morrow's assistant] letters what splendid comments and reviews the work has received. It was great good luck to receive, on the same day, the wonderful letters from Havelock Ellis and Dr. Malinowski. We almost staged a celebration when we read them. We got out a bright red band to put around the book with part of Havelock Ellis's comment on the front. That stunt helped the sales materially.
>
> You will, I am sure, be specially interest in the results. Up to December 31st, we sold in the United States, 3,144 copies, and in Canada, about 80

copies. This is better than I expected in view of the small advance sales. The encouraging fact is that sales have been maintained at a good rate from the start. So far, there has been no let-down.

I spent an evening with George Dorsey about the middle of December, and found him greatly delighted over the way we handled the book. We spent nearly $1,500.00 in various forms of advertising and promotion, and I am very glad we did because although this is a substantial sum for a book of its kind, I am confident the expenditure of that sum and further expenditures we are now planning will be justified by the continued sales. Let us hope we are both right . . .

If there is any chance to get a line through to us, I hope you will take advantage of it. We want to hear from you personally . . . and then, if you can add some news that we can make use of to help *COMING OF AGE IN SAMOA*, we shall, of course, be very glad.

Faithfully yours,
William Morrow[23]

George Dorsey, the Jared Diamond of his day whom Morrow refers to in his letter, was a former curator of anthropology at the Field Museum of Natural History who taught at the University of Chicago. His book, *Why We Behave Like Humans* (1925), was an account of how and why various aspects of human behavior developed; aimed at a general audience, it was a popular success.[24] Dorsey shared a similar theoretical outlook as Mead, one that emphasized the role of human creativity and intelligence in shaping human behavior, in contrast to the innate behavior of other animals.

Dorsey's endorsement of Mead's book said, "I wonder if we shall ever be as sensible about sex as the Samoans are?" Along with the endorsements of Ellis and Malinowski, Dorsey's comment would have helped to solidify the association between *Coming of Age in Samoa* and the topic of sex in the public's mind.

"Sex in the South Seas": The Beginning of the Iconization of Margaret Mead

Given that the 1920s in America was a time when sexual mores were in transition, driven in large part by changes in the sexual conduct of young women, Mead's observations about sexuality in Samoan society hit a responsive chord. If the groundwork for an association between Mead, free love, and the study of the sex lives of South Seas islanders had been laid by her publisher, it was more firmly established by reviewers such as Freda Kirchwey. Her review of *Coming of Age* for *The Nation* led with the eye-catching phrase, "This Week: Sex in the South Seas." Kirchwey, a feminist as well as a left-leaning journalist and former editor of *The Nation*, appealed to readers' stereotypical image of a South Seas island as an alternative to the complex reality of life in the modern American city by reporting that "when you read *Coming of Age in Samoa*—which you should do—you will probably be astonished to discover how like a South Sea island that South Sea island can be." Linking the South Seas with sexual freedom, she goes on to note in almost clinical terms that "sex experience is frequent before marriage, almost to the point of promiscuity. Jealousy is rare. Violent and possessive emotion is held to be in poor taste, but frigidity does not exist."[25] However, Kirchwey realized that there are societal and personal costs that Americans might not be willing or able to make in order to "be as sensible about sex as the Samoans are."[26]

A review in the *Times Literary Supplement* also focused on the topic of sexuality in the book with the opening comment: "Anthropologists are at last waking to the realization that in order to study the family systems of primitive peoples a scientific investigation into their sexual tabus and puberty rites is a first essential." The reviewer then mentions two other works by anthropologists that also focus on sexuality: Malinowski's recently published *Sexual Lives of Savages* (1929) and Ling Roth's "unfortunately named work on the aborigines of Australia" (Roth's book was titled *Ethnopornography*).[27]

Reviews such as these led enthusiastic readers to send Mead fan letters, including the following from Henry Neil of Battle Creek, Michigan:

> My dear Miss. Mead,
> Your book, "Coming of Age in Samoe" [*sic*] next to the Bible is the most interesting book that I have ever read.
>
> I am going to one of the South Sea Islands to get local color for my new novel, "Go Into All the World."
>
> Yours truly,
> Henry Neil

Neil already had written several nonfiction books under the pseudonym Marshall Everett, including one about the St. Louis Exposition with its living dioramas of Bontocs from the Philippines and other exotic non-Western peoples.[28] Although he apparently never wrote a novel set in the South Seas, many years later popular fiction writers Irving Wallace and James Michener did. In his novel *The Three Sirens*, Wallace includes a thinly disguised Margaret Mead–like character, as does Michener in *Return to Paradise*, his sequel to *Tales of the South Pacific*.[29]

There were also letters such as one from Professor W. A. Brownell, a psychologist of education at George Peabody College for Teachers in Nashville, Tennessee. Peabody wrote Mead about the difficulty he faced in using her book in a classroom in the South because of the frank nature of the material on sex. "I do not dare to do so," he wrote, "for fear of being charged by certain individuals whom you can imagine as being guilty of disseminating salacious material."[30] His solution was to present students with the last two chapters of the book, those in which Mead wrote about the implications of the Samoan material for the education of adolescents in America.

In these two quite different letters we see the range of responses readers had to *Coming of Age in Samoa*, from the enthusiastic embrace of the book specifically because of its graphic nature to a fear that the presentation of such material to college students in the conservative South would lead to an accusation of the promulgation of prurient material. Reflected in these two extremes is the profundity of the social change that was in the process of revolutionizing American attitudes and practices regarding sex. *Coming of Age in Samoa* was considered to exhibit the new attitude of openness toward the topic of sexuality as well as to promote the practice of it.

However, we gain a slightly different perspective on the topic of sex from a review by the feminist writer Mary Austin. Her piece appeared in the *Birth Control Review*, a journal published by Margaret Sanger that publicized birth control activities and also served as a forum for the discussion of scientific and social policy related to birth control.[31] As a writer, feminist, and student of Native American folklore, Mary Austin's reputation as a regional writer of the American West and Southwest was established in 1903 when she published a collection of sketches about California titled *The Land of Little Rain*.[32]

Austin made the telling observation that "what interests me is not so much Miss Mead's lively picture of Samoan society, as the unanimity with which American reviewers have accepted the conclusion that a total absence of sex inhibitions can be held responsible for the want of adolescent stress, even though Miss Mead is far from being as convinced as her readers."[33] According to Austin, reviewers were reading what they wanted into Mead's book.

She was the first person to acknowledge that the media's interest in Mead's description of the permissiveness regarding Samoan adolescent sexuality played an important role in determining—and shaping the nature of—the popular success of *Coming of Age in Samoa*. Many reviews of the book by the popular press demonstrate the Western fascination with "the primitive"—especially with "primitive sexuality," a fascination that erases the actual complexity of non-Western societies and extracts from them idealized versions of what we want them to be. Moreover, in these reviews we see the beginning of the iconization of Mead, a process whereby she is made to represent something more than simply herself or what she has said.

"The Problem with Adolescents"

In addition to the topic of sexuality, other reviewers highlighted another subject that was of major interest to them in the book—adolescence. "Youth in Samoa: A Land with No Neuroses" read a review in the *Honolulu Star-Bulletin*. "The Younger Generation with a Difference" read another.[34] Many of the reviews of *Coming of Age in Samoa* noted the contribution the book made to broadening readers' understanding of adolescence in general, a problem of current concern in the United States, through a comparative study of adolescence in Samoa. As the reference to neuroses in the *Honolulu Star-Bulletin* review reminds us, Mead's interest in, and familiarity with, Freudian theories of adolescence and sexuality made the book of current interest to scholars and also to the educated layman who wanted to keep up with the latest scientific and social ideas.

"Richly Readable in Its Style"

From the beginning of her publishing career, reviewers praised Mead for her writing style. The *New York Times*'s review of *Coming of Age in Samoa* stated that just "as Miss Mead's careful scientific work deserves the most earnest tribute, so her method of presenting its results calls for the highest praise. Her book, broad in its canvas and keen in its detail, is sympathetic throughout, warmly human yet never sentimental, frank with the clean, clear frankness of the scientist, unbiased, richly readable in its style. It is a remarkable contribution to our knowledge of humanity."[35]

Mary Austin also praised Mead's lucid writing style, saying that "as a folk study, Miss Mead's work is cool, competent, and commendably free from the shibboleths of formal science, so often a stumbling block to the layman."[36] Such praise of Mead's writing and the accessibility of her prose highlight a key factor in the public success of her books: people enjoyed reading them. Beginning with *Coming of Age in Samoa* Mead distinguished herself from her academic colleagues by her clear, engaging writing style.

Mead consciously wrote *Coming of Age in Samoa* using jargon-free prose with a general readership in mind. But she also published a more technical description of Samoan society. This second volume, *Social Organization in Manu'a*, published by the Bernice P. Bishop Museum, describes the social structure of the societies in the Samoan archipelago of Manu'a, where Mead conducted her research, and uses the technical kinship terminology and social categories that anthropologists employ in order to make comparative analyses of different forms of social organization.[37] Mead followed this pattern of writing a popular book as well as specialized volumes and articles for a scholarly audience with most of her subsequent research.[38] Beginning with her Samoan research, she also wrote short pieces for popular magazines and cultivated a following among editors and readers who welcomed these short, accessible articles.

"South Seas Hints on Bringing Up Children"

The articles she wrote about Samoa for popular magazines were of two types: those about politics and current events and those of general interest. The former pieces she wrote for magazines such *The Nation* ("Civil Government for Samoa") and the *American Mercury* ("Americanization in Samoa") in which she argued that the American Navy's governance of American Samoa had been beneficial to the Samoans.[39] The general interest articles included "South Seas Hints on Bringing Up Children," written for *Parents* (a relatively new magazine aimed at giving American parents advice about raising their children), and "Standardized American vs. Romantic South Seas," in *Scribner's Magazine* that built upon the popular stereotypes and literary associations American readers had with Samoa.[40]

In these two sets of articles we see Mead writing for two different audiences, one a more highly educated, intellectual audience interested in issues of current political and social concern such as America's presence in Samoa, the other, such as the readers of *Parents Magazine*, more broadly middle class. Throughout her career Mead sought to address both of these audiences in her books, editorials, and public lectures. These early articles represent the genesis of a pattern of "popularization" of her anthropological findings that Mead engaged in from the beginning of her career. Reporters, editors, and publishers found that Mead was a willing subject and was very able at providing them with the type of material they wanted.[41]

Anthropologists' Reviews of *Coming of Age in Samoa*

Given that we now know about the intimate personal relationship between Mead and Ruth Benedict, we read Benedict's review of *Coming of Age in Samoa* in the *New Republic* with knowledge of the complex ways in which she was not an unbiased reviewer. Yet it is still interesting to see what she chose to highlight and what she wanted the well-educated general reader of the *New Republic* to gain from the book. For Benedict the book was important because its findings "turn our attention from the theory of the inevitable and biologically fixed causes of adolescent upheaval" and allow us to "take note of the enormously variable social determinants that fashion our flexible human nature."[42] She stressed the most general and, at the time, most provocative and important finding of Mead's study that underscored Boas's broader research agenda to refute the theory of biological determinism as the overriding mechanism that shaped human behavior. Benedict sought to convey the importance of the fact—without identifying it in these terms—that in discovering a society in which adolescence for the Samoan girl is not a time of conflict and emotional stress, Mead had added to the scientific arsenal Boas was accumulating to deflect the then reigning theory of biological determinism.[43]

Although Alfred Kroeber, one of Boas's first students, did not write a published review of *Coming of Age in Samoa*, he sent Mead a personal letter in which he commended her on the book, while at the same time pointing out possible shortcomings: "I think you have been able more successfully than anyone else to sketch the place of the individual in his particular culture. While some people complain that you do not give enough data to allow them to check up, this leaves me cold. Somehow I have confidence that your diagnoses are right even when your facts are few or not printed in full. I think you have given us all a mark to shoot at."[44]

However, Robert Lowie, another of Boas's students and a colleague of Kroeber's at Berkeley, was more critical of Mead in his review of *Coming of Age in Samoa* in the *American Anthropologist*, the premier journal of the profession in the United States.[45] He begins by acknowledging that Mead "deliberately set herself a task distinct from the traditional ethnographer's. Ignoring the conventional descriptive pattern, she concentrated on the individual's reaction to his social setting—specifically, the adolescent girl's adjustment." He goes on to say that "the author further departs from ordinary practice in pointing a moral." Of this practice, which he labels "applied anthropology," he scathingly retorts, "fortunately readers of this journal are not concerned with pedagogical sermonizing."[46]

Furthermore, he chastises Mead for burying her knowledge of the differences between Samoan attitudes toward adolescent sexuality in the past and the 1920s in the book's appendix, where she acknowledges that in the past adolescent girls would have been severely punished if discovered having premarital sex. And finally, he is skeptical of statements such as "the Samoan girl never tastes the rewards of romantic love as we know it." Clearly thinking that Mead has overstepped the boundaries of credulity here, he writes: "Query: What, never? And: Who are 'we'?"[47] Nonetheless, he ends his review by saying, "These reservations should not be taken to obscure the value of Dr. Mead's achievement. Dealing with problems incomparably subtler than those which usually engage the ethnographer's attention, she has not merely added much in the way of illuminating information but also illustrated a new method of study that is bound to find followers and to yield an even richer harvest."[48]

Thus, in contrast to the popular press's enthusiasm for *Coming of Age in Samoa*, Lowie's review encapsulates all of the complex and contradictory reactions anthropologists (and other scholars) were to have to Mead's work over the course of her career. On the one hand, she broke new ground in the research she undertook and the type of ethnography she wrote, for which she was both praised and condemned by her peers. On the other hand, while the public liked Mead's "pedagogical sermonizing," most anthropologists dismissed it for what it was—Mead's own ideas and opinions. From Lowie's review we get the image of Mead as an iconoclast, someone who was part of the profession but also was set apart from the mainstream—a relationship she would have with her profession throughout her career.

Mead and the Concept of "the Primitive"

Mead set off on her Samoan fieldwork at a time when westerners' fascination with the Primitive Other was at a peak. As industrialization and urbanization became rampant in the West, the desire for the simpler, more natural world that so-called primitive peoples represented to westerners became even stronger: "primitivism" as a concept, a mode of thought, and an aesthetic came into being. *Coming of Age in Samoa* and Mead's subsequent books about New Guinea cultures were published at a time when Western society was nostalgic for a simpler way of life that was rapidly disappearing in the west, but was also highly ambivalent about the ways of life of those technologically simpler peoples who yet remained in remote parts of the world. There were those individuals—missionaries, imperial officers, and other representatives of empire—who saw their role as westerners to civilize the remaining non-Western populations that were under their authority. And in contrast, there were individuals who were critical of Western industrial society and its antihuman, destructive forces—including pacifists, artists, writers, and intellectuals who were alienated from modern society and who saw in indigenous cultures alternative ways of life to that being created by modernity.[49] Among these latter individuals was an avid interest in the art, rituals, and beliefs of non-Western peoples and thus in the books that anthropologists published about these cultures, as well as interest in anthropologists themselves.[50]

There was a "rage for the dark" that went beyond merely enthusiasm for jazz and "slumming it" in Harlem. As journalist Peter Jennings later noted: "In the 1920s, the tanned body became suddenly stylish (*Vogue* carried its first advertisements for sunlamps in 1923), and America's fasci-

An American Princess of the South Seas

The Fascinating Experience of a Young American Girl Who Lived Among the Natives of the South Sea Islands and was Adopted by Them and Made a Princess

By E. R. BRAND

"When the native boys call on girls in Samoa," said Miss Mead, "they take with them the gift of a devil fish—often a spoiled one"

A High Chief of Samoa accompanied by his two daughters

A LETTER written by Robert Louis Stevenson to a Samoan chief in the South Sea Islands was discovered last year and sent to Columbia University to be translated. After one baffled look, the officials there forwarded it to the only person in America who is able to speak the Samoan language.

She is Margaret Mead, a charming American girl who, two years ago, at the age of twenty-three went, all alone, to live among the natives of Samoa.

"Ever since I was a little girl I have wanted to visit strange places," she said to me in her office in the Museum of Natural History where she functions as curator, ethnologist and, unofficially, youthful prodigy of the anthropology department. "Even today, I spend my spare moments studying that map on the wall over my desk, looking at places I want to visit. I'd like to work next in each of the large areas of the Pacific, Malaysia, Micronesia and Melonesia."

Sitting behind a big roll-top desk on which was a curious array of Fijian necklaces of whales' teeth, cocoanut shell kava cups, palm leaf fans and rolls of banana fruitcake sent as a Christmas present from Samoa, Margaret Mead looks much like any other girl. No divine fire of adventure or genius burns on the surface. She is slight, short, young looking; her speech clear, simple and friendly. Her hands, perhaps, are the surest tokens of her skill; capable and swift, they are efficient and at the same time graceful. As she talks, the impression of her general efficiency, poise and sureness becomes ever more striking.

She was born twenty-five years ago in Philadelphia, her mother a sociologist and her father a professor of economics. "You see, I came by my interest in sociology quite naturally," she said. Since her college days at Barnard, she has paid her own way, lived apart from her family and, apparently, is as efficient in domestic arts as in scientific research.

"I like cooking," she explained, "and all domestic things. I live now in a sort of community housekeeping scheme with three other girls. But please don't say we are 'college girls' as a newspaper interviewer recently wrote! Say 'professional women.'"

There are probably few professional women who wouldn't rather be taken for college girls, but then, this is no usual order of the species.

After digging out her anthropology thesis on the subject of Polynesian culture, in the safe precincts of New York libraries, she was struck with the notion of going to Samoa to see first-hand the things of which she had read and written. She went, all alone. Financed by a National Research Council fellowship which her brilliant record as a student helped to secure, she set sail for far Samoa, that little group of Southern Pacific islets, located by Stevenson as "the first stop after Honolulu on the way to Australia."

Here Margaret Mead was often the only white person in a village of natives. She lived in the native houses, which are more picturesque than private, boasting no walls, but simply pillars of bread-fruit trunks and beehive roofs thatched with sugar cane. The floor was coral rubble, pebbly like our driveways. On this she slept with what comfort could be derived from a mat of about a quarter-inch thickness. Fifteen or more natives shared the floor, sleeping beside each other, as she put it, "cheek by jowl." Sometimes, as a mark of special deference to her, she was walled off from the others by a screen of mosquito netting. In any case, the unwalled house was open to all the village outside.

She ate the native food—cocoanut in various forms, yam, bread fruit, taro which tastes like soap, and kava, the ceremonial drink with a flavor of quinine. The only water in the village was seepage and salt water. Milk, other than that of cocoanuts, was unknown. So was salt, except that derived from sea water. Fish was a delicacy. "And especially delicious," said Miss Mead, "was rotten devil fish.

"When I planned to go to Samoa, I was warned by friends in Honolulu not to eat spoiled fish. At the time I thought the warning hardly necessary, but once at Samoa I found myself greatly tempted. It is really delicious—like cheese, strong and high

Views of Samoa, which is literally a tropic paradise

Photos by Galloway

Miss Mead and two of the daughters of a High Chief

Salisbury, from Galloway

A typical Samoan girl, charming, gracious and with a complexion that is more golden than anything else

Figure 3.3 Headlines such as this that pronounced Mead "a Princess of the South Seas" heightened readers' interest in the exotic, almost fairytale-like adventures she had had in Samoa, while the article itself, since it described her as looking "much like any other girl," encouraged female readers' identification with the young Margaret Mead, 1931. (Mead Archives, Manuscript Division, Library of Congress) nation with 'primitive' cultures continued. American anthropologist Margaret Mead made the Pacific Island of Samoa the subject of a best-selling book when she reported in 1928 that the people there practiced recreational sex without guilt. For a decade wild with curiosity for anything in the realm of the erotic, the news was positively riveting."[51]

In part, individuals such as members of the Surrealist movement in Paris were interested in Primitivism as a reaction against those elements of modernity that were creating a new culture of desire based upon the idea that happiness could be achieved through purchasing things.[52] Even earlier museums and expositions such as the 1893 World's Columbian Exposition in Chicago and the Saint Louis World's Fair of 1904 were introducing large numbers of Americans to the indigenous cultures of the Pacific Northwest and the Philippines, as well as to the discipline of anthropology.[53] And anthropologists such as Boas, Benedict, and Mead, as well as Robert Lowie, Edward Sapir, Alfred Kroeber, and Elsie Clews Parsons were writing about the anthropological concept of culture. They introduced American intellectuals to a new, more inclusive concept of culture than had hitherto been associated with the term through their books and the essays they published in influential literary magazines such as the *New Republic*, *Harper's Monthly*, *Century*, and the *Atlantic Monthly*.[54]

The discipline of anthropology, and in particular the aforementioned anthropologists, were thus active participants in a discourse that took place in the United States during the first half of the twentieth century in which intellectuals in general and scholars in the social sciences in particular were debating the meaning, content, and social implications of concepts such as culture, race, mind, sexuality, personality, psychology, and psychoanalysis. The important feature that anthropologists such as Mead brought to these discussions was a cross-cultural perspective that aimed at dissolving the boundaries of difference between "civilized" and "primitive" people that most westerners assumed existed.

The Legacy of *Coming of Age in Samoa*

From Henry Neil's gushing fan letter to Irving Wallace's creation of a Mead-like character in *The Three Sirens*, from psychology professor Brownell's quandary to Howard Mumford Jones's ditty and an *Esquire*

"But I came of age in Samoa!"

Figure 3.4 Cartoon by Jan Langan, *Esquire* magazine. (Mead Archives, Manuscript Division, Library of Congress and *Esquire* magazine) cartoon, *Coming of Age in Samoa* has reverberated throughout American culture from its publication in the heyday of the Roaring Twenties onward, becoming a symbol of changing American mores with regard to sex, and thus a book that was either celebrated or excoriated, depending upon one's morals and politics. *The Timetables of American History* lists it as a notable event in American science for the year 1928 and the U.S. commemorative stamp honoring Mead alludes to it through the symbolism of Samoan bark cloth behind her portrait.[55] After her death it became the focus of the media once again when Derek Freeman published his critique of Mead's Samoan research. Even today, *Coming of Age in Samoa* raises the hackles of conservatives, some of whom still regard it as among the twenty or so most harmful books of the nineteenth and twentieth centuries.[56]

The media's response to the publication of *Coming of Age in Samoa* created several enduring images of Mead. The positive reviews the book received from the popular press established her reputation as an engaging writer and provocative mind, as someone who had insightful things to say about her own culture as well as about primitive cultures. With the addition of the book's two final chapters that discuss the implications of her Samoan research for American society, Mead established what was to become her signature modus operandi, her practice of cultural critique based on the cross-cultural comparison between less complicated non-Western cultures and our own.

In recent years anthropologists have been divided in their evaluations of the merits of this type of "edificatory ethnography." Some anthropologists consider Mead's development of the genre as a laudatory practice, one they label "cultural critique," or an "engaged anthropology" that can use insights gained from other cultures to criticize aspects of one's own culture, thus helping people to think about ways in which their own cultural practices might be amended or transformed.[57] Others such as Micaela di Leonardo have labeled Mead a "social engineer," someone who used her social science expertise to dictate how to reform societies.[58] While Lowie and others objected to the "sermonizing" aspects of Mead's ethnography on scientific grounds, contemporary critics see it in political and moral terms.

The practice, coupled with her decision to write a jargon-free book that would appeal to a broad audience, opened Mead to professional criticism. Despite publishing a popular book and also a scholarly study of Samoan kinship and social organization, most anthropologists focused their critical attention on her popular work, often neglecting to mention or being unaware of the academic monograph she had also written. Thus, one result of the popular success of *Coming of Age in Samoa* was that the distinction between Mead as a popularizer and Mead as a serious scholar was set in motion. It is a distinction that hounded her throughout her entire career.[59]

The discussion of adolescent sexuality in *Coming of Age in Samoa* also reinforced an association already established in the public's imagination between the practice of free love or sexual promiscuity (depending upon one's perspective) and South Seas islanders.[60] Thus, according to writer and filmmaker Roger Sandall, *Coming of Age in Samoa* is one of the prime texts that has contributed to "the culture cult," a term he uses to refer to the type of "romantic primitivism" that many twentieth-century westerners developed as a reaction to the ills of bourgeois consumer society. It is a false philosophy that he feels much anthropological literature—especially Mead's—has fed through its lush language and cultural relativist stance. According to Sandall, *Coming of Age in Samoa* was important in fostering Mead's role as "guru" of the countercultural revolution of the 1960s, enticing gullible young minds with idyllic visions of non-Western cultures as utopian alternatives to the ills of Western capitalist society.[61]

With its discussion of the sexual practices of the Samoans, *Coming of Age in Samoa* also reaffirmed an image in people's minds of anthropologists as individuals fixated on the study of the sex lives of non-Western people. And it served to sexualize the image of Mead herself (something that did not happen to male anthropologists).[62] Even an elderly Mead was sexualized—unflatteringly, and thus ironically—in David Levine's caricature of her, bare-breasted, in the *New York Review of Books*.

Mead in Samoa with Fa'amotu

Levine's caricature is based on several iconic images of a younger Mead in Samoa. Although she published no photographs of herself in the original edition of *Coming of Age in Samoa*, Mead included one of herself in Samoan garb in her autobiography. She appears there in a full-page photo wearing a bark cloth (*tapa*) skirt and top standing next to a Samoan girl named Fa'amotu, holding hands with her.

Figure 3.5 This iconic David Levine caricature appeared in the December 6, 1984 issue of the *New York Review of Books* to illustrate a review of Jane Howard's biography, *Margaret Mead: A Life*, and Mary Catherine Bateson's memoir of her parents, *With a Daughter's Eye*. (Caricature courtesy of David Levine)

This photograph of Mead the anthropologist and Fa'amotu, a Samoan *taupou*, or ceremonial princess—an honorary position available only to girls of high status—has subsequently become one of the most frequently reproduced images of Mead.[63] A Xerox reproduction of the picture was even used by feminist graduate students at the University of Michigan on a postcard that ironically juxtaposes the image of Mead and Fa'amotu with Allan Bloom's derogatory quote about Mead as a "sexual adventur-

Figure 3.6 Mead in Samoan dress with her friend Fa'amotu, 1925. (Courtesy of the Library of Congress and the Institute for Intercultural Studies)

Figure 3.7 This ironic postcard designed by graduate students in the Department of Anthropology, University of Michigan, juxtaposes the image of Mead and her Samoan friend Fa'amotu with Allan Bloom's disparaging quote about Mead as a "sexual adventuress," from *The Closing of the American Mind* (1983). Postcard circa 1992.

ess" from *The Closing of the American Mind*. Although the image has taken on iconic status, it has a range of contradictory meanings.

To anthropologist Micaela di Leonardo, who has written a scathing critique of Mead as emblematic of the worst kind of anthropologist—racist, imperialist, *and* sexist—one assumes that her use of the photo of the two women is meant to signify the false consciousness, or more precisely, the hypocritical nature, of Mead's relationship to Fa'amotu and therefore, in di Leonardo's words, of Mead's "trafficking in the skin trade."[64] That is, while superficially the two women appear to be friends and equals, in reality, according to di Leonardo, Mead only sought to further her career through writing about Fa'amotu and her Samoan friends as "dusky maidens" whose sex lives allowed Mead to present a tantalizing portrait of sensuality and lasciviousness to Western readers. Perhaps to illustrate her point, di Leonardo includes the photo of Mead and Fa'amotu, but chooses not to identify Fa'amotu by name, hence erasing her identity and individuality. The caption simply reads: "Margaret Mead with Samoan Informant."[65]

Literary critic Marianna Torgovnick uses a similar photograph of Mead with another Samoan woman—whose identity actually *is* unknown—to contrast Mead's and Bronislaw Malinowski's relationships to the brown-skinned "natives" among whom they worked. She suggests that both anthropologists were very aware of the physical bodies of their informants. But, according to Torgovnick, while Malinowski was afraid of that corporeality and commended himself on his ability to resist any desire to experience it firsthand, in contrast, Mead wrote of the importance of understanding how the body was treated in other cultures and how cultures experienced, controlled, and regarded bodily functions. Aiming to be witty, Torgovnick captions the picture "A toga party, Samoan Style, 1928," and uses the photograph of Mead with her arm around the Samoan woman as evidence that Mead did not shy away from the dark-skinned bodies of her informants. Instead, she tried to learn what it might feel like to a Samoan to dance in a tapa cloth skirt or sleep on fine mats on a floor of crushed coral.[66] To Torgovnick, Mead was less hypocritical and less fearful of intimate contact with the Other than Malinowski. However, like di Leonardo, Torgovnick is ultimately critical of Mead for having "used" the Samoan adolescents self-servingly to further her career.[67]

Figure 3.8 Mead in Samoan garb posing with another (unidentified) Samoan friend, 1925. (Courtesy of the Library of Congress and the Institute for Intercultural Studies)

Historian Susan Ware uses the photograph of Mead and Fa'amotu to emphasize her point about Mead's small stature and her youthful appearance. Her caption for the photograph reads: "Margaret Mead never told her Samoan hosts that she was married, and the 24-year-old anthropologist could easily have passed for an adolescent. Here she is in Samoan dress with Fa'amotu, the daughter of a local chief with whom she stayed at the beginning of her research trip."[68] Ware's use of the photograph also underscores the point she wants to make about Mead as a popular heroine who as a single woman went off to distant Samoa to do fieldwork and live among the natives. Her caption for the photo underscores the fact that Mead was playing a role, not simply the role in the picture of being dressed up as a Samoan, but also the role of being a young, unmarried girl like the subjects she was studying.

The appearance of a new edition of *Coming of Age in Samoa* in 2001, Mead's centenary year, with the photograph of Mead in Samoan garb along with two Samoan girls on the cover, completes the iconization of images of Mead in Samoa.[69] The book has gone from its original edition, which was devoid of any photographs of Mead but featured an image of clandestine Samoan lovers, to a cover that foregrounds Mead as much as the Samoan girls who were the subject of the book. The inclusion of a photograph of Mead on the cover of the 2001 edition could be seen as signifying the fact that the public's interest in the book, now, is as much, or more, because of its interest in the controversy Derek Freeman stirred up about Mead and the book in 1983 than because of its interest in Samoan adolescent sexuality.

From yet another perspective the photograph represents a now-vanished moment in the history of anthropology, a time when it was still unusual for a single white Western woman to go off on her own to do fieldwork in a remote and exotic locale. The photograph also indicates another historical dimension of the book—that it is an ethnography about Samoan adolescent girls *as they were* in 1925-26. The image of the two Samoan women dressed in ceremonial attire represents a bygone era in Samoan culture too. Today the majority of Samoan adolescent girls do not even live in Samoa, but in Hawaii, New Zealand, or California. Rather than wearing tapa cloth skirts, they are most likely to be found wearing blue jeans, t-shirts, and flip-flops. Even a few years after the picture of Mead with Fa'amotu was taken, Fa'amotu's life had changed dramatically. She married a U.S. Navy officer she met in Samoa and the two of them moved to San Diego, from where she wrote to Mead in 1931 to say that she hoped that Mead would not be too disappointed in her loss of her Samoan ways.[70]

There is one other reading of the photographs of Mead with Fa'amotu and the other Samoan girls that has emerged with the revelation that Mead enjoyed sexual relations with women as well as men. As Torgovnick and others have suggested, perhaps these photographs hide a more intimate physical relationship that Mead had with some young Samoan woman—or man.[71]

Mead, Samoa, and American Imperialism

After the Vietnam War had ended, a younger generation of Americans began to be critical of both anthropology and Margaret Mead. In 1976, political cartoonist Garry Trudeau and social satirist Nicholas von Hoffman called their critical parody of American politics and cultural hegemony in American Samoa *Tales from the Margaret Mead Taproom.*[72] Trudeau's alter ego, the cartoon character Doonesbury, visits his Uncle Duke, who has been appointed governor of American Samoa. Although reference to Mead is minimal in the book, its back cover shows Uncle Duke sitting at his piano singing:

Drinkin' Again
Jes' Margaret Mead n' Meee . . .
Jes' getting' spaced
With Amazin' Grace
Ain't no place we'd rather beee . . .
Than Pago Pago . . .

Oh, my Margaret, you . . .
Note that I could surely die . . .
Who's here to cry but you . . .
In Pago Pago?

Pago Pago . . . Pago Pago . . .
You were the island's rage
When we both came of age . . .
In Pago Paaago

Duke's Samoan factotum, who clearly does not recognize the name Margaret Mead, says to him: "That's . . . that's beautiful, Governor. You must have really loved her." To which Duke replies, "Naah, she was just required reading."[73]

The references to Mead, in the title of the book and in the concluding cartoon segment, bookend the description of a trip that Trudeau and von Hoffman took to American Samoa and their scathing indictment of the effects of the American presence on Samoan culture. Invoking Mead's name highlights the fact that Americans know very little about American Samoa, and that what they *do* know often came from having been required to read *Coming of Age in Samoa* in a college course. Trudeau and von Hoffman attribute the tawdry quality of life they find in 1970s American Samoa to the benign neglect of U.S. imperialism, interested only in the islands as a naval base and site for R&R for American soldiers fighting in Vietnam. The picture they paint of Samoa in the 1970s stands in stark contrast to the idyllic images of Samoan life that Mead portrayed in *Coming of Age in Samoa*. They also take a jab at anthropology, seeing it as one of the main activities that Americans have engaged in on the islands, in addition to "madcap social welfareism," neither of which they see as having helped the Samoans much.

In this respect Trudeau and von Hoffman's comments represent a more general critique of anthropology that began to emerge during the 1970s in which the entire anthropological enterprise came under scrutiny from within as well as without and was criticized for its imperialist origins.[74] In this instance, Mead has become a symbol of the entire anthropological enterprise and the focus of the critiques that a younger, more politically disillusioned and socially cynical generation of Americans was making of both anthropology and American society.[75]

In contrast to these postcolonial critiques, feminist scholars have put forth a different image of Mead and *Coming of Age in Samoa*. They embrace her book as bold, experimental, and theoretically significant, a work that was in the forefront of what was later to become the genre of feminist ethnography.[76] For example, Sharon Tiffany notes that Mead was one of the first anthropologists—male or female—to focus on the lives of women and adolescent girls at a time when most anthropologists were men. Male anthropologists tended to focus on the study of political institutions, leadership, and the economic organization of societies and seldom dealt with questions about the individual in society, let alone singling out women for study.[77] Thus, within the burgeoning subfield of feminist anthropology that began in the 1970s, Mead's most innovative and lasting contributions to anthropology are her decision to take seriously the lives of women, children, and adolescents as a focus of study.[78]

Another image of Mead that *Coming of Age in Samoa* generated was that of her as an expert on adolescence, that phase in an individual's life between puberty and adulthood metaphorically referred to as "coming of age." As with the study of sex, the study of adolescence was also a relatively new area of investigation when Mead began her research in Samoa. The idea of adolescence and the related notion of "teenager" were twentieth-century developments that grew out of the new understanding of human development delineated by researchers in the United States and abroad, and Mead was recognized as a contributor to this new field of knowledge.[79]

Mead added the concept of culture and its role in shaping adolescent behavior, contributing to our understanding of adolescence as a social process. She described adolescence as a phase in an individual's life the characteristic behavior and emotional tenor of which is predominantly shaped not by physiological factors but by the social, historical, and cultural milieu in which it is experienced.[80] This insight aligned her with her fellow Boasians who argued for the importance of culture in the determination of human behavior and more broadly with "metaphysical" philosophers such as John Dewey, William James, and Charles Sanders Peirce, who from the late nineteenth century on argued for the importance of ideas and the imagination in shaping social life as well as individual behavior.[81]

Mead's growing interest in psychoanalytic theory and the relationship between culture and personality led her to shift the focus of her next research from the study of adolescence and sexuality to the study of children preadolescent and younger (and thus a less emotionally charged period of development) in order to understand the role that culture played in the socialization of children into becoming adult members of a particular society. In order to do so, her next research took her to Manus Island in New Guinea and an island society that was in many ways diametrically opposed to the relatively easy-going, sensuous culture of the Samoans.

CHAPTER 4

Mead as Anthropologist: "To Study Cannibals"

The youthful scientist hopes to win the confidence of the natives with gifts of cigarette lighters, hairpins, and plug tobacco.
—*Hammonton News*, September 14, 1928

In September of 1928, just after the publication of *Coming of Age in Samoa*, Margaret Mead left the United States to join Reo Fortune in Australia.[1] They were on their way to the Admiralty Islands in the Territory of Papua and New Guinea for their first major stint of fieldwork together.[2] Continuing her interest in the effects of culture on behavior and personality, Mead intended to study the socialization of children to observe how early childhood experience might contribute to shaping adult personality.

As with her earlier departure for fieldwork in Samoa, a local newspaper in Hammonton, New Jersey (where Mead's family had resided off and on while her mother had studied the local Italian residents for her doctoral dissertation), reported the event with the following headline:

TO STUDY CANNIBALS
Dr. Margaret Meade [*sic*], Former Resident Leaves for Work among Natives of South Seas

followed by the text, "The youthful scientist hopes to win the confidence of the natives with gifts of cigarette lighters, hairpins, and plug tobacco. She will carry a complete kindergarten equipment for the entertainment of the children."[3]

The article's headline, "To Study Cannibals," stands in stark contrast to the more mundane reality of Mead's research intentions. Aiming to grab the reader's attention, the newspaper employed the clichéd Western trope of cannibals to refer to non-Western peoples by playing up the danger and exotic nature of Mead's endeavor. By 1928, the Manus Islanders, with whom she and Fortune would be working, had long been pacified, first by the Germans and then the Australians. Moreover, they claimed that they had never been cannibals.

Further emphasizing the Otherness of these dangerous "cannibals," the article says that Mead "hopes to win their confidence"—with what?—trifles such as "cigarette lighters, hairpins, and plug tobacco." Although this particular trope is evocative of numerous first contact scenes, from the Dutch purchase of Manhattan onward, in which westerners gained the friendship as well as more tangible items through inherently unequal exchanges, in Mead's case, she wanted the confidence of the Manus Islanders so that she could acquire knowledge of their culture and society.

Although the article reports Mead's plan to make a study of the Manus children, the reader is not told *why* she might be interested in studying children age two to seven. The article seems more intent on mentioning the fact that Mead is bringing kindergarten equipment for "the entertainment of the children,"—thereby evoking the image of a kindergarten teacher rather than a serious scientist—than on explaining what she would actually be studying.

In the Admiralties, Mead intended to conduct a comparative study between the lives and minds of so-called primitive children and Western children. Her interest in this topic was stimulated by the writing of Freud and the French scholar Lucien Lévy-Bruhl, both of whom equated the minds of primitive adults with the intellectual capabilities of Western children and the mentally ill.[4] If this equation was valid, Mead wondered what the minds of non-Western children were like in comparison to those of Western children and Manus adults. She was continuing an interest she had in determining if there were significant differences in the mental capacities of different races and the influence of biology versus the environment on the development of children that she had begun with her study of adolescent girls in Samoa. Her research also would contribute to the broader Boasian project to question the assumption of innate biological differences between members of different races.

What the newspaper article probably achieved was the reinforcement of the stereotype of the anthropologist as an adventurer who goes off to study "primitive cannibals."

Growing Up in New Guinea (1930)

While *Coming of Age in Samoa* was becoming a best seller in the United States, Mead and Fortune were engaged in their study of the Manus people, initially oblivious to the book's success. When they returned to New York City in September of 1929, Mead wrote that, "We were caught up in the excitement of meeting my friends, who informed me that I had already achieved a wide reputation as an author-anthropologist, something I vaguely knew but had not yet fully comprehended."[5] The success of *Coming of Age in Samoa* meant that numerous journalists wanted to interview Mead, as they sensed a good adventure story that involved a female heroine. For example, Frances D. McMullen titled her article about Mead in the *Women's Journal* "Going Native for Science: Dr. Margaret Mead, Ethnologist, Tells How She Lived in a Grass Hut in the Admiralty Islands and Became a Princess in Samoa to Study the Life of Her Primitive Neighbors."[6] McMullen introduces Mead by contrasting the exoticism of her anthropological research with the starkness of her office in the American Museum of Natural History, where "her talk summoned up strange scenes in that grim-looking museum room, without trace of the life under discussion save the carved coconut shell 'kava cup' into which Dr. Mead flicked her cigarette."[7]

Trying to convey to the reader exactly what anthropologists are and how they work, McMullen writes,

> The nature of her business is the way of living and thinking of primitive folk . . . but if the attitude presupposes equipment and point of view that are highly scientific, it is not strictly so; for the personal equation enters into these studies with emphasis. To solve it one needs to be as pleasing as intelligent, as sympathetic as analytical, as confidence-winning as statistical. In doing the particular jobs to which Dr. Mead applied herself—the intimate study of primitive childhood and adolescence—youth is an added asset.[8]

Once again we find an emphasis on Mead's youthfulness and, as the article was for a women's magazine, an emphasis on Mead's comments about the suitability of anthropology for women: "The striking beauty about her profession at present from the woman's point of view, Dr. Mead added, is that it offers plenty of room. Women scientists of any kind are scarce, and of anthropologists there are not even enough to fill those jobs that beckon to women especially."[9]

While Mead seems not to have had any qualms about granting interviews with magazine and newspaper journalists, she did have second thoughts about publishing her work in popular magazines. In a letter from her editor about an article Mead had been thinking of submitting to either *Cosmopolitan* magazine or *Smart Set*, Morrow advises her that she "should be cautious in arranging for magazine articles, and should take into account the possible attitude of your fellow-scholars whose opinions would count in connection with your further career as a scholar and scientist."[10] Perhaps chastened by Morrow's words, Mead apparently decided not to publish an article in either magazine.

In November 1929, Mead held a press conference at the American Museum of Natural History to describe her New Guinea research. She said that she had found the Manus Islanders less pleasant than the Samoans, more materialistic and more sexually prudish. She also introduced the theme of the Manus people as "primitive capitalists," a description of the islanders that played well with the press.[11] As did a photograph of Mead dressed in a Manus ceremonial headdress that appeared in several newspapers across the country.

Not surprisingly, the newspapers chose to highlight details of Manus culture that would strike the American reader as bizarre or scandalous or heathen and humorous. In contrast to how they had portrayed the lithesome, brown-skinned Polynesian Samoans, the press described the darker, more savage-looking Manus people by playing up their primitiveness. The Manus men, with their frizzy heads of hair, scantily dressed in narrow loincloths with necklaces of dogs' teeth and shells hanging down their chests, were indeed exotic looking to the American public. The *New York Times*, however, chose to foreground a different aspect of Manus society, one that pointed to similarities as well as differences between American and Manus culture. Taking off from Mead's description of the Manus as middlemen and traders par excellence, the *Times* ran the headline "Tooth Money Panic Rocks South Seas," followed by the subheading "Admiralty Islands' Inflation in Dog-Molar Currency Is Told by Woman Explorer."[12] The article played off New Yorkers' immediate concerns with their own

Figure 4.1 Mead dressed in Manus ceremonial headdress, Manus, 1929. (Courtesy of the Library of Congress and the Institute for Intercultural Studies)

shaky economy and the panic caused the previous month by the stock market crash on Black Thursday, October 24, 1929. The juxtaposition of the notion of "inflation," an economic concept most Americans associated with capitalism and a money-based economy, affecting something as seemingly simple and barbaric as an economy based on dogs' teeth must have amused readers, or at least grabbed their attention.

The Associated Press avoided the topic of the Manus economy and focused on the children instead. It ran a short piece with the headline

"Children Smoke at Three," while the *New York Herald Tribune* announced "Woman Studies Smoking Babies of Pacific Isles."[13] At a time when young women were asserting their independence by smoking cigarettes (as Mead did), and specialists in child development were alerting parents to the necessity of keeping their children on strict schedules,[14] the thought of three-year-olds smoking cigarettes must have struck Americans as a particularly uncouth, to say nothing of unhealthy, practice and a definitive sign of the uncivilized nature of the Manus people.

When writing *Growing Up in New Guinea*, Mead followed the successful model of *Coming of Age in Samoa* and subtitled her new book *A Comparative Study of Primitive Education.* The first half of the book was devoted to a description of the socialization of Manus children from birth to marriage, while the entire second half of the book was devoted to Mead's discussion of the similarities between Manus and American society, especially in the area of education, and the implications she drew from the Manus case for changes in the American system of education. A blurb for a 1953 edition of the book read: "With brilliant insight, humor, and warm sympathy, a noted anthropologist explores the family life of a primitive island people—their attitude toward sex, marriage and the raising of children—and finds intriguing parallels with problems of modern life."[15]

"Just a Puff"

There are twenty-four photographs in the first edition of *Growing Up in New Guinea*, including one of a young Manus child smoking a cigarette. Mead's decision to include this latter photo of a naked Manus boy three or four years old puffing on a limp hand-rolled cigarette may have been influenced by the curiosity the press had shown in this unusual custom.[16] All of the photos, but especially those of the naked Manus children, would have helped reinforce the contrast between the "civilized" life of the reader and the "primitive" life of the Manus.

There is only one photograph of Mead (and none of Fortune) in the book. Captioned "Research Methods" (ironically?!), the photograph of Mead shows her seated with a group of Manus children playfully decorating their hair with strands of celluloid ribbon.[17] This photograph is typical of the pictures that she later chose to publish in her autobiography to

Figure 4.2 "Just a Puff," Manus, 1929. Photograph from the first edition of *Growing Up in New Guinea*, 1930. (Courtesy of the Library of Congress and the Institute for Intercultural Studies)

Figure 4.3 "Research Methods," Manus, 1929. Photograph by Reo Fortune. Mead included this picture of herself in the field in the first edition of *Growing Up in New Guinea*, 1930. (Courtesy of the Library of Congress and the Institute of Intercultural Studies)

represent her doing fieldwork, such as one from Manus that shows a young Mead, still girlish in appearance, seated holding a child on her lap and another that she used in *Letters from the Field* that shows her carrying a small Manus child on her back.[18] These photos emphasize particular aspects of her public persona that she cultivated: the feminine Mead who played with and loved children; the scientific Mead who studied children's behavior and childhood development; and, beginning with *Growing Up in New Guinea*, the maternal Mead, and, later, Mead the protector of the world's children.

Marketing *Growing Up in New Guinea*

The success of *Coming of Age in Samoa* had taught Mead and William Morrow much about the marketing of her work, especially the impor-

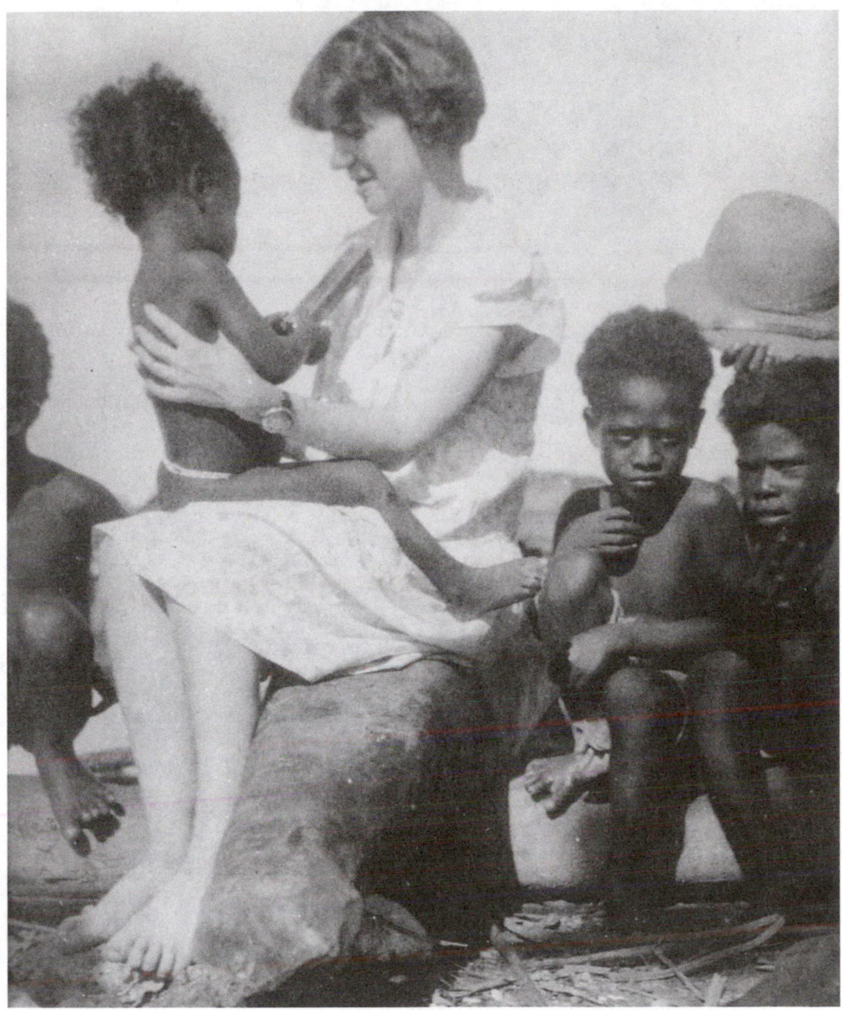

Figure 4.4 Mead with Ponkiau, Bopau and Tchokal, Manus, 1929. Photograph by Reo Fortune. (Courtesy of the Library of Congress and the Institute for Intercultural Studies)

tance of getting her book out to a wide range of scholars and intellectuals who might find it of interest. A letter Mead wrote to Morrow suggested that the following people, categorized by profession, be sent a copy of *Growing Up in New Guinea*. She also suggested which chapters in the book specific individuals or groups might find of particular interest:

Figure 4.5 Mead carrying Piwen, Manus 1929. Photograph by Reo Fortune. (Courtesy of the Library of Congress and the Institute for Intercultural Studies)

Psychologists: Watson, Adler, Woodworth.[19] Chapter on the content of the child's world, stressing the dependence of the child upon traditional material and the void which exists when this is absent. Chapter on development of personality, the role played by identification.

Sociologists: W. F. Ogburn, University of Chicago, W. I. Thomas.[20] Analysis of the way in which a society without political organization impresses its mores upon the growing individual, discussion of the role of the family, the projection of the family picture into the religious system (Chap. On Child and Religion). Disciplinary methods used by society (The Triumph of the Adult Chap.).

Psychoanalysts: White (St. Elizabeth's Hospital, Washington), Brill, Dr. Marian Kentworthy (NY School of Social Work).[21] Interchange of the mother's role and the father's role and effect upon the development of boys and girls, association between sexual defections and a general anxiety attitude in the society, discussion of identification and the elaboration of the life after death. Chap. On Scope of Imagination. Relationship between child's attitude to father and the attitude towards the spirits of the dead. Projection upon the spirits of the dead of ideas of guilt. (Last two points in chap. On Child and Religion.)

Educationalists: John Dewey, Bertrand Russell, and Meiklejohn (University of Wisconsin).[22] This is the first scientific study ever made of the educational process in a primitive society. Brings out the interesting points: (a) results of leaving children without guidance in their play, how empty it is. (b) dependence of children upon tradition. (c) harshness of the methods of subjection which must be used by a society which permits its youth to grow up in anarchy, (d) relation of this kind of growing up to the values of the adult society and the curious analogy between Manus and America, both societies stressing acquisition of material objects at the expense of other values.

Economists: (I am having a bunch of reprints of an article called "Melanesian Middlemen" sent down to you which should be slipped into the copies sent to any one with an economic interest, as bait).[23] Interesting study of a commercial-minded primitive people with highly developed ideas of private property, division of labor, exchange, money, etc. See esp. Chpt on Child and Adult World, and Appendix on Ethnography and Contact with White Culture. Educational values developed by such a society. Send to Mitchell (National Bureau Economic Research), John Keynes (Cambridge, England), R. H. Tawney (London School of Economics), James Harvey Robinson, (combine economic and sociological points for him), and add the point that Manus is curiously like a far away echo of our own historical development with its emphasis on commercial Puritanism and it's almost identical spiritualistic cult.[24]

Sex People: Havelock Ellis, [G.] V. Hamilton and Kenneth Macgowan, Floyd Dell, Dr. Katharine B. Davis, analysis of the effect on individuals where sexual freedom is disallowed for women, romantic love is culturally unknown, marriage is an economic lever, the arrangement of kin groups militates against any happiness in marriage, rape is the ideal of the men and frigidity the rule for women.[25] Primitive puritans who contradict many of the popular ideas about sex among primitive peoples.

Special People: Gilbert Murray, Oxford (I think he's a Sir), mention his known interest in Pacific Island[s] because of his brother, Sir Herbert [*sic*] Murray's notable contributions to Pacific administrative problems and his interest in League of Nations Mandates.[26] If there are any other English names on the League of Nations list with publicity value (think there are) it will be possible to play up the book as the first scientific account published of any of the primitive peoples in the Mandated Territory since Australia assumed the Mandate (Better say first complete account).[27] And draw their attention to the chapter on Culture Contact in the Appendix.

Malinowski doesn't need any special points. Sir James Frazer, author of the *Golden Bough*, stressing first time the child's attitudes towards a primitive religion has even been studied (Chap. On religion); Westermarck, University of London, author of *History of Human Marriage*, stresses inside account of the working in the lives of the individuals of arranged marriages which are key points in an elaborate economic system. H. G. Wells, in the light of his contention that men of the future will be without tradition, in the way in which it controls our lives today, discussion of the effect in education of bringing children up physically perfect and mentally alert, in a kind of vacuum. (Chap. Content of Child World.) Hilaire Belloc and G. K. Chesterton, this is an inside picture of the effect upon the lives of individuals of a society which values commercialism and has thrust all artistic values aside in the interest of commercialism.[28] I think it would be worth trying Aldous Huxley, emphasizing the detailed psychological study of a group of primitive puritans and also Ernest Hemingway, J. B. S. Haldane, should get the same line as the educationalists.[29]

For general interest people, stress inside account of education among an untouched people, spiritualism, Puritanism, caricature of American attitudes, result of giving children perfect freedom![30]

It is revealing to see whom Mead targeted and what sections of the book she thought different specialists might find of interest. Bolstered by the success of her first book, Mead sought to interest some of the most highly regarded intellectuals and social scientists of the time in her work, many of whom were reformers or outspoken critics of modern society. Her choices also demonstrate her conviction that her Manus research and its implications for Western society would be of interest to a wide range of scholars in the social sciences and human genetics in the United States and England, but also novelists and public intellectuals such as H. G. Wells, Aldous Huxley, and Bertrand Russell, who had started his own school for progressive education in England.

Popular Reviews of *Growing Up in New Guinea*

As with *Coming of Age in Samoa*, reviews of *Growing Up in New Guinea* in the popular press commended Mead on the clarity of her writing. "Miss Mead," a review in the *New York Times* said, "has the rare faculty of combining scientific observation with happiness of literary expression." The reviewer is particularly interested in the fact that while childhood in Manus is a time of great freedom and happiness, the adult Manus Islander, "a product of this childhood of undisciplined freedom . . . is not a happy individual." The reviewer then notes that in the second half of her book Mead "throws an illuminating and rather disconcerting light on the similarity of Manus civilization and our own."[31]

The "disconcerting similarity" is the emphasis upon material goods and commercialism in the two societies as well as a parallel between the undisciplined freedom of Manus childhood and the experimentation in American schools that was underway at the time, with "most of the experiments being directed toward greater freedom and less discipline for the growing child." The reviewer finds the book excellent not only for the portrait it paints of Manus society but also because it serves to prod readers to think critically about American society.[32]

Anthropologists' Reviews of *Growing Up in New Guinea*

The most damning review of *Growing Up in New Guinea* written by an anthropologist was C. W. R. Hart's in the British journal *Man*. Hart, a student of Malinowski, was searing in his censure of Mead. He began his review by referring to the book's success in the United States, as well as that of *Coming of Age in Samoa*:

> On the basis of these two studies Miss Mead has been hailed by some critics in America as one of the leading anthropologists of the day. English students to the contrary will be strongly inclined to query whether she is an anthropologist at all.[33]

These, of course, were fighting words as they struck at the heart of Mead's professional identity. Hart underscored his accusation by pointing out, in a rather condescending manner, that:

> In itself residence for a period of time among a native community does not make a person an anthropologist, as certain travelers and most publishers seem to think. The criterion of whether work among natives is anthropology or something else lies in the sort of phenomena investigated there and the sort of generalizations attempted in any published account of the work.[34]

Heaping one insult upon another, Hart continues:

> Miss Mead went to Manus, but while there was not apparently interested in any of the problems with which anthropologists (both in England and in America) are normally concerned. Her whole interest lay not in seeing what the culture was, but what effect living in a certain group had on an individual of that group. The result is that such glimpses as we get of the structure of Manus society are only obtained incidentally in somewhat the same way as we may obtain an idea of the houses used by a tribe from a medical report on the causes of pneumonia among that tribe.[35]

He accuses Mead of not having studied the structure of Manus society, that is, of not having presented a detailed analysis of the kinship system and related social organization of the society, as these topics were the central focus of British structural-functionalist anthropology at that time.[36]

Hart dismissed the second section of the book, "Reflections on the Educational Problems of Today in the Light of Manus Experience," as "of no value in anthropology," and then in a sweeping statement added, "and one imagines of very little value to any other of the social sciences." In this respect, Hart echoes Robert Lowie in his review of *Coming of Age in Samoa*. Both men thought that this type of "pedagogical sermonizing" had no role to play in the science of anthropology. Once again, it was precisely what attracted the interest of the general public to Mead's books that was denounced by other anthropologists.

Both Reo Fortune and Ruth Benedict wrote letters to the editor of *Man* defending Mead's book. Benedict's response is particularly interesting as she points out that "the essential misunderstanding on the part of your reviewer has to do with the dilemma of anthropological publication in America. There is not in America a publishers' list of prospective subscribers interested in colonial affairs and native peoples. In England the existence of this market, even though it is small, makes possible the commercial publication of ethnological monographs."[37] Therefore, she says, American ethnographers must present their material in a manner that will appeal to the general public, and thus English students "cannot at the present look to such publications for the detailed account of the formal structure of the culture, nor take its absence as an indication that such a study was overlooked by the investigators."[38]

Fortune, on the other hand, attacks Hart's criticisms of Mead head on. For example, in response to Hart's statement that Mead was not apparently interested in any of the problems with which anthropologists (both in England and America) are normally concerned, Fortune throws back the fact that both Dr. Haddon in England and Dr. Boas in America, "the pioneers in anthropology on either side of the Atlantic, have both for many years been anxious to secure just such an account of a primitive culture and have both acknowledged that in Dr. Mead's work the desired object has been achieved."[39] Adding a more personal attack, he remarks that "Mr. Hart has a most curious conception of anthropology, for he appears to think that it should be confined to the purely codified forms of culture. He would study the Code Napoleon and believe that he has studied the French people."[40]

In a more tempered critique of the book for the *American Anthropologist*, A. L. Kroeber conceded that Mead was an outstanding writer: "To judge Margaret Mead by the standards inherent in her work," he wrote, "her gift is essentially aesthetic, suffused by the power of conceptualization, and holding a legitimate and stimulating place in anthropology; and she possesses this gift in a degree approaching genius."[41] Kroeber, unlike some of his colleagues, was willing to acknowledge that there was a place within anthropology for work such as Mead's.

Kroeber, reiterating the comment he had made to Mead about *Coming of Age in Samoa*, also suggested, "If she will add the substantiating body of fact, her work will be unusually influential in the science."[42] He concluded by cautioning Mead, saying that, "When she leaves her vein to intellectualize about American educational tenets of 1930, or to compromise between the amount of cultural fact that ethnologists want and the public will stand, her own peculiar quality rapidly evaporates. If she can learn to satisfy only herself, she should do finer and profounder work than Samoa or New Guinea."[43] Unlike Hart, Kroeber respected aspects of Mead's work, lauding her for her ability as a writer, while at the same time sternly urging her to be a more thorough and detailed ethnographer.

Angered by Hart's critical remarks, Mead postponed a field trip to the mainland of New Guinea that she and Fortune were about to embark on and spent the next several months writing a book about Manus kinship and social organization.[44] Her decision to delay their fieldwork to write the kinship monograph indicates how important she felt it was to prove herself technically competent as a professional anthropologist. Given the popular success of her first two books, she must have sensed that this was all the more incumbent upon her than had these books not been as popular as they were with the general public.

The Legacy of *Growing Up in New Guinea*

The iconic image of Mead with children—holding babies, playing with toddlers, extending a doll to a bemused child—started with the publication of *Growing Up in New Guinea* and the picture of Mead surrounded by a group of naked Manus boys and girls. The Manus photo shows Mead as a young, girlish-looking woman, but even as she grew older the format stayed the same: a maternal Mead with a child or children (often dark-skinned in contrast to Mead). There is a subtle change in the image of Mead from *Coming of Age in Samoa* to *Growing Up in New Guinea* that marks a shift from Mead as the flapperesque ingenue to a more mature, married, and maternal Mead, a change that also signals a shift in her research interests from the study of adolescent girls to the study of infants and children. Although the association between Mead and the study of sexuality continues, another image of Mead develops alongside it: that of the maternal caretaker interested in and concerned for the welfare of children the world over. The repetition over the years of the image of the maternal Mead will eventually transform her into "grandmother to the world."

With the publication of *Growing Up in New Guinea*, Mead's image as an expert on childhood and education was established, and she became a pioneer in the cross-cultural study of education and socialization.[45] For the rest of her career she would be called upon for advice about education and the raising of children. With increasing frequency she was asked to give talks such as one she presented to the Philadelphia chapter of the American Association of University Women in 1931 in which she argued *against* both the permissiveness of Manus parents and the growing permissiveness among American parents who did not instill a sense of respect for adults in their children or establish guidelines for discipline. What she did advocate, reiterating what she had written in *Coming of Age in Samoa*, was that Americans should educate their children about how to make informed choices from among the many different possibilities that life in modern American society offered them.

As Mead later pointed out, when she wrote *Growing Up in New Guinea* questions about education were uppermost in many American's minds: "Under the influence of the progressive-education movement and a quick and partial interpretation of the first flush of success in Russian educational experiments, educators and philosophers were saying, 'Yes, the child is malleable, he takes the form you wish him to take; therefore, if you train him sufficiently differently from the way his unfortunate parents were trained, in no time at all you will produce a new generation which will built a new world.' "[46] What Mead's Manus research contributed to this debate was that "human nature is flexible, but it is also elastic. It will tend to return to the form that was impressed upon it in earliest years"—an insight that later led to the creation of programs such as Head Start.[47] A more curious legacy was the association Reagan-era conservatives made between Mead and the "permissiveness" they bemoaned in the American education system, especially since what Mead actually *did* say about Manus society and its implications for American education was quite to the contrary.[48]

The Changing Culture of an Indian Tribe (1932)

Mead and Fortune had returned to New York City in the fall of 1929 to begin writing up their Manus material. The following summer, at the request of Clark Wissler, Mead's superior in the Department of Anthropology at the American Museum of Natural History, they had agreed to accept research stipends to conduct a few months research among the Omaha Indians in Nebraska.[49] Mead was to study the role of women and change.[50] They spent the fall of 1930 writing up their Omaha material. The book Mead published based on her fieldwork among the Omaha, *The Changing Culture of an Indian Tribe*, remains one of her least known studies.

The public's response to the book, or, more precisely, its lack of enthusiasm, indicates how important it was to Mead's popular success that she had done her anthropological research in remote places such as Samoa and New Guinea. These Pacific islands, albeit in very different ways, piqued the American public's curiosity about exotic cultures. In contrast to Mead's first two books, the narrative she had to tell about the Omaha Indians (whom she thinly disguised in her book as "the Antlers") was a depressing and familiar one. By the summer of 1930, when Mead went to study Omaha women, the tribe, former buffalo hunters who had once roamed across the Great Plains, had long been settled on reservations in Nebraska. Moreover, Mead had not wanted to do the three months summer research upon which the book was based in the first place, only agreeing to do so under duress. It was the only fieldwork she ever did that she had not chosen to do herself. As Maureen Molloy has observed, "to write about *The Changing Culture of an Indian Tribe* . . . [is] to write about . . . a repression both by Mead herself and by the many intellectuals, journalists, and educators who seized her other books and made them into best-sellers."[51]

Why, after the resounding success of *Coming of Age in Samoa* and the lesser, but still noteworthy, popularity of *Growing Up in New Guinea*, did both Mead and the popular press ignore her third book? Unlike her previous two books, Mead did little to promote *The Changing Culture of an Indian Tribe*. There are various reasons she may not have. The book's location—Nebraska and the Great Plains of the American Midwest—did little to excite either her or the public's imagination. Further indication of her ambivalence toward the research project can be gathered from the fact that rather than telling the Omaha women that she was an anthropologist, she kept her own identity as a researcher a secret and hid under the pretense of accompanying Reo Fortune while he did fieldwork.[52]

Most importantly, there was the nature of Mead's findings. She described the situation as one in which as the result of many years of mistreatment at the hands of the American government, "there was the dismal sense that the people themselves were going backward."[53] Because Omaha culture was so despoiled, she felt as though the research she had done was not really "anthropological," and thus of little scientific value. Real anthropology, Mead said, could only be conducted in societies that were still intact and had not suffered the kind of cultural degradation that had affected the Omaha.[54] Perhaps because she found the Omaha situation so bleak, or because of the short period of time she did research, Mead eschewed making suggestions for ways to change their condition. Thus, there was no "sermonizing"—as with her previous books.

For all these reasons, Mead did little to promote the book and chose not to seek publication with a trade publisher, letting Columbia University Press publish the study instead. Subsequently, she seldom referred to her Omaha research in articles or books she wrote.[55] Even years later in her autobiography she says very little about her Omaha research, focusing instead on Fortune's unrecognized success in finding the answer to the research question Benedict had originally set for him as to why was there no evidence of vision quests among the Omaha.[56] It was, as Molloy suggests, as though Mead repressed her negative experience with the Omaha, both soon after the event as well as decades later.

Published during the depth of the Great Depression, *The Changing Culture of an Indian Tribe*, unlike Mead's earlier volumes, did not offer the vision of escape to an idyllic South Seas paradise, as had Samoa, or even to the site of bustling primitive commerce that Mead had portrayed as characteristic of the Manus people. Instead, it recorded the effects on hapless individuals of a resounding social and economic failure. Perhaps the book's story of cultural demise presented a parallel between the depleted and downtrodden lives of the Omaha and Depression-era Americans that was too starkly familiar. For, as a brief review in *The Nation* noted, Mead's conclusion regarding the Omaha was that "the individual . . . is left floundering in a heterogeneous welter of meaningless, uncoordinated and disintegrating institutions."[57]

Although Mead may have relegated the Omaha book to the dustbin of her mind, subconsciously she seems to have registered the impact of its discordant note on both herself and the public. Twenty-five years later, when she observed the very different reaction of the Manus people to culture contact and acculturation, she was eager to write about their experience in her popular book *New Lives for Old* and to appear in the television documentary it inspired.[58]

Other anthropologists, however, were enthusiastic about Mead's Omaha work. Writing for the *American Anthropologist*, Alexander Goldenweiser admiringly stated that, "Margaret Mead has made a signal contribution to our knowledge of the reactions of a typical Indian tribe to the impact of white civilization."[59] According to Goldenweiser, despite the abundant amount of research that American anthropologists had done among Native American tribes, until Mead's study there had been little work done on the topic of what was to become the study of "culture contact." He even predicted that because "the result of her investigation is so interesting and far-reaching . . . her pioneering study is bound to be followed by other such studies, opportunity for which abounds among the North American Indians."[60]

Praise for the book was not limited to the United States. In the British journal *Man*, in addition to commending Mead's vivid writing style, the reviewer observed that Mead's study "shows the great importance to both the ethnographer and the sociologist of investigating the results of these extreme examples of diffusion and culture change."[61] Thus, according to these and other anthropologists, *The Changing Culture of an Indian Tribe* represented a pioneering effort at a new kind of research, research that focused on the problem of acculturation and culture change, defined as the study of the social processes whereby a culture adapted to the beliefs and practices of a new, more dominant culture. It was a subfield of political anthropology that was to become increasingly important during the 1930s. For acculturation theory, as it came to be called, "contained, albeit implicitly, the attack on racial domination, imperialism, and monopoly capitalism that has been a subterranean trend within the discipline on both sides of the Atlantic from the beginning."[62]

Ironically, although *The Changing Culture of an Indian Tribe* remains one of Mead's least known works, among her professional peers the book added to her reputation as an innovative and serious anthropologist. Nonetheless, neither the profession nor the public ever associated Mead with the study of Native American cultures, and soon after the book's publication Mead returned to New Guinea to embark upon the research that resulted in *Sex and Temperament in Three Primitive Societies*, the book she later claimed was the most misunderstood of all her work.

CHAPTER 5

Mead as Anthropologist: "To Find Out How Girls Learn to Be Girls"

> . . . what she saw was profoundly disconcerting . . . there was a differentiation so shattering in its contrast to all we know that hardly the nicest and most magnanimous woman could be trusted to read it without happy guffaws. They are getting what they deserve back in Tchambuli—they are being taught what it feels like.
>
> —Rebecca West, Review of *Sex and Temperament*, the *Sunday Times* (London)[1]

During the summer of 1931, having postponed her return to New Guinea while she wrote *Kinship in the Admiralty Islands*, her response to anthropologist C. W. R. Hart's stinging critique of *Growing Up in New Guinea*, various articles appeared in New York City newspapers that described Mead's impending research trip:

> **DR. MARGARET MEAD TO JOIN THIRD EXPEDITION**
>
> **To Find Out How Girls Learn to Be Girls, she says.**
>
> She has a suspicion, she said yesterday, that a great part of what we believe to be fundamental sex differences is not biological at all but is implanted by the way boys and girls are brought up.[2]

This headline—as well as another in the *New York Herald Tribune* that announced: "Jungle Expected to Reveal Why Boys Are Boys"[3]—shows that the media was interested in telling readers that Mead was off again to the remote South Pacific, this time to study a question that continued to fascinate Americans: What makes girls different from boys? Is it a matter of nature or nurture? While the prevailing thought at the time was that sex differences between males and females were determined biologically, Mead was among a dissenting minority of scientists who were intent on investigating the extent to which one's social environment—the way that a boy or girl is brought up—determines whether one behaves like a man or a woman.

The *New York Herald Tribune* article was accompanied by a photograph of Mead standing next to an elaborately decorated orator's stool, an example of the type of sculpture found in the Sepik River region of New Guinea where Mead and Fortune were headed for their next research. The photo, with its caption's reference to the carved stool as an "idol," titillates the public with notions of pagan non-Western religions and images of primitive supernatural spirits.

Other writers, enthralled by the idea of Mead as a woman setting off for a remote and hostile environment, juxtaposed sexuality, danger, and primitivism in the service of Western science:

> GOING AND GETTING IT FOR SCIENCE:
> WHITE WOMAN STUDIES GHOST-RULED SAVAGES IN MELANESIA
>
> New Yorkers today are piercing dark jungles. They are crossing far deserts. They are facing strange hazards. It's a matter of course. They're truth hunters. They're members of expeditions of the American Museum of Natural History. They go and get odd, new facts. They bring them back and interpret them for the sake of science.[4]

This article was one in a series published by the *New York World-Telegram* that focused on scientists at the American Museum of Natural History and highlighted their quest for "adventure and truth both in laboratory and down dim, distant trails." It once again demonstrates how the press, in seeking to entice readers by appealing to their sense of adventure and kindling their imaginations by implying intrigue and danger, contributed to the iconic image of Mead as anthropologist and intrepid explorer.

The article also reminds us of how important it was to Mead's fame that she worked at a museum rather than a university. The dual function of the American Museum of Natural History as research center and locus of informal public education meant that the media often turned to the

Exhibiting Something Rare in Idols

Herald Tribune photo—Zerbe

Dr. Margaret Mead, pictured yesterday at the American Museum of Natural History, where she is an assistant curator, at the opening of a special loan exhibition of the Morner collection

Jungle Expected To Reveal Why Boys Are Boys

Dr. Margaret Mead, of Natural History Museum, Sailing for New Guinea Study

Figure 5.1 "Exhibiting Something Rare in Idols," 1931. (Mead Archives, Manuscript Division, Library of Congress)

New York World-Telegram

SECOND SECTION

NEW YORK, WEDNESDAY, JUNE 17, 1931. 21

GOING AND GETTING IT FOR SCIENCE

White Woman Studies Ghost-Ruled Savages in Melanesia

Islanders Rely on Beneficent Spirits to Protect Them from Evil Machinations of Mainland Bogies, Diagnose Sickness and Preserve Morality.

New Yorkers today are piercing dark jungles. They are crossing far deserts. They are facing strange hazards. It's a matter of course. They're truth hunters. They're members of expeditions of the American Museum of Natural History. They go and get odd, new facts. They bring them back and interpret them for the sake of science. In a series of six articles, of which this is the third, William Engle, New York World-Telegram staff writer, is revealing how the American Museum quests adventure and truth both in laboratory and down dim, distant trails.

By WILLIAM ENGLE.
World-Telegram Staff Writer.

(Copyright, 1931, by The New York Telegram Corp.)

THAT venerable gentleman, Manewai, transformed four suns ago by the protozoans of malaria from a Melanesian grandfather to a competent ghost, was fated at midnight to drop in from the interstellar spaces; he was destined to take up in spectral guise his abode there in the sago leaf thatched hut perched on spindling piles above the equatorial lagoon, where he had dwelt in the frailty of the flesh.

So on the living room floor the folks ceremoniously spread the yams and taro and mud hen eggs for the funeral feast.

He came. His missus and the others of the household vouched for it. For the next morning, they said, they discovered that in the night he had eaten, though sparingly, of the feast. And they therefore knew that thenceforth he would remain invisibly but faithfully hovering on guard over their home.

Where Ghosts Rule.

They counted twenty suns. Then, with that which yet was mortal of Grandfather Manewai, they did what there was to be done. They hung his head in ritualistic state in the parlor.

They suspended it from the ceiling near the front of the room in the position of highest honor, to remain there until the astute ghost of some outsider should outwit grandfather in the duties of his thatched protectorate. They then bore the residuum of the mortal Manewai to far-away sand dunes where the sun and wind might have their way, as was proper.

Manus ghosts rule those hot lagoons off the island Great Admiralty in Melanesia.

They protect the Manus fishermen from rigors of dry season, and rainy, three one degree above the equator. They match ...

... time children elsewhere take to velocipedes, think it is a lie. But they outgrow, as their sagacious elders outgrew, that early skepticism.

Ghosts do sturdily survive there in the huts precariously huddled above the shallow lagoons. Ghosts do marry, and give in marriage, and irk one another, and sometimes grant cause for a New York State divorce. And they do consistently put potent spells upon the bogies of the mangroves.

A Manus child lay gravely stricken ...

Dr. Margaret Mead Pursues Ethnological Studies to Malarial Tropics.

... course heard a spectral whisper, clear enough, anyway, to conclude that probably it was Pataliwan, whose didoes were back of it all, clear enough to divine that the end of his didoes would mean the end of illness.

When the patriarchal ghost errs in pronouncement, and death comes on despite obedience to his orders, the family nevertheless has a ready explanation.

It was not the patriarch, after all, who visited affliction on a happy home. Some brash outsider ghost was too smart for that patriarch, and despite the patriarch's will, the outsider wrought evil.

So, as in the theologies that get into print, the faithful remain faithful even when faith sometimes is sorely burdened.

Encompassed by Bogies.

Faith, to the Manus people, is as necessary as the betel nut and pepper leaves they chew. It is as definitely a part of daily humdrum as their barter with dogs' teeth and turtles. It has to be kept as sharply in mind as the phases of the moon that presage the great runs of spawning fish in warm, shallow lagoons.

Bogies encompass them. Sorcery of the "man-o-bush" beats about them. Demons of the tangled swamps threaten direly through all the ceremonials that attend life ...

Two Faces In Fashion For Women

Athletic Make-Up for Sport Gives Way to Something Fragile at Night.

By ALICE HUGHES.

Paul Gallico, sports writer for Vanity Fair, has thrown this country's cosmeticians into confusion. They are all a-dither among their creams, unguents and lotions. He scorns the lady athlete whose face gets tanned and weathered, whose limbs are knotty with bulging muscles. "Muscle Molls," Gallico calls them, and declares himself as preferring those limper lilies who recline white and languishing in the shade while the horsey-torsey ones whip themselves into a lather on the tennis court.

Alice Hughes.

Helena Rubinstein, caretaker of this country's feminine complexion, steps into the breach. All this week her sister, Manka Rubinstein, is telling those who come to the Abraham & Straus store for beauty consultations that a woman may romp in the sun and be as boisterous as she likes and still maintain a delicate skin. She may be a ruddy out-of-doors girl from 9 to 5, and a hothouse lily after dark.

It's all in the make-up. A sunproof foundation cream, suitable for the beach and for all outdoor sports, shields the face better than a sunshade. Over this a suntan powder gives the skin a bronzy glow. Waterproof lipstick and rouge added to this permit even water sports, all under a smooth, cafe au lait finish.

Sundown tells a different tale. A new make-up, creamy and fragile-looking, gives the lie to the athlete of but a few hours back. Manka Rubinstein is showing Brooklyn women how to make their faces lead this double life.

* * *

Avedon Shop to Reopen.

The Avedon specialty shop on Fifth Ave., near 40th St., reopens on Saturday of this week after closing its doors several months ago when depression overtook it. It will ...

Figure 5.2 "Going and Getting It for Science," 1931. (Mead Archives, Manuscript Division, Library of Congress)

museum's curators as experts, and they became not only sources of information but intellectual and cultural symbols as well. Being employed by the museum offered Mead the imprimatur of expert and a platform from which she could reach a larger public than had she taught at a university.

In 1935, Mead published *Sex and Temperament in Three Primitive Societies*. Along with Ruth Benedict's *Patterns of Culture*, published in 1934, *Sex and Temperament* served to bring anthropology once again into the public spotlight. Based upon research Mead and Reo Fortune carried out from 1931 to 1933 in the Sepik region of New Guinea, *Sex and Temperament* presents comparative data from the Arapesh, Mundugumor, and Tchambuli (now called the Chambri) societies about male and female behavior and personality. It was the third major popular book Mead had published about Pacific Island societies in less than ten years.

Publicity for *Sex and Temperament*

After reading the manuscript for *Sex and Temperament,* Frances Phillips, Mead's editor at William Morrow, wrote to her:

> We want to congratulate you on a superb piece of work—first the research and then the creative thinking from M. M. that so lights up the scene not only of New Guinea but of Ameriky. It will stir up a lot of controversy and should get you a wider audience, as well as new laurels.[5]

Phillips, as well as others at William Morrow, sensed that Mead's challenge to the idea that male and female behaviors were biologically determined, and thus immutable, would be controversial and spark considerable interest in the book and its author. Discussing publicity for the book, Phillips wrote Mead that:

> We all agree that Bertrand Russell is a fine name to have on the jacket so will you write and ask him? H. G. Wells is also good, but Russell is better, we think. However, if you can start working on Wells, do so and we'll send him galleys, too.[6]

Mead wrote to Bertrand Russell, the eminent British philosopher, pacifist, and outspoken social critic, with a request for a blurb endorsing *Sex and Temperament*, described her book as "an analysis of the psycho-sexual roles of both sexes in three New Guinea tribes with which I worked in 1931–33, and a discussion of the bearing of these findings on the problem of sex temperament."[7] Russell, an advocate of trial marriage, among other unconventional ideas, had recently written a hugely successful and controversial book titled *Marriage and Morals* (1929), which described his "free-thinking" ideas about the relations between men and women.[8] Since Russell was a frequent lecturer in the United States, many Americans would have been more familiar with his books and articles about social issues than his work on mathematics and analytical philosophy, for which he later received a Nobel Prize.[9]

Phillips also thought that Mead should ask the British author H. G. Wells for a blurb. He was renowned worldwide for his popular science fiction, books such as *The Time Machine*, *The War of the Worlds*, and *The Invisible Man.* A racy figure in the literary and intellectual world, Wells was also known for his progressive social ideas, his socialist politics, and his call for a World State and free love (as well as for his womanizing and his reputation as a lothario). In short, he was a major British intellectual, an eminent writer whose broad interests in science and the psychology of the human mind and libido made him someone who was likely to be interested in what Mead had to say about human sexuality and the behavior of men and women. Moreover, because Wells had just published his widely read *Experiment in Autobiography*, in which he discussed his progressive ideas about sexual relations between men and women, it would have been advantageous for the promotion of *Sex and Temperament* for Mead to have had an endorsement for her book from him.[10] Phillips wrote Mead that "a word from him, while that book [*Experiment in Autobiography*] is in the limelight, would be helpful. If I were you, I'd go after him."[11]

After Russell had replied to Mead that he did not think an author's third book warranted an endorsement, since by that point the author should be sufficiently well known that the work should stand on its own merits, she decided not to contact Wells.[12] The exchange between Mead and her editor about endorsements indicates the desire both author and publisher had to get Mead's book as much recognition as possible from eminent writers and intellectuals of the time, especially individuals associated with progressive ideas about subjects such as marriage and sexuality. They wanted to demonstrate that the book was of interest to a broad spectrum of readers, not simply to specialists or scholars.

Rebecca West's Review of *Sex and Temperament*

Sex and Temperament was indeed widely reviewed and well received by the popular press. Ironically, it was Rebecca West, H. G. Wells's former lover and a respected, albeit unconventional journalist and intellectual with an international reputation, who reviewed *Sex and Temperament* in Britain for the *Sunday Times*.[13] Outspoken and gutsy, West began her career in the early 1920s writing for the feminist journal the *Freewoman*. Thus, it is not surprising that she welcomed what Mead had to say about the malleability of men's and women's behavior, for she herself was an example of a woman who had defied the conventional roles for women that the Edwardian society in which she had been raised had set out for her.

West began her review by citing Ruth Benedict's argument in *Patterns of Culture* that human nature is more malleable than we commonly think. "Now there is another American anthropologist," West continued, "who produces further evidence supporting this theory. It is even more startling than anything in *Patterns of Culture* because it concerns the differentiation in the characters of men and women which we are most apt to take as inherent in human structure."[14] Welcoming Mead's conclusions about the variability of women's and men's characters, West concluded with a discussion of the implications of Mead's theory for different specialists. Referring to her own profession first, she mentioned its import for literary criticism and writers: "Writers of bad fiction," she said, "take for granted that males and females have the sharply differentiated characteristics the pattern of our Western culture alleges." While "the authors of the second [good fiction] see themselves as possessed of an infinite range of common qualities which the environment draws out differently at different times."[15]

West also suggested that Mead's findings had important bearing on psychology and education, observing that "a great deal of psychiatric work is vitiated by the tendency to treat people who deviate from the role prescribed them by the pattern of their culture as if they were deviating from a norm established by nature." Like West herself, the product of an unconventional upbringing in turn-of-the-century England, and an individual who had made choices about how to live her life that were not the norm for Edwardian women, she implored educationists to "read Miss Mead's lucid and moving last chapter, in which she recounts the actual losses suffered by all members of communities which believe too credulously in their pattern and plead for a less arbitrary social fabric, one in which each diverse human gift will find a fitting place."[16]

That West was asked to review *Sex and Temperament* and considered it to be an important intellectual contribution shows that the book was in step with the intellectual and social currents of the time. Whether in the fields of fiction or of science, people were challenging the traditional roles assigned to men and women, and ideas from one domain of activity bolstered and stimulated ideas in other domains.[17] It is not surprising that West wrote in praise of Mead's findings about the social construction of male and female behavior. Both West and Mead represent modern twentieth-century women who challenged the limited traditional roles for women that Western society had ascribed to them through their work and the way they lived their lives.[18]

Anthropologists' Reviews of *Sex and Temperament*

Mead once commented that *Sex and Temperament* was her most misunderstood book.[19] This was so, she surmised, because unlike Rebecca West—who got Mead's point about the malleability of male and female personalities and behavior—many readers thought that Mead was suggesting that there were *no* differences between men and women.[20] Other critics, especially anthropologists, thought her descriptions of the three societies she described—the Arapesh, the Mundugumor, and the Tchambuli—could not be true. It was not possible, they thought, for Mead to have found within a fairly circumscribed radius of the Sepik River three societies that illustrated so neatly the three contrasting models of male/female behavior she attributed to them. Among the Arapesh, both males and females exhibited what Mead described as "nurturing" behavior. In other words, Arapesh men as well as Arapesh women behaved in ways that Western society would describe as feminine. While among the Mundugumor, a belligerent and recently pacified society of warriors and former headhunters, both women and men exhibited behavior that we would label as masculine: aggressive, boastful, nonnurturing; even Mundugumor mothers disliked babies and children. Finally, Mead characterized the dominant behavior of Tchambuli men and women as being exactly opposite that of Western men and women. In Tchambuli society the men liked to preen and dress up, painting their faces and adorning themselves with feathers, dog's teeth, and shell finery. In contrast, Tchambuli women were the workers and the economic support of their families. While Tchambuli men stayed home with their children, Tchambuli women went off in their canoes to fish and trade at distant markets.

Once again, in contrast to adulatory reviews of *Sex and Temperament* such as West's in the popular press, Mead received negative reviews of her work from anthropologists. The review of *Sex and Temperament* that appeared in the *American Anthropologist* was written by a German anthropologist, Richard Thurnwald, an "old New Guinea hand" who as a young man had worked in the same region of the Sepik as Mead and Fortune. Thurnwald, who was currently teaching at Yale along with Edward Sapir, voiced similar reservations to those of other anthropologists who had reviewed her earlier books. He too dismissed what he referred to as Mead's moralizing, although in more polite terms than either Lowie or Hart, and observed that "the attempt to mingle anthropological research work with educational planning makes the book attractive for large groups of people, but may sometimes lead the student of anthropology astray."[21] He then questioned the accuracy of Mead's data, the validity of her interpretations, and her knowledge of the local languages. In particular, as Fortune and other anthropologists would do later, Thurnwald questioned Mead's conclusion that the Arapesh were a nonviolent, docile people. However, after what reads as a very damning review of her work, Thurnwald ends by saying, "After all these remarks, I do not want to leave this book without acknowledging its merits. It provides a store of information about women and sex, children and education. It offers a fascinating description of daily life and the psychology of human beings. . . . It is very well written and will recruit friends for anthropology."[22]

Thurnwald's review reiterates several recurring themes regarding anthropologists' reactions to Mead's books and her proficiency as an anthropologist. On the one hand, there is the professional's dislike of what they considered to be her moralizing and skepticism regarding her ability to produce sufficient accurate data when working for such a short period of time in any one particular society. On the other hand, the familiar recognition of how well Mead writes was coupled with anthropologists' acknowledgment that her skill as a writer attracted readers and aroused the public's interest in anthropology. Mead, displeased with Thurnwald's review, wrote a lengthy response to his criticisms.[23]

Sex and Temperament Seventy Years Later

At the time Mead published her argument in *Sex and Temperament* that masculine and feminine behaviors are socially constructed and vary from society to society established her as one of a group of prominent social scientists and intellectuals who were outspoken in their opposition to a lingering nineteenth-century social Darwinism, the eugenics movement of the early twentieth century that it had spawned, and the racist ideologies that European fascisms were beginning to propagate during the 1930s. Feminist-minded intellectuals such as Rebecca West and, thirty years later, feminist leader Betty Friedan, praised Mead's conclusions.

In *The Feminine Mystique*, Friedan wrote that Mead was to be commended for her insights into the malleability of women's and men's roles.

Citing an oft-quoted statement in the book, in which Mead wrote that "we may say that many, if not all, of the personality traits which we have called masculine or feminine are as lightly linked to sex as are the clothing, the manners, and the form of headdress that a society at a given period assigns to either sex," Friedan said that Mead's conclusions helped to strike a blow against biological determinists' theories of innate differences between men and women.[24]

Just as *Coming of Age in Samoa* came to represent Mead's stance as a cultural determinist and advocate of sexual freedom among adolescents, *Sex and Temperament* came to represent Mead's contribution to feminist scholarship and female equality with men. As we have seen, beginning in the mid-1970s feminist anthropologists started to cite Mead's work, especially *Coming of Age in Samoa* and *Sex and Temperament*, as important contributions to the anthropological study of women and our understanding of the social construction of gender roles.[25] More recently, feminist anthropologist Kamala Visweswaran has also written admiringly of Mead's work, especially of *Sex and Temperament*, seeing it as an important contribution to a feminist perspective in the social sciences and as exemplary of the genre of feminist ethnography. Visweswaran cites the same statement about masculine and feminine personality traits as Friedan, bolstering its status as a foundational statement about gender identity.[26]

"The Triangular Situation": Mead, Fortune, and Bateson in New Guinea

While Mead and Fortune were in New Guinea conducting the research that Mead would analyze in *Sex and Temperament*, they met Gregory Bateson, who was doing ethnographic research in Tambunum village on the Sepik River. While visiting Bateson in the field, Mead wrote in *Blackberry Winter*, the two of them began to fall in love.[27] At a time when the separation between private and public life was clearly delineated, even if the resident Australian colonials in New Guinea or colleagues who saw the three of them when they arrived in Sydney suspected Mead and Bateson's mutual attraction, no comment about the "triangular situation" would have been made in public.

Two generations later, however, this incident—and speculation about it—has piqued the curiosity of scholars and laymen alike and even spawned two films that reference it—a dramatization of a scene with the three anthropologists on the Sepik in the documentary *Margaret Mead: An Observer Observed* and a feature film, *In a Savage Land*, by Australian director Bill Bennett.[28] The scene in *An Observer Observed,* while conveying information about Mead and anthropology, is also filled with amorous innuendos as the actors playing Mead and Bateson gaze meaningfully into each other's eyes, a palpable unspoken emotional connection established between them.

Although *In a Savage Land* is also about anthropologists and similarly set in New Guinea during the 1930s, it takes place in the more eroticized Trobriand Islands, a place well known to many westerners from Bronislaw Malinowski's ethnography of the islanders, *The Sexual Life of Savages.*[29] Although the film's location is different, the parallel between the actual ménage à trois of Mead, Fortune, and Bateson reverberates in *In a Savage Land*, as the story also focuses on the emotional life of a female anthropologist and her romantic involvement with two men, one of whom is her husband. Thus, both films play upon the sexual tension ignited by the different personalities of the anthropologists and subtly, or not so subtly, perpetuate the stereotype of anthropologists as either fixated on the study of sex or on performing it.

Building on this and other permutations of Mead's "triangular situation," feminist scholars and anthropologists have given us a new image of Mead as anthropologist, one that stresses the dialogical nature of her research and writing; of the importance, that is, of the conversations Mead had with colleagues, lovers, and friends to her intellectual work.[30] For example, drawing upon archival material, especially Mead's correspondence, historian Lois Banner and psychologist Hilary Lapsley present the image of Mead as a young woman who was questioning her own sexual identity and whose research, especially her research on the three Sepik cultures in New Guinea, was motivated in part by a personal quest to understand the nature of her own identity.[31] More substantively, they also highlight the social nature of the production of knowledge by foregrounding the intimate physical, emotional, and intellectual relationship between Mead and Benedict. Banner, for instance, argues that Mead wrote much of *Sex and Temperament* in response to Benedict's *Patterns of Culture*. She suggests that throughout *Sex and Temperament*

THE

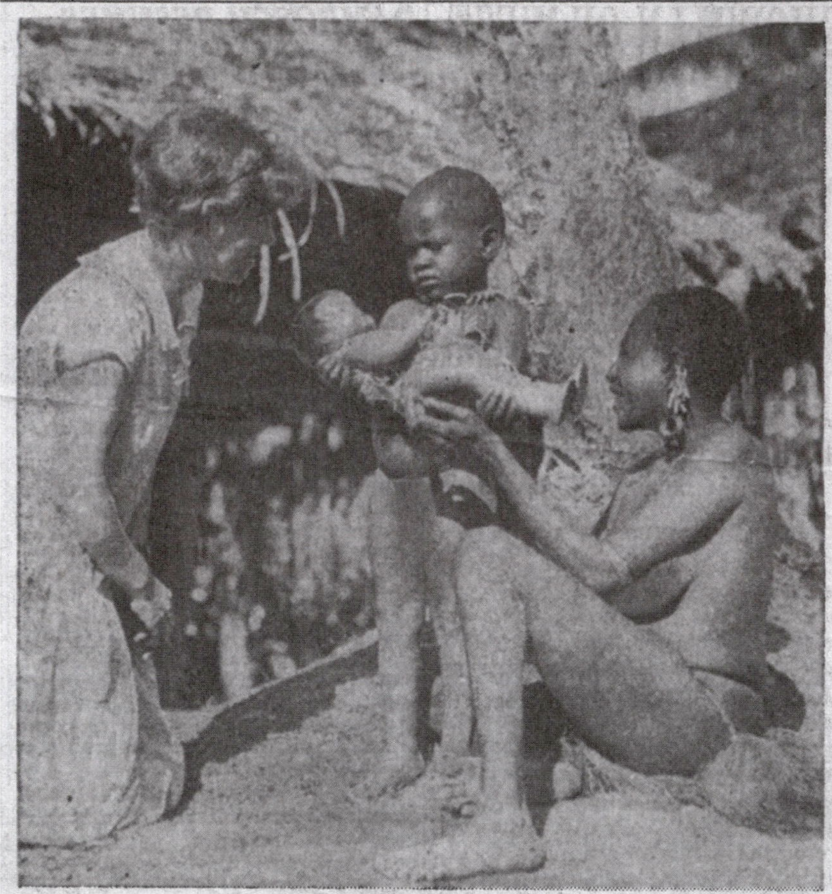

Times Wide World Photo.

THE FIRST DOLL STIRS INTEREST IN NEW GUINEA.

Dr. Margaret Mead, who headed the expedition of the American Museum of Natural History, watches the reaction of a native child. Women of the tribe had to be persuaded that the doll was not a mummified baby.

Figure 5.3 Mead with an Arapesh mother and child, New Guinea, 1933. (Courtesy of the Library of Congress and the Institute for Intercultural Studies)

Mead articulated points of view and conclusions about the nature of sexuality that were at variance with statements Benedict had made in *Patterns of Culture*.[32]

Anthropologist Paul Roscoe, in contrast, has recently suggested that Mead was unduly influenced by Benedict's *Patterns of Culture*, to the extent that she mischaracterized Arapesh culture and either ignored or downplayed data that did not conform to the cultural pattern she was invested in seeing.[33] Agreeing with Fortune, who first challenged Mead's interpretation of the Arapesh as nonaggressive and not practicing warfare, Roscoe and other anthropologists who have also worked among the Arapesh present data that challenges Mead's interpretation of Arapesh men's character as nonaggressive and maternal.[34]

In many ways Roscoe's 2003 critique of Mead's interpretation of the Arapesh is more damning than Derek Freeman's earlier refutation of Mead's Samoan data because it presents a more carefully argued and less polemical critique. Yet with the exception of a flurry of attention in New Zealand when Roscoe's article first appeared, the media has hardly picked up on the challenge. The interest in New Zealand in Roscoe's article no doubt was due to the fact that Fortune was a New Zealander. Roscoe's argument not only vindicates Fortune's interpretation of the Arapesh but also promotes Kiwi pride at the expense of Mead, the Yankee.

Roscoe's article may have received little attention from American media because it was the second time, rather than the first, that Mead's work had been challenged. From the standpoint of the media, Mead, already dead for twenty-five years when Roscoe published his article, was of far less importance to American society than she was when Freeman's book appeared just five years after her death. And finally, it may be that Roscoe was challenging her interpretation of her data, not the validity of the data itself. He praises Mead for the quality and quantity of her Arapesh data, and he also attributes her with giving anthropology the first detailed description of the Big Man as a political type, a concept that became central to political anthropology.[35]

Roscoe is not the only anthropologist to have challenged aspects of Mead's research in the Sepik. Deborah Gewertz has criticized her conclusions about the Tchambuli (Chambri) based on her own research with the Chambri beginning in the 1970s. While she takes exception to Mead's overly westernized image of the Chambri as individualistic, she too has admiration for Mead as an ethnographer.[36] Similarly, Nancy McDowell, who painstakingly combed through Mead's notes on the Mundugumor in order to reconstruct an ethnography based on her 1930s notes, also has admiration for the detail and thoroughness of Mead's fieldwork.[37] These anthropologists, all of whom have worked in the same societies as Mead, often question aspects of her interpretation of her data, but find the data itself to be rich in detail. They present a contradictory image of Mead as an anthropologist. She is a flawed interpreter of data, often reading more into it than the facts allow, but nonetheless she is an excellent fieldworker and observer of human behavior.

As with *Coming of Age in Samoa,* in recent years anthropologists and historians have returned to *Sex and Temperament*, either to challenge aspects of Mead's interpretation of her ethnographic data or to look in more detail at the intellectual and social forces that contributed to Mead's argument about sex and gender. For example, in her introduction to the 2001 centennial edition of *Sex and Temperament*, biological anthropologist Helen Fisher writes admiringly of Mead's research goals and comparative methods, placing the book and its theoretical perspective within its historical milieu—the eve of World War II and the rise of Hitler and German fascism. Fisher notes, however, that Mead might amend what she had to say in *Sex and Temperament* if she knew what scientists now know about the role of the mind as a third factor that interacts with human biology and culture to shape human behavior.[38]

Today within anthropology, although the responses to her conclusions in *Sex and Temperament* are ambivalent, criticisms of her interpretations of her data are tempered by admiration for the quality and quantity of data she collected. And among area specialists, the extensiveness of her fieldwork and the detail of her raw data still draw admiration.[39]

Images of Mead as Anthropologist

In less than ten years—between 1928 and 1935—Mead had conducted fieldwork in five different Pacific Island societies and had written three widely acclaimed books about them, along with numerous articles in popular magazines and journals, a feat that few other anthropologists have matched.[40] With the publication of *Sex and Temperament in Three Primitive Tribes* in 1935, Mead's popular reputation as an anthropologist who was an expert on non-Western peoples and their psychology was firmly established.

In the media and the public's mind Mead had come to represent a set of ideas about anthropologists and the practice of anthropology. By 1935, both in the United States and abroad, anthropology was still a profession that employed relatively few individuals, either within or outside of academia. Yet the publicity that Mead's books (as well as the work of Malinowski, Boas, Benedict, and others) had generated meant that most educated Americans had heard of anthropologists, even if they were not entirely sure of what they did. In this regard, Mead came to epitomize the anthropologist as fieldworker, for not only had she studied a large number of societies in the South Seas, she had also studied people who fit both popular stereotypes of non-Western peoples: that of the Noble Savage (the sensuous and seemingly carefree Samoans) and the Savage Barbarian (the Manus Islanders and the three Sepik groups described in *Sex and Temperament*, some of whom formerly had been headhunters). Mead as an anthropologist came to represent Western civilization's knowledge of and dominance over the non-Western peoples anthropologists studied. The new inflection Mead gave to this stereotypical image of the anthropologist was that she studied the lives of women and children.

Another image of Mead as anthropologist was that she studied the sex lives of primitive people. On the one hand, as poet Howard Mumford Jones expressed in "The Anthropologist," to some individuals this focus on the study of sex led to an image of Mead as prurient and voyeuristic. On the other hand, Mead's study of adolescent girls and their sexual practices aligned her with the development of the scientific study of sexuality that had begun with the work of Freud and other sexologists. The public associated Mead with those progressive scientists, scholars, intellectuals, and social reformers interested in the fields of psychology, psychiatry, and psychoanalysis whose ideas about the centrality of sexuality to human behavior and human fulfillment were gradually reforming American society's sexual mores and practices.[41] Thus, another image of Mead is that of a modernist, both with regard to her own sexual behavior and in terms of her theoretical conclusions about the varied nature of men's and women's sexual relationships, erotic desire, and the cultural patterning of gendered behavior.

According to Mead, the study of adolescence in Samoa led her realize that in order to understand the effect of culture on the development of personality she first needed to study children and childhood.[42] This decision reflected the influence of Freud and psychoanalytic theory on her desire to understand how culture shaped adult personality. It also aligned her with a growing number of American social scientists and educators who were engaged in the study of childhood and child development, another relatively new field of research being supported by the Rockefeller Foundation under the guidance of Lawrence Frank.[43] Frank, who became a personal friend and mentor to Mead, helped shape the field of child development in America, and in doing so, influenced Mead's involvement in it. Mead's research on children and child rearing in New Guinea, published in both *Growing Up in New Guinea* and *Sex and Temperament in Three Primitive Societies*, contributed to her image as an expert on the study of child development, parenting, and the family.

This image of Mead developed at a time when twentieth-century American parents were becoming more and more dependent upon the advice of experts for information about how to bring up their children. Raised by a mother who had instructed her to record her observations of her younger siblings' development, Mead was eager to formalize her study of child development by learning from other researchers interested in the scientific study of child development.[44]

Mead first met her friend and colleague Benjamin Spock at a meeting of the New York Psychoanalytic Association, as they both shared a professional interest in psychoanalytic theory. During the 1930s, Mead was a key figure in the development of the subdiscipline of anthropology known as culture and personality, a field of inquiry that sought to integrate psychoanalytic theories of the individual with anthropology, thus expanding the scope of psychoanalytic theory beyond its culture-bound sphere of Western societies. As historian Warren Sussman has demonstrated, the idea of *personality*—as a phenomena of investigation, a personal attribute, and as a focus of research and potential disorder—was very much a twentieth-century development.[45]

Along with Edward Sapir, Ruth Benedict, Ralph Linton, and other anthropologists in the New York area and psychoanalysts and psychologists such Abram Kardiner, Harry Stack Sullivan, Karen Horney, and Erik Erikson, Mead participated in seminars and research projects that sought to integrate traditional Freudian psychoanalytic theory about individual personality with anthropological theory about culture. Practitioners of this neo-Freudian perspective sought to understand the role that culture played in the shaping of individual personality and national character, as well as the dominant types of personalities associated with particular countries or cultures.[46] Mead's interest in psychoanalysis, psychology, and psychiatry led to her lifelong professional association with individuals such as Erik Erikson and Karl Menninger, major contributors to theoretical and practical developments in the fields of psychoanalysis and psychiatry.[47] It also led to her involvement with the creation of the National and World Federations for Mental Health and her participation in organizations such as the Menninger Foundation, the Department of Psychiatry at the University of Cincinnati's School of Medicine, the Merrill-Palmer Institute in Detroit, and the Society of Orthopsychiatry.

Another image of Mead that circulated within the social sciences was that of Mead the neo-Freudian and proponent of culture and personality, the subfield of anthropology mentioned above. In its positive valence, this image of Mead credits her with contributing to the foundation of what today is known as the field of psychological anthropology. However, when later in her career Mead defended fellow anthropologist Geoffrey Gorer's argument about the influence of swaddling Russian infants on their later adult personality, Mead also became labeled derisively as an adherent of the "diaperology" school of anthropology.[48]

The development of these areas of inquiry with which Mead was associated represent the growing importance of the social sciences in American intellectual, political, and cultural life during the twentieth century. The public's enthusiastic response to Mead also reflects the increasingly powerful role that experts were coming to play in advising Americans how to live their lives. Their response also mirrors the growth of anthropology from an esoteric field that focused solely on the study of remote, exotic people and their customs to a social science that engaged in dialogues with many other disciplines and that addressed issues of contemporary concern to Americans.

This transformation in the popular understanding of anthropology occurred in part because Mead wrote and spoke in a style that the general public could understand and appreciate. As a result, the media and the public came to see Mead—and anthropologists in general—not simply as adventurers who went off to study the esoteric sexual habits of indigenous peoples, but more broadly as scientists and experts in the study of human behavior. Nonetheless, as we have seen by the media's representations of Mead and her work, these two images of the anthropologist—

adventurer and purveyor of the exotic and esoteric versus human behavior expert—have remained juxtaposed against each other in the public's mind, as represented in popular culture. In the next chapter we will take a closer look at the contributions of the images of Mead to the development of the popular image of the anthropologist. In doing so we will gain further insight into the meanings the "primitive" assumed in twentieth-century American society and the role anthropology played in shaping the modern American identity, an identity defined in contrast to the image of "the primitive."

CHAPTER 6

Mead and the Image of the Anthropologist

> The development of the fieldworker's image in America, from Frank Hamilton Cushing (an oddball) to Margaret Mead (a national figure) is significant . . . a particular form of ethnographic authority was created—an authority both scientifically validated and based on a unique personal experience.
>
> —James Clifford, "On Ethnographic Authority"[1]

As we have seen, the media's responses to Mead's South Pacific books illustrate that from the beginning of her career there was a powerful confluence between its interest in her as an exceptional young woman and the American public's fascination with her study of exotic "primitive" peoples. These two interests intersected to create a stereotype of Mead as anthropologist, a stereotype based on the popular image of the anthropologist as an authority on the cultures of indigenous peoples, especially their sex lives.[2] Taken together, the topics of sexuality and the study of exotic "primitives" provided her with an avid audience. While Mead's increasing fame had much to do with the burgeoning influence of mass media, it was also dependent upon her choice of career, her decisions to go to Samoa and New Guinea, and the American public's curiosity about the so-called primitive Other. In this chapter our focus shifts from Mead as anthropologist to a consideration of her contribution to media representations of the anthropologist in general.

Other Famous Anthropologists

Although a handful of other anthropologists have achieved some degree of fame and recognition, none has ever achieved the same popular recognition worldwide as Mead. Limiting our scope to American anthropologists, the first anthropologist to catch the American public's attention was, as James Clifford notes, the flamboyant Frank Hamilton Cushing. At the turn of the nineteenth century Cushing's lively stories about the five years he spent living among the Zuni Indians captivated readers of *Century* and other popular magazines.[3] A member of the Bureau of Ethnology's first official expedition to the Southwest, Cushing's eccentric behavior, which included posing for an audience dressed in Zuni ritual attire, contributed to the stereotype of anthropologists as nonconformists and led Clifford to characterize him as "an odd ball."

By far the most influential anthropologist in twentieth-century America was Mead's mentor, Franz Boas. More than sixty years after his death, scholars and authors interested in the intellectual and cultural history of race and the study of human behavior are still analyzing his legacy.[4] Throughout his lengthy career Boas constantly wrote newspaper editorials and engaged in public debates about issues of race, intelligence, eugenics, and cultural versus biological determinism. As a public figure, Boas's renown reached its apex in 1936 when his picture appeared on the cover of *Time* magazine, "a national hero" for his stance against eugenics and scientific racism at a time when the specter of Hitler's racial policies were beginning to haunt Europe.[5] But despite his role as a public intellectual and his media exposure, Boas's name was never as well known by the general American public as Mead's. This is in large part because the fieldwork he undertook among the Eskimos of Baffin Island and Northwest Coast Indians as well as his books for the general public never caught the public's imagination in the same way as Mead's.[6]

Likewise, although Boas's male students such as Robert Lowie, Alexander Goldenweiser, Edward Sapir, and Alfred Kroeber also wrote for the general public and used their anthropological insights to engage in discussions of contemporary social issues, they too never achieved the public acclaim or national visibility that Mead did.[7] During the 1920s, several of these anthropologists contributed to debates about the nature of civilization and the notion of culture. In 1922, anthropologists Robert Lowie and Elsie Clews Parsons, along with other prominent intellectuals such as H. L. Mencken, Lewis Mumford, and Van Wyck Brooks, contributed to a volume titled *Civilization in the United States: An Inquiry by Thirty Americans*, whose purpose was to "work towards the advance of intellectual life in America."[8]

Of all these individuals, Kroeber's name is probably the most recognizable today. Having founded the Department of Anthropology at Berkeley in 1901, he achieved a degree of notoriety during his lifetime and after for his relationship with Ishi, the last member of a northern California tribe.[9] Because of the interest subsequent generations of Americans, especially in California, have had in Ishi's unfortunate demise after Kroeber befriended him, Kroeber's public image today is an ambivalent one, symbolizing to some the disappearance of Native American cultures in general.[10]

Although Mead was married to three anthropologists, none of them ever achieved the same degree of public renown as Mead. Luther Cressman received a limited amount of recognition for his work on the archaeology of the American West.[11] And although Fortune wrote several books based on his ethnographic research in New Guinea, with and without Mead, since he did not pitch his work toward a popular audience he never achieved popular acclaim.[12]

Gregory Bateson did become something of a celebrity in his own right, but only after he had divorced Mead and moved to California. Although his first book, *Naven*, an ethnography of the Iatmul people of the Middle Sepik region of New Guinea, has achieved the status of a classic in anthropology, Bateson's fame was the result of his being "discovered" in the late 1960s and 70s by Jerry Brown, governor of California, and Steward Brand, counterculture publisher of the *Whole Earth Catalogue*.[13] Brown and Brand valued Bateson's unconventional but insightful thinking about the paradoxes of human behavior as well as his intellectual forays into the newly emerging field of cybernetics. They saw in Bateson a bold and provocative mind and a mentor well suited for the rebellious thinkers of the counterculture. Governor Brown appointed Bateson, who at the time was affiliated with the University of California at Santa Cruz, as a regent of the University of California. A product of a very specific moment in American culture, Bateson's fame never garnered the same broad public appeal as Mead's and was mostly limited to college campuses across America and the West Coast.[14]

What about other famous *female* anthropologists? Margaret Mead was neither the first nor the only female anthropologist to gain public recognition in the United States. Both here and abroad, anthropology has had a lengthy history of colorful and strong female practitioners. Long before Mead sailed for Samoa, when anthropology was still in its infancy in nineteenth-century America and was associated primarily with the study of Native Americans, there were women engaged in ethnographic research whose work caught the attention of the media. One of them, Alice Fletcher, was an independent scholar who wrote popular articles about life among the Omaha Indians for *Century Magazine*, as well as scientific papers. By 1890, Fletcher was a famous woman, honored for both her philanthropic and scientific work.[15] When an endowed chair was established for her at Harvard University in 1891, eight hundred people came to shake her hand at a reception given in her honor in Washington, DC.[16]

In contrast to Fletcher, there was Matilda Stevenson, who, along with her husband Colonel James Stevenson and the flamboyant Frank Hamilton Cushing, worked among the Zuni in 1891. She and her husband titillated Washington society in 1885 when they brought a Zuni "princess" named We'wha back east to live with them for six months; We'wha later was discovered to be a man.[17] A year later, Stevenson made the pages of the *Illustrated Police News* with the headline, "Cowed by a Woman. A Craven Red Devil Weakens in the Face of a Resolute Heroine. Exciting Adventure in an Indian Village in Arizona." Ignoring warnings that they were forbidden to enter the sacred inner sanctum of a Hopi kiva, the Stevensons had found themselves held captive by angry Hopi men, particularly incensed that a woman had entered their kiva. The article included an artist's sketch of a fearless Matilda Stevenson brandishing her umbrella at a disgruntled Indian while its headline utilized the familiar tropes of adventure, danger, and conflict with primitive heathens that the public associated with anthropologists and, as its pièce de résistance, the resolute heroine.[18]

Closer in age to Mead, but still a generation older, was Elsie Clews Parsons; Mead knew Parsons because of her association with the Department of Anthropology at Columbia University. Parsons had begun her career as a sociologist and feminist, teaching sociology at Barnard College, but later transformed herself into an ethnographer and folklorist via her friendship with Franz Boas and his students and her enthusiasm for fieldwork among Pueblo Indians in the Southwest.[19] From a wealthy family, Parsons had established her reputation among the New York City intelligentsia and Greenwich Village bohemians as a writer, social critic, and progressive, even radical, thinker whose work captured the attention and admiration of fellow social critics H. L. Mencken and Walter Lippmann.[20] As a member of Heterodoxy, a group of feminist women who gathered regularly in Greenwich Village to discuss political and social issues of concern to women, Parsons participated in the bohemian culture of New York City that thrived during the early years of the twentieth century and was an important precursor and exemplar for Mead of the female social scientist as public intellectual.[21]

As a result of World War I, feminism, and Boas's respect for women—as well as Parsons's support for their fieldwork—during the 1920s and 30s many of Mead's fellow graduate students at Columbia were women.[22] In addition to Mead's mentor, Ruth Benedict, they included Ruth Bunzel, Ruth Landes, Gladys Reichard, Esther Goldfrank, Gene Weltfish, and Zora Neale Hurston. Like Benedict and Parsons, Bunzel, Reichard, Goldfrank, and Weltfish all did fieldwork in the Southwest.[23] After her initial fieldwork among the Ojibwa, Landes conducted fieldwork in Brazil, and Hurston, in addition to the work she initially carried out in the rural south, also did fieldwork in Haiti and Jamaica.[24] Of all these women, Zora Neale Hurston has become the best known, but less as an anthropologist than as a writer. During her lifetime, Hurston was relatively unknown to the American public; she was only discovered well after her death when writer Alice Walker rescued her work and her reputation from obscurity.[25]

Unlike Hurston, whose work remained unknown by much of the public during her lifetime, Ruth Benedict's work did receive public acclaim while she was still alive. And even though she had a hearing impediment that made public appearances difficult for her, Benedict eventually became a public figure as well. Although Mead's fame from the publication of *Coming of Age in Samoa* preceded Benedict's, when Benedict published *Patterns of Culture* in 1934 it too became a best seller. *Patterns of Culture* not only established Benedict's reputation for writing accessible prose, it also contributed to a paradigm shift in American thought that had been initiated by Boas and his students: the idea that culture played a greater role in shaping human behavior than did biology. *Patterns of Culture* remains the best-selling anthropological book ever, with more than two million copies having been published in more than two dozen languages.[26]

With the publication twelve years later of *The Chrysanthemum and the Sword*, her study of Japanese culture written during World War II, Benedict again came to the public's attention. Her book played a role in President Harry S. Truman's treatment of the Japanese emperor.[27] Another area in which Benedict made important contributions as a popular writer was the subject of race. At the time of her death at sixty-one she had a national reputation as a public intellectual, social scientist, and scholar.[28]

If Mead was not the only female anthropologist doing fieldwork in exotic cultures during the 1920s and 30s, why did *she* become more famous than these other women? In contrast to Parsons and Benedict, who by the time they set off to do fieldwork were mature women, Mead's youthfulness and flapperesque physique captured the media's attention. And by the time they and Mead's cohort of female graduate students did their research among the Pueblo Indians, the advent of the transcontinental railroad had long made trips to the Southwest relatively accessible to the general public, thus reducing the "exoticness" factor of these research locations. In contrast, Samoa and New Guinea were still remote and highly exotic locales for much of the general public.

Additionally, despite the impact of the Harlem Renaissance and the newfound interest of the urban white bourgeoisie in jazz and other facets of Negro culture, the fact that Zora Neale Hurston was African American worked against her achieving greater acclaim during her lifetime. In 1920s America, race was still an issue that kept an individual out of the mainstream press, and because Hurston's work portrayed rural backwoods Negroes and their culture, even her fellow African American writers denigrated her work, feeling that it perpetuated the very stereotypes of black Americans they were trying to undermine through their own work.

There was also Hortense Powdermaker, an American trained by Malinowski at the London School of Economics, who returned to teach in the United States after having done fieldwork in New Guinea. Powdermaker provides another interesting comparison with Mead. Close in age to Mead, she too had gone to an exotic location for her initial fieldwork, living on the small island of Lesu in the Territory of New Guinea. However, Powdermaker's first book, *Life in Lesu*, was a traditional structural-functionalist ethnography and did not gain a wide public audience. Although Powdermaker's subsequent work, especially *Hollywood, the Dream Factory*, an ethnography of Hollywood she published in the 1950s, received more popular acclaim, by then Mead was already firmly established as the most famous woman anthropologist in the country.[29]

Examining the careers of these other female anthropologists, we see that while Mead was not unique in what she did, she displayed a unique and timely combination of traits: youthfulness, fieldwork in exotic locations, tantalizing topics of research, a felicitous writing style, and an ease in talking to journalists and the public. These five elements combined to make her a more alluring figure to the media and the American public than other female (or male) anthropologists.

Popular Images of the Anthropologist

While anthropologists were working hard to establish themselves as sober scientific researchers, how did the wider public come to view them? Perhaps the most frequent image of the anthropologist that circulated in the popular media during the twentieth century is the anthropologist as explorer. Hence the ubiquitous figure of the anthropologist—whether male or female—dressed in khaki wearing a pith helmet, looking much like a colonial district officer at the height of European empire. In this role the image of the anthropologist is often interchangeable with that of the missionary, explorer, or colonial officer, an elision seen frequently in cartoons.[30] When I requested images of anthropologists from the *New Yorker* magazine's cartoon bank, the selection of thirty-five cartoons they sent me from the period 1933 to 1996 included more cartoons about missionaries and explorers than those explicitly about anthropologists. In addition to cartoons that focused specifically on these three colonial stereotypes, the selection also included several that focused solely on exotic "natives"—black, naked, or scantily dressed individuals living in the jungle. These cartoons often depicted the natives in association with some sort of tribal "witch doctor." The inclusion of cartoons depicting natives, missionaries, and explorers in a selection that was to focus on anthropologists gives us some insight into cartoonists', and the cartoon bank researcher's, interpretation of anthropologists: they were associated with "primitive" people and their pagan religious practices, colonial exploration, and missionization.[31]

Most of the cartoons featured men—whether explorer, missionary, or "witch doctor"—as indeed in real life these individuals tended to be male. However, as the two *New Yorker* cartoons illustrate, in American cartoonists' imaginations the specific image of an *anthropologist* is often female. This fact, I think, attests to the prominent role Margaret Mead had assumed by the late 1930s in American popular culture, a

"I'm already seeing an anthropologist."

Figure 6.1 Even as late as the 1990s Mead remained a stereotype of the female anthropologist, as seen in this 1992 *New Yorker* cartoon. (© The New Yorker Collection 1992 Victoria Roberts from cartoonbank.com. All Rights Reserved)

role that indicated the (middle class, educated) public's consciousness of her as "an anthropologist," even if they did not always know exactly what an anthropologist was.[32] While the allusion to Mead is oblique in the first cartoon (only the spectacles and short dark hair signal the figure as evocative of Mead), certainly the emphasis on sexuality fits squarely into the stereotype of a female anthropologist such as Mead being a "sexual adventuress." It also plays upon other stereotypes prevalent in our society: that female scientists are unattractive (the female version of the scientist as nerd), that female anthropologists might therefore be interested in studying "the natives" so that she could get a date, as that is something that she might otherwise have had difficulty doing in her own society.[33]

"Young men, you've now reached the age when it is essential that you know the rites and rituals, the customs and taboos of our island, Rather than go into them in detail, however, I'm simply going to present each of you with a copy of this excellent book by Margaret Mead."

Figure 6.2 This cartoon about male initiation in New Guinea was an allusion to Mead's best-selling book *Sex and Temperament in Three Primitive Societies*, 1956. (© The New Yorker Collection 1956 Alain from cartoonbank.com. All Rights Reserved)

The second cartoon explicitly refers to Mead. Inside what is probably meant to be a New Guinea men's spirit house (*haus tambaran*), such as Mead wrote about in *Sex and Temperament* and *Male and Female*, a tribal elder stands next to a stack of books and addresses the group of youths assembled in front of him. The cultural knowledge necessary to appreciate the humor in this cartoon includes recognition of Mead and her occupation as an anthropologist as well as knowledge of what she has written about (male initiation rituals among tribal societies in New Guinea in her books *Sex and Temperament in Three Primitive Societies* and *Male and Female*). Unlike the first cartoon that satirized female anthropologists, this joke is subtler. It presumes that American readers will enjoy the incongruous idea that tribal elders might prefer to bypass performing their own rituals and simply teach their youth their customs by providing them with a book about them written by an anthropologist.

Finally, recall the cartoon from *Esquire* magazine seen in chapter 3 that showed a young white woman at a tea party seated holding a teacup in her hand, while completely naked. Seated across from her dressed in formal afternoon attire was an elderly grand dame, also holding a teacup. In response to the look of surprise on the older woman's face the naked woman offered the explanation, "But I came of age in Samoa." The cartoon works on the assumption that many of *Esquire*'s middle-class American readers may have read *Coming of Age in Samoa* in college, or were at least familiar with its title and subject matter.

The Anthropologist as Hero(ine)

Cartoons like these have given rise to stereotypes of anthropologists in popular culture, but the popular media has not been the only source to celebrate the figure of the anthropologist as adventurer and hero. The literary critic Susan Sontag wrote an essay about the French anthropologist Claude Lévi-Strauss titled "The Anthropologist as Hero." The piece was about Lévi-Strauss's compelling memoir *Tristes tropiques*, in which he reflects upon his experience during the 1930s conducting research among tribes in the interior of Brazil.[34] Sontag's reflection on the profoundly existential as well as intensely physical nature of Lévi-Strauss's ethnographic endeavor now reads as an elegy to the traditional enterprise of anthropological fieldwork as it was once practiced. While Mead had noted the suitability of anthropology as a career for women, Sontag observed that anthropology was "one of the rare intellectual vocations that do not demand a sacrifice of one's manhood," since "the attributes of courage, love of adventure, and physical hardiness—as well as brains—are all called upon."[35]

Here lies the common ground between the popular press's interest in an anthropological expedition as high adventure and the literal meaning of Sontag's anthropologist as hero. Fieldwork in exotic places, especially in the late nineteenth and first half of the twentieth centuries, entailed the same kinds of physical hardships, grueling forms of travel, risks of disease and injury that adventurers and explorers encountered. In the general reader's mind the distinction between traveler/explorer and anthropologist was often blurred. And, as we have seen in the media's coverage of Mead, in pandering to their readers' interests the media often accentuated the image of anthropological fieldwork as adventure.

However, beyond the physical heroics, Sontag identifies a heroic philosophical and psychological transformation that the anthropologist experiences in doing fieldwork. Thus, "the field," she says, "where every ethnological career begins, is the mother and nursemaid of doubt, the philosophical attitude par excellence." As Sontag observes, "To be an anthropologist is thus to adopt a very ingenious stance vis-à-vis one's own doubts, one's own intellectual uncertainties." Doubt, skepticism, and the willingness to have one's certainties about how the world operates turned upside down, these are the necessary attitudes an anthropologist takes into the field. This second meaning most interests and impresses Sontag.[36]

Anthropology as practiced by someone like Lévi-Strauss, she says, is "a total occupation, one involving a spiritual commitment like that of the creative artist or the adventurer or the psychoanalyst."[37] Moreover, it is one of a number of modern activities that seek knowledge of the Self through an understanding of its Other. In the case of Europe and the United States, the Other is looked for in the exotic—in Asia, in the Middle East, and among preliterate peoples in the Americas and beyond. Sontag identifies anthropology as a quintessentially modernist endeavor because of its practitioners' search for alternatives to the alienation they experience in the modern world. The anthropologist is thus "a man [*sic*] in control of, and even consciously exploiting, his own intellectual alienation." As such, the anthropologist in the field becomes "the very model of the twentieth century consciousness: a 'critic at home' but a 'conformist elsewhere.' " That is, while not hesitating to criticize the way things are "at home," by contrast, in order to learn the rules of how things are done elsewhere, the anthropologist has to learn to be a conformist in another culture.[38]

For Sontag then, the heroic action of the anthropologist is his (or her) willingness to totally submit himself to the experience of living in a completely strange and exotic world in order to comprehend more fully through the *dépaysement*, or removal, from the familiar and secure world of home what is valuable and mutable in that world. To do so according to Sontag is a noble, indeed heroic, endeavor.

Relating Sontag's lofty words about Lévi-Strauss and the anthropological endeavor to Margaret Mead, we have seen that in addition to the public's enjoyment in reading about Mead's adventures in Samoa as a "Samoan princess" or among the "cannibals of the South Seas," a similar reason for people's interest in her and her work has been the insights she revealed about ourselves and our own culture through her exploration of the "primitive" Other.

While *Tristes tropiques* appealed to Sontag (she called it "one of the great books of our century") and other intellectuals, Mead's books appealed to a broader readership—but for many of the same reasons: her reflections upon what we have to learn from less sophisticated cultures, her critique of Western civilization, and her identification of what we have lost at the expense of modernity's technological sophistication. However, in contrast to Lévi-Strauss, who wrote from a philosophical stance of pessimism, Mead was ever the optimist. (This is also a contrast that explains many intellectuals' attraction to Lévi-Strauss and their aversion to Mead.) Her unflagging optimism also helped endear her to her American audience.

Anthropology, Modernism, and the "Savage Slot"

By the end of the nineteenth century, anthropology came to fill a thematic and symbolic "savage slot" that had already been constituted by literature and the travel accounts of explorers and adventurers of previous centuries.[39] As historian James Clifford reminds us, early twentieth-century anthropologists sought to separate the science of anthropology from these other discourses through their emphasis on the professional practice of fieldwork. The intense process of extended fieldwork, modeled after the field research of the natural scientist, was meant to systematize and introduce scientific rigor into ethnographic practice, distancing it from the accounts of adventurers.[40] Thus, anthropology today recognizes Bronislaw Malinowski, who spent two years in the Trobriand Islands between 1915 and 1918, as a model of the anthropologist as field researcher. Although

Mead stayed in the field for much shorter periods of time than Malinowski, she is also recognized for her contributions to anthropological fieldwork because of the detailed observations she recorded.[41]

In *Gone Primitive*, literary scholar Marianna Torgovnick's study of the meaning of "the primitive" in twentieth-century Western culture, Torgovnick has chosen the ethnographer to symbolize the West's relationship to non-Western indigenous peoples. Because ethnographers' lives are so closely tied to indigenous societies (albeit only "for a narrow shaft of time"), Torgovnick suggests that they serve as a metaphor for modernism's involvement and fascination with "the primitive." Like Sontag, Torgovnick also sees the West's fascination with "the primitive" as largely a male project. One of the aims of male primitivism, Torgovnick says, was to critique and escape the confines of masculinity as the modern masculine role was defined in Western society.[42]

But, she argues, modernist authors' and artists' fascination with "the primitive" was produced at the expense of the lives of indigenous people, and she criticizes this appropriation of the primitive Other for Western intellectuals' personal ends. Thinking that modernist women perhaps were different in their treatment of the primitive Other, she compares Malinowski's and Mead's ethnographies in order to see if gender affected an ethnographer's engagement with his/her non-Western subjects. For Torgovnick, Malinowski exhibits two common but paradoxical Western responses to "the primitive": the primitive as erotically desirable and the primitive as physically repugnant. In contrast, as we saw earlier, Torgovnick found Mead much more willing to engage physically with her indigenous subjects.

But ultimately, "Mead used the primitive for purposes of her own—research, fund-raising, fame, the advocacy of specific goals in the West. Her career testifies to and advances inexplicable, irrational connections often made covertly between gender, race, and versions of the primitive."[43] For Torgovnick, Mead exemplifies the stereotype of "the Evil Imperialist Anthropologist" that anthropologist Micaela di Leonardo has identified as one of five contemporary images of anthropologists.[44] It is also the stereotype of the anthropologist most frequently found in circulation among scholars and academics who see the discipline's interest in other cultures as motivated more by self-advancement than by any intrinsic interest in or concern for these other cultures.[45]

Torgovnick offers a postmodernist critique of modernist ethnographers such as Mead that highlights anthropology's role in shaping and perpetuating the Western fascination with the primitive Other.[46] However, as Sontag's essay and the *New Yorker* and *Esquire* cartoons demonstrate, intellectuals and the popular media have also played a powerful role in shaping and promoting the image of the anthropologist as purveyor of the exotic, the erotic, and the heroic. Nonetheless, as James Clifford's comments about the anthropologist's image reminds us, juxtaposed alongside this popular image of the anthropologist is another, that of an expert whose authority is scientifically validated. In the next chapter we will explore some of the origins and expressions of that image by looking at the image of Mead as scientist.

CHAPTER 7

Mead as Scientist

If I went to a scientific convention, and I spotted Margaret Mead, I'd go up and start interviewing her. Margaret Mead is positive feedback, a household name; she's good copy; she's a sure thing.
—Science writer cited by Rae Goodell, *The Visible Scientists* (1975)[1]

The media and popular culture in America not only embraced Mead as an icon of the modern woman and of anthropology, they also promoted her as a scientist, in particular as a woman scientist. In 1949, the Associated Press named Mead "Outstanding Woman of the Year in Science," while in 1955 author Edna Yost included her in *American Women of Science*—the only social scientist among the twelve female scientists Yost profiled in her book.[2] More recently, at Walt Disney's Epcot Center in Orlando, Florida, Mead was the only woman included in a pantheon of six scientists whose images once adorned the walls of the center.

This chapter explores the media's image of Mead as a scientist and also scrutinizes some of the ways that Mead perceived of herself as a scientist and promoted anthropology as a scientific endeavor. Whether anthropology in general—traditionally categorized as a social science, in contrast to the natural and physical sciences—and the type of interpretative cultural anthropology that Mead practiced in particular should be considered a science has been debated. That issue, however, does not concern us here; what is relevant is the fact that the media and the general public very often did, and thus labeled Mead a scientist. During the 1950s, television expanded throughout middle-class America as it became the nation's most pervasive form of mass media. Thus, we will look at the role television came to play in cementing the public's identification of Mead as a scientist and public figure. And because Mead promoted the use of visual technology—especially photography and film—as scientific research tools, we will also consider Mead's influence on the use of visual media in ethnographic research.

Three post–World War II media events are of particular interest: Mead's response to the publication of Alfred Kinsey's study of the *Sexual Behavior in the Human Male* in 1948; her appearance in the 1950s on the CBS television series *Adventure*; and her participation in *Margaret Mead's New Guinea Journal* (1968), a public television project that filmed her return to Manus Island. Each event presents a slightly different image of Mead as a scientist. The print media's portrayal of Mead's response to Kinsey's book created an image of Mead as scientist that she was later to perfect in her television appearances, that of an expert criticizing another scientist, as well as chastising the American public for its unquestioning acceptance of facts. Mead's appearances on the CBS *Adventure* series portray her as translator of scientific knowledge to the public, and thus as a willing (although somewhat stiff-figured) participant in a new undertaking to use television to bring science to the masses. In *Margaret Mead's New Guinea Journal* viewers had the opportunity for the very first time to see an anthropologist at work in the field. Although this format would become commonplace on American television during the 1970s and 80s, when it first appeared in 1968 this made-for-television documentary was groundbreaking and established a new genre of ethnographic documentary. Finally, we consider Mead's legacy as a *female* scientist, the identity most frequently perpetuated in popular books about her written for children and young adults. In addition to lauding her for her achievements as a woman in a sphere dominated by men, these books frequently symbolize Mead's work as furthering our understanding of cultural diversity and human universals.

Mead regarded the dropping of atomic bombs in 1945 as a watershed in human history. For her and many others the development of the bomb underscored the fact that scientific knowledge and technology was not inherently benign, and therefore scientists bore a heavy responsibility to ensure its positive use.[3] To this end, throughout the cold war period she participated in organizations such as the United Nations and its UNESCO project on culture and technological change, SIPI (Scientists' Institute for

Public Information), and the American Rocket Scientists' committee on Space Law and Sociology. Her role in these organizations was as a social scientist concerned with the social use and dissemination of technological innovation and scientific knowledge.[4]

Mead on "The Kinsey Report": The Scientific Study of Sexual Behavior

One might think that Mead would have wholeheartedly endorsed Alfred Kinsey's 1948 book, *Sexual Behavior in the Human Male*,[5] as his findings would appear to have substantiated the flexible nature of sexual identity and the variability in human sexual practices that Mead had experienced personally and had scientifically propounded. This was not the case, however. Along with her colleagues Ruth Benedict and Geoffrey Gorer, Mead was one of a group of prominent social scientists, psychologists, psychoanalysts, and intellectuals who castigated Kinsey's research. While Kinsey had anticipated resistance to his findings among religious conservatives, he was particularly surprised and distraught at the criticisms of Mead and her fellow anthropologists.[6]

As viewers of the film *Kinsey* have been reminded, when *Sexual Behavior in the Human Male* was first published, it was a phenomenal bestseller.[7] The meteoric success of the book became a headline story across the United States. It was an astonishing accomplishment for a nonfiction book that was 801 pages long, written in a turgid technical language, and filled with numerous statistical charts and graphs. Kinsey became a celebrity overnight and was dubbed a "second Darwin" by the media. The startling revelations the Kinsey report (as it was soon referred to) made about the wide variety and frequency of sexual practices that a large number of American men admitted to engaging in—extramarital sex, sex with prostitutes, masturbation, and homosexuality—shocked, titillated, and captivated the American public.[8] An entomologist by training who had originally specialized in studying the life cycle of the gall wasp, Kinsey's goal in the publication of his research findings was to alert the American public to the fact that human sexual practices were far more varied than the narrowly prescribed set of standards that society put forth. He hoped the sheer weight of evidence provided by the quantity of data he produced would cause people to adjust their ideas as to what was and was not normal sexual behavior, thus expanding their understanding of what was natural human sexual practice.

Kinsey was well disposed toward anthropologists. At the suggestion of Harvard anthropologist Clyde Kluckhohn, Kinsey had hired one of Kluckhohn's graduate students, Paul Gebhard, as a research assistant. Kinsey's rationale for hiring Gebhard was that anthropologists should make good researchers in the field of human sexuality because they were trained to respect practices and beliefs different from their own. As good cultural relativists they would be neither judgmental nor fainthearted when confronted with evidence of a wide variety of sexual behavior.[9]

Mead met Kinsey in New York City early in March 1946, almost two years before he had published *Sexual Behavior in the Human Male*.[10] Mead undoubtedly would have been interested in Kinsey's research on human sexuality as it was an area in which she claimed expertise. Her own book on men, women, and sexuality, *Male and Female*, would be published the following year. And she was likely to have heard about Kinsey's research because the prestigious Rockefeller Foundation, where her close friend and colleague Lawrence Frank worked, funded it. She may even have been skeptical of his research techniques—wondering exactly how a zoologist went about studying human sexuality.

Correspondence between Mead and Kinsey indicates that Mead may have offered or agreed to a request to be interviewed by Kinsey, perhaps in order to observe the methods and questions he and his researchers were employing in their extensive collection of interview data from over 12,000 American men and women.[11] Kinsey, in his search for a diverse and extensive set of interviewees, sought out volunteers who would provide histories of their sexual activities from all walks of life, including his sponsors at the Rockefeller Foundation and the National Research Council as well as inmates of penitentiaries and denizens of skid row.

However, it appears that Mead did not have the opportunity to give Kinsey an interview; he wrote to her in January 1947: "I am sorry that my stay in New York was not long enough to contact all the persons who offered histories. I should very much like to have you go through a history with us someday to see how the material is handled. It will probably be fall or winter before we get back to New York. If you would not object, I shall get in touch with you then and try to make a date for a history."[12] There is no indication in Mead's scheduling records that she ever did so, and Kinsey's research associate, Paul Gebhard, confirmed that she had not.[13]

Two months after the publication of Kinsey's book, Mead was invited to speak in New York City at a conference organized by the American Social Hygiene Association to discuss Kinsey's findings. Mead was one of a group of experts that included a lawyer, a psychoanalyst, a sociologist, and a statistician. The conference, whose speakers were generally critical of the book, received extensive coverage by the New York press. Mead aimed her critique at both Kinsey and the American public. After first chastising Kinsey for the nonrandom nature of his research sample, she stated that ". . . the anthropological comments I can make best on this material are, I think, based on treating the Kinsey report as a cultural phenomenon, just as if I were to go to a South Sea island and attend a cremation ceremony, or a cannibal feast, or a puberty rite."[14] She identified two aspects of Kinsey's book that made it a cultural phenomenon, its scale and the amount of publicity it had received, but not its findings. According to Mead, Kinsey's findings were not new to experts on human sexuality.[15] She focused her comments on the book as a media event because of the enormous amount of publicity the book had garnered before and after its publication and its huge sales.

"Until Kinsey came along," Mead said sardonically, "people did not know whether one should have more sex expression, or less sex longer, or more sex shorter, or more or less frequent sex—this was something one just couldn't find the answer to. It has been making a great many Americans miserable for a very long time because they didn't know whether they were happy or not."[16] How could they keep up with the Joneses if they did not know what the Joneses were doing? This discomfort—bred of the ethnic diversity of Americans—led to the tendency "to build our ethics out of what other people are doing this week."[17] Mead also cited the nation's penchant for the trappings of science:

> Dr. Kinsey's book, by purporting to give norms and ranges laid down for sex behavior of the male, does what the Gesell book does for babies, what Emily Post does for manners and quiz books do for one's education, giving a way of placing oneself and feeling more comfortable . . . . One can find out where oneself or one's spouse really is. This paraphernalia of statistics is something we approve of, something that we are used to, and something that gives us security.[18]

Mead objected most to Kinsey ignoring the emotional dimension of sex, a perspective she called "extraordinarily destructive of interpsychic and interpersonal relationships."[19] Moreover:

> Dr. Kinsey has limited himself to a description of a non-interpersonal and meaningless act. He simply perpetuates the American tradition that we should think about sex as we would about any bodily act.
>
> The major abstraction that an anthropologist from Mars would get from reading the Kinsey report is that sex in this country is an important, meaningless physical act which men have to perform fairly often, but more often if they have not gone to college.[20]

Mead found Kinsey's mechanistic language of "outlets" and "emissions" to be a perpetuation of a typically American prudish attitude toward sex, much like a Puritan tract.[21] "Nowhere," she said, "have I been able to find a single suggestion that sex is any fun, not anywhere in the book, not a suggestion."[22]

In contrast to Kinsey, Mead argued for a different view of human sexuality, one that did not remove it from the messy, often highly charged, world of emotions, interpersonal relationships, and pleasure. With understated wit and a touch of sarcasm, she ended her comments by saying:

> You see, one of the curious things from the Kinsey report is that this emphasis is on the fact that there will be outlets and then you tell somebody that there is going to be an outlet anyway, so it's just a question of which outlet and the book suggests no way of choosing between a woman and a sheep.[23]

The press conveyed the image of a contentious Mead. Moreover, her use of humor, irony, and paradox to puncture what she considered to be a veil of "scientism" surrounding information that she asserted was basically not new made her all the more quotable by the press.

Mead probably made a bigger splash in the media because of her criticism of Kinsey's book than had she simply been another voice that praised it. However, although she was critical of the study, she was no fuddy-duddy about sex. Rather, to the contrary, true to her earlier image as a sexual libertarian, she criticized Kinsey for his failure to convey sex as a pleasurable activity. Like Lionel Trilling, her fellow New York public intellectual who criticized Kinsey along similar lines, Mead represented a modern liberal humanist who bemoaned the lack of attention Kinsey paid to the virtues as well as the interpersonal complexities of human sexual behavior.

Kinsey biographer, James H. Jones, cites correspondence between Mead and British anthropologist Geoffrey Gorer as evidence of Mead's behind-the-scenes manipulation of the media in order to assure that there would be multiple sources of bad press for the book. Jones shows that when Mead declined a request from the *New York Herald Tribune* to write a review of *Sexual Behavior of the Human Male* she suggested Geoffrey Gorer's name instead, knowing that he too would be critical of it.[24] Gorer's review of the book, titled "A Statistical Study of Sex," concluded that it was not valid for Kinsey to claim that his sample was actually representative of the American male population at large, let alone, as the title of the book proclaimed, of "the human male" in general.[25]

Kinsey was upset by Gorer's review. Speculating on the reason for Gorer's opposition to the book, he surmised that "this is due in part to the fact that Margaret Mead objects strenuously to the materialism of masculine sexuality this book deals with."[26] He attributed Gorer's negative review in part to his association with Mead, while Kinsey's biographer Jones attributes Mead's reaction to jealousy at Kinsey's success, and "aggravated spite."[27]

These representations of Mead's response to Kinsey's book present a range of images. The newspaper coverage of her portrays a feisty Mead who is not afraid to question—or even to mock—scientific expertise or to generate controversy. They also convey the image of a liberal humanist—someone whose attitudes are not puritanical toward sex, but, rather, emphasize the emotional dimension of sexual behavior. In contrast, Jones presents the image of a jealous and spiteful academic, as well as a conniving woman. Kinsey imagines a feminine (feminist?) Mead incensed at the "materialism" of male sexuality. Together these images create a complex picture of how science, expertise, sexism, and fame interact, and also of Mead as scientist, woman, and public intellectual.

The Televisual Mead

In 1949, Mead wrote: "I worry about our children growing up in a world where radio and television and comics and the threat of the atomic bomb are every day realities."[28] Despite her concerns (and she was not alone in her concern over their ill effects on children[29]), or perhaps because of them, beginning in 1953, Mead appeared on television in a new series about science called *Adventure* that the Columbia Broadcasting System launched as part of its public service programming. Her appearance on the program marked the beginning of a new phase of public exposure for her, as she proved to be a highly telegenic personality, the type of pundit and public intellectual—articulate, often humorous, and a master at repartee—that commercial television eagerly sought. Eventually, Mead also became a favorite with late night talk show host Johnny Carson and appeared on the *Tonight Show* and other talk shows with some regularity. (She was the first, and perhaps the only, anthropologist in the country eligible for membership in the American Federation of Television and Radio Artists union as a result of her frequent appearances on major TV programs.) Mead's appearances on television helped make her name and face recognizable to a larger segment of the American population than her books and speaking engagements ever had.

Television launched Mead into the role of a celebrity and an American icon. But when she first appeared on television in the 1950s the networks were interested in her because she was a scientist and expert and she still had much to learn about performing live on TV.

"Experiments in Television": Mead and the CBS *Adventure* Series

When CBS began to air its *Adventure* series in May 1953, there were no public television or cable stations to provide alternatives to the standard prime time evening television fare of quiz shows, family sitcoms, variety programs, and live drama anthologies such as the *Kraft Television Theater.*

Unlike these programs that had major corporate sponsors, CBS offered the *Adventure* series as part of its public service programming. As Perry Wolff, the producer of the series, explained, it was conceived of as being in the tradition of CBS radio, which provided public service programming that aired during unsold time.[30] With science as its focus, CBS executives also saw the series as demonstrating to the public the network's commitment to serious subjects, not just light entertainment. Moreover, the new medium of television was considered to have great potential as a means to educate a broad spectrum of Americans about science.[31]

During the 1950s, William Paley, the president of CBS, was on the board of directors of The Museum of Modern Art in New York City. In contrast to that museum, which he and others considered to be an elite institution that catered to more refined and sophisticated tastes, Paley thought of the American Museum of Natural History as "the people's museum." What could be better, Paley apparently thought, than a public service television program about science, natural history, and diverse cultures that was generated right from the museum?[32]

So in 1952, Wolff got the go ahead to explore a collaboration with the American Museum of Natural History on the *Adventure* series. The museum agreed to provide CBS with space in its capacious building on Central Park West, thus allowing the CBS crew to produce programs directly from the museum and to use the museum's collections and exhibits as the sets for the programs and its curators as the series' scientific experts. As Wolff has reminisced, it was a moment in the development of commercial television when risks could still be taken and experiments made in programming that financial considerations would rule out later.[33] It was also a golden moment in the history of television programming because the audience, still new to the medium, had few preconceived ideas of what to expect and was excited by the novelty of seeing new things presented visually.

The *Adventure* series, a precursor to travelogue and science programs such as *Wild Kingdom* and *Nova* and today's *Discovery* and *National Geographic* channels, focused on everything from evolution to wildlife and exotic indigenous peoples in remote areas of the world. The series began rather inauspiciously, according to a review in the *New Yorker*, with a somewhat inane and tepid conversation about space travel between the director of the museum's Hayden Planetarium, Joe Chamberlain, and moderator Mike Wallace.[34]

Mead appeared in one of the earliest of the *Adventure* programs on Sunday, May 24, 1953. Charles Collingwood introduced the program, saying, "This is the third in a series of experiments in television—an experiment we call a science nonfiction show." The audience then heard slow, haunting flute music that accompanies the credits, apparently chosen to create a sense of mystery and anticipation about the "experiment" to follow.[35]

Preceded by segments about bighorn sheep and dinosaurs, the final segment of the program featured Mead discussing Balinese culture. It began with moderator Douglas Edwards holding a scary-looking mask up to the camera while saying, "I don't suppose you'd care to meet up with this gentleman on a dark night." Edwards is holding a Balinese mask that represents the supernatural witch Rangda, a character who features prominently in Balinese trance dances and other ritual ceremonies. He then holds up a shadow puppet: "And this is a kind of puppet which is used in a dramatic form. . . . He's used by a people on an island in the Java Sea, one of the famous islands known as Bali." The television screen then darkens, Balinese gamelan music is heard in the background, and gradually the silhouette of the shadow puppet fills the television screen. Compared to the previous two segments of the program, this scene is exciting and dramatic, creating an aura of mystery and anticipation.

As Mead explains to Edwards: "The shadow play in Bali, why you might almost call it a primitive television, where plays are given for the people by throwing the shadows of puppets like these on the screen. And then also it is important because of the theme. This is a witch, coming from the witch play which is one of the most important stories you see in Bali."

Setting the stage for what is going to happen next, Edwards asks if it would be possible to watch a shadow puppet performance, to which Mead replies, "If we were in Bali . . ."

Then Edwards demonstrates the "magic" of television. He says, "Perhaps through television we can do it. We do it this way. We wipe out the puppet"—Edwards moves his right arm across the image of the shadow puppet. The lights dim and the image of the puppet disappears. The audience is left seeing only the silhouettes of Mead and Edwards on the screen and Edwards speaks again—"And then we bring in Bali . . ."

When the lights come up we see the two of them standing in front of a decidedly fake-looking model of the entrance to a Balinese temple. It is meant to appear as if in an instant we have been magically transported to Bali. As they turn toward the temple yard the lights dim and images from Mead and Bateson's film *Trance and Dance in Bali* appear on the screen.[36] Again, it is meant to appear as if the audience, along with Mead and Edwards, has happened upon a Balinese dance performance. The film depicts Balinese dancers going into trance and turning their daggers upon themselves without being harmed. It is dramatic footage, and the writhing figures on the screen are accompanied by loud, clanging gamelan music. During the screening Mead keeps up a running commentary, pointing out specific characters, explaining the meaning of different symbols or actions, and answering questions Edwards periodically poses. Perhaps echoing a question in the audience's mind, Edwards twice asks if the dancers are really in trance or just pretending.[37]

"Why would a scientist be interested in watching a play?" Edwards asks Mead.

"I know it sounds a little odd," Mead replies, "but one of the things we are interested in is the relationship between the way people live in society and how they stay as sane and happy and healthy as they are."

What Mead did not mention was that her research had been funded by the Committee on Dementia Praecox (a term formerly used to refer to schizophrenia). It had entailed studying the role trance behavior—physiologically similar in some ways to schizophrenia as it produced a temporary altered state of consciousness in individuals—might play in the emotional health of the Balinese.[38] Caught up in the drama and movement of the dance, the participants go into trance. Thus, Mead explains, the worst fears and dreams of the Balinese are acted out. "Fears," she says, "become shared rituals." "Ah," Edwards suggests, "A sort of shock treatment . . . a syncopated psychiatry."

In his review of the series for the *New Yorker*, Philip Hamburger commented that the film "was stunning beyond measure." The segments from *Trance and Dance in Bali* were riveting; television viewers watched slow-motion footage that showed the lithe female dancers in trance, their long, loosened hair flowing and intertwining with wisps of incense, and the tense drama of the male trance dancers as they turn their sharp twisted daggers toward their own chests. Hamburger's concluding comment praises Mead's "fascinating contribution to the program and her explanation of the important role that the dances played in the mental health of the Balinese."[39]

Mead appeared in two other *Adventure* programs, one about her return to the Admiralty Islands in the early 1950s, and another about the Iatmul people of New Guinea.[40] In the Admiralty Islands segment Mead discussed the sociological, economic, cultural, and political changes that had taken place on Manus Island in the twenty-five years between her first and second visits to the Admiralty Islands. Photographs and artifacts from Mead's first trip were contrasted with film footage of the Manus people taken in 1953 and a newsreel of American troops landing on the island during World War II.[41]

Having been on radio extensively and having spoken before public audiences for several decades, one might have thought that Mead would have little to learn about performing on television, but as her early appearances on *Adventure* show, Mead had yet to acquire the self-confident ease and affability she displayed in her later on-camera television persona. In these early programs we still see a stiff and rather formal Mead. Dressed primly in fussy-looking 1950s frocks, belted at the waist and full-skirted, she looked more like a member of the PTA than a scientist. Careful to articulate clearly and slowly, Mead answered the moderator's questions with schoolmarm precision and with a slightly sing-song, unmodulated voice. These early programs represent Mead's television debut, and they provided her with the opportunity to hone her on-camera skills. She eventually learned to direct her attention to the moderator rather than the monitor, becoming proficient in the two-minute interview and in producing memorable sound bites.

The image Mead projected was nonthreatening—she appears to be an ordinary looking middle-aged woman—but also a bit remote. She was somewhat stern in her demeanor, like a solicitous librarian. Science, Mead implied—even when it entailed adventures like traveling to New Guinea or exotic spectacles like the Balinese trance dancers—was serious business. Nonetheless, Mead still did not look like the average person's image of a scientist. She could be that matronly looking woman down the street. Thus, in addition to challenging the public's stereotype of the anthropologist as a man dressed in khakis and a pith helmet, Mead's appearance on the *Adventure* programs also broadened the public's image of a scientist and increased her own visibility.

Mead and Visual Media: Bali and the Scientific Documentation of Culture

What allowed the director of the *Adventure* program to stage the illusion of transporting television viewers into the world of Balinese trance and dance was the fact that sixteen years earlier Mead and Gregory Bateson had shot thousands of feet of movie film while doing research in Bali.[42]

Their decision to do so had been motivated by their desire to be as scientifically precise as possible about the data they collected. Movie film and photographs, they argued in their research proposals, would allow others to view the same material they had observed, to make their own independent interpretations of the data, and provide data for the comparative study of human infants. It would also allow them to show the footage to the Balinese themselves in order to elicit their comments and reactions to it.[43] Their emphasis on visual data marks a turning point in Mead and Bateson's thinking about ethnographic research methods and in anthropology in general. With their Balinese research they sought to demonstrate the value of visual data in the scientific study of culture.

When Mead and Bateson arrived in Bali in 1936, they quickly became associated with a group of European and American artists and scholars, some of whom had been living as expatriates in Bali since the 1920s. Charlie Chaplin and the playwright Noël Coward arrived on Bali the same time they did. Like these other individuals, Mead and Bateson soon became infatuated by the artistic elements of Balinese culture—in particular, dance, music, and sculpture—and, of course, ritual and trance.[44]

Bateson calculated that he took some 25,000 photographs in Bali and shot some 20,000 feet of movie film. He and Mead developed an innovative two-person research methodology for recording behavior that combined Bateson taking photographs or shooting film while Mead was simultaneously writing notes.[45] While other anthropologists had taken photographs and shot film to illustrate their research, Mead and Bateson's Balinese research was the first to utilize visual data as a central research tool. Subsequently, especially with the advent of more portable camera equipment, visual records have become an increasingly common and important aspect of data collection. At the time, however, Mead and Bateson's extensive visual record of Balinese culture was groundbreaking.[46]

Mead published two scholarly studies of Balinese culture and personality based on the analysis of Bateson's Balinese photographs. The first of these, *Balinese Character: A Photographic Analysis* (1942), she wrote with Bateson. The second, *Growth and Culture: A Photographic Study of Balinese Childhood* (1951) was coauthored with Frances Cooke Macgregor.[47] The books differed in their approaches to the analysis of photographic material. While *Balinese Character* has been criticized for its lack of a theoretical premise upon which photographs were selected as evidence, in *Growth and Culture* Mead and her coauthor Frances Macgregor, a photographer who had been trained in the Gesell-Ilg method of photographic analysis, utilized the theoretical framework of child psychologist Arnold Gesell and the categories of child development he had determined in his research as the basis for their analysis of Balinese childhood and character formation.[48] However, Mead never published a full-scale ethnographic monograph about the Balinese for either a popular or a scholarly audience. This may have been in part because she and Bateson had plans to return to Bali for an extensive interdisciplinary research project that were cut short by the advent of World War II, as well as the fact that after the war she and Bateson were divorced.[49] After the war she did create a series of films about child development using the Balinese footage, as well as *Trance and Dance in Bali*.[50]

Had Mead and Bateson not commissioned the dance performances that were used to compose *Trance and Dance in Bali* (they had requested that the rituals be performed during daylight rather than at night, when they usually occurred, in order for the dances to be filmed), viewers of the *Adventure* series that featured Mead's work in Bali would not have seen this fascinating footage, nor would subsequent generations of anthropology and film students who continue to be intrigued by the aesthetics of the film, while wondering if the Balinese were really in trance and not simply "faking it."[51] While *Trance and Dance in Bali* has become a classic ethnographic film, Mead and Bateson's extensive visual documentation of the Balinese produced little information to further our understanding of the etiology of schizophrenia and multiple personality disorder—the stated purpose of their Balinese research.[52] Mead and Bateson's research on Balinese children, along with the comparative work they did on a short return visit to the Iatmul of New Guinea in 1938,[53] was influential in initiating the cross-cultural study of childhood, child development, and socialization that subsequently developed in anthropology and psychology.[54]

Mead and Bateson's visual materials—the photographs and film footage they shot and the collection of paintings and sculptures they commissioned during their stay in Bali—have also provided rich fodder for subsequent anthropologists. Due to their extensive visual documentation we have a detailed record of certain aspects of village life—in particular the interactions between parents and infants and ritual activities—in and around the highland Balinese village of Bayung Gedé between 1936 and 1939.[55] Moreover, their visual research in Bali transformed Mead into an

Figure 7.1 "Goodbye and Good Luck to Margaret Mead and Gregory Bateson," 1938. Painting by Balinese artist I Ketut Ngendon commissioned as a farewell gift by their Balinese research assistant. The painting shows Mead and Bateson seated in a canoe. Mead waves goodbye to the Balinese while Bateson waves hello to the New Guinea villagers on the opposite shore. (Courtesy of Lois Bateson and Mary Catherine Bateson and the Institute for Intercultural Studies)

advocate for visual data, which she promoted the remainder of her career; she is regarded as an early champion of the use of film in the scientific study of culture.[56]

Mead on Bali: Popular Press versus Academic Publications

As with her previous research, Mead segregated her comments about the Balinese into two different modes of communication: the popular press and scholarly publications. For the popular press Mead embedded the Balinese in contemporary world politics, talking about their geopolitical significance to the war that had recently erupted between Japan and the United States.

"Bali," Mead said, "is significant today on two scores, first because it is the little piece of land that the Japanese need and second because these people give a promise of the possibility of constructing a society in which we can live [harmoniously]. . . . The people of Bali are wonderfully balanced. If the plan of society were as well founded everywhere as it is in Bali, this would be a far better world."[57] In these comments we see two familiar sides of Mead—the pragmatist, represented by her first statement, and the idealist, seen when she expounds upon the value of Balinese society as a model for America and other societies.[58]

In contrast to such comments, Mead's academic publications did not attempt to situate Bali in the present moment. In both *Balinese Character* and *Growth and Culture*, Balinese culture is discussed in atemporal terms, as if it was suspended in a vacuum of timelessness and ahistoricity. This was largely due to the fact that Mead believed that the culture and the cultural processes they were investigating—the cultural conditioning during childhood that transformed an infant into an adult member of Balinese society—were little affected by historical change.

Although the methods she developed for the visual analysis of the relationship between Balinese child development and personality have been criticized, traces of the influence of the Balinese films she made about childhood can be found today in such programs as the PBS series *Childhood*, and even before that, the Canadian Broadcasting Corporation's documentary *Four Families*, made in collaboration with Mead.[59] In the world of public television Mead's visual work is an iconic reference for subsequent generations of media producers when thinking about new forms of "popular ethnography" for public consumption.[60]

Public Television and the Impact of *Margaret Mead's New Guinea Journal*

During the week of December 1, 1968, on public television channels across the nation, people turned their TV sets on to a ninety-minute special titled *Margaret Mead's New Guinea Journal.* The documentary was an NET (National Educational Television) production. "Don't miss this beautiful South Sea adventure!" announced an ad in the *Washington Post.*[61] "The celebrated author of *Growing Up in New Guinea* takes you on a moving and entertaining visit to people she has studied for forty years—as they leaped from the stone age into the 20th century," the ad continued. The premise for the film was Dr. Mead's "final return" to Pere village in the Admiralty Islands, a place she had first visited in 1928 with anthropologist Reo Fortune.[62] Since that initial visit to Pere, Mead had returned twice, first in 1953 and again in 1964, to observe the huge "leap" the Manus Islanders had made into the twentieth century.

Mead had written about her initial return trip in her book *New Lives for Old: Cultural Transformation—Manus, 1928-1953*, which she published in 1956. In the book she documented the rapid, and what she viewed as successful, transformation of Manus society from its isolated pre–World War II condition into a twentieth-century community, linked by radio to the world at large. Before the NET documentary, Mead had already told the story of the Manus Islanders and their astonishing transformation for a segment of the CBS *Adventure* series a decade earlier and had made a short twenty-minute educational film titled *New Lives for Old.*[63] But director Craig Gilbert convinced Mead—and his superiors at WNET, the local New York City affiliate of NET—that there was still another exciting story to be told about Manus society, a story that would feature Mead as prominently as the Manus people. Gilbert proposed that he and his film crew accompany Mead on her return trip to Manus.

The film is ostensibly about the changes that had occurred in Manus society since Mead was first there in 1928, but it is also a visual narrative in which Mead not only "plays" herself but also comes to symbolize, among other things, the post–World War II emergence of the United States as a world leader, America as a paternalistic champion of decolonization and independence for former third world colonies, and American cold war intervention in international development.

According to Gilbert, his superiors at WNET were looking for "a blockbuster."[64] Having read a brief newspaper account of Mead's return to Manus in 1964,[65] he thought that there was potential for a visually exciting story about Mead's lengthy relationship with the people of Pere village and the dramatic changes they had undergone, especially since these changes had come about largely as a result of World War II and the American presence in the Admiralty Islands.[66] Gilbert thought that elements in that story would appeal to a variety of individuals, among them American veterans of World War II, fans of Margaret Mead, and viewers still intrigued by the exotic South Seas location.

For people who had read Mead's books and popular articles in magazines such as *Redbook*, to see her in action and to travel with her to a remote locale in the Pacific had a tremendous impact; for others who had not known about her and her work, the television special introduced them to someone they found intriguing and inspiring. Moreover, Gilbert had seen that in Mead's story there was a larger story to be told, one that directly spoke to many Americans who had had wartime experiences in the Pacific, or to others who were dismayed and discouraged by political and social events at home who could take heart in the inspiring story of positive change and development that Mead had to tell about the Manus people. Once he had gotten the go ahead to make the film, all Gilbert had to do was to convince Mead that she wanted to make a film with him. Although Gilbert said that Mead would have preferred to have made a film in Bali, eventually she did agree to return to Manus with him and his film crew.[67]

In the letters that Mead received from friends, fans, and strangers encountering her for the first time through the documentary we gain insight into several different images of Mead that the film elicited in viewers: "Mead as friend and adventurer," "Mead as a character who plays herself in the movie version of her life," "Mead as ideal woman," "Mead as scientist," and "Mead as either the Good or the Ugly [Imperialist] American."

Figure 7.2 Margaret Mead in Pere Village preparing the Manus Islanders for participation in democratic elections by explaining the American ballot to them, 1963. (Photograph by Lola Romanucci-Ross. Courtesy of the Library of Congress and the Institute for Intercultural Studies)

Margaret Mead's New Guinea Journal as Travelogue and Biopic

For individuals already familiar with her, as the following letter indicates, the documentary gave them the opportunity to see a place they had read about in her books and thus to feel as though they were accompanying Mead on her trip to New Guinea.

> This is a note to say "thank you" to you and your team for the wonderful television program on the Manus. Last night, I was transported with you to that remote island and felt that I, too, was renewing old acquaintances. I have read your books and *Redbook* articles through the years and this filmed account of your most recent visit brought everything into focus. I only hope you will be able to return one day and bring us another Journal from Peri.[68]

The film offered individuals an opportunity—albeit a mediated one—to spend an extended period of time with Mead in an exotic locale and to see her in action, as well as to "meet" individual Manus men and women whom they had previously encountered in Mead's books. For this viewer the film provided the image of Mead as friend, confidante, and expert guide on a trip to a remote part of the world they had previously read about. Another viewer wrote:

> Dear Margaret,
> I saw you on Ch. 13 on television, and I must tell you how much I enjoyed your "New Guinea Journal." You were wonderful. Your staff was so meaningful; it was the shepherd's crook when you were among all these people who were looking up to you; it was the Bishop's crozier when you were settling their disputes, and it was a pilgrim's staff when you walked. It was so symbolic of your relationship with the people of New Guinea. I hope to see more of your travels on television.[69]

The ninety-minute documentary gave this viewer an inspirational picture of Mead replete with biblical connotations. It is an image of Mead as an Old Testament prophet or Christ-like figure among her followers, a pilgrim with a mission. As Mead only began using her thumb stick in the early 1960s, this letter highlights its visual impact and one set of meanings associated with what was to become an iconic image of Mead with her signifying staff. Embedded in this image of Mead with her thumb stick, which the viewer also saw as symbolic of "her relationship with the people of New Guinea," is that of a paternalistic (in this case maternalistic) figure offering guidance and leadership to the needy, less knowledgeable inhabitants of New Guinea.

Further insight into Mead's image comes from comments made by her colleague, psychologist Martha Wolfenstein. Wolfenstein had written a psychological study of the movies and was struck by Mead's naturalness in front of the camera:[70]

> She and an old black woman fall into each other's arms and she's just as much herself there. . . . The way she comes through in this film is just like Humphrey Bogart, an American actor whose acting consists in being himself all the time, in a very vivid, forceful way. She's really a marvelous movie actress, in the best tradition of American acting, which isn't acting but being yourself.[71]

Wolfenstein celebrates the fact that Mead was simply "being herself" in this film, even though she knew that the footage would be screened across

Figure 7.3 Mead embraced by a Manus woman, 1963. (Photograph by Lola Romanucci-Ross. Courtesy of the Library of Congress and the Institute for Intercultural Studies)

the nation by thousands of Americans. Her comments imply that Mead was playing a role, albeit one that she could play unselfconsciously. It was a role in which Mead was leader, arbitrator, sage, and friend of the common man (and woman), literally embracing people with no regard for the color of their skin. She was also equally at ease berating the Manus people, never hesitant or fearful that she might be viewed as scolding or domineering.

Margaret Mead's New Guinea Journal exhibits what Christina Klein has identified as "middlebrow universalism," a value that flourished in cold war America that accepted—indeed celebrated—cultural variation while asserting a larger human sameness.[72] According to the terms of *The Ugly American*, a popular novel of the period in which Americans working in Asia are identified as being either "ugly Americans" or "non-ugly Americans" depending upon their willingness to embrace other cultures, other languages, and other ways of life, Mead's anthropological message of tolerance for cultural variety and the existence of a larger human universalism not only made her a "non-ugly American," but also one of universalism's strongest exemplars.[73]

However, today when watching this film viewers often react uneasily to Mead, whose manner they find overbearing and paternalistic toward the Manus people, whether young or old. By 1968, both the antiwar movement and the Black Power movement had emerged in the United States, as well as many of the independence movements in Africa, and white dominance and authority over black people was no longer uniformly accepted either in the United States or abroad. For younger viewers, Mead's "sermon" to the schoolchildren about their future paints an uncomfortable picture of Americans as, at best, meddlesome and, at worst, representatives of an imperialistic America and its misguided policies toward Vietnam and Southeast Asia in general.

Manus, World War II, and the Pacific Theater

Letters Mead received show that the documentary resonated with viewers in different ways depending upon the their background and whether they were male or female. In 1968, anyone over thirty would have had memories of World War II, and most veterans who had served in the Pacific were still alive. Even older men and women who had not been to New Guinea were familiar with the names of place such as Rabaul, Manus, and the Admiralty Islands. Most of the letters that referred to the war in the Pacific were written by men, while in contrast letters that expressed admiration or vicarious pleasure and excitement about Mead's enterprise as an anthropologist were usually from women.

Letters from World War II veterans included comments such as those of Thomas W. Russell Jr.:

> Dear Dr. Mead,
> Just a note to thank you and the producer for the splendid evening. I spent a year outside of Port Moresby and then Dobodura and six months on Manus and Mauote. I'm afraid I was one of the fomenters of change although I never really was able to learn *talk talk*. I hope you were as pleased by the record of your exciting work as I was.[74]

Russell seems to have been prompted to write to Mead because the film made him realize that having spent a year and a half in New Guinea, including Manus itself, he had been part of the very process of change that Mead was talking about in the film. Perhaps it had caused him to reflect in a new way upon his wartime experience, or, at the very least, to remember it years later and to realize that he might have had an impact on the Papua New Guineans he had come into contact with.

For the segment of the American public who had fought in the Pacific, the documentary allowed them to revisit that part of the world, with Manus metaphorically representing all the Pacific islands and villages through out Melanesia and Micronesia, including Dutch New Guinea and the port of Hollandia where General MacArthur's Pacific fleet had been stationed; the Solomon Islands (the site of James Michener's *Tales of the South Pacific*); and Buna and the Bulldog trail in eastern New Guinea, where twenty-five years earlier as young men and women, in a time of danger and fear, they had spent time in a part of the world that many of them had never dreamed of visiting before, nor thought of returning to later.

It was coincidental of course that the Admiralty Islands, where Mead and Fortune had first worked with the Manus people in 1928, would a dozen or so years later become a staging ground for more than a million American troops, becoming one of the largest American bases between Pearl Harbor and Guam.[75] As a result of this major world conflagration the Manus Islanders were precipitously forced into contact first with the Japanese military forces and then with the Americans. From the Manus people's standpoint there was much to admire and emulate in the Americans: their abundant supplies of equipment and provisions, the seemingly egalitarian relations between black and white U.S. soldiers, and the American troops' generous and friendly treatment of the Manus Islanders.[76]

As these letters from former servicemen reveal, for many viewers the film was not just about Margaret Mead and what anthropologists do, or about the Manus people and the changes their society had undergone since World War II. For them the documentary was a narrative about their own lives and the role they played as Americans in the Pacific wartime theater. It allowed them to reconnect via Mead and her return to New Guinea with a distant time and place experienced under very trying circumstances. In this context the Manus Islanders came to represent all the various Pacific islanders whom they had come into contact with. Watching Mead's upbeat story about the strides the Manus people had made since the end of the war and her positive interpretation of the inspirational role the American servicemen had played in their transformation would have been gratifying for these veterans.

"From the Stone Age to the 20th Century": Metaphors of Transformation

The cliché of the Manus Islanders transforming themselves from a Stone Age culture into a modern culture used to advertise *Margaret Mead's New Guinea Journal* was based on Mead's description of the changes in Manus culture in her book *New Lives for Old*. It provided an image that appealed to Americans in particular with their admiration for progress and rapid change. It also exuded a sense of the exotic and the magical—from the Stone Age, a temporally distant, hence unreachable, place—to modernity. What connects these two temporally distinct places is the process of transformation, here posed as a semimagical state of affairs whereby an entire society seemingly overnight finds itself moving from one temporal mode of existence to another. A large factor that facilitated this transformation among the Manus Islanders was the powerful agency of World War II—more precisely, the presence of thousands of American troops who were stationed in the Admiralties as the Allied forces strove to keep the Japanese from advancing into Australia. Thus, as a Coca-Cola ad from October 1945 illustrated, many aspects of American culture were introduced to the Manus people as a result of the presence of so many American soldiers in the archipelago for an extended period of time.

In the film, Mead acts as a mediator between the Manus Islanders and America. While in 1945 Coca-Cola may have been a symbol of the American way of life ("a bit of America") to U.S. service men and Admiralty Islanders alike, in the documentary it is Mead who symbolizes America and modernity.[77] She is also the television viewer's connection between the so-called Stone Age of the Manus past, which she had witnessed when she first visited the Manus in 1928, and the modern twentieth century that the Manus people now actively participate in via radio, the Beatles, and other forms of American and European pop culture; formal education (from elementary school to university); and the development activities of the Australian government, the United Nations, and other international agencies focused at the time on preparing the territories of Papua and New Guinea for impending independence from Australian trusteeship in 1975. The film is more than just the story of Mead's involvement with the Manus people. Her story becomes metonymic of *our* story—the story, that is, of the impact of American soldiers on the Manus Islanders and the model for a new type of society they provided Manus leaders. More generally, it is metonymic of America's development as a world power during the twentieth century. Although New Guinea had been divided in 1884 into colonies ruled by the Dutch, the Germans, and the British, by 1968, it was preparing for independence. It was preparing to take its place as one nation among many with a voice, a vote, and a physical presence at the United Nations.

Since the end of World War II and the beginning of the cold war, Mead had been concerned that the United States not remain isolationist in its foreign policy. Because she believed that America had an important role to play in assuring world peace and in ending poverty, famine, and disease worldwide, she, along with other prominent liberal American women such as Eleanor Roosevelt and Pearl Buck, had argued vehemently for the creation of the United Nations and America's participation in it.

As she did in *New Lives for Old*, Mead suggests in *New Guinea Journal* that the Manus people provide Americans with a model of successful and rapid social change as well as an example of peaceful decolonization and the ability of third world peoples to successfully adapt to nationhood and modernization.[78] Given the extensive postwar political upheavals that accompanied decolonization, the process of decolonization and methods for the successful development of new nations were of prime concern to Western democratic states.

Thus, from a postcolonial perspective, the film, like the book it was based on, is a narrative about the changing role of the United States as a world power over the course of the twentieth century and of the role that Mead and other anthropologists were playing in this process.[79]

New Guinea Journal as Inspirational Woman's Journey

Dear Dr. Mead,
Seldom am I inspired to write to a "celebrity" . . . however . . . I watched the Tuesday special on Channel 13 about your work . . . and I cried. I saw your eyes saying "goodbye" to your beloved Peri and wondered with you whether you would ever return to your "Camelot." Perhaps I am being over sentimental. . . . I did not only cry for you, but selfishly, I must admit, for myself as

> well. I am 40 years old and have nothing . . . nothing . . . and have let talents go to waste. To see a woman so revered by those natives because of the expectation of fulfillment you have instilled in them is astounding to me. Here, in this asphalt jungle, the tumultuous behavior of our natives is unbearable and unbelievable, and we have no Dr. Margaret Mead to help enlighten them, and lead them out of the maze of blunder and blight they have ensued upon. The headhunters have ceased in Peri, but not so here . . . here leaders like Dr. Martin Luther King, John F. Kennedy, and Robert F. Kennedy are hunted down and destroyed and the murderers are glorified . . . what a sick society we have.
>
> I should love to go to your beloved Peri one day and bring knowledge and understanding as you have . . . however, this is only one of my unfilled hopes amongst so many. I am the dreamer, you are the Accomplisher. I hereby salute you, Madam Dr Margaret Mead, may you LIVE, LIVE, LIVE, and continue your blessed worthwhile work.[80]

Viewing *Margaret Mead's New Guinea Journal* had inspired this forty-year-old woman from Long Island to compare her own life with Mead's. Finding her life lacking in any lasting accomplishments, she wrote to Mead to express her admiration for all that Mead had achieved. In this letter we glimpse another major audience for Mead and her work: women of her own generation and younger who long to have achieved something more with their lives than they have thus far. For these women, the "adventure" in the film's South Seas adventure is less one of a daydream of escape to an idyllic tropical island and more one of a yearning for self-fulfillment, for the career never embarked upon, the risks never taken, the challenges never met.

To watch Mead return to Pere village and reminisce about her first visit there when she was twenty-seven years old, and then to see her forty years later, an aging, matronly figure, now more a grandmother to the young Manus children than a mother, the very ordinariness of Mead's appearance, her bulky body and plain, wrinkled face hidden underneath her floppy broad-brimmed hat, made it seem like any other woman who had had the courage and conviction could also have gone off to far-flung places and done something exciting and worthwhile with her life. For many of the documentary's female viewers there may also have been a similar identification between themselves and Mead, as stated explicitly by the writer above. The image of Mead as the "Accomplisher" stands in this woman's mind in stark contrast to herself, the dreamer left at age forty with only her unfilled hopes and aspirations. Captured in the raw honesty of this woman's letter are the feelings that a great number of fortyish American women may have felt. These were the women who had married at the end of World War II and settled down to become housewives and mothers. They were also the women to whom Betty Friedan had directed her clarion call in 1963 in *The Feminine Mystique*.

The letter writer romanticizes Mead's experiences as well as the reality of the lives of the Manus people, exchanging the clichéd notion of a South Seas paradise for that of a primitive Camelot. The second theme in this woman's letter is that of despair over the state of the nation in 1968. The sixties had been a time of civil strife throughout urban America, first focusing on civil rights, then on the draft and the war in Vietnam. Her reference to Pere as Mead's "Camelot" was an allusion to the short-lived John F. Kennedy administration whose reign had been cut short by the president's assassination in 1963. That event, along with the subsequent assassinations of Martin Luther King and Robert Kennedy, riots in urban ghettoes across America, and the country's increasing involvement in Vietnam and Cambodia led the woman who wrote this letter to Mead to call the United States a sick society. Along with her personal despair, she quickly cited parallels between Manus and America and bemoaned the "heathenness" of her own culture.

An Anthropologist at Work

For some viewers, *Margaret Mead's New Guinea Journal* was also a film about anthropology and how anthropologists work:

> Dear Margaret,
> It was some days after I had first seen the program before I realized that in a very subtle way the film makes a definite statement about the mechanics of anthropology. So that's what an anthropologist actually does, belatedly came into my awareness—careful and specific recordations [*sic*], observations and conversations.

> Subsequent viewings further revealed something quite interesting about anthropologist's equipment—it is really quite light, consists of little hardware, and is in the main related to mind and spirit, with little external machinery involved.[81]

Some colleagues wrote to ask her how they could get a print of the film to use in teaching students how anthropologists work in the field.[82] Others acknowledged that Mead had provided them with an intimate portrait of the nature of her relationship with her research subjects. Harvard sociologist David Riesman, author of *The Lonely Crowd*, wrote Mead: "I think you are very courageous to reveal what anthropologists often hide, namely, their involvement with the lives of the people they study, and their awareness of the dilemmas of progress and development."[83]

While in 1968 Riesman praised Mead for her honesty in revealing her involvement in the lives of the Manus Islanders, beginning in the 1970s some anthropologists and Manus people themselves began to criticize her for her portrayal of Manus society in her books and for meddling in the islanders' lives. They saw her actions as neocolonialist and racist. Such comments became part of a larger critique of the field of anthropology as a whole that culminated in another television documentary titled *Anthropology on Trial*.[84] In this film, college students from Manus criticized Mead's portrayal of their culture. It marked the dawn of a new era in which the subject of anthropological descriptions could now talk back via the media, holding anthropologists responsible for their representations of themselves and their ancestors.

"Ethnography on the Airwaves" and "Popular Ethnography"

As Faye Ginsburg has noted, in 1953 the CBS *Adventure* series was the first television series to use anthropologists as consultants and guests on a program.[85] Providing another first, *Margaret Mead's New Guinea Journal* was arguably the first example of what has become a familiar genre: "popular ethnography" or "ethnography on the airwaves."[86] Today, when college students and television viewers have been raised on documentary channels such as Discovery and National Geographic, it is hard to remember that when *Margaret Mead's New Guinea Journal* aired in 1968 it was the first television documentary of its genre. Perhaps it is not surprising, given Mead's enthusiasm for television as a new medium of mass communication and her renown as a popularizer of anthropology, that it was she who blazed the way and provided these subsequent series with the model of a television documentary based on showing an anthropologist at work in the field.

As British television producer Leslie Woodhead and anthropologist-producer André Singer note, "partly as a result of [Mead's] enthusiasm for new ways of reaching the public, film took on an ever greater importance in anthropology. By the 1960s and 1970s, film was reaching millions in their living rooms through the spread of television, and anthropologists had an exciting new medium to use."[87] Thus, added to the image of Mead as an advocate of film and photography as research tools for anthropologists is that of Mead as a proponent of television as a means to teach the general public about the goals and significance of anthropology.

Mead did not live to see the development of inexpensive, portable video equipment that allows today's anthropologists to shoot their own projects, edit on their laptop computers while in the field, and work on collaborative projects with informants. However, she believed that what she and Gilbert had accomplished in their collaboration was merely the first of more such endeavors, and she regularly invited Gilbert to come to her graduate seminar in ethnographic research methods at Columbia to discuss the use of new types of film equipment in field research.[88] Gilbert too had been influenced by his involvement with Mead, and their paths would continue to cross in the future.

Margaret Mead, *An American Family*, and the Origins of Reality TV

In 1973, Mead's name appeared in the press in association with a daring new television documentary series, *An American Family.* Twelve episodes in length, shown weekly on PBS stations nationwide, millions of Americans viewed seven months in the lives of the Louds, a white, middle-class family who lived in Santa Barbara, California. During the series, viewers witnessed the unraveling of Pat and Bill Loud's twenty-year marriage, as well as the antics of the five Loud children, Lance, Kevin, Grant, Delilah, and Michele. In a particularly controversial segment, Americans gained a peephole onto the gay lifestyle of the Loud's oldest son, Lance, who was then living in New York City. Neither Mead nor her friend Craig Gilbert, the producer of the series, ever suspected that *An American Family* was destined to become the precursor of MTV's *The Real World*, *Survivor*, and the other reality TV programs of today that have become the new cash cows of the television industry.[89]

Having worked intimately with Gilbert on the production of *Margaret Mead's New Guinea Journal*, Mead had become a steadfast ally and sounding board for Gilbert. It may even have been because of his association with Mead that Gilbert developed his idea for a study of the everyday life of an American family. Mead did her part to promote the series, writing in an article for *TV Guide* that *An American Family* was "as new and significant as the invention of drama or the novel—a new way in which people can learn to look at life, by seeing the real life of others interpreted by the camera."[90]

Two months later in an interview for the *Los Angeles Times* titled "Some Second Thoughts from *An American Family*," Pat Loud, the wife and mother whose life had been laid out before the American public week after week, said:

> Margaret Mead, bless her friendly voice, has written glowingly that the series constituted some sort of breakthrough, a demonstration of a new tool for use in sociology and anthropology. Having been the object of that tool, I think I am competent to say that it won't work.[91]

It is not surprising to find conflicting opinions about a new technological innovation voiced in the press. What was surprising was that the subject of the "new tool," or technological innovation under discussion, spoke back, telling Mead, in ways that the characters in a novel or play cannot, that this new mode of representation she has spoken of so glowingly won't work. In this exchange we see a precursor to the arguments that have reverberated throughout anthropology and the media in general about the representation of the Other.

Pat Loud's objection to the use of the video camera as an observational tool—even though she and her family had willingly agreed to its presence—was offered as a warning to others not to do as she had done.[92] She and her family had no control over their images once they were on videotape and broadcast into millions of American homes. In retrospect, the

Louds were naive to agree to subject themselves to the scrutiny of the television public, and Mead was naive to believe in the objectivity of the camera. We now acknowledge not only the degree to which the person operating the camera can shape the images that the camera produces, but also the important role that individuals involved in editing can play in creating the final product an audience views.

However, if we consider Mead's statement about *An American Family* as a forecast of the importance and impact of a new visual technology—small-format, relatively inexpensive, video—as both a new method of observation and a new mode of representing reality on television, we see her as very prescient. As film scholar Jeffrey Ruoff notes: "*An American Family* represents a new stage in filming of everyday lives of ordinary individuals, a landmark in the history of nonfiction film. In its aftermath, the American documentary would never be the same."[93] It is hard not to see in the voyeuristic enthusiasm of the American television audience for the real life spectacle and drama provided by *An American Family* the seed of today's plethora of reality TV programs.

Mead: The Nonstereotypical Scientist

In 1957, in the aftermath of the United States' shock and dismay that the Soviet Union had launched a satellite into orbit before it had, Mead and her colleague Rhoda Metraux published an article in *Science* magazine titled "Image of the Scientist among High-School Students." It presented the results of a survey they had conducted for the American Association for the Advancement of Science that asked students a series of questions aimed at finding out what they thought about scientists and what they did. Perhaps not surprisingly, Mead and Metraux found that the average student thought of a scientist as "a man who wears a white coat and works in a laboratory. He is elderly or middle aged and wears glasses . . . he may wear a beard . . . he is unshaven and unkempt. He may be stooped and tired. He is surrounded by equipment: test tubes, Bunsen burners, flasks and bottles, a jungle gym of blown glass tubes and weird machines with dials."[94]

Students also thought that a scientist "neglects his body for his mind." He also neglects his family: "[he] pays no attention to his wife, never plays with his children. He has no social life . . . a scientist should not marry. No one wants to be such a scientist or to marry him." They also thought of scientists as "geniuses" who invented or discovered new and better products that improved people's lives. There was also a sense of respect—even awe—that students felt toward scientists.[95]

Even before C. P. Snow pointed out the great gulf that existed between the practitioners of science and literature—a gulf so great that Snow characterized them as inhabiting two different cultures—Mead and Metraux found that students saw scientists as a distinct cultural group.[96] As the high school students' responses indicate, foremost among these features was that a scientist was thought to be a man.

Mead, however, did not fit the common stereotype of a scientist. In fashioning an image of herself as a scientist she adopted some features characteristic of the culture of science while defying others, or adapting them to her own purposes. For example, she enjoyed being and looking like a woman. She liked to dress up, she liked frilly clothes, and she liked to wear lipstick and nail polish. Even when doing fieldwork in New Guinea she never donned the stereotypical pith helmet and safari gear Western cartoonists associated with colonial explorers and anthropologists in the jungle (not many anthropologists ever did!), but preferred to wear dresses and broad-brimmed hats. Yet while at work in her office at the museum she often wore a smock over her regular clothes to keep them clean, her symbolic lab coat (although hers were feminized, being either bright colors or embroidered with flowers).

Perhaps because she was an eldest child, perhaps because her parents had encouraged her to speak up and to voice her opinions, Mead never had any difficulty interjecting her ideas into a debate with male colleagues or speaking in front of an audience at a professional meeting. Thus her verbal style was never hampered by the quality of reticence associated with women, especially when in the company of men.[97] In fact, Mead found the format of the small conference at which an interdisciplinary group of scholars gathered to discuss a particular issue to be the ideal mode of communication to stimulate new ideas and to generate new forms of knowledge.[98]

Mead's ability to defy some aspects of the masculine culture of science while easily conforming to others was the result of personal characteristics as well as her choice of anthropology for her field of research. The social sciences in general and anthropology in particular have been characterized as having cultures that were far more receptive to women than

Figure 7.4 Mead looking at a diorama of Pere Village as it was when she first visited Manus in 1928. The diorama was created in 1971 for the new Hall of the Pacific at the American Museum of Natural History. Notice Mead's plaid variation of the traditional, more austere, white scientist's "lab coat." (Photograph courtesy of Ken Heyman)

the "hard" sciences such as physics, chemistry, or biology. As a social science, anthropology is viewed by these hard sciences as a "soft science," in terms of research methods and focus of study, and as a "small science," in terms of its impact and the nature of the questions it seeks to answer. Because of these qualities, it is also viewed as a rather marginal science. At the same time, these qualities have also contributed to the relative ease with which women entered the profession. While the media characterize Mead as a scientist, from the perspective of many practitioners of the hard sciences, because she was a social scientist she was an "inferior breed" of scientist.

Nonetheless, the media's interest in Mead as a scientist, especially as an expert on the topic of human behavior, was extensive during her lifetime—and continues today. It is particularly evident in literature written for children and young adults and especially in books intent on presenting girls with role models of women in science. Mead contributed to this genre herself by writing *People and Places*, a book about anthropology for young adults in which she uses her ethnographic experiences to describe the training an anthropologist needs to do field research. First published in 1959, the book was described as "a study for young readers of the diverse ways in which human beings have solved their common problems."[99] With its Boasian emphasis on cultural diversity within a basic human universalism (the common problems all humans face and the common physiological and psychological characteristics we share as human beings) as its underlying message, the book fit perfectly with the tenor of cold war era America and its new emphasis on the acceptance of cultural difference.[100]

Mead situates anthropology as a science in *People and Places* by embedding it within a larger discourse on human curiosity about the natural world, a curiosity that gave rise to such sciences as astronomy, geology, and physics, as well as speculation about humans in comparison to other species—which gave rise to sciences such as linguistics, psychology, and anthropology. While *People and Places* introduced young readers to anthropology as a science, other authors have written books for young readers that celebrate Mead's achievements as a pioneering female anthropologist and scientist. It is a common narrative about her. For example, in *Women in Profile: Scientists*, Carlotta Hacker includes Mead as one of six women scientists she singles out for an extended profile.[101] The intent of the book is clearly to celebrate women who have made contributions as scientists and to stress how unusual it has been for women to become scientists. Yet not all books about Mead emphasize that she is a *female* scientist. Others, such as the *Oxford Series in Science* simply include her as an outstanding scientist.[102]

Other books for young adults include Mead as an example of an outstanding woman; her status as a scientist is of secondary import. Thus *Women of Our Time,* a series of biographies that focus on the lives of twentieth-century women, includes a volume titled *Margaret Mead: The World Was Her Family.*[103] The series aims to provide exemplary models for seven- to eleven-year-olds because "today more than ever, children need role models whose lives can give them the inspiration and guidance to cope with a changing world."[104]

The titles of other books about Mead in this genre of exemplary, or *representational* (in Emerson's sense of the term), biography are revealing: *Margaret Mead: Student of the Global Village, She Never Looked Back: Margaret Mead in Samoa,* and *The Value of Understanding: The Story of Margaret Mead.*[105] These and other short biographies of Mead written for young readers all tend to focus on similar aspects of Mead's life and career, in particular, her early research in Samoa and New Guinea.[106] They also share a common message—that Mead valued the diversity of cultures (or diverse ways of being male or female, diverse ways of raising children, and so forth) while considering all cultures to be part of one great human society. Although Mead is often singled out for being a scientist, and in particular, for being a female scientist, she is most celebrated as an icon of cross-cultural understanding, cultural relativism, and the underlying unity of humankind as a species.[107]

One book that does not obviously fit into this genre of representational literature is the delightfully imaginative children's picture book, *We're Back! A Dinosaur Story.* Given high school students' stereotypic image of a scientist as someone who wears a lab coat and is elderly, it is not hard to see where artist/author Hudson Talbott came up with his rendition of the imaginary Dr. Miriam Bleeb, the grandmotherly heroine who works at the American Museum of Natural History. In her white lab coat and practical black shoes, Dr. Bleeb is a parodic transformation of Margaret Mead, complete with bobbed hair, bangs, and glasses. (Rather than a thumb stick, however, Dr. Bleeb walks with cane.)[108] In the story, Dr. Bleeb protects the dinosaurs from being harmed by New York's finest. The police want to arrest the dinosaurs for disturbing the peace. In Talbott's tale

Figure 7.5 Dr. Miriam Bleeb talking to New York City policemen as she leads them through the Hall of the Dinosaurs at the American Museum of Natural History in *We're Back! A Dinosaur's Story.* (Illustration courtesy of Hudson Talbott)

Figure 7.6 Dr. Miriam Bleeb talking to one of the dinosaurs from outer space in *We're Back! A Dinosaur's Story*, 1987. (Illustration courtesy of Hudson Talbott)

of alien dinosaurs—the inhabitants of a distant planet who mistakenly return to earth where they have the misfortune of landing on present-day Manhattan—the prehistoric creatures have become surrogate "primitives" whose lives need to be protected by a kindly and clever scientist, a female scientist who, like the real Dr. Mead, works at the American Museum of Natural History. In the end, Dr. Bleeb helps the dinosaurs return to their home in outer space. Talbott's thinly veiled Margaret Mead, complete with lab coat and glasses, is yet another permutation of Mead as an iconic figure in American popular culture. For some parents and grandparents reading *We're Back!* to a child, there may be the pleasure of "getting" Talbott's visual pun about Dr. Miriam Bleeb, while for children there is the pleasure and excitement of her heroic deed. In both instances, Bleeb/Mead is a kindly maternal figure, wise as well as sly and a bit mischievous.

The Image of Mead as Scientist

We have considered two interrelated sets of images of Mead as a scientist: Mead as a proponent of new forms of visual technology to be used both for research and the dissemination of scientific knowledge and Mead as a particular type of scientist—a social scientist whose area of expertise is the study of human behavior.

The first set of images is based upon Mead's interest in new forms of visual technology and mass media—photography, cinema, television, and video—developed or refined over the course of the twentieth century. Thus we saw how Mead came to represent the subfield of visual anthropology as a result of the extensive and innovative use of film and photography she and Bateson devised for their fieldwork in Bali. Almost twenty years later some of this Balinese film footage launched Mead's television career when she appeared on the CBS science series *Adventure*. In her enthusiastic endorsement of the use of video cameras to record everyday life in the television documentary *An American Family*, we see her unalloyed support for the depth and breadth that documentary video could provide specialist and lay viewer alike.

The second set of images includes those that specifically refer to Mead as a scientist, in particular as a social scientist and expert on human behavior and a female scientist. We saw how the media portrayed her as an expert on human sexuality and relished her barbed critique of the first Kinsey report and the gullible American public that eagerly consumed it. We read how viewers responded to *Margaret Mead's New Guinea Journal*, seeing in Mead's description of the changes occurring to the Manus Islanders reflections of themselves, their personal histories, and a parable about the role that the United States and the United Nations should play in helping them develop into twentieth-century societies. Lastly, in books written for children and young adults we saw Mead's iconic role as a female scientist and intellectual whose life serves as an inspirational narrative and model of success for younger generations of women.

Mead also came to represent scientists who believed in the importance of providing scientific information to the populace at large. Despite her initial worries about radio and television, she eventually embraced them as forms of electronic chautauqua; as a means, that is, of educating the populace and thus as useful tools that could nurture participatory democracy.[109] Much like the venerable nineteenth-century American institution of small town tent chautauquas where rural Americans could hear the likes of William Jennings Bryan and Booker T. Washington (and its contemporary offshoot, the Chautauqua Institute in upstate New York where Mead was a regularly featured speaker), Mead considered radio and television to be useful venues where important contemporary issues and ideas could be presented to a popular audience.[110]

From viewers' responses to *Margaret Mead's New Guinea Journal* and her appearances on numerous talk shows, Mead also learned the value of television in increasing her recognition. Television was not simply a means of reaching a vast number of viewers spread across the nation, it was also a way to stimulate individuals to read more of her books or to want to hear her speak in person. As she told Rae Goodell:

> Television is the best medium. It is not a good medium for a long substantive communication, but the more you are on television, the more others pay attention, read your books, come to your lectures. There is nothing like it, because television appears to be extremely frustrating. Americans want to be in the same room with people and they don't feel that television puts them in the same room. So if they have seen you on television, they read your book or they go to a lecture. They drive fifty miles to sit in the back of a hall with two thousand people, because they have seen somebody on television.[111]

These comments reveal Mead as very media savvy, someone who cultivated the use of television appearances not simply as an end but as a means of increasing the circulation of her name and image, as well as her ideas. Mead's emphasis on the value of television to create desire for the real person herself, rather than the image of a person on the television screen, the simulacra, is perceptive. This process of Mead becoming more widely known to the public, of becoming a media celebrity, will be dealt with more fully in the next chapter.

CHAPTER 8

Mead as Public Intellectual and Celebrity

> Margaret Mead was perhaps the only anthropologist ever to become a household word in America. Through her films, best-selling books, her column in *Redbook* magazine, and her counsel to world figures, she attained truly international stature.
>
> —*Thinkers of the Twentieth Century*, 1983[1]

Margaret Mead stills remains the only anthropologist to have become a household name in America. This chapter looks at examples of various media events that contributed to making Mead's name so recognizable. They include Mead's role as a *visible scientist*—one of a group of American scientists who were well known to the general public and an early example of the present-day phenomenon of academic and intellectual superstars; the circulation of Mead's name, ideas, and image on radio and television and in popular middle-class magazines such as *Life* and *Redbook*; and a grass-roots campaign to launch her as a candidate for president of the United States in the 1972 presidential election. These examples track Mead's role as a transitional figure between an earlier type of public intellectual and today's media academics whose fame is fanned by the ascendancy of celebrity as an increasingly dominant American value. We will also see the ways in which the media and the public embraced Mead as an American icon who stood for such long-standing American values as the American Dream, the importance of the family, peace, and freedom of speech. A look at the FBI files kept on Mead, however, will also demonstrate the suspicion with which J. Edgar Hoover and others regarded her during the cold war era as potentially subversive and anti-American.

Mead as Visible Scientist

Visible scientist is a term that communications scholar Rae Goodell first used in 1975 to refer to what she identified as a new breed of scientists. She observed that visible scientists were quite different in behavior and appearance from the public's popular image of a scientist. They did not go around wearing lab coats, for example, nor did they all sport heads of unruly hair like Einstein, and they were not all men.[2] Most important, however, was that visible scientists were known not for their discoveries, or for their popularization of their particular scientific field of expertise, but rather for their activities, in particular, their participation in controversial contemporary political and social issues. They offered their opinions and conclusions about a broad range of science-related policy issues that included such topics as overpopulation, race and intelligence, drugs, genetic engineering, nuclear power, pollution, and arms control.

Mead was one of several visible scientists Goodell interviewed, including Paul Ehrlich, Linus Pauling, B. F. Skinner, Carl Sagan, Barry Commoner, and William Shockley. Issues upon which Mead spoke before the public or testified at congressional hearings included the legalization of marijuana, the need for stricter controls over nuclear power plants, racism and Black Power, air pollution and the environment, and the generation gap.[3] She was also a founding member of SIPI (Scientists' Institute for Public Information), an organization that had grown out of the public information activities initiated by nuclear physicists involved with the creation of the atomic bombs during and after World War II.[4]

The existence of scientists who spoke out about social and political issues was not new; individuals such as Bertrand Russell and Albert Einstein had assumed the role of public intellectual earlier in the twentieth century. What *was* new was the magnitude of these scientists' fame and public recognition—the fact that they had become "household names." Goodell contends that visible scientists were unique to contemporary electronic media. They were the product of the needs and demands of new communications media and their audiences who no longer wanted "scientists as heroes," as was true of earlier decades, but rather yearned for "science-celebrities."[5]

We still have individuals who function as the twenty-first century's visible scientists. There is primatologist Jane Goodall with her concern not only for chimpanzees but also for the endangered African environments in which they live, and Pulitzer Prize–winning biogeographer and physiologist, Jared Diamond, who like Mead worked extensively in Papua New Guinea before turning his attention to the world as a whole. And before his death in 2002, evolutionary biologist, writer, and Harvard professor Stephen Jay Gould was one of America's best-known scientists.[6] During their lifetimes Gould and Mead were the best-known scientist of their respective disciplines. Both were also committed to conveying complex ideas to the general public through writing and speaking clear, non-jargon-filled, simple prose, and both experienced ambivalence from members of their own disciplines largely as a result of their celebrity status as "intellectual superstars." While some of his peers eulogized Gould as a "latter-day Darwin," like Mead, others dismissed him as "a simple-minded popularizer of science."[7]

Mead: From Public Intellectual to "Academostar"

Stephen Jay Gould, Margaret Mead, and Jared Diamond are but three of a small number of academics who have achieved superstar status within their own disciplines and among the general public. Other such individuals include historians Gail Kern Goodwin and Howard Zinn and a plethora of scholars from philosopher Judith Butler to African Americanist Cornel West. Linguist Noam Chomsky and literary scholar Edward Said occupy a slightly different category, as their name recognition or celebrity among the general public has been generated as much, or more so, from their political activism as from their academic expertise.

These individuals differ from earlier generations of public intellectuals in one important respect: they are all associated with academia. Much has been written in the last twenty years about the demise of the independent public intellectual who wrote for the educated reader. While a newer breed of academics far outnumbers the traditional public intellectuals, "since they do not employ the vernacular, outsiders rarely know of them."[8]

In response, scholars have described new breeds of intellectuals,[9] one type of which they have labeled the *academostar.*[10] This new academic-cum-celebrity has become more prevalent in recent years as universities, like sports teams and movie producers, have sought to hire *stars* at inflated salaries in order to boost their institutions' reputations and rankings.

The public intellectual and the academic superstar represent two historically specific social roles that intellectuals have played in twentieth-century American society. The public intellectual described by intellectual historian Russell Jacoby arose during the first half of the twentieth century and included mostly men born during the first two decades of the century. (He includes a few exceptional women such as Jane Jacobs and Mary McCarthy, as well as Susan Sontag a generation or so later.)[11] It was primarily an urban type. Even more specific, intellectuals were often immigrants to the United States. Most were Jewish, and if they did not already start out there, most of them eventually made their way to New York City, many of them lived in Greenwich Village or were otherwise considered to be *bohemians* because of their independent lifestyles and iconoclastic ideas. They included individuals such as Lewis Mumford and Edmund Wilson, critics and polemicists who "deferred to no one."[12] An important freedom their independence afforded them was the ability to critique the society at large as they saw it, and to make suggestions as to ways in which society could or should change. "In a precise sense," Jacoby says, "they are obsolete."[13]

Although Jacoby did not include Mead in his discussion of public intellectuals, she had many of the characteristics associated with them. She was born during the period he refers to; she held an independent status from a university; she used jargon-free language; she desired to reach out to a broad general public; she admired and emulated the role of writer; she thrived in her urban location of New York City during exactly the period Jacoby refers to; and she brought an oppositional and critical perspective to bear on a broad range of issues.

I suggest Mead represents a transitional figure between the old-fashioned intellectual Jacoby is referring to and the new breed of intellectual "academostars." The fact that she was not ensconced in a university allowed her greater freedom to pursue an iconoclastic career course, as well as more latitude to pursue the cultivation of a public persona. It also allowed her, in Edward Said's term, to cultivate her role as an intellectual *amateur* rather than becoming overly concerned with the narrow specialization encouraged by the intellectual professionalization of today.[14]

As one of the first academostars, Mead and her fellow visible scientists were the prototype for today's academic celebrities. Her successful engagement with—indeed, her eager embracing of—the mass media, especially radio and television, but also women's and other popular magazines, contributed to her transformation into one of the first academic superstars. The academic as celebrity replaces an earlier representation of the academic as austere, remote, and dispassionate, as well as invisible to the public.[15] Instead, a new emphasis on the academic as performer and public personality is consistent with the general increase in importance of celebrity as a mode of being in our culture.

The acceptability of the new role has also been reinforced by the new entrepreneurial thrust of universities, who see academic stars as useful marketing tools. As universities modernized during the course of the twentieth century they became increasingly bureaucratized and professionalized. This led to universities today being run more like business firms with attention paid to the students as customers or clients, rather than as guilds with students as apprentices whose minds are to be shaped and guided by knowledgeable mentors and masters, as in the past. It has also meant that the name recognition of a university—its brand or "trademark" value—has become increasingly important as a means of "product differentiation."[16] One way in which a university increases its name recognition is by the star academics it attracts to its faculty. It is not so much a matter of *what* the celebrity academic has to say, but simply the name recognition of the celebrity that is important to the university as a means of attracting students.[17]

Academic stardom was aided by the increased mobility of academics and the rise of the conference circuit. The increase in professional conferences has meant that there are more opportunities for fellow academics to see one another in action, performing for one another as well as the press who cover such events. As Martin Jay has pointed out in his discussion of female academics such as Gayatri Spivak and Judith Butler, whom he calls "performance artists," there is indeed a performative dimension to academia.[18] As Said pointed out, "an intellectual is an individual endowed with a faculty for representing, embodying, articulating a message . . . to as well as for, a public." Furthermore, "Not enough stock [has been] taken of the image, the signature, the actual intervention and performance, all of which taken together constitute the very lifeblood of every real intellectual."[19]

Although the academostar is a relatively recent phenomenon, its roots are to be found in the Hollywood star system and the spread of television into middle-class American households.[20] In the past leading scholars may have been influential, even famous, within their disciplines, yet they were almost always invisible to the public. This began to change with the rise of television as a popular medium of information and entertainment. The early 1950s were a period in the history of television when a university professor could become a television star, as the CBS station in Los Angeles learned in 1953 when Frank Baxter, an English professor at the University of Southern California, hosted *Shakespeare on TV.* To the network's surprise, the program became a hit throughout the country. In 1954, Baxter received two Emmy awards for "most outstanding male performer" and "best public affairs program."[21]

Unlike Baxter, Mead was not an immediate television hit after her initial appearances on the *Adventure* program. No one from a television network sought her out, as they did Baxter, to preside over her own series. Her television persona developed over time as she became more at ease with the medium. Throughout the 1950s and 60s Mead became known to an increasingly broad audience through her frequent appearances on commercial television where she was asked to comment on a variety of social issues ranging from the changing nature of the American family to Jacqueline Kennedy's role as first lady.

Making Mead a Celebrity

After the serendipitous success of *Coming of Age in Samoa*, Mead began to employ the services of a clipping agency to keep track of reviews of her books and the appearance of her name in the press.[22] She did not shy away from coverage by the press, well aware of how helpful it could be for the sale of her books. Her willingness to give generously of her time to journalists was one factor that contributed to her rise as a visible scientist. Beginning in 1930 she engaged a literary agent to promote her writing for the public.[23]

Although Mead's transformation into a media celebrity began with the success of *Coming of Age in Samoa* and continued with the publication of her next two books, it expanded exponentially in the postwar period.

Mead embraced every form of mass media available: she gave interviews to newspapers, appeared on radio talk shows, and wrote articles or was featured in numerous magazines from the *New Yorker* and the *Saturday Review* to *Mademoiselle*, *Life*, and *Time*. She also appeared in films that were televised in the United States and Canada and received worldwide attention through a United States Information Agency documentary about her.[24]

All this media exposure contributed to Mead's increasing fame, as evidenced by her name appearing in lists such one in the *Washington Post* in 1943 that included her as one of eight "outstanding woman in the modern world," along with Eleanor Roosevelt, Madame Chiang Kai-shek, and the Queen of England.[25] Mead, long an admirer of Eleanor Roosevelt, was probably pleased to have been included among such illustrious company.[26]

Hope Ridings Miller, the journalist who compiled the list, chose Mead because she was "one of the few women who have made their way brilliantly in a man's world and has become one of the world's foremost anthropologists. Because her business is the study of humanity and she has made a sensational success of it and because she is one of the most unassuming and yet more engaging persons it has even been my pleasure to meet."[27] Lists such as this one are personal, and thus idiosyncratic, but they also have a predictability to them, with specific names appearing again and again. Beginning in the 1940s, Miller's was just one of a number of such lists on which Mead's name began to be included.[28]

Ephemera of Fame

Upon her return from a trip to Europe in February of 1959, Mead attended a party in Greenwich Village where one of the guests, who worked for *Modern Screen* magazine, mentioned that he had just read about her in the *Celebrity Service Bulletin*, a daily publication that listed the comings and goings of the rich and famous.[29] Mead was included along with such stars of the entertainment world as Rosemary Clooney, Gary Cooper, the McGuire Sisters, Walter Winchell, and Douglas Fairbanks.[30] The entry about her said:

> Arriving in New York from Europe yesterday was the noted author and anthropologist MARGARET MEAD. Here to publicize her new book, *An Anthropologist at Work* (Houghton Mifflin), Miss Mead is recognized as one of America's foremost anthropologists today . . . Dr. Mead . . . recently told a meeting of the World Federation for Mental Health in Berlin, that utmost attention should be directed to the mental health of the world leaders who decide the prosperity or disaster of the entire human race. . . . Today, better known for her paperbound books and popular lectures than for her latest research on anthropology, Dr. Mead became famous at the age of twenty-seven with the publication of her first report, *Coming of Age in Samoa*. People all over the world were enchanted with the idea of this young woman who had gone off alone among the natives of a South Pacific island to see life on a lonely and lush patch of land in the sea. By concentrating on children she opened to herself and to science a realm of research—the living quarters of native women forever barred to men. During the war she returned to this country and worked in Washington—developing a new dimension of struggle, psychological warfare. She then turned to expand her interests to other scientific disciplines and new lands—England, France and Australia.[31]

While the bulletin mentions that Mead is an anthropologist and that she is returning to New York to publicize her new book, *An Anthropologist at Work* (a biography of Ruth Benedict), whoever wrote the entry thought it necessary to say that Mead was better known by the public for her "paperbound books and popular lectures than for her latest research on anthropology." Once again we see that by 1959 Mead is being singled out not simply because she is an anthropologist but also because she has become a well-known author and public speaker. Not so well known, however, that it was unnecessary to explain to readers of the bulletin exactly who Margaret Mead was and what she had initially become famous for. However, as the guest from the party remarked to Mead, the bulletin gave her more copy than most of their usual "celebrities of the day."[32]

Crossword puzzles are also useful indicators of a nation's collective (popular) cultural literacy at specific points in time. By 1959, Mead had become so widely known to the American public that her name and profession were used in a crossword puzzle, a sign, her twelve-year-old daughter Mary Catherine had once said, that one was truly famous.[33] The puzzle's clue asked for "a contemporary anthropologist."[34] Crossword puzzles, cartoons, and other ephemera of popular culture indicate that by

CROSSWORD PUZZLE

HORIZONTAL

1 Neglects
6 Convey
10 Small barracuda
14 Purposeful
15 Lily plant
16 Girl's name
17 Venture: 3 words
19 Garlands
20 Seraglio salon
21 —— Abner
22 Whimpers
24 Antilles Indian
26 Hold back
27 Energy
30 Anderson's "High ——"
32 Heath genus
35 Esau
36 Boundaries
38 Sinecure: slang
39 Unharmed
40 Proclamation
41 Favorites
42 Man's name: abbr.
43 Relish
44 Formerly
45 Great artery
47 Chinese "Yang and ——"
48 Insects
49 Tolerate
51 British historian
53 Cook partially
56 World War II battleground
57 Military decoration
60 Figment of the mind
61 Drastic remedy: comp.
64 Fashion
65 Subject, "Grapes of Wrath"
66 Atelier gear
67 City in Iowa
68 Cape
69 Harden

VERTICAL

1 10th century German king
2 Contemporary anthropologist
3 —— Chase
4 Bond
5 Undirected quantity: math.
6 Knock off work: 4 words
7 —— Khan
8 Small deer
9 Gull-like bird
10 Symbol of wealth: 2 words
11 Outstanding
12 Ludwig or Jannings
13 Soviet news agency
18 Evergreen
23 Native of: suff.
24 Food
25 Sucre is one of its capitals
27 Match
28 Boise's state
29 Shoot the works: 3 words
31 Settles
33 Apprehend
34 Church recesses
36 Foot: Latin
37 Vessel: abbreviation
46 Fuss
48 Victor and Thomas
50 Image: Greek
52 Duo
53 Egyptian cotton
54 Furniture style
55 Counterpart
57 Italian actress
58 Unhampered
59 Cubicle
62 Fleur de ——
63 Grimalkin

Solution to Saturday's Puzzle

Margaret: You have really attained distinction as the above testifies!

Tom Park 21/July/1959

Figure 8.1 "Mead" as the answer to the crossword puzzle clue: "Contemporary Anthropologist," 1959. (Newspaper unknown. Mead Archives, Manuscript Division, Library of Congress)

1959 Mead's reputation—her state of being famous for being famous—was sufficiently widespread that her comings and goings were worth being noted by a business whose business was celebrity.

The Rise of Talk Radio: Mead and the *Martha Deane Show*

While Mead's initial fame was the result of the success of her books and her steady stream of public lectures and articles in the popular press, beginning in the 1940s her appearance on radio talk shows such as the long-running syndicated program the *Martha Deane Show* extended her national renown even further.[35]

One of the first nationally broadcast talk radio programs, and one of the only shows hosted by a woman, the *Martha Dean Show* was produced in New York City. Between 1941 and 1973, when it ended, Mead appeared at least once a year on the program, often to promote a new book. In 1972, for example, when she published both *Blackberry Winter* and her book *Twentieth Century Faith*, she appeared on the program twice.[36] Because it was syndicated, listeners all over the country were introduced to Mead and her work, as well as to her sense of humor and pithy insights into American culture.

Margaret Mead, Henry Luce, and *Life* Magazine

Not only did Mead become a regular contributor to new radio and television programs that were being produced in New York City, she was also often featured in many of the mass-circulation magazines published there, such as *Life* and *Time*. A part of publishing magnate Henry Luce's Time corporation, Luce had started *Life* in 1936 as a magazine whose aim was to be an eyewitness to events great and small through the medium of photography. Much has been written about the role *Life* played in twentieth-century American culture in reinforcing certain images of an American way of life that Luce felt beneficial to the nation,[37] as well as the magazine's use of photography as "a microcosm of the ways in which a photographic aesthetic suffused not only the [American] Dream but the entire imagery of American modernity."[38]

Luce originated the concept of "The American Century," the idea that the twentieth century was the period in which the United States became the political, economic, social, and technological leader of the world. His larger goal with his Time, Inc. publications was to strengthen the American nation through a celebration of its diversity while at the same time uniting that diversity in the name of a stronger nation. He shared this goal with Mead.[39] Luce thought it was important that Americans know more about their nation and its diverse regions and ethnicities, and he found photography to be a particularly useful medium for this goal.

Iconoclastic and outspoken, Mead did not fit many of the stereotypes *Life* magazine promoted. Yet her concerns—the nature of the American family, the changes in post–World War II American culture, male-female relations—caused her to be embraced by magazines such as *Life* whose readers were eager to read what an expert had to say about American culture. In fact, the people at Time, Inc. had been tracking Mead for some time before she first appeared in *Life* magazine in 1959. As far back as 1940, a staff member at *Time* had written a memo suggesting that Mead was someone they should keep an eye on in the future:

Office Memorandum: Time, Inc.
To: Thomas Krug
From: Mary Johnson
Subject: Margaret Mead
Date: June 5, 1940

Apparently well known in the field of anthropology is Margaret Mead who is considered by many of the more serious men in the field to have prostituted the science by popularizing it in best-selling books. She is attached to the staff of the Museum of Natural History and is usually off on one of their junkets.

Some people were talking about her the other night and she seems to be worth a take-out when her next book appears. Not a particularly attractive woman she has nevertheless snared three husbands, all fellow-anthropologists I believe.

Suspiciously coincidental to anthropologists is her ability to decide to study one particular problem, take a junket to a remote part of the world and invariably find the answer to just that problem.

Much of the criticism of her from her colleagues is said to be because they too would like to make money—but don't know how.[40]

The memo writer is most interested in the controversial aspects of Mead's personality, as well as the innuendos about her that she gleaned from

Mead's fellow anthropologists. The memo shows the role that good old-fashioned gossip played in creating and perpetuating some of the stereotypes about Mead. Someone said something to someone else at a party, or a reception, or a lecture, and down it goes in a memo. It just so happens that the writer of this particular memo worked for a major national news magazine—one that did eventually pick up on Mead as a colorful personality.[41]

"Meadisms": The Original "Sound Bites"

In 1959, Ken Heyman, a young photographer working for *Life*, shot photographs of Mead to accompany an article about her titled "Close Up: Student and Teacher of Human Ways."[42] (Heyman had earlier shot the iconic image of Mead with a Balinese baby we saw in the Introduction.) The focal point of the article was a photograph of Mead seated in a comfortable chair surrounded by a bevy of attentive students, like a mother duck with her ducklings.

The article characterized Mead as "America's best-known woman scientist [a description that she probably bristled at as she resented being singled out for being a woman] and a shrewd critic of the natives at home in the U.S."[43] To provide evidence of Mead's insights into American culture—the real purpose of the piece—the article included a section titled "Meaty Meadisms about America." These nuggets of wisdom quote Mead on a smorgasbord of topics that range from American mothers ("motherhood is like being a crack tennis player or ballet dancer—it lasts just so long, then it's over") and fathers ("fathers are spending too much time taking care of babies") to leisure (of which Mead said there was not enough in contemporary America) and suburbia. An avid proponent of cities and the myriad of different ways of life they encompassed, Mead criticized suburbia as stunting children's knowledge of the world: "We're bringing up our children in one-class areas. When they grow up and move to a city or go abroad, they're not accustomed to variety and they get uncertain and insecure. We should bring up our children where they're exposed to all types of people."[44]

These "Meadisms" illustrate why journalists found Mead such a delight to interview, for she was highly quotable. She inevitably came up with snappy responses that were often quite novel or sharply critical of

Figure 8.2 Mead surrounded by students at International House, Columbia University; they are intently focused on what she has to say. The photograph was originally published in the "Close-Up" section of *Life* magazine, 1959. (Photograph courtesy of Ken Heyman)

the status quo. In this *Life* article, for example, Mead first came out with her oft-quoted statement about menopause. In talking about motherhood Mead had noted that, "We've found no way of using the resources of women in the 25 years of post-menopausal zest."[45]

We also see in the *Life* article the idea that anthropologists not only study "primitive," non-Western societies, but they also have insights into their own society. Although this idea had been associated with Mead since she first published *Coming of Age in Samoa*, beginning in the 1960s she gradually began to be associated more and more with the analysis of American society and the problems of the modern world as a whole.

Mead and the Problems of the Urban Jungle

In 1967, *Life* ran another interview with Mead titled "Close Up: We Must Learn to See What's Really New."[46] Like the earlier *Life* article about her, the focus of the piece was on what Mead had to say about contemporary American culture; it was subtitled, "Margaret Mead's Sound Insights into the Furor over Shifting American Morals."[47] In 1967, the United States was now in the midst of the Vietnam War, there were student protests on campuses across the nation, and the generation gap had threatened to split the American family apart. The nation seemed to be divided between old and young in a manner that it had not experienced since the 1920s when parents bemoaned the behavior of their children, especially of their young upstart daughters. As in the 1920s, Mead again had much to say to the American public about its youth, the generation gap, and its changing values.[48]

The article introduced Mead by saying that, "Most Americans picture her in pith helmet pursuing primitive tribes in the jungles of the South Seas. But Dr. Mead's home base is Manhattan. . . . It is the problems of urban jungles and family patterns of sexually liberated modern man—and woman—that she and her fellow anthropologists are increasingly called upon to examine."[49] Here we see the well-worn trope of "anthropologist as explorer" juxtaposed with the image of anthropologists at work in "the urban jungle" studying their own cultures' changing habits. What appealed to the editors of *Life* were Mead's provocative and original opinions that "spoke to both an alarmed older generation and to a restless youth." The article was accompanied by two photographs of Mead, one showing her at her desk in her office at the American Museum of Natural History studiously reading a text, the other—a rather unusual pose for Mead—pictured her seated with a colleague on the rocks that abut the reservoir in Central Park, the skyline of Manhattan silhouetted in the background. Using the same observational skills she honed "in the field" (represented by a small photo of her looking at a decorated skull from the Sepik region of New Guinea), Mead is "learning to see what's really new" in her own culture, represented here by the urban world of New York City.

Mead, Ken Heyman, and *Family*

If *Life* magazine's photography played an important role in the creation of a uniquely American style of twentieth-century modernity, then indirectly Mead played a role in the creation of that style through her influence on photographer Ken Heyman, who often took photos for the magazine. Heyman credits Mead with having discovered him and launching his career as a photographer.[50] They met in 1954 when he was a student in an anthropology course Mead taught at Columbia University. He was dumbfounded at her interest in him, especially when she invited him to accompany her as a photographer on a return research trip she made to Bali in 1957.[51]

Heyman not only accompanied Mead on several of her field trips, he also collaborated with her on two large-format, coffee-table-style books of photo essays, *Family* (1965) and *World Enough: Rethinking the Future* (1975). Mead wrote the text for both books and Heyman contributed the photographs. The title *Family* evoked that of an earlier book of photographs, *The Family of Man*, based on the hugely successful photography exhibition that Edward Steichen had curated at The Museum of Modern Art in New York City in 1955.[52]

Ten years later, Mead and Heyman published *Family*.[53] The theme of both *The Family of Man* and *Family* was the universality of the family as a social institution, as well as the metaphorical notion of the exhibition's title that all humans living on earth belong to one extended family. While a subtext of *The Family of Man*, exhibited in the aftermath of Hiroshima and Nagasaki and during the cold war had been an antinuclear weapons message, this part of the exhibition was excluded from *The Family of Man* book. Similarly, *Family* made no reference to the nuclear threat, and it was ostensibly nonpolitical. Instead, it stressed a basic anthropological premise—the universality, yet infinite diversity, of the family as the fundamental building block of human society.

Unlike *The Family of Man*, whose images were expected to speak for themselves, Mead's text guides one through the images. It was vintage Mead, extolling the numerous cultural permutations in the composition of the family worldwide, the role grandparents play in families, the roles of mothers and fathers, and the joys and frustrations shared among siblings.[54]

Selected as a Book-of-the-Month Club offering, the book club's blurb described *Family* as a "fascinating sort of world conference" where "the guests all seem somehow to know one another, because they have so much in common."[55] To assure the potential reader that the book was not just "warm and fuzzy," the reviewer noted: "there is no treacle about 'togetherness' in Mead's text. Dr. Mead never was a treacly writer anyhow, and all those cute youngsters aren't going to beguile her now. Her writing is generally in the measured tones of a scholar, with Mr. Heyman providing a sort of graphic counterpoint, variously amusing, spirited, comic, pathetic."[56]

Family was very much of its time, the period of postwar prosperity and the baby boom in the United States, and it also fit with the new postwar American ideology of "unity with diversity," the same message promoted by *The Family of Man* and one that Mead had been promoting for years. But *Family* was published at a moment when the generation gap was beginning to threaten the very foundations of the American family, providing all the more reason perhaps to wax nostalgic about such a fundamental institution. And as a Book-of-the-Month Club selection, the book helped Mead reach an ever-widening mainstream, middle-class audience.[57]

Mead as Environmentalist and "Earth Mother"

With the publication of *Family*, Mead had begun to produce a very different genre of popular work from her earlier ethnographies. Given its coffee-table format, *Family* did not pretend to be a scholarly work but was intended instead for a very broad general audience. A decade later, Mead and Heyman collaborated on a second photo-essay book titled *World Enough: Rethinking the Future*.[58] In contrast to the basically benign tone of *Family*, the aim of *World Enough* was to provoke people to think about their future and the future of our planet. While *Family* was grounded in a basic anthropological premise about the variability of this universal human institution, *World Enough*, while still reflecting anthropological topics (cultural evolution, the role of technology in culture change, and the inequities of technological development), was a more polemical and didactic book. It was Mead's clarion call to people to develop alternatives to the destructive course she saw humanity currently following. "While it is too late to return to the situation of the past," she said, "it is not too late to reverse the 'wrong turn' made a quarter of a century ago." The "wrong turn" to which she referred was what she believed to be the misguided effort of both developed and developing nations since 1945 "to solve all the major problems by extending to the poor countries the high technology and political centralization of the rich." Mead felt that we needed "to reassess our conceptions of progress, see the world as a fragile, endangered whole, and consider nature's and our own biological rhythms as sources of knowledge."[59]

What was innovative about *World Enough* was the decision to present Mead's argument visually. "Seeing" was an important dimension of the project, and the book's aim was "to view the contemporary world, in all its complexity, diversity, and rich contradiction, by condensing it to manageable size" and by "sharpening the focus of our eyes and thought."[60] The metaphors of vision, focus, and condensation of the vast and complex image of the diversity of the world's societies was juxtaposed with the metaphor of a "macroscopic" view of that diversity through the range of images gathered together in the book. The camera lens and the ethnographer's pen could collect a sample of the vast array of human diversity and focus the reader's thoughts on how this interconnected complexity could be dealt with. However, the pictures and the text remained separate from each other, two parallel experiences bound together by the uniting covers of the book.

Although *World Enough* made little impact on the public when it was published in 1975, and has subsequently been all but forgotten, the book represented Mead's increasing involvement with environmental concerns, as well as her belief in the value of images and their emotional impact. In this respect, *World Enough* symbolized her role during the 1960s and 70s as a "visible scientist" who offered her opinions on a range of environmental issues and the impact of technology on the quality of human life. She attended United Nations conferences on the Environment (Stockholm, 1972) and Urban Settlements (Vancouver, 1975) as a delegate of the United States.[61] She addressed congressional hearings on nuclear power reactors, air quality, and pollution. She participated in groups such as the American Rocket Society's Space Law and Sociology Committee that discussed the peaceful use of outer space and argued that social scientists should be included in the development of all scientific policies to ensure that scientists considered the impact of new technologies on society.[62] For example, since its inception in 1970, she also participated each year in Earth Day activities. Wrapped in her cape with her thumb stick in hand, her presence at these events added to her Earth Mother image.

While it has been said that anthropology ceased to be Mead's main focus after World War II, as she increasingly played the broader role of public intellectual and visible scientist,[63] it is more accurate to say that as a result of her activities during World War II, Mead transformed herself into a new kind of applied anthropologist, the precursor to today's public anthropologist. In this respect, she was the harbinger of the changes that continue to transform the field of anthropology today. One of a group of anthropologists who had worked for the government during World War II adapting anthropological methods to the study of a range of problems, from the rationing of food to psychological warfare, she had to rethink anthropology, its methods, and its uses.[64] Similarly, her return to Manus in 1953 led her to think more broadly about the effects of technological change on small-scale third world countries. Rather than simply limiting her focus to Manus, however, Mead used the insights she gained there to think about technology and cultural change more generally in her activities with newly created organizations such as the World Federation for Mental Health and the United Nation's UNESCO project on technology and change.[65] Thus, by the time Mead came to write the text for *World Enough*, she had been thinking about and observing the impact of technology on cultural change for over twenty years. Although the format for presenting her ideas might be new, for Mead, what she was doing was still anthropology.

Redbook Magazine: Mead's Grandmotherly "Expert Advice"

From 1965 until her death in 1978, Mead wrote a monthly column for the popular women's magazine *Redbook* that brought her name and her ideas to another significant sector of American society: young, primarily college-educated, married women in their twenties and thirties. Writing for popular magazines was nothing new for Mead; she had done so from the very beginning of her academic career. Also during the 1920s and 30s, Mead had often been the *subject* of articles in women's magazines and on the "women's pages" in newspapers that sought material about young women who were doing new and exciting things.

When Mead agreed to become a monthly columnist for *Redbook*, she was also following in the tradition of other opinionated and worldly women such as Eleanor Roosevelt and foreign correspondent Dorothy Thompson.[66] She was joined at *Redbook* by her longtime friend, Benjamin Spock, who contributed his own monthly column to the magazine.[67] The editors of *Redbook*, especially Sey Chassler, editor-in-chief of the magazine from 1965 until 1981, and his predecessor Robert Stein, saw themselves as publishing a magazine that was different from the long-standing women's magazines such as *Mademoiselle*, *Glamour*, *McCall's*, or the *Ladies' Home Journal*. Chassler considered *Redbook* to be less conservative politically and more willing to take risks in publishing controversial material than these other women's magazines.[68]

Although she began to write for *Redbook* late in her career (she was sixty-four when her first column appeared), it was also a propitious moment. During the mid-1960s and 1970s, American society was in the throes of several major social upheavals—the civil rights movement, the antiwar movement, the women's liberation movement, the Black Power movement—and magazines such as *Redbook* felt they could not simply defend the status quo. Instead, through the columns that Mead wrote, as well as through the polls the magazine conducted, *Redbook* attempted to offer a range of ideas and information about what readers and experts such as Mead and Spock thought about issues of current import. Their practice of polling readers began in 1960 as the result of the enormous number of responses they received when they asked them to write about their feelings of discontent with their role as housewives.[69] *Redbook* went on to poll readers on abortion, sex, the media's representation of women, and the women's movement. Using a social science firm to analyze the data, they then published the results in the magazine.

Chassler, although part of the old guard—in the sense that the editor-in-chief of a women's magazine was still a man (this changed in the 1980s)—was politically progressive and concerned about women's rights. He even credits himself with having pushed Mead further in her own acceptance of the feminist movement. "In the beginning," he said, "I think if you've read some of Mead's books you know that she dealt with the differences between men and women [by] arguing for a full world for each and equal contributions from each. She therefore did not want, at least I've always felt this, to confuse the argument by pushing women forward at the rate that the more active feminists were doing it at the time. But she came around."[70]

Chassler served on the committee that organized the first National Conference of Women, working alongside Bella Abzug and Shirley Chisholm. Indeed, it was Chassler who suggested that Mead be asked to be the keynote speaker at the convention, and it was he who helped persuade her to participate in the event. "There was a period," he said, "when Mead saw the ERA [Equal Rights Amendment] as simply a wistful symbol, but she came around to be a very strong advocate about three years before she died, and made a rousing speech at the National Conference of Women in Houston in 1977. That was one thing about Margaret—she would insist on not changing her mind, but she changed her mind when she was convinced."[71] In contrast to images of Mead as a champion of the feminist movement that often circulated in the media, Chassler gives us an image of Mead as someone who was cautious about the women's liberation movement as it developed during the 1960s and 70s, only slowly coming around to accepting aspects of it rather late in her life.

Mead's *Redbook* column offered a forum where she could express her ideas and opinions about a wide range of issues, not all of which were confined to the sphere of "women's issues" or "domestic issues," and most of which were infused with her anthropological brand of cultural relativism.[72] She chose topics in consultation with Chassler and Rhoda Metraux, her colleague and longtime companion.[73] To be sure, Mead used the column to advertise her own projects, such as *Margaret Mead's New Guinea Journal*, but she also listened to the *Redbook* readers, answering letters she received in response to her columns and following suggestions to write about specific issues. And she tried out new ideas. Her *Redbook* column, for example, was where she first wrote about curtailing the development of nuclear energy. Chassler remembers that he received a considerable amount of criticism for publishing that particular column: "There was a big fight on the matter of nuclear energy. The chief lobbyists threatened us with getting major advertisers to stop running ads in the magazine, General Electric, for example. But we didn't back down. Mead originally took up the idea in the late 1960s for us and then we followed with other pieces."[74]

As we saw earlier, it was also in *Redbook* that Mead published her first and only piece about bisexuality.[75] "Today," Mead wrote, "the recognition of bisexuality, in oneself and in others, is part of the whole mid-20th century movement to accord to each individual, regardless of race, class, nationality, age or sex, the right to be a person who is unique and who has a social identity that is worthy of dignity and respect."[76] Not many women, feminist or not, were able to publish such open-minded—indeed radical at the time—statements in a mainstream women's magazine.

The fact that Mead published provocative and challenging pieces in a popular magazine such as *Redbook* added to her credibility with many liberal middle-class Americans that she was a progressive, yet moderate, voice of wisdom during a period when Americans both young and old were unmoored and searching for answers. The grandmotherly figure of Dr. Mead (coupled with the equally grandfatherly, paternal figure of Dr. Spock) provided *Redbook*'s young married women, the predominant readership of the magazine, a source of sage advice and a comforting as well as thought-provoking voice—but one that was not that of their mothers!

"Urge Dr. Mead to Run for President"

—*Courier-Post*, Camden, New Jersey, April 2, 1971[77]

Perhaps the best insight into how Mead was perceived by liberal Americans in her later years is an attempt to draft Mead to run for president in the 1972 election. In 1971, Mrs. Mildred Rogers Crary, a former journalist and wife of a Washington, DC bureaucrat, launched a grass-roots campaign to get Mead to run. At the time, Richard Nixon was the incumbent president. Disgusted over Nixon's first campaign, the nation was increasingly divided over the war in Vietnam.

Mildred Crary had never even met Margaret Mead. But, dissatisfied with Nixon and the course of the nation during his presidency, Crary drafted a letter that called on American citizens to write to Mead and ask her to become a candidate for president in the 1972 election. She sent copies of her letter to newspaper editors throughout the United States, and local papers across the country published it. Crary's reasons for trying to draft Mead were varied, but foremost among them was Mead's image: "Candidate Mead," Crary wrote, "will not need an 'image' manufactured by Madison Avenue, because her 'image' is already clear and well known. Her 'image' is 'the real thing,' not a hypocritical put-on at all."[78]

The issue of *image* was important in the 1972 presidential election because the American public had been astonished to learn that both presidential candidates had used public relations firms in the 1968 presidential campaigns. Joe McGinniss, a young journalist from the *Philadelphia En-*

Figure 8.3 Cartoon of "Mead for President" that accompanied Mildred Rodgers Crary's letter to the editor published in the *St. Louis Post-Dispatch*, April 7, 1971. (Courtesy Mead Archives, Manuscript Division, Library of Congress)

quirer, published *The Selling of the President* in 1969. The book was McGinniss's account of the role PR men, former television producers, and admen from Madison Avenue had played in shaping Nixon's 1968 campaign strategy and the manipulation of his TV image.[79] While we take this practice for granted today, in 1969 people were outraged that candidates were being packaged and sold to the public by Madison Avenue. Hence, Mrs. Crary's emphasis on Mead's image as "the real thing."

In a backhanded reference to Nixon's penchant for changing his position on difficult or controversial issues, Crary pointed out that Mead was "possessed of a firm and organized basic philosophy and an integrity which will preclude wishy-washy shifts with political winds."[80] Then in order to substantiate Mead's ability to be the head of state, Crary cites Mead's decades of work as an anthropologist as evidence of her "profound knowledge of human relations, the basis of politics," as well as her ability to organize and successfully carry out scientific expeditions "to the far corners of the earth." She also felt that Mead's extensive contact with peoples and governments all over the world would be invaluable in the conduct of foreign affairs.[81]

Finally, and this seems to lie at the heart of Crary's promotion of Mead as a presidential candidate, Mead could "restore a bit of dignity to the office of President—or at least to the office of candidate for the President and to the campaign itself, a dignity sorely lacking nowadays." Only after having enumerated these substantial qualifications does Crary refer to the fact that Mead is a woman. Summing up her argument, she said that Mead's candidacy would "benefit from the reputation which she has already earned, from the respect she generates in both old and young, and from her appeal to both intellectuals and the common people. In short, Margaret Mead can win."[82]

Mrs. Crary's campaign to launch public support for Mead's candidacy did cause a number of people to write to Mead urging her to run for president. As the following letters demonstrate, for these individuals Mead represented the virtues of honesty, kindness, and all that was good in America:

> Dear Margaret:
> Please run for President next year! The White House needs some one honest and kind like you. You stand for all that is good in America. Like the American Dream. For the sake of the nation, Margaret, run for President in 1972.
> Sincerely,
> Al Mattera[83]

> Dear Margaret,
> . . . It really doesn't matter to me which ticket you run under—I'm voting for you no matter what. I'll be 18 years old on October 1. . . . We need somebody like you in Washington. Women's Lib is for you, youth is for you, ecologists are for you, doves (like me) are for you. How can you lose? Even the Lord is for you (I just asked him). So, the only real way you can be defeated is if you don't run! Margaret—for the sake of the Nation—I BEG you to run for President next year. Thank you!
> Sincerely and faithfully,
> John Gillerlair,
> Philadelphia, Pa.[84]

For this second writer, Mead's opposition to the Vietnam War and her antiwar stance was important.[85]

Mead wrote a letter in response to Crary's write-in campaign that was also carried by many newspapers. She said that even if she was asked by a large number of Americans she would not run for president because she felt that she could do more good for the country as a nonpartisan activist for the cause of peace. Moreover, she wrote, "I take political life seriously. I think a candidate must spend a lifetime apprenticeship, and I've been doing other things."[86]

Although Mead declined to be considered as a presidential candidate (a victorious election would have been a long shot anyhow), Crary's support of Mead and that of others provide insight into the public's view of her in the early 1970s, or at least the perspective of the antiwar, anti-Nixon element of the American public. Their letters present clear statements of what some liberal-minded Americans felt Mead represented—integrity, lack of pretense and dissemblance, maturity, wisdom, and the American Dream—as well as what they felt was lacking in American leadership at the time. Although Crary's movement to get Mead to run for president never got off the ground, the fact that she chose Mead as an alternative to the traditional male Republican and Democratic candidates was indicative of new ways of thinking about American democracy and the political process among mainstream, middle-class Americans, as well as the extent to which some Americans were disillusioned and frustrated with the status quo. The fact that Mead was female was incidental in Crary's mind. "Mead," she said, "can run for President as an individual, a learned, well known and loved person, who incidentally is a woman. Without depending or harping on feminism at all, she can do much to foster respect for women in public office just by demonstrating her capabilities as a human being."[87] She also represented integrity, industriousness, and intelligence, all qualities Crary and others felt should be associated with the role of the president.

Of course, there were many Americans both conservative and liberal who would have been opposed to Mead had she actually become a presidential candidate. Some of them who were of the more liberal persuasion would have opposed her not because of her politics, with which they might have been sympathetic, but because they were not impressed with her popular wisdom, which they found either simplistic or inane. One such critic was David Cort. His explanation for why so many Americans were enthralled by Mead was that we longed for a Mother Figure.[88] Well before Crary's actual bid to draft Mead, he wrote a satirical piece about "Mead for President" that was accompanied by a drawing of a young, prim, schoolmarmish Mead dressed in a conservative scholarly looking skirt and jacket, complete with Mead's signature eyeglasses and bobbed hair. The pièce de résistance was a small shrunken head that she dangled in one hand pendulum-like from a tuft of long hair.

In addition to individuals such as David Cort, there was also a group of antiwar activist anthropologists who will never forgive Mead for the stance she took in support of several anthropologists working in Thailand who were denounced by members of the American Anthropological Association for the role they had played during the Vietnam War as informants for the CIA in Southeast Asia.[89] And on the right there was J. Edgar Hoover, then head of the Federal Bureau of Investigation, and other political conservatives who viewed Mead as dangerous because of her antiwar stance and her progressive views on everything from sex and marriage to marijuana.

Mead and the FBI

The files on Mead kept by the Federal Bureau of Investigation began in 1941 and continued until 1975, just three years prior to her death. They were started because Mead needed clearance to help with the war effort by working in Washington for the National Research Council as secretary of the Committee on Food and Nutrition. (She initially did *not* receive clearance because her husband Gregory Bateson was considered an "alien" as he was a British citizen.[90]) Over the course of a decade Mead was interviewed five more times for government-related jobs for which she needed to undergo Loyalty of Government Employee investigations.[91]

Files on Mead between 1949 and 1954 indicate that as McCarthyism escalated in the United States, the FBI delved ever deeper into Mead's activities, questioning the politics of even such seemingly innocuous organizations as the Foster Parents' Plan for War Children (which Mead said she had joined because the organization supported and published the work of Dr. Anna Freud on the effects of war trauma on children), the Institute for Pacific Affairs (which the California Committee on Un-American Activities cited as a Communist front organization), and the United

Figure 8.4 Illustration for David Cort's article "Mead for President," *Monocle* magazine, 1963. (Illustration by Paul Davis. Courtesy Jane Temple Howard Archives, Rare Book and Manuscript Library, Columbia University)

China Relief (an organization author Pearl Buck had invited her to join in 1942). When asked if she had known that the organization was a Communist front, she said that she had thought the fact that Henry R. Luce and John D. Rockefeller where on the board of directors would have been sufficient evidence that the organization was not run by Communists.[92]

Reading page after page of FBI reports that repeatedly question the purpose and politics of such organizations one gains insight into the fears and suspicions that pervaded Washington, DC during the McCarthy era. But we also see how Mead learned to handle these investigations with a combination of forbearance and pique. For example, a detailed letter she wrote to the FBI in 1953 from Pere village in New Guinea shows that she had learned by then what aspects of her activities and background raised suspicion or confusion among FBI investigators. Mead went to great lengths to aid the investigators in their work, hoping to expedite the process, while trying to impress upon her interrogators the benign yet personally very important nature of her research. She was requesting government clearance so that she could serve as a U.S. representative to a meeting of the United Nations World Health Organization on "The Psychobiological Development of the Child":

> October 15, 1953
> (Written by Dr. Margaret Mead from the primitive village of Peri, Manus, Territory of Papua and New Guinea via Sydney, Australia. Recopied in her New York office.)
> These forms will have to be filled out in the inappropriate bustle of a primitive village, interrupted by requests to come and pull people out of fainting fits from cerebral malaria, or revive someone who had made an unsuccessful attempt at suicide, or to negotiate with wild-eyed bush people for enough fruit for my next meal. It is obviously a perfectly abominable place to try to fill out forms—and the time is short because I am so far from civilization, eight hours at least by small native canoe from the government station. But I do want very much to go to the conference, for which this clearance is required. It is the most important conference in my field, and the matters that come up there will shape my work for several years to come. Part of the work that I am doing here in New Guinea is designed for this conference—on the Psychobiological Development of the Child, and it is going to be pretty disappointing to have done all this work, endured all the privations and vexation of living on smoked fish in a native village, and then not to be able to present my material.

She continues:

> It seems to me that the least I can do, in getting these forms in late, and it being the sort of clearance it is—filled with little known words and small, obscure scientific endeavors—is to provide as many clues as possible to make the work of the investigator easier . . .
>
> After I have done all this, the investigator will probably wish that somebody else had been handed this one, and I don't blame him a bit. At the same time, if the leads I give are followed, a great many of these things can be checked by methods which are easier than those often used by investigators who have to deal with so many kinds of people that they never have time to perfect all the appropriate short cuts.[93]

It is obvious that Mead is pulling out all the stops when she describes herself filling out these forms in the remote "primitive" village of Pere, in between thwarting suicides and attacks of malaria, at least eight hours away (by small native canoe no less!) from civilization. At the same time, she wants to appear sympathetic and helpful to the investigators who will have to deal with her case (although it is also clear that she considers the whole thing to be an incredible imposition on her and a waste of everyone's time—hers as well as the poor investigators). This is pure vintage Mead at her most manipulative and, at the same time, ingratiating best. In the end, she was allowed to attend the conference. On the five different occasions that Mead was interviewed by the FBI and other government agencies, she always received clearance for her government employment. However, the FBI continued to be interested in Mead because she had been studying the Soviet Union, even though this study had been conducted "at a distance," using Russian informants currently living in the United States. When her former supervisor for the project, which had been conducted for the RAND Corporation, was asked to testify on her behalf, he stated that the results of her study were published in her book, *Soviet Attitudes towards Authority* (1951) and that "since the book was critical of the Soviet system that surely was testimony to Dr. Mead's anti-Communist attitude."[94]

Repeatedly, individuals who knew Mead were asked to testify on behalf of her loyalty to the United States and to American democracy, which they always answered affirmatively.[95] And yet the files also include allegations that stem as far back as 1933 that "one Margaret Meade [*sic*], of New York City, was a communist and a secretary of the League of Homeless Women." "This information," the report states, "was obtained from the August 18, 1933 issue of the *Daily Worker*, a Communist newspaper." The report concludes by saying that, "No other substantiating information was developed in this connection in this investigation."[96]

In the reports from the 1960s, more immediate concerns about Mead stemmed directly from her antiwar activities as well as other controversial positions she took during that turbulent decade. A detailed report from November 8, 1962, gives an account of how a Special Agent (SA) of the FBI had ascertained that Mead had traveled to Montreal, Canada, to deliver a speech advocating world peace as part of a conference held in conjunction with Women for International Cooperation Year. The SA had obtained the information "telephonically," that is, by placing a call to the "subject's secretary under a guise of a student interested in subject's efforts on behalf of world peace."[97]

One of the final entries in the files is a letter sent from a resident of Bronxville addressed to the president of the National Broadcasting Corporation, with a copy sent to J. Edgar Hoover, dated October 29, 1969. The author stated his objections to NBC, having presented Mead's testimony to a congressional committee in which she gave evidence favoring the use of "pot." "This was a real shocker," the letter writer proclaimed, as, "in short, the presentation in question indirectly condoned the use of 'pot' by the youth of this country." The letter concluded with the statement: "The audio and audio visual news media, by gearing itself to the ultra-left and presenting editorial matter as news is abusing its privileges under the constitution and causing a polarization of thinking that is already leading to extremism right and left and could ultimately lead to revolution."[98]

Such accusations of the news media's "left-wing politics" are not new, and the letter writer was not the only individual to be shocked by Mead's testimony—the governor of Florida, disapproving of Mead's condoning of marijuana, called her "a dirty old lady."[99] At a time when the Students for a Democratic Society were bombing government facilities and campus protests were shutting down universities across the country, Mead was far from radical in her politics. However, the fact that the letter writer sent a copy of his letter to the FBI, who dutifully filed it away in their Mead files along with other reports of Mead's attendance at antiwar rallies in New York, her televised conversations with "Negro" author James Baldwin,[100] and her attempts to bring about an exchange of Soviet and

American children in an effort to convince parents—and the governments—of both the USSR and the United States that cooperation and disarmament was the sanest and healthiest choice for the future citizens of both countries,[101] demonstrates that a conservative segment of the American public—and the government—continued to view Mead's liberal politics and activities with suspicion. No wonder Mead had been content to stay out of presidential politics, rightly arguing that she was more effective if she did not hold an elected office.

Mead's Celebrity, or "Mead as Mead"

Although Mead received many awards and honorary degrees during her life, there was one award that eluded her: the Nobel Peace Prize. She once voiced her disappointment, to a former student, in having been overlooked for the prize.[102] While on the one hand one might see her desire to receive the prize as hubris, on the other hand it was not unreasonable for her to have aspired to receive it. She had achieved a level of international fame and recognition for her work as an anthropologist and as a humanitarian that put her in the running for the award; her fellow "visible scientist," Linus Pauling, had received the prize in 1962, and individuals or organizations associated with the United Nations had also been favored as laureates.[103] Moreover, her desire for this particular prize also reveals what was important to her and her image of herself: to have made an effort toward ensuring that human beings and human society would continue in the future; to have worked toward achieving some small modicum of peace among warring nations and peoples, and to have done so with the tools of anthropology, the discipline she had championed throughout her career.

At the American Museum of Natural History in New York the exhibition about Mead at the entrance to the Hall of the Peoples of the Pacific—a hall that Mead had originally designed—highlights her public persona. Along with other Mead memorabilia, such as the Presidential Medal of Honor that she received posthumously from President Jimmy Carter, there is a mannequin draped in one of her red wool capes with a thumb stick nearby. A placard notes that if Mead wanted to escape being recognized on the street, she said that all she had to do was *not* wear her cape

Figure 8.5 Margaret Mead's signature cape and thumb stick on display outside the Hall of the Pacific, American Museum of Natural History, May 2007. (Photograph by the author)

or carry her thumb stick. Mead's celebrity—like celebrity in general—was based in part on her personal style and eccentricity. Paradoxically, Mead was also liked by the media and the public precisely because she was considered *not* to be contrived or eccentric, but because she was always herself—or was perceived to be so.[104] As her colleague Martha Wolfenstein had said about Mead, "She's really a marvelous movie actress . . . which isn't acting but being yourself."[105]

The idea of people playing themselves is not unique to movies or television. As Wendy Doniger, a scholar of mythology and religion, has written, the theme of self-imitation is found in the myths and literature of many different cultures throughout history. Especially as people age it is not uncommon for them to become caricatures of themselves, consciously attempting to give the people who know them well the version of themselves that they expect. This practice of self-impersonation is even more common among people who are famous and well known to the public.[106] Thus, as Mead became better known to the American viewing public, people expected a certain kind of behavior from her, as well as a certain image. And the person Mead became best at performing was herself.

We have seen ways—both large and small—in which Mead and the media capitalized on certain of her attributes and accomplishments so that over the course of the twentieth century her celebrity increased. I have suggested that Mead was one of the last independent public intellectuals, a type associated with the first half of the twentieth century, and also the first of a new type of celebrity academic, or "academostar," that has become increasingly prevalent today. Using Rae Goodell's category "visible scientist," we have seen Mead as an exemplar of the type of media-savvy intellectual who was willing to speak out on a range of social, scientific, and political issues beyond her immediate area of expertise at a time when the public increasingly desired such individuals.

In Mead's case, we can see very clearly that the confluence of different forms of mass media—magazines, newspapers, radio, and especially television—played a crucial role in the escalation of her fame. It was a condition that Mead thrived in. She worked hard at maintaining her fame: writing, lecturing, appearing before congressional hearings, and participating in meetings, conferences, and symposia. She was also very media savvy in her creation of a particular image, one that fit her body type, her age, and her personality.

But Mead also believed that anthropology should be of interest and of use to everyone. She thought that the interdisciplinary nature of her research, the fact that she collaborated with psychologists and psychiatrists, nutritionists, child development and education specialists, sociologists, urban planners, and theologians, also made her work appealing to the public. She attributed her foresight or ability to discern and anticipate what issues would be of vital interest and concern to people to her acute powers of observation and a particular worldview. When she traveled to different countries or parts of the United States to attend conferences or give talks, she said, "I pay attention. I think I see more of what's happening. Most scientists most of the time are pretty busy with their own material, and they go to another country, meet the chemists there or the physicists there, and they don't look at the whole country."[107] Finally, she said (one suspects she said it with a mischievous twinkle in her eye), "I make much better newspaper copy as a woman than I would as a man."[108]

Mead was aware of how important her gender was to her success. But that was not all; as Goodell noted: "For the public and the press, Mead had a remarkable and successful combination of ingredients: she was readable, relevant, colorful, controversial. Journalists were quick to appreciate these characteristics, which have matured and magnified over the years, as she continues to lecture, write, and speak out in the press on a variety of issues, changing topics with changing times."[109] Goodell's observations are underscored by David Dempsey in a 1970 profile of Mead for the *New York Times Magazine*: "Unlike most of her colleagues, who bury themselves in the tribal customs of primitive man, Mead is visible, a willing plunger into modern social controversy who projects herself as a prophetess on almost every subject that concerns the human condition. To a society troubled by its own shifting folkways, and hungry for guidance in coping with them, she is a poor man's anthropologist."[110]

C H A P T E R 9

The Posthumous Mead, or Mead, the Public Anthropologist

I have been publicly discussed, lambasted and lampooned, lionized and mythologized, called an institution and a stormy petrel . . .
—Margaret Mead[1]

Death, the cliché assures us, is the great leveler; but it obviously levels some a great deal more than others.
—Alden Whitman, obituary writer, *New York Times*[2]

Death was the major event in Mead's life that she was not able to control. Her fame, hard work, intelligence, the unfinished projects waiting for her, all these things were supposed to protect her from the inevitable. She was not ready to die and she was angry at the prospect of dying.[3] However, after several months of illness she died of pancreatic cancer on November 15, 1978. Her death was announced nationwide on evening news broadcasts, and soon after obituaries, appreciations, and editorials about her appeared in newspapers throughout the country. These offer more images of Mead. In reading her obituaries today it is apparent that many of them took their lead, as well as much information, from the obituary Alden Whitman wrote for Mead that appeared on November 16 on the front page of the *New York Times*.[4]

Whitman described Mead as "not only an anthropologist and ethnologist of the first rank but also something of a national oracle on other subjects ranging from atomic politics to feminism."[5] The following week, Elizabeth Peer also described Mead as an oracle in *Newsweek*: "For 50 years Margaret Mead was the world's most visible—and most vocal—

anthropologist. Her research into primitive societies cast light on our own, and when she died last week at 76, she had become a national oracle with her unpredictable and peppery views on every issue from nuclear family to nuclear war."[6] Anthropologist Clive Kessler elaborated on the oracle image, saying, "She became a public or national institution, a secular oracle, a modern sphinx, invoking her anthropological understanding to pose the riddles of her own discordant culture."[7]

In addition to the image of Mead as oracle or prophet, another image in a *New York Times* editorial was Mead as "Grandmother to the World," a variation on the theme of Mead as "Mother to the World" that *Time* magazine had initiated a decade earlier.[8] However, when *Time* ran its own obituary for Mead, it had adjusted its description of her accordingly, now calling her "fond grandmother to the global village."[9] The *New York Times* began its editorial with a description of Mead: "Draped in her grandmotherly shawl, brandishing her staff, she would command attention—and admonish an errant world to mend its ways." Noting that she was probably the best known scientist in contemporary America, it gave the following insight into her renown: "Journalists who visited her cluttered office at the American Museum of Natural History found her compulsively quotable . . . with the advent of electronic journalism, she mastered the two-minute interview and talk show banter."[10]

Mead as "Global (American) Citizen"

In addition to the epithet "grandmother to the global village," the press also labeled Mead a "citizen of the world," in part because she had spent so much of her life living in and studying cultures other than her own. They also did so because she had been an internationalist who, along with other women such as Eleanor Roosevelt and author Pearl Buck, had championed the creation of the United Nations and the United States' support of it. And they did so because Mead had been global in her vision, seeing postwar nations new and old becoming ever more interconnected in terms of economics, technology, communication, travel, and social institutions. Even her interest toward the end of her life in human settlements, housing, and urban planning had a global perspective as she considered the significance that the majority of the world's population now lived in cities.[11]

Mead's death occurred within a week of that of another well-known American, the painter Norman Rockwell. Reflecting on this coincidence, Guy Wright, a columnist for the *San Francisco Examiner*, wrote an editorial that contrasted these two very different individuals and their contributions to American society. On the surface, Wright said, the two of them had little in common: "Rockwell was an unassuming giant. Dr. Mead enjoyed her towering fame. She used it to 'give the country a scolding,' as she put it, when she felt one was needed."[12] Rockwell was famous for his realistic paintings that showed an idealized, often romanticized, America, paintings that had appeared on the cover of the weekly magazine *Saturday Evening Post* during the Great Depression and throughout World War II. As Wright suggested, Rockwell's paintings "showed us how we were supposed to be."[13]

In contrast, Mead had left the United States for long sojourns in the South Pacific in order to "show us that the American Way isn't the only way at a time when we needed a lesson in tolerance." The similarity between Rockwell and Mead, according to Wright, was the role each played as social commentator. Working in quite different ways, they were "curiously complementary in what they contributed."[14]

Implicit in Wright's description of Mead is the image of her as a scolding mother seeking to discipline her sometimes-unruly children—the American public—and to set them on the right track by reminding us that we were not the only "kids on the block." For Wright, at least, Mead symbolized a curb on our ethnocentrism and a reminder of America's need to be tolerant of the way of life of others, both at home and abroad. But also, Wright seems to imply, underlying Mead's harangues was a benevolent maternal affection for her country and her desire for America to improve itself. As he points out, Mead "showed us hidden realities in our lives, often painful realities. But she wasn't just twisting the knife. By turning to cultures of the South Pacific for comparisons and contrasts, she helped us to understand and accept ourselves, maybe even improve ourselves."[15]

Mead also died within a week of Janet Flanner, a journalist for the *New Yorker* who was the magazine's longtime Paris correspondent.[16] Newspaper columnist Paul Greenberg wrote an editorial commenting on the loss of these two remarkable women. The connection he saw between them was that they were both "writers whose descriptions of other cultures brought to life the people, events, and ways of life of far away places."[17] Greenberg's discussion of Flanner and Mead not only indicates his personal admiration for them, but his reference to the *New Yorker* also reminds us that both Flanner and Mead—who had been the subject of a *New Yorker* profile—were known primarily to middle- and upper-middle-class Americans, the individuals who typically subscribed to the *New Yorker.*[18]

Mead, however, was known to a wider public, and Greenberg appreciated that throughout her career she had "retained the no-nonsense, plain-Jane style that made *Coming of Age* not only instructive but a good read. Whatever the quality of the ideas whizzing through her always open mind, she never developed airs; she handled abstract sociological theories like Julia Child working on a good slab of meat." She had also come to "symbolize the challenges and triumphs of her sex in twentieth century America."[19] Greenberg's reference to Julia Child alluded to another quintessentially American woman who also became an icon, a symbol of middle-class America's postwar embrace of gourmet food and continental cooking. However, although all three women represent the hard won achievements of independent, career-minded American women, Greenberg singles out Mead for the distinction of having become a symbol both of and for twentieth-century American women.[20]

Another editorial about Mead's death made her populist appeal more explicit. Titled "2 Kinds of Leaders—Making Us Better," it noted that fifty years earlier, in 1928, two events had occurred that "began to shape the American way of life. Margaret Mead published a book. Walt Disney drew Mickey Mouse. Each event made America—and the world—better."[21] Mead, the editorial pointed out, had become a leading scientist in a male-dominated profession as well as "an idol and advisor to young and old." It also noted that, "with *Coming of Age in Samoa* . . . [Mead] suggested that Americans might just look at themselves as causing problems in the American way of life."[22] Echoing sentiments similar to those of Guy Wright, this editorial also celebrated Mead for calling her fellow Americans to task and thus helping to make "America—and the world—better."

Margaret Mead, Mickey Mouse, Janet Flanner (and the *New Yorker* magazine), Julia Child, and Norman Rockwell have all come to represent different aspects of American culture to various segments of the American population over the course of the twentieth century. What is striking about this constellation of symbols, however, is the fact that Mead, unlike Flanner and Child, transcended the bounds of her own social class and came to be known—as did Mickey Mouse and Norman Rockwell's paintings—by a much broader range of American society than the more limited worlds of the readers of the *New Yorker* or *Mastering the Art of French Cooking*.[23]

Finally, it is informative to see what foreigners had to say about Mead. In his obituary for *Nature* magazine, the British anthropologist Meyer Fortes acknowledged Mead's "unique career" and "her boundless energy and phenomenal productivity" that earned her "world-wide fame." He pronounced that she had "a place in the social history of the United States" because of her dynamic influence "on the development of education and moral ideas and values after World War II."[24]

He ended his essay with the observation that "a phenomenon like Margaret Mead could perhaps not have emerged in any other country than modern America."[25] Although he does not explain why he considers Mead to have been a distinctly American creation, it is telling that he made the observation.[26] For it is true that Mead was a distinctly modern American phenomenon, both in the sense that modern America, more than other country, has during the twentieth century perfected the creation of "phenomenon" such as Mead, of media celebrities in general and of academics as celebrities in particular. It is also true in the sense that Mead, more so than any of the other "visible scientists" with whom she has been associated, came to be a truly *American* phenomenon, representing not only the achievements and struggles of twentieth-century American women but also a set of ideas and values that represent America and how Americans like to think of themselves: energetic, independent, open-minded, good-hearted, sometimes willful and sharp-tongued, but ultimately open to criticism and willing to change. Of course, as we will soon see, some of the very qualities that had endeared Mead to many Americans, also made her—and her fame—objectionable, especially to non-Americans.

The Mead-Freeman Controversy as Media Spectacle

Five years after her death Mead's name was in the news again. On January 31, 1983, the *New York Times* published a front-page article announcing that a "New Samoa Book Challenges Margaret Mead's Conclusions."[27] What was astonishing, in addition to the fact that the article appeared on the front page of the paper, was that the book would not be published for another two months. Harvard University Press gave the *Times* an advance copy of *Margaret Mead and Samoa: The Making and Unmaking of an Anthropological Myth*, written by Derek Freeman, a professor emeritus of anthropology at the Australian National University (ANU), assuming correctly that Freeman's attack on Mead's Samoan research—work that she had done in the 1920s—was so provocative they could not resist the scoop. And, indeed, for several months that spring, talk about Freeman's accusations that Mead had simply been outright wrong in her conclusions about Samoan society reverberated through the halls of academia and throughout the media as well.

Talk show hosts such as Phil Donahue devoted entire programs to the controversy. Since Mead had already been dead for five years it was impossible to hear her side of the story, but Freeman was flown over from Australia, and Mead's daughter Mary Catherine Bateson (a linguistic anthropologist) often appeared on television in lieu of her mother, as did several other sociocultural anthropologists who had done research in Samoa.

Derek Freeman, seventeen years Mead's junior, had been born in New Zealand and received his doctorate in anthropology from Cambridge University. He later went to Canberra to teach at ANU. After having been expelled from conducting further research in Borneo, where he had suffered a mental breakdown, in 1965 he went to Western Samoa to conduct research there, since he thought that Mead had been wrong in many of her Samoan findings. Although Freeman published a few technical articles about Samoan culture, he had published nothing critical of Mead's Samoan research until his 1983 book.[28] He waited so long, he said, because he needed access to archival records in American Samoa, which he was only able to get in 1981.[29] Freeman asserted that the Samoan people are intensely competitive; that they have high rates of homicide, assault, and rape; that they are extremely prone to fits of jealousy; and that not only are they *not* permissive of casual lovemaking, but that they practice a "cult of female virginity that is carried to a greater extreme than in any other culture known to anthropology."[30] On many accounts Freeman's description of Samoan culture was diametrically opposed to Mead's.

In addition to the *New York Times*, many newspapers; magazines such as *Time*, *Newsweek*, and *Life*; and a slew of other popular and professional science journals reviewed the book or covered the controversy.[31]

Science writer Hal Hellman even included the controversy in his book *Great Feuds in Science: Ten of the Liveliest Disputes Ever.*[32] Anthropologists cited example after example of erroneous and self-serving scholarship in Freeman's book: his use of partial quotes, his lifting material out of context, the spurious logic of some of his conclusions.[33] While the initial *New York Times* article reported that "several of Professor Freeman's professional colleagues note that his own personality has complicated the dispute," saying that, "He is, unfortunately, a difficult person," the press did not mentioned Freeman's personal history of mental breakdowns and his notoriously tempestuous temper.[34]

Despite the many sound criticisms made of Freeman's book, there are several reasons why his attack on Mead became such a media event. Foremost among them was Mead's fame. By the time Freeman published his attack, Mead was internationally renowned, dead, and unable to respond. Moreover, here was a little known David from "Down Under" taking on the reputation of a mighty American Goliath, albeit one unable to defend herself. The media loves controversy and the public is always eager to read or hear about the tarnishing of the reputation of the famous.

Two additional dimensions of Freeman's critique caused his book to be newsworthy. One was the impact *Coming of Age in Samoa* had on American society. The media suggested that if Mead had been mistaken about aspects of Samoan culture then perhaps the American public had been misled in making changes to their own culture based on insights Mead had drawn from her Samoan research. In an article titled "Bursting the South Seas Bubble: An Anthropologist Attacks Margaret Mead's Research in Samoa," *Time* magazine stated the issue succinctly:

> The book [*Coming of Age in Samoa*] made Mead a hero among scholars and non-scholars alike. Bertrand Russell and Havelock Ellis liked her findings on sex, marriage, and child rearing and cited them often. Mead became the natural ally of those who promoted free education, relaxed sexual norms and green-light parenting intended to give American youngsters the trouble-free adolescence enjoyed in Samoa. Says Manhattan Psychologist Otto Klineberg, "She had a very definite influence in shaping public opinion, similar to that of Dr. Spock. Mead and Spock reduced the emphasis on the biological side of childhood and adolescence and changed the pattern of child rearing."[35]

The article ended by saying that "if Freeman is correct, Mead succeeded in swaying the minds of liberal educators and psychologists mostly by dramatic but mistaken references to primitive living."[36] The connections that *Time* alleged existed between Mead's statements in *Coming of Age in Samoa* and the beliefs and practices of liberal educators and psychologists were later expanded upon by Allan Bloom in *The Closing of the American Mind*. According to Bloom, "sexual adventurers like Margaret Mead and others who found America too narrow told us that not only must we know other cultures and learn to respect them, but we could also profit from them. We could follow their lead and loosen up, liberating ourselves from the opinion that our taboos are anything other than social constraints. We could go to the bazaar of cultures and find reinforcement for inclinations that are repressed by puritanical guilt feelings."[37]

Bloom felt that the greatest damage to higher education and American democracy was caused by the idea of cultural relativism (a concept that he sometimes glosses as *openness*) that anthropologists like Mead introduced to Americans. "History and social science," Bloom lamented, have been "used in a variety of ways to overcome prejudice. We should not be ethnocentric, a term drawn from anthropology, which tells us more about the meaning of openness. We should not think our way is better than others. The intention is not so much to teach the students about other times and places as to make them aware of the fact that their preferences are only that—accidents of their time and place."[38] For Bloom, "all such teachers of openness had either no interest in or were actively hostile to the Declaration of Independence and the Constitution," because both these documents *already* protect the rights of the individual regardless of race, sex, or class. Instead, what cultural relativism has done is eliminate the possibility of the quest for "the truth" and "the Good."[39]

Bloom published *The Closing of the American Mind* in 1987 during a decade when the country was experiencing a period of political conservatism under the leadership of President Ronald Reagan, his fellow Republicans, and the New Right. Freeman's critique of Mead offered individuals such as Bloom, who considered the principle of cultural relativism that Mead and her fellow Boasians had expounded to be the source of many of the nation's contemporary problems, additional fuel for their antiliberal, antimulticulturalist arguments.[40]

Directly related to the issue of cultural relativism is the more general and long-standing debate within various fields of science referred to as "the nature-nurture debate." The two are related through the concept of cultural determinism. Other terms for *nurture* include *the* [social] *envi-*

ronment or *cultural determinism* versus biological determinism or *innate human nature*. Mead was associated with the concept of cultural relativism and also with the notion that cultural factors play as dominant a role in determining aspects of human behavior as biological factors. It was this issue—nature versus nurture, or biological versus cultural determinism—that Boas had charged Mead to investigate in Samoa.

Just as E. O. Wilson had argued in his controversial 1975 book, *Sociobiology: The New Synthesis*,[41] Freeman proposed a synthesis between biology and culture. And like Wilson he too emphasized the role of biology as the *primary* determinant of human behavior. Freeman's ultimate goal in his critique of *Coming of Age in Samoa* was to demonstrate the falsity of Mead's conclusions about the importance of culture in the determination of human behavior: "Mead was in error in her depiction of the nature of adolescence in Samoa. . . . This being so, her assertion in *Coming of Age in Samoa* of the absolute sovereignty of culture over biology is clearly invalid."[42]

While neither Mead nor Boas had ever claimed "the absolute sovereignty" of culture over biology, Freeman claimed that Mead's emphasis on cultural determinism had set anthropology on the wrong track. He felt it was his mission to rectify this mistake. Unlike Wilson, however, Freeman never provided a model or theory that explained how a synthesis of biological and cultural factors would work. However, science journalists used Freeman's denunciation of Mead's theory of cultural determinism as an opportunity to promote Wilson's version of sociobiology as an alternative explanation of human behavior.[43]

It was exactly this aspect of the debate that prompted members of the Department of Anthropology at Columbia University to write a letter to the editor of the *New York Times*, published the day after the paper's front-page article about Freeman's book, that chastised the *Times* for uncritically accepting Freeman's argument. They argued that, "the Mead-Freeman issue casts little light on heredity, or environment." In fact, they said, "Freeman's position is that the oppressiveness of Samoan society was the source of manifold behavioral disturbance among young people, a radically different view from Mead's but still a cultural interpretation." Moreover, "whatever may be the Samoan facts, subsequent research in other parts of the world has substantiated [Mead's] essential theoretical stance" that was the position that most anthropologists supported. They concluded by noting that, "As for the reliability of ethnological data, this is hardly the first time that anthropologists—and sociologists and physicists—have looked at the same thing and seen different facets of reality. This is called science."[44]

But the damage had already been done. As Professor Bradd Shore said at a symposium about the controversy at Barnard that April: "The publicity surrounding Derek Freeman's unhappy book about Mead and Samoa has taken on something of a life of its own, strangely unconnected with anything approaching fact. In some corners one senses that peculiarly American joy at deconstructing yet another American hero, and in the process Margaret Mead and the enterprise of anthropology she helped to found have been distorted and trivialized."[45]

Looking at the public image of anthropology and anthropologists from an angle that had received far less attention in the press than the focus on Mead and Freeman, James Sterba, a reporter for the *Wall Street Journal*, actually traveled to American Samoa in order to find out what impact Freeman's book had on the Samoans.[46] Sterba found himself to be but another notebook-toting visitor to the "tranquil" islands: "To disrupt this modern, heavily subsidized tranquility has come of late an assortment of what Samoans call Palagis, or foreigners, with free love on the brain. They arrive in commuter planes from Pago Pago, carrying cameras, notebooks, TV equipment and word of a hubbub beyond the horizons." Local Samoans, who had seen anthropologists come and go over the years, simply regarded Freeman as "the latest to assert that the Mead study was essentially bunk" and greeted the revelation "with the Samoan words for 'So what's new?' "[47]

Doing a little investigative reporting, Sterba visited the local library, where he discovered that *Coming of Age in Samoa* had been checked out only twice in the last six years: "Much more popular is a book called *Tales from the Margaret Mead Taproom*, featuring Doonesbury comic strips by Garry Trudeau and satirical musings on modern Samoa by Nicholas von Hoffman, who wrote that Samoans 'say they just made up every kind of sexy story for the funny *palagi* lady because she dug dirt.' "[48]

Sterba also visited a village where he found an eighty-four-year-old woman, Soaifetu Taula, who had known Mead when she was in Samoa. Taula said that she had accompanied Mead on a sixty-mile boat trip to the village of Loaloa so that Mead could get her thighs tattooed in the traditional island manner. Although Taula warned Mead that the process would be painful, Mead had told Taula that she wanted the mark "so that when she went back to America, people would pay to see her dance."[49] If one needed any additional proof to back up the statement that Samoans like to accommodate people by telling them what they want to hear, Taula's story about Mead's tattoo certainly provides it, along with evidence that they also have a great sense of humor!

While Sterba spoke with American Samoans about Freeman and his criticisms of Mead's Samoan research, a reporter for the *New York Times* spoke with the prime minister of Western Samoa about controversy. "To be frank," Prime Minister Tofilau Eti said in his interview, "I think that both anthropologists are wrong. The best type of person to write about Samoa is a Samoan," to which he added that his country has many qualified scholars educated mostly in New Zealand and Australian universities. Moreover, while he agreed with Freeman's critique of Mead's account of youthful sexuality being condoned by Samoans, he was incensed by Freeman's assertions of high rates of rape, jealousy, and aggression in Samoan society.[50] Samoan scholars also spoke out against both Mead and Freeman, finding each of their descriptions to be negative caricatures of more complex and nuanced behavior.[51]

More Media Spectacles

The irony of the Mead-Freeman controversy is, of course, that it made Freeman a media celebrity himself and acquired symbolic meaning.[52] It was no longer simply "Margaret and the Giant-Killer," as one magazine described the controversy, but "the Anthropologist from the Antipodes"[53] (Australia and New Zealand) against the mighty Mead, symbol of the United States. This symbolic transformation occurred in two forms—a documentary film made for television by an Australian filmmaker, Fred Heimans, and a play titled *Heretic*, written by David Williamson, one of Australia's best-known playwrights whose work for the stage and movie screen was widely known in Australia and internationally.[54]

The documentary, also titled *Margaret Mead and Samoa*, is not a balanced journalistic overview of the Mead-Freeman controversy but a contribution to the debate in its own right, as it purports to present startling new evidence that proves that Mead was duped by her Samoan informants, and thus wrong in her conclusions about Samoan culture.

SYDNEY**THEATRE**COMPANY
presents the world premiere of

Figure 9.1 *Heretic* playbill, 1995. (Playbill reproduced courtesy of the Sydney Theatre Company Archives)

Although the film's main character is Freeman, its dramatic climax is the revelation made by Fa'apua'a Fa'amu, an elderly Samoan woman who claims to have been one of Mead's young informants. She tells us, via her Samoan interpreter, that she and her friends deliberately lied to Mead about their adolescent lovemaking in order to humor her by telling her what they thought she wanted to hear. As critics of the film have been quick to point out, this kind of evidence does not prove anything. An admission of having lied to someone raises the suspicion that such an informant might easily lie again, perhaps even in the film.[55]

Williamson's play *Heretic*, which is also based on Freeman's version of the Mead-Freeman controversy, is far more intriguing than Heimans's rather pedestrian film. When Penguin Books Australia published the script in 1996, the year the play was first produced, they advertised it as "the most controversial play of the 1990s."[56] Although Williamson makes Freeman the hero of the play—he is "the heretic" of the play's title—he allows himself to probe into the psyches of both Mead and Freeman, speculating as to what personality traits, sexual proclivities, and marital dramas might have led both individuals to take their respective intellectual positions. Williamson plays fast and loose with aspects of Mead's personal life and career. For example, he suggests that Mead wrote *Coming of Age in Samoa* as a sexual fantasy story that resulted from an affair she had with a Samoan youth while in the field. He also probes deeply into Freeman's past, giving his audience an image of a much more complex individual than Freeman himself ever reveals.[57] Even Williamson, however, does not allude to the mental breakdown that Freeman had while doing research in Borneo.

Clearly, Freeman relished the role of the heretic, for when Penguin reissued his book *Margaret Mead and Samoa* in 1996, it was given a new title: *Margaret Mead and the Heretic*.[58] In his own way, Freeman, like Mead, was an indefatigable self-promoter. After he read in the *Anthropology Newsletter* that I was writing a book about Mead and the media, he began to send me copies of articles he had written in response to critiques of his book and reviews of *Heretic*'s successful runs in Sydney and Auckland.[59] But unlike Mead, who never saw herself cast in the role of "the heretic," or the outsider, Freeman was always fighting against being the underdog. His last attempt came in 1998 when he published another book, titled *The Fateful Hoaxing of Margaret Mead*. By this time the mainstream media took little note of yet another Freeman book on the same issue he had been pursuing for fifteen years. The anthropological community seemed to have tired of the tirade too, having suffered the negative effects of much of the publicity his first book had stirred up in the media. University of Chicago anthropologist David Schneider summed up the feelings of many anthropologists when he wrote: "Freeman's book is not a serious, scholarly work but an unscientific personal attack on Margaret Mead, who stands, in the eyes of many, for rationalist values. It is a work that celebrates a particular political climate [the ascendancy in the 1980s of what Schneider called 'materialist, biologistic' thinking] by denigrating another [the period of the 1920s when talk of the 'science' of eugenics was influencing political decisions such as immigration quotas in the United States]."[60]

When Freeman died in 2001, an obituary in the *New York Times* read "Derek Freeman, Who Challenged Margaret Mead on Samoa, Dies at 84." Despite all the public critiques of Freeman's books that anthropologists had made, according to the *Times*, Freeman's challenge to Mead, although initially "greeted with disbelief or anger . . . gradually won wide—although not complete—acceptance."[61]

As the *Times* obituary confirms, despite the fact that within anthropology Freeman's attack on Mead led to a reevaluation of her work that not only acknowledged errors in her research but also vindicated her theoretical argument regarding the role of culture in determining important aspects of human behavior, outside the discipline, in the wider world of the general public and mainstream media, Mead's reputation had been tarnished.[62] What many individuals remember are not the detailed arguments anthropologists presented in her defense, but only that someone had "proven her to be wrong." Reflecting—and helping to confirm—this popular opinion, in 1999, in its end-of-the-century issue on "The Century's Greatest Minds," *Time* magazine relegated Mead to a sidebar with the comment:

> The century's foremost woman anthropologist, Margaret Mead was an American icon. On dozens of field trips to study the ways of primitive societies, she found evidence to support her strong belief that cultural conditioning, not genetics, molded human behavior. That theme was struck most forcefully in Mead's 1928 classic, *Coming of Age in Samoa*. It described an idyllic pre-industrial society, free of sexual restraint and devoid of violence, guilt and anger. Her portrait of free-loving primitives shocked contemporaries and inspired generations of college students—especially during the 1960s sexual

> revolution. But it may have been too good to be true. While few question Mead's brilliance or integrity, subsequent research showed that Samoan society is no more or less uptight than any other. It seems Mead accepted as fact tribal gossip embellished by adolescent Samoan girls happy to tell the visiting scientist what she wanted to hear.[63]

Thus, long after most anthropologists—especially those who had worked in the South Pacific themselves—had dismissed Freeman's book as unscholarly and unscientific, even going so far as to have the members of the American Anthropological Association vote to censure the book as "poorly written, unscientific, irresponsible and misleading," the media had accepted at face value Freeman's argument that Mead had been duped by her adolescent informers.[64] It was not even an original idea, having already been suggested, albeit in jest, by Nicholas von Hoffman and Garry Trudeau in 1976, a full decade before Freeman and Heimans presented it in the film *Margaret Mead and Samoa*.[65]

The media had initially built Mead up as a popular heroine, and the media undermined her reputation with their handling of the Mead-Freeman controversy. Nonetheless, the media has not always been correct in its declarations about her. In 1983, for example, *Time* magazine predicted that as a result of Freeman's attack on Mead, *Coming of Age in Samoa* would come to be regarded as "a curious artifact from an ancient war."[66] However, the book has not become a relic of the past. Not only did HarperCollins Perennial reissue a new edition of *Coming of Age* in 2001 during the Mead centennial year, but as recently as May 2005, *Human Events Online*, a Web publication of the National Conservative Weekly, included *Coming of Age* among the books it felt worthy of an honorable mention in its selection of the "Ten Most Harmful Books of the 19th and 20th Centuries."[67] Thus, while the Mead-Freeman controversy made Mead an equivocal icon, it did not entirely diminish her renown. In recent years, due to changes within the field of American anthropology and the growth of the Internet, Mead has apotheosized as the discipline's totemic public anthropologist.

The Mead Centennial Year

The year 2001 saw a flurry of official activities at various universities, scholarly institutes, and professional meetings in honor of the one-hundredth year of Mead's birth on December 16, 1901. These events are particularly interesting in light of the Mead-Freeman debacle and its effects on Mead's public image. How was Mead now regarded professionally and popularly after her reputation had undergone such a public drubbing?

Not surprisingly, the American Anthropological Association (AAA) sponsored a series of organized sessions at which anthropologists and historians were invited to present papers assessing Mead's contributions to anthropology and her role as a public intellectual. As similar sessions had been held at the AAA meetings soon after Mead's death, one might wonder what else there was to say about Mead and her career. While the presentations made at the earlier sessions had been eulogistic in tone, extolling Mead's many achievements,[68] by 2001 scholars had access to the voluminous Mead archives housed at the Library of Congress. The new perspectives on Mead presented at the AAA meetings and other scholarly symposia were based on detailed analyses of Mead's field notes, correspondence, drafts of her various book manuscripts, and related ephemera—newspaper clippings, announcements, cartoons, and memos—thus offering new insights into her innovative contributions to anthropology and American public life. Moreover, by this time the concept of public anthropology had emerged, and Mead was celebrated for her pioneering role as a public anthropologist.[69] The Library of Congress also mounted a special exhibition about Mead titled "Margaret Mead: Human Nature and the Power of Culture" that focused on Mead's life and career as an anthropologist and featured material from the Margaret Mead Papers and South Pacific Ethnographic Archives at the library.[70]

As we have seen, new archival research and fieldwork has also led to new critiques of other research of Mead's—in particular, her interpretation of her Arapesh data in *Sex and Temperament in Three Primitive Societies*.[71] Once again, although anthropologists fault Mead for her errors, there is also acknowledgment of how much she *did* get right in her Arapesh and other research.[72] However, unlike Freeman's critique of *Coming of Age in Samoa*, no one has challenged the soundness of the larger theoretical point she made in *Sex and Temperament* about the cultural construction of what we now call gender, nor have any of these ethnographic critiques attracted the same degree of media attention.

Much less attention was paid to Mead's centennial by the popular media than by anthropologists. HarperCollins Perennial Classics (which had incorporated William Morrow) reissued Mead's best-known books along with new introductions written by well-known individuals who had expertise in areas related to the topics of each book.[73] Another media event with national impact was a two-hour special about Mead on the nationally syndicated radio program, the *Diane Rehm Show.* Given that Mead had a lengthy history of interacting with female radio talk show personalities from the 1940s on, it was telling that the most extensive media tribute to Mead was Diane Rehm, herself of a generation that would have grown up admiring Mead.[74] To judge by the mass media's response, Mead at one hundred was of interest to an increasingly narrow public audience.

Mead's Legacy as Public Anthropologist

Within anthropology things were different. As I noted in the Introduction, today many anthropologists regard Mead as one of the first—if not *the* first—public anthropologists, and certainly the best-known anthropologist who championed the use of anthropology for social change and for the betterment of her own society as well as non-Western cultures around the world. Thus, for example, undergraduate students at the University of Rochester used Mead's well-known quote, "Never doubt that a small group of thoughtful committed citizens can change the world," as the focus for a conference they organized around the theme "Change the World" in celebration of her centennial.[75] These students cared little about the details of the Mead-Freeman controversy, or what it might mean for Mead's reputation as an anthropologist and social scientist. What was important to them was how Mead had made anthropology relevant to the world around her. For this new cohort of budding anthropologists (or at least of anthropology majors), she represented a set of beliefs and practices that demonstrated how useful an anthropological perspective and anthropological methods could be in grappling with social, economic, and political issues in the real world.

For the Rochester students and others like them, Mead's participation in UN-sponsored conferences on the environment, housing, and mental health; her interest in nutrition and culture; her role in the antinuclear movement; and her participation in the Scientists' Institute for Public Information and the American Association for the Advancement of Sci-

Figure 9.2 Internet image of Mead used by the Better World Project as part of their "HeroPix" Project. (Image Courtesy of The Better World Project, www.betterworldheroes.com/mead.htm)

ence—in short, her role as a visible scientist, a social activist, and a concerned American citizen—had impressed them. This was the legacy that Mead had bequeathed to a younger generation who no longer yearn to go off to distant and exotic climes, but who instead are seeking to work right in their own backyards. It was also the image of Margaret Mead that the editors of the American Anthropological Association's monthly newsletter referred to when in 1998 they called for a discussion among anthropologists of the relevance of anthropology to contemporary American society. Projects such as *The Wagon and the Star: A Study of American Community Initiative* that Mead collaborated on in 1966 with social psychologist Muriel Brown—an analysis of a series of successful community projects found across the United States—have contributed to Mead's role as a symbol of the importance of anthropology not only to addressing problems of today's complex, transnational world, but problems at home in our own neighborhoods, towns and cities as well.

Why There Is No "Margaret Mead" in Anthropology Today

In his discussion of the uses of great men, Ralph Waldo Emerson makes the humorous, but nonetheless perceptive, point that "every hero becomes a bore at last."[76] Once a hero dies, another individual will appear on the horizon to take his (or her) place. However, as Emerson also noted, the next man or woman who appears to the fill that role will not be the same type of hero as before, but from a quite different field: "now a great salesman; then a road-contractor; then a student of fishes; then a buffalo-hunting explorer."[77] He was aware that every generation, every epoch, every culture, has its own particular heroes, specific to their own particular time and needs. It is useful to keep Emerson's words in mind as we consider why anthropology has not produced another Margaret Mead.[78] A more relevant question to ask might be, "What was it about Mead and the era in which she lived that allowed her, an anthropologist, to achieve the degree of national and international fame she had during and after her lifetime?"

The answer lies in several quite specific attributes of Mead as an anthropologist and the ways in which these attributes and the discipline of anthropology resonated with the period in which she lived. It was perhaps most significant that she was a woman. Mead understood this when she said, "I make much better newspaper copy as a woman than I would as a man."[79] She came of age during a period of great change in the roles of women in American society. She was instrumental in shaping some of those changes and was in turn shaped by them. It was newsworthy when she transgressed various boundaries—professional, social, sexual, and gender—in what she did, what she said, and how she lived her life.

Mead lived during a period when an anthropologist could become both a heroine and a celebrity. It is unlikely that any anthropologist will ever achieve the same degree of fame as Mead did. This is not because anthropology will never attract anyone as smart and as media-savvy as she was. It is because the moment when an anthropologist could capture the public's imagination and serve as a "representative" figure for much of American society has ended. During the first half of the twentieth century in the United States, there was great intellectual and popular preoccupation with questions concerning race, sex, gender, culture, and civilization—questions that anthropology and anthropologists addressed either directly or indirectly in their work. In the marketplace of ideas, anthropology was a hot new commodity. For example, Mead first became famous as a popular heroine at a time when American intellectuals were wrestling with the idea of culture—what exactly was culture? Did Americans have culture? What was the difference between culture and cultures? Were some cultures superior to others? It was also a time when "the primitivist project," that is, the Western fascination with "primitive societies," was in vogue. Mead's early fame also corresponded with the height of the imperialist moment. Even the United States was engaged in imperial endeavors in the Pacific that entailed ruling and containing non-Western populations. There was interest in understanding these "savage" societies. Even into the 1960s it was a time when intellectuals such as Susan Sontag could still write about "the anthropologist as hero," without being either ironic or cynical about the anthropological endeavor.

Since Mead's death, not only have other academics become critical of the twentieth-century anthropological enterprise, but anthropologists themselves have also engaged in a soul-searching "crisis of representation," rethinking traditional ethnographic practices, in terms of how and where their research is conducted and in terms of how they write about that research and represent other cultures.[80]

In other respects, anthropology may have been *too* successful. The ethnographic concept of culture is now widely accepted, and its use is ubiquitous in common parlance. The practice of ethnography has expanded beyond the narrow confines of the discipline and is now performed by scholars in a broad range of academic fields from sociology to film studies to English, American, and cultural studies. Any scholar who actually talks to someone these days claims to be "doing ethnography." And "practicing" anthropologists are hired by businesses, government agencies, and international organizations that run the gamut from public relations firms and furniture manufacturers to the automotive industry and beyond. With the demise of "primitive cultures"—and thus the subject matter that gave the discipline its distinct identity—anthropology, as Micaela di Leonardo has succinctly put it, has a PR problem.[81]

However, at the same time anthropology has evolved in ways that Mead would appreciate and approve of. Many of the current developments of a more public anthropology are actually practices that Mead either initiated or paved the way for through her own projects and her broad conception of what anthropology could do. One reason to look anew at Margaret Mead is that the trajectory of her career as an anthropologist, which began with her work in the Pacific in the 1920s and 1930s, continued with her application of anthropological methods to the study of national problems during World War II, and culminated with her critiques of American culture and a focus on global social issues in the 1950s through the 1970s, presaged the parallel trajectory of anthropology during the twentieth century and into the twenty-first.

Examples of some of these developments include work in the field of medical anthropology, especially the ethnographic study of the practice of medicine, and anthropological work in the field of mental health and health care delivery[82] and media anthropology.[83] Mead was among the first anthropologists to suggest not only that films, photographs, and other media products could provide valuable insights into culture, but also that the study of the organization and process of their production was also culturally determined.[84] She was one of a group of anthropologists who transformed their wartime experiences adapting anthropological methods to the study of practical problems into the subdiscipline of applied anthropology.[85] Her study of nutrition during World War II, for example, initiated the anthropological study of food and nutrition in the United States.[86] Mead's initial work in the area of culture and personality has been transformed into various approaches to the study of psychological anthropology and cultural psychology, the latter an interdisciplinary field that has attracted both anthropologists and psychologists. Anthropologist William Beeman has even argued recently that Mead's work during the 1940s on the study of culture at a distance was the intellectual and methodological precursor of today's cultural studies.[87]

Mead's contributions to the development of the anthropological study of education began in 1930 with *Growing Up in New Guinea* and continued throughout her career.[88] It can be argued that the study she and Rhoda Metraux undertook to determine the image of the scientist among American high school students was a precursor to today's Science and Technology Studies (STS), as was her attention to the study of the impact of new technologies on different cultures.[89] Although at the time many of Mead's anthropological colleagues were disdainful of her interest in applying anthropological methods to everyday problems, today Mead's forays into these areas are recognized as groundbreaking, leading to the development of the discipline's present focus on public anthropology. With this development of a more broad-based set of issues and wider range of audiences for anthropological studies we see the achievement of what Mead might have meant when she said to *New Yorker* journalist Winthrop Sargeant, "It's All Anthropology."[90]

Mead's Legacy: At Home, In Cyberspace, and Beyond

When I visited former *Life* photographer Ken Heyman in his New York City apartment to talk with him about his lengthy friendship with Mead, he told me that he was in frequent spiritual contact with her. Before I left he showed me an altar he had dedicated to her, like a Chinese shrine to the ancestors, complete with incense and bright red cloth. Placed prominently in the center was a photograph of a smiling Margaret—one mostly likely that he had taken of her. For Heyman, Mead is still a strong spiritual presence in his life.[91]

Within the collective memory of many American anthropologists (at least those in their forties and older), Mead is also still a vivid presence, someone who manifests herself in a shared repertoire of anecdotes and legends that circulate whenever her name is mentioned. I cannot count how many times, upon mentioning that I was writing about Mead, that I was told the same story about her at the annual meetings of the American Anthropological Association (an event that Mead seldom missed if she could help it): A group of anthropologists were packed together in a hotel elevator. The elevator stopped and Mead got in. She stood there with her forked thumb stick grasped firmly in her hand, looked around her, and announced in a loud voice: "Someone has been having sex. I can smell it!"

Whether this story is apocryphal or not does not really matter. As anthropologists know, what matters is that I was told the story on numerous occasions, in different places, by different individuals when they found out that I was writing about Margaret Mead. The story reveals several things, both about what anthropologists thought about Mead and what they think about anthropologists. The subject matter of the story—sex—is one that has been associated with Mead ever since she wrote *Coming of Age in Samoa*. The fact that Mead would blurt out in public something that was usually kept private indicates what some people thought about Mead's style and personality; Mead had a reputation for saying controversial and provocative things. This anecdote certainly illustrated that dimension of her image. And finally, there is the aspect of the story that alludes to insiders' shared knowledge, or a stereotype of it: that anthropologists were thought to have affairs with their colleagues (and even more transgressive, sometimes with their graduate students) at the meetings. Mead had simply made public what many anthropologists privately knew—or believed, or wished—was going on.

The telling of stories such as this one, an example of the informal dimension of the myth-making process, is as important as the formal dimensions such as the symposia held during Mead's centennial year and the textbooks and films that place Mead's work within the official history of the discipline.[92] Although her name may no longer be a household word or as readily recognized as when she was alive and seen frequently on television, there is one public domain in which Mead's legacy continues to live on, and even grow, and that is cyberspace.

The Internet has provided a new means of immortality for Mead. Yahoo alone lists 3,840,000 links to "Margaret Mead," while Google lists 1,950,000 and Google Images another 35,100, and these are just the largest and best known of the search engines.[93] Public schools in the United States and Papua New Guinea have been named for her; awards created in her honor such as the Society for Applied Anthropology's Margaret Mead Award that is given to an individual who has brought anthropology to bear on wider social and cultural issues;[94] one can download one's favorite Mead quote and emblazon it on T-shirts, coffee mugs, or screen savers and mouse pads; and her image is used to promote everything from the legalization of marijuana to fat people's pride. Mead lives on in popular culture.

Aside from the omnipresent references to Mead as a twentieth-century female icon and role model for young women and girls (on the Internet Mead has returned to her original status as a popular heroine), another frequent reference to Mead on the Internet, on posters, and as the epigraph for various organizations' flyers and Web sites is the now famous quote used by the University of Rochester anthropology students: "Never doubt that a small group of thoughtful committed citizens can change the world; indeed, it's the only thing that ever has." There is a huge number of organizations and grassroots causes that use these words of Mead's as an epigram, from the Cayuga Nation, a Native American group that is fighting to regain land in upstate New York, to the U.S. Environmental Protection Agency.[95]

Although the exact origins of the quote have not been located in any of Mead's published work (some attribute it to the first Earth Day celebration in 1970, others think it may have first appeared in a newspaper article quoting Mead), the essence of the quote is directly related to the project Mead engaged in for *The Wagon and the Star: A Study of American Community Initiative*.[96] The community projects analyzed in the book were exactly the type of small group, community-based, local endeavor that the quote refers to. Both the quote and the book are emblematic of another set of ideas and values that Mead has come to represent to Americans: the pioneering "can do" spirit that helped people settle the United States in the first place, and the importance of community, of a group of people taking the initiative to work together toward a common goal. The use of the quote also expresses a sense of Mead the Populist; that is, Mead as a symbol of "the populace," the common people, and their democratic right to the freedom to control their own lives.[97] The popularity of the quote and the frequency of its appearance on the Internet is an entirely new development in Americans' popular response to Mead and a new source for the ongoing creation of Mead's symbolic meaning in twenty-first-century American culture.

In this book I have analyzed Margaret Mead as an American culture hero. I have examined how and why a young, outspoken female anthropologist who studied a series of small Pacific Island societies became an American celebrity and icon and what she would come to symbolize to American society over the course of the twentieth century. I have also sought to explain why Derek Freeman's accusations of Mead were of such interest to the media and the American public. And why, despite the mainstream media's uncritical acceptance of Freeman's critique as valid, Mead remains an important figure within anthropology, to the study of twentieth-century American intellectual and cultural history, and to a broad range of the American public. Many Americans have not been concerned with the details of Samoan ethnography or the issue of cultural versus biological determinism; what has been important to them has been Mead's symbolism as a role model to other women, her brook-no-nonsense attitude and willingness to criticize her fellow Americans combined with her intrinsic optimism, humanism, and wit, as well as her fundamental faith in the ability of individuals to grapple with problems and to find solutions—to come up with new social inventions, as she liked to say.

She played a key role in our contemporary understanding of the social construction of gender roles—the different ways different cultures define what it means to be masculine or feminine. She was a champion for a more open attitude toward the expression of sexuality and for more tolerance toward different forms of sexuality. And she supported equal rights and opportunities for all women and showed that women could both be good mothers and have a career. For these reasons, as well as the way in which she lived her own life, she has been seen as an icon of the modern twentieth-century woman.

Because of the popular success of her early books about Samoa and New Guinea and because of her later unflagging efforts to bring an anthropological perspective to bear on the study of a wide range of modern issues—from the generation gap to the impact of technology on developing countries to the image of the scientist in American society—and her extensive public appearances, Mead came to symbolize anthropology for the American public. Underlying that symbolism are a substantive set of contributions that anthropology has made to modern American culture, including the ethnographic concept of culture now used in everyday discourse, the concept that race is a cultural category not a biological reality, and the concept of cultural relativism that has infused twentieth-century American political liberalism with a sense of the importance of recognizing cultural differences.[98]

As a result of Mead's role as a "visible scientist," someone who not only acted upon her conviction that science could help solve many of the problems of the modern world but who also believed that scientists have a duty to inform the public about the risks as well as the benefits of new technologies, Mead became a symbol of the scientist as involved citizen and the ethnographer as a public anthropologist. And as a scholar and a scientist who embraced and mastered the media, Mead not only became a media celebrity but also a symbol of the social scientist and public intellectual. Finally, although she was considered "a citizen of the world" because of her far-flung travels and her anthropological research, Mead remained first and foremost an *American* phenomenon and a complicated and contradictory American icon.

ABBREVIATIONS OF ARCHIVAL SOURCES

AMNH	American Museum of Natural History, Margaret Mead Archives.
CU	Columbia University, Rare Book and Manuscript Collections, Butler Library, Jane Temple Howard Papers.
CU-OHP	Columbia University, Oral History Project, Rare Book and Manuscript Collections.
LC	Library of Congress, Manuscript Division. Margaret Mead Papers and the South Pacific Ethnographic Archives.
UH	University of Hawaii, Hawaiiana Collection.
VC	Vassar College, Archives and Special Collections. Ruth Fulton Benedict Papers.

NOTES

Preface

1. Nancy Lutkehaus, "Margaret Mead as Cultural Icon: Anthropology and the Media in American Culture," *Anthropology Newsletter*, December 1996, 45; and Nancy Lutkehaus, "Margaret Mead as Media Icon," unpublished paper presented at the Annual Meetings of the American Anthropology Association, Washington, DC, November, 1993.

2. Margaret Mead, *People and Places* (New York: World Publishing Company, 1959).

3. See Patricia Grinager, *Uncommon Lives: My Lifelong Friendship with Margaret Mead* (Boulder, CO: Rowman and Littlefield, 1999) for another description of working for Mead.

4. In addition to an administrative assistant there was also a correspondence assistant, a publications assistant, and a part-time bibliographer to find references for her books and articles.

5. These two courses were a study in contrast. A research methods course was a small seminar aimed at graduate students in anthropology, who were required to do their own ethnographic research as a team somewhere in New York City. The other, Culture and Communication, was a huge lecture course that attracted graduate students from throughout the university. Mead met a broad range of people through this course, including journalist and popular author Gail Sheehy. See Gail Sheehy, "She Was a Mentor to Us All," *Newsday*, November 19, 1978.

6. Margaret Mead, *Blackberry Winter: My Earlier Years* (New York: William Morrow, 1972).

7. Ethnographic filmmakers and theorists of documentary film's awareness of the highly constructed and thus often subjective and idiosyncratic nature of nonfiction film long preceded the so-called crisis in representation in written ethnography (see note 9); Nancy C. Lutkehaus and Jenny Cool, "Paradigms Lost and Found," in *Collecting Visible Evidence*, ed. Michael Renov and Jane M. Gaines (Minneapolis: University of Minnesota Press, 1999), 116–39.

8. Ann Peck, *Margaret Mead, Taking Note*, Odyssey Series, edited by Michael Ambrosino, videocassette, color, sound, 60 minutes (Boston: Public Broadcasting

Associates, 1981); and Virginia Yans-McLaughlin and Alan Berliner, *Margaret Mead: An Observer Observed*, videocassette, color, sound, 85 minutes (New York: Filmmakers Library, 1995).

9. The essays in *Writing Culture: The Poetics and Politics of Ethnography*, ed. James Clifford and George E. Marcus (Berkeley: University of California Press, 1986), initiated a far-reaching self-critique within anthropology of the practice of writing ethnography and the representation of cultures.

10. I took part in this process of representing Mead as well, as I was asked to write an introduction to a new edition of Mead's memoir, *Blackberry Winter* (New York: Kodansha International, 1995) and to contribute an article about Mead as a writer to the volume *Women Writing Culture* (edited by Ruth Behar and Deborah Gordon [Berkeley: University of California Press, 1995]).

11. Nancy Lutkehaus, "Margaret Mead: Anthropology's Liminal Figure," in *Reading Benedict/Reading Mead: Feminism, Race, and Imperial Visions*, ed. Dolores Janiewski and Lois W. Banner (Baltimore: Johns Hopkins University Press, 2004), 193–204.

Introduction
Mead as American Icon

1. *The Works of William James*, vol. 1, *The Principles of Psychology*, ed. Frederick H. Burkhardt (Cambridge, MA: Harvard University Press, 1981), 281–82.

2. Derek Freeman, *Margaret Mead and Samoa: The Making and Unmaking of an Anthropological Myth* (Cambridge, MA: Harvard University Press, 1983). See chapter 9 for a more detailed discussion of Freeman's accusation of Mead and the media's response to it. Margaret Mead, *Coming of Age in Samoa: A Psychological Study of Primitive Youth for Western Civilization* (New York: William Morrow, 1928); citations are to the 1961 Morrow edition.

3. Mary Catherine Bateson, *With a Daughter's Eye: A Memoir of Margaret Mead and Gregory Bateson* (New York: William Morrow, 1984). Jane Howard has written the most extensive biography of Mead, *Margaret Mead: A Life* (New York: Simon and Schuster, 1984). Other biographies include Phyllis Grosskurth, *Margaret Mead: A Life of Controversy* (New York: Penguin, 1988); Robert Cassidy's *Margaret Mead: A Voice for the Century* (New York: Universe Books, 1982); Hilary Lapsley, *Margaret Mead and Ruth Benedict: The Kinship of Women* (Amherst: University of Massachusetts Press, 1999); and Lois Banner, *Intertwined Lives: Margaret Mead, Ruth Benedict, and Their Circle* (New York: Knopf, 2003).

4. Daniel Boorstin, *The Image: A Guide to Pseudo-Events in America* (New York: Atheneum, 1985), originally published as *The Image, or What Happened to the American Dream* (New York: Atheneum, 1961). All references to *The Image* are to the 1985 edition.

5. Ralph Waldo Emerson, *Representative Men: Seven Lectures*, 1850, with an introduction by Pamela Schirmeister (New York: Marsilio, 1995), 7.

6. See, for example, Michael Rogin's analysis of political demonology, *Ronald Reagan, the Movie, and Other Episodes in Political Demonology* (Berkeley: University of California Press, 1987).

7. Garry Wills, *John Wayne's America: The Politics of Celebrity* (New York: Simon and Schuster, 1997); S. Paige Baty, *American Monroe: The Making of a Body Politic* (Berkeley: University of California Press, 1995); Ronald Steel, *In Love with Night: The American Romance with Robert Kennedy* (New York: Simon and Schuster, 2000); Larry McMurtry, *The Colonel and Little Missie: Buffalo Bill, Annie Oakley, and the Beginnings of Superstardom in America* (New York: Simon and Schuster, 2005).

8. Wayne Koestenbaum, *Jackie under My Skin: Interpreting an Icon* (New York: Farrar, Straus, and Giroux, 1995); Tina Brown, *The Diana Chronicles* (New York: Doubleday, 2007); Carl E. Rollyson and Lisa Olson Paddock, *Susan Sontag: The Making of an Icon* (New York: W. W. Norton, 2000); and Brenda R. Silver, *Virginia Woolf Icon* (Chicago: University of Chicago Press, 1999).

9. "Margaret Mead: 1901–1978," *Time* magazine, November 27, 1978, 57.

10. Lucy O'Brien, *Expedition: Treasures from 125 Years of Discovery* (New York: American Museum of Natural History, 1995), 26.

11. Allan Bloom, *The Closing of the American Mind: How Higher Education Has Failed Democracy and Impoverished the Souls of Today's Students* (New York: Simon and Schuster, 1987); Freeman, *Margaret Mead and the Making of an Anthropological Myth*.

12. David Williamson, *Heretic: Based on the Life of Derek Freeman* (Melbourne and New York: Penguin, 1996).

13. See, for example, Brainy Quote, Margaret Mead, at http://www.brainyquote.com.

14. See chapter 9 for a discussion of this quote.

15. *Time* magazine, 1999; Susan Ware, *Letter to the World: Seven Women Who Shaped the American Century* (New York: W. W. Norton, 1998). Ware also includes Eleanor Roosevelt, Dorothy Thompson, Katharine Hepburn, Babe Didrikson Zaharias, Martha Graham, and Marian Anderson.

16. Catherine Besterman and Hugh Gusterson, eds. *Why America's Top Pundits Are Wrong: Anthropologists Talk Back* (Berkeley: University of California Press, 2005).

17. Virginia Yans-McLaughlin, "Science, Democracy, and Ethics: Mobilizing Culture and Personality for World War II," in *Malinowski, Rivers, Benedict, and Others: Essays on Culture and Personality*, ed. George W. Stocking Jr. (Madison: University of Wisconsin Press, 1986), 184–217.

18. There has been much written about public anthropology within the past decade. See, for example, Robert Borofsky, www.publicanthropology.org; Louise Lamphere, "The Convergence of Applied, Practicing, and Public Anthropology in the 21st Century," *Human Organization* 63 (Winter 2004): 431–33; George Marcus, "The Passion of Anthropology in the U.S., circa 2004," *Anthropological Quarterly* 78, no. 3 (2005): 673–95; Jeremy MacClancy, ed., *Exotic No More: Anthropology on the Front Lines* (Chicago: University of Chicago Press, 2002).

19. See, for example, Margaret Mead, *World Enough: Rethinking the Future* (Boston: Little, Brown, 1975) and the collection of essays by Mead in Margaret Mead, *The World Ahead: An Anthropologist Anticipates the Future*, ed. Robert B. Textor (New York and Oxford: Berghahn Books, 2005).

20. *Time* magazine, March 29, 1999, 183.

21. Russell Baker, "The Blathery Gibberish," *New York Times Magazine*, April 29, 1997.

22. William Safire, "Many Icons, Few Iconoclasts," *New York Times Magazine*, November 24, 1996.

23. Silver, *Virginia Woolf Icon*, 12.

24. O'Brien, *Expedition,* 26. The text that accompanies Mead as Treasure No. 38 reads: "Margaret Mead taught generations of Americans about the value of looking carefully and openly at other cultures to better understand the complexities of being human."

25. *Time* magazine, 1999.

26. See Nancy Lutkehaus, "Margaret Mead: Anthropology's Liminal Figure," in *Reading Benedict/Reading Mead: Feminism, Race, and Imperial Visions*, ed. Dolores Janiewski and Lois W. Banner (Baltimore: Johns Hopkins University Press, 2004), 193–204, and Virginia Yans, "On the Political Anatomy of Mead-Bashing, or Re-Thinking Margaret Mead," in *Reading Benedict/Reading Mead*, ed. Janiewski and Banner, 229–48.

27. Boorstin was the first to develop a cogent argument for the dominance of the image, or visual media, in American culture. Other important sources on the dominance of images in modernity include John Berger's *Ways of Seeing* (New York: Viking Press, 1972) and W. J. Thomas Mitchell, *Picture Theory: Essays on Verbal and Visual Representation* (Chicago: University of Chicago Press, 1994).

28. It is because of the importance of visual media in the creation of meaning that I have chosen to look at Mead as an icon rather than simply a symbol or trope. I also consider discourse and textual representations along with visual images. However, given my argument that visual media have played a dominant role in the creation of Mead as a famous—indeed legendary—figure as well as an important twentieth-century American intellectual, the use of the term *icon* reflects a particular theoretical stance. See Marita Sturken and Lisa Cartwright,

Practices of Looking: An Introduction to Visual Culture (New York: Oxford University Press, 2001).

29. Boorstin, *The Image*.

30. See William Leach, *Land of Desire: Merchants, Power, and the Rise of a New American Culture* (New York: Pantheon, 1993), and Richard Wightman Fox and T. J. Jackson Lears, *The Culture of Consumption* (New York: Pantheon, 1983).

31. Neil Postman, *Amusing Ourselves to Death: Public Discourse in the Age of Show Business* (New York: Penguin, 1985), and Neal Gabler, *Life the Movie: How Entertainment Conquered Reality* (New York: Vintage, 1998).

32. Richard Schickel, *Intimate Strangers: The Culture of Celebrity* (Garden City, NY: Doubleday, 1985), viii.

33. Ware, *Letter to the World*, 118.

34. See Margaret M. Caffrey and Patricia A. Francis, eds., *To Cherish the Life of the World: Selected Letters of Margaret Mead* (New York: Basic Books, 2006).

35. Ann Hulbert, *Raising America: Experts, Parents, and a Century of Advice about Children* (New York: Knopf, 2003).

36. Kevin Markey, *100 Most Important Women of the 20th Century* (Des Moines, IA: Ladies' Home Journal Books), 1998, 71. The category of women scientists included paleoarchaeologist Mary Leakey and primatologist Jane Goodall.

37. For a more detailed discussion of Mead's writing, see Nancy C. Lutkehaus, "Margaret Mead and the 'Wind-Rustling-in-the-Palm-Trees' School of Ethnographic Writing," in *Women Writing Culture*, ed. Ruth Behar and Deborah A. Gordon (Berkeley: University of California Press, 1995), 186–206, and Deborah A. Gordon, "The Politics of Ethnographic Authority: Race and Writing in the Ethnography of Margaret Mead and Zora Neale Hurston," in *Modernist Anthropology*, ed. Marc Manganaro (Princeton, NJ: Princeton University Press, 1990), 146–62.

38. Roy Richard Grinker, *In the Arms of Africa: The Life of Colin M. Turnbull* (New York: St. Martin's Press, 2000). Turnbull wrote *The Forest People* (New York: Simon and Schuster, 1961) and *The Mountain People* (New York: Simon and Schuster, 1973).

39. Emerson, *Representative Men*, 175.

40. See Margaret Mead, "Visual Culture in a World of Words," in *Principles of Visual Anthropology*, ed. Paul Hockings (The Hague: Mouton, 1975), 3–10.

41. This was true for anthropology far more than other social sciences. See Elizabeth Edwards, ed., *Anthropology and Photography, 1860–1920* (New Haven, CT: Yale University Press, 1992).

42. See Alison Griffiths, *Wondrous Difference: Cinema, Anthropology, and Turn-of-the-Century Visual Culture* (New York: Columbia University Press, 2002).

43. See Sol Worth, "Margaret Mead and the Shift from 'Visual Anthropology' to the 'Anthropology of Visual Communication,' " in his *Studying Visual Communication*, ed. Larry Gross (Philadelphia: University of Pennsylvania Press, 1981), 185–99. See also Ray L. Birdwhistell, *Kinesics and Context: Essays on Body Motion Communication* (Philadelphia: University of Pennsylvania Press, 1970); Edward T. Hall, *The Silent Language* (Greenwich, CT: Fawcett, 1959) and *The Hidden Dimension* (Garden City, NY: Doubleday, 1966); and Edmund Carpenter, *Oh, What a Blow That Phantom Gave Me* (New York: Holt, Rinehart, and Winston, 1973).

44. In Jean Rouch, *Margaret Mead: A Portrait of a Friend*, videocassette, color, sound, 28 minutes (New York: American Museum of Natural History, 1978).

45. For a comprehensive list of articles that Mead wrote for both popular magazines and scientific journals, see Joan Gordan, ed., *Margaret Mead: The Complete Bibliography, 1925–1975* (The Hague: Mouton, 1976).

46. Michele Hilmes and Jason Loviglio, eds., *Radio Reader: Essays in the Cultural History of Radio* (New York and London: Routledge, 2002).

47. Susan Ware, *It's One O'Clock and Here Is Mary Margaret McBride: A Radio Biography* (New York: New York University Press, 2005). McBride was the original host of the nationally syndicated radio program the *Martha Deane Show*.

48. See chapter 7 for a discussion of Mead and the *Adventure* series.

49. See, for example, *Barnard Alumnae News*, 1931. See also Rouch, *A Portrait of a Friend*, which shows Mead in the museum.

50. Andrews was famous for his discovery of fossilized dinosaur eggs in the Gobi desert in the 1920s.

51. For more about the masculine iconography of the American Museum of Natural History, see Donna Haraway, "Teddy Bear Patriarchy: Taxidermy in the Garden of Eden, New York City, 1908–1936," in *Primate Visions: Gender, Race, and Nature in the World of Modern Science* (New York: Routledge, 1989), 26–58.

52. Meyer Fortes, "Obituary: Margaret Mead, 1901–1978," *Nature* 278 (March 1979): 289–90.

53. United States Information Agency, *Reflections: Margaret Mead*, 16 mm, color, sound, 58 minutes (Washington, DC: USIA, 1975).

54. Margaret Mead, *And Keep Your Powder Dry: An Anthropologist Looks at America* (New York: William Morrow, 1942).

55. See, for example, Richard Handler, "American Culture in the World: Margaret Mead's *And Keep Your Powder Dry*," in his *Critics against Culture: Anthropological Observers of Mass Society* (Madison: University of Wisconsin Press, 2005), 141–53, and Hervé Varenne, Introduction to *And Keep Your Powder Dry*,

by Margaret Mead, in The Study of Contemporary Cultures, vol. 2. (New York and Oxford: Berghahn Books, 2000), x–xxx.

56. Mead, *And Keep Your Powder Dry*, 10–11.

57. Margaret Mead, *Blackberry Winter: My Earlier Years* (New York: William Morrow, 1972), 41.

58. For more about the postwar American political ideology of cultural pluralism and its relationship to the Boasian concept of cultural relativism, see Christina Klein, *Cold War Orientalism: Asia in the Middlebrow Imagination, 1945–1961* (Berkeley: University of California Press, 2003).

59. I deal with Mead's FBI files in chapter 8.

60. See Micaela di Leonardo, *Exotics at Home: Anthropologies, Others, American Modernity* (Chicago: University of Chicago Press, 1998); Lenore Foerstel and Angela Gilliam, eds., *Confronting the Margaret Mead Legacy: Scholarship, Empire, and the South Pacific* (Philadelphia: Temple University Press, 1992); Eric Wakin, *Anthropology Goes to War: Professional Ethics and Counterinsurgency in Thailand* (Madison: University of Wisconsin Press, 1992); Marianna Torgovnick, *Gone Primitive: Savage Intellects, Modern Lives* (Chicago: University of Chicago Press, 1990); Nicholas von Hoffman and Garry Trudeau, *Tales from the Margaret Mead Taproom* (Kansas City, MO: Sheed and Ward, 1976); and Barbara Gullahorn-Holocek, *Anthropology On Trial*, videocassette, color, sound, 60 minutes (New York: Time-Life Video, 1983).

Chapter 1
Mead as Modern Woman

1. Mary Ellin Barrett, "Margaret Mead: First of the Libbies," *Cosmopolitan*, September 1972, 160–65. "Libbie" was short for a member of the "women's liberation movement."

2. Supersisters™, "Margaret Mead," New York, 1979.

3. Betty Friedan, *The Feminine Mystique* (New York: W. W. Norton, 1963).

4. For more discussion of Bloom's argument, see chapter 9. Allan Bloom, *The Closing of the American Mind: How Higher Education Has Failed Democracy and Impoverished the Souls of Today's Students* (New York: Simon and Schuster, 1987).

5. Playwright David Williamson makes explicit the association of Mead with the sexual revolution of the 1960s in *Heretic*, his play based on the life of Derek Freeman and Freeman's controversy with Margaret Mead's Samoan research. See David Williamson, *Heretic: Based on the Life of Derek Freeman* (Melbourne and New York: Penguin, 1996). So does Roger Sandall in *The Culture Cult: Designer Tribalism and Other Essays* (Boulder, CO: Westview Press, 2001), 65.

6. Feminists, who were often characterized as "New Women," were different from suffragists. While the suffragists who initiated the women's movement in the nineteenth century had concentrated on the issue of gaining equality for women through gaining the right to vote, in the nineteen teens there developed a group of women, and men, who called themselves *feminists*. For them, female emancipation meant more than simply the right to vote; it also meant the freedom to choose new roles, values, and beliefs, a rejection of the past conventions that surrounded what it meant for middle- and upper-class women to be "female." See Nancy Cott, *The Grounding of Modern Feminism* (New Haven, CT: Yale University Press, 1987); Desley Deacon, *Elsie Clews Parsons: Inventing Modern Life* (Chicago: University of Chicago Press, 1997); Rosalind Rosenberg, *Beyond Separate Spheres: Intellectual Roots of Modern Feminism* (New Haven, CT: Yale University Press, 1982); and Christine Stansell, *American Moderns: Bohemian New York and the Creation of a New Century* (New York: Henry Holt, 2000)

7. The term "New Woman" is used with reference to Mead in the 1920s. See Hilary Lapsley, *Margaret Mead and Ruth Benedict: The Kinship of Women* (Amherst: University of Massachusetts Press, 1999), 125.

8. Margaret Cussler, quoted in Jane Howard, *Margaret Mead: A Life* (New York: Simon and Schuster, 1983), 235.

9. Carolyn Heilbrun, "Margaret Mead and the Question of Woman's Biography," in *Hamlet's Mother and Other Women* (New York: Ballantine, 1990), 25–32, quotation is on p. 26.

10. Heilbrun, "Margaret Mead," 25–32, quotation is on p. 25.

11. Susan Ware, *Still Missing: Amelia Earhart and the Search for Modern Feminism* (New York: W. W. Norton, 1993).

12. Ware, *Still Missing*. In her book *Letter to the World: Seven Women Who Shaped the American Century* (New York: W. W. Norton, 1998), Ware includes Mead along with Eleanor Roosevelt, Katharine Hepburn, Martha Graham, Dorothy Thompson, Babe Didrikson Zaharias, and Marian Anderson as important 20th century American women.

13. See Richard Dyer, *Stars* (London: Educational Advisory Service, British Film Institute, 1979); and Richard deCordova, *Picture Personalities: The Emergence of the Star System in America* (Urbana: University of Illinois Press, 1990) on the Hollywood's development of the star system. See also Neal Gabler, *Winchell: Gossip, Power, and the Culture of Celebrity* (New York: Knopf, 1994).

14. Ware, *Still Missing*, 175.

15. Ibid., 24–25.

16. For more information about Mead's parents and childhood, see Margaret Mead, *Blackberry Winter: My Earlier Years* (New York: William Morrow, 1972); Lois W. Banner, *Intertwined Lives: Margaret Mead, Ruth Benedict, and Their*

Circle (New York: Knopf, 2003); Howard, *Margaret Mead: A Life*; Lapsley, *Margaret Mead and Ruth Benedict*; and Rosenberg, *Beyond Separate Spheres*.

17. See Margaret Mead, "Margaret Mead," in *A History of Psychology in Autobiography*, vol. 6, ed. Gardner Lindzey (Englewood Cliffs, NJ: Prentice-Hall, 1974), 293–326.

18. Mead, "Margaret Mead," 302.

19. Edward Sherwood Mead was born in 1874 to Martha Ramsey Mead and Giles F. Mead in Winchester, Ohio. An only child, Edward's father died when he was six.

20. It appears that Emily Mead was attracted to the newly established University of Chicago in part because of its progressive attitude toward women and women's education.

21. For more about the intellectual milieu Emily Fogg entered in 1894 at the University of Chicago, see Jackson Lears, "Beyond Veblen: Rethinking Consumer Culture in America," in *Consuming Visions: Accumulation and Display of Goods in America, 1880–1920*, ed. Simon J. Bronner (New York: W. W. Norton, 1989), 73–98; and Eugene Rochberg-Halton, "Life, Literature, and Sociology in Turn-of-the-Century Chicago," in Bronner, ed., *Consuming Visions*, 311–38.

22. A fifth child, a girl named Katharine, was born after Richard, but died when only nine months old.

23. Emily Fogg Mead, "The Place of Advertising in Modern Business," *Journal of Political Economy* (March 1901); reprinted in *Fame* 10 (April 1901): 165.

24. Fogg Mead, "The Place of Advertising in Business," 220. She did distinguish between what she identified as "false advertising" and truthful advertising, criticizing the former and praising the latter.

25. After she completed her undergraduate degree at the University of Chicago, she enrolled as a graduate student in Sociology at Bryn Mawr College. Although she wrote a master's thesis, she never completed her PhD.

26. Emily Fogg Meade [*sic*], "Italians on the Land: A Study in Immigration," U.S. Bureau Labor Bulletin 14 (May 1907): 473–533, reprinted as *The Italian on the Land: A Study in Immigration; Italian Immigration into the South* (Hammonton, NJ: Hammonton Historical Society, 1992). The Mead family moved several times a year, from urban Philadelphia to a farmhouse in Hammonton, New Jersey, during the spring and summer so that Emily could continue her research on the nearby Italian immigrants.

27. See Mead, *Blackberry Winter*, 28, and Banner, *Intertwined Lives*, 66.

28. Mead, *Blackberry Winter*, 257. See also Margaret Mead, *And Keep Your Powder Dry* (New York: William Morrow, 1942).

29. Mead, *Blackberry Winter*, 20.

30. Ibid., 37.

31. See Ann Hulbert, *Raising America: Experts, Parents, and a Century of Advice about Children* (New York: Knopf, 2003), 63–67.

32. See Catherine Mary Bateson, *With a Daughter's Eye: A Memoir of Margaret Mead and Gregory Bateson* (New York: William Morrow, 1984), 28–30.

33. Mead, "Margaret Mead," 302.

34. Ibid.

35. See Ware, *Letter to the World.*

36. Mead, "Margaret Mead," 307.

37. Mead's father had an affair "with an attractive redhead," *Blackberry Winter*, 35.

38. Mead had wanted to attend Wellesley College, but her father objected to the expense. They reached a compromise with the decision that Mead would attend her father's alma mater. Mead, *Blackberry Winter*, 85–86.

39. See Mead, "College DePauw," chap. 8 in *Blackberry Winter*, for details about Mead's experiences at DePauw. See also Howard, "Now We're All Bobbed," chap. 2 in *Margaret Mead: A Life*, esp. 37–40.

40. Mead, *Blackberry Winter*, 99; Howard, *Margaret Mead: A Life*, 39.

41. As a result of her stay at DePauw she gained insight into various forms of discrimination. For the very first time she experienced being ostracized by her peers, who found her taste in clothing, books, and pictures too individualistic and idiosyncratic for their midwestern taste and refused her admittance to a sorority. The sorority members even mocked her East Coast accent. She was one of a group of five friends there who called themselves "The Minority," because they were all ostracized by other students. One was black; another Roman Catholic; Katharine Rothenberger, a Lutheran; Mead, Episcopalian; and the fifth, the only Jewish student at the university. One of the few times in her life that she was rejected by a group because of being "different," Mead said the experience left her with a lifelong distaste for the elitism exhibited by individuals impressed with their membership in exclusionary groups. See Mead, *Blackberry Winter*, 92–101.

42. Katharine Rothenberger to Margaret Mead, February 25, April 8, 1922, C-1, LC.

43. Lapsley, *Margaret Mead and Ruth Benedict,* 23–26; Banner, *Intertwined Lives*. Banner is the more circumspect of the two scholars with regard to Mead's intimate involvement with Katharine Rothenberger. She notes that "what went on between Margaret and Katharine is unclear, although Margaret later described her to Gregory Bateson as so secure in her Midwestern ideals that she was willing to try anything." She implies that they may have experimented with sexual intimacy, since "in a note between them that survives from that time, Katharine writes to Margaret . . . and asks her to come and 'tuck her in.' " She sums up their behavior with the comment that the two "acted in accordance with the system of

gender socialization of Margaret's childhood, with its encouragement of both same-sex and heterosexual affection" (Banner, *Intertwined Lives*, 157).

Lapsley argues that Katharine may have been Mead's first lover—male or female. She bases her conjecture on several pieces of evidence, among them a conversation with Mead's daughter about Rothenberger in which Mary Catherine Bateson suggested that the two were lovers "because there was a certain coyness in her mother's tone whenever she spoke of Katharine" and data from dreams that Mead recorded during her mid-twenties along with interpretive notes Mead made some years later that indicate the strength of her attachment to Katharine and her anxieties about whether this attachment meant that she was homosexual (Lapsley, *Margaret Mead and Ruth Benedict*, 24–26).

44. Mead, *Blackberry Winter*, 164; also Bateson, *With a Daughter's Eye*, 22, and Barbara Roll, in Virginia Yans-McLaughlin and Alan Berliner, *Margaret Mead: An Observer Observed*, videocassette, color, sound, 85 minutes (New York: Filmmakers Library, 1995).

45. See, for example, Banner's discussion of Mead and sexual orientation in Lois Banner, "Mannish Women, Passive Men, and Constitutional Types: Margaret Mead's *Sex and Temperament in Three Primitive Societies* as a Response to Ruth Benedict's *Patterns of Culture*, *Signs: Journal of Women in Culture and Society* 28, no. 3 (2003): 833–58.

46. She added, "And Luther Cressman was in New York." Mead, *Blackberry Winter*, 100.

47. F. Scott Fitzgerald, the author perhaps most closely associated with the 1920s, claimed credit for naming the decade the Jazz Age, and for proclaiming its beginning and demise. See F. Scott Fitzgerald letter to Maxwell Perkins, May 1931, in *The Letters of F. Scott Fitzgerald*, ed. Andre Turnbull (New York: Charles Scribner's Sons, 1963), 225. See also Frederick Lewis Allen, *Only Yesterday: An Informal History of the Nineteen-Twenties* (New York: Harper and Brothers, 1931); Malcolm Cowley and Robert Cowley, *Fitzgerald and the Jazz Age* (New York: Charles Scribner's Sons, 1966).

48. F. Scott Fitzgerald, "Echoes of the Jazz Age," *Scribner's Magazine*, 1931.

49. Fitzgerald, quoted in Cowley and Cowley, *Fitzgerald and the Jazz Age*, 3.

50. Mead, *Blackberry Winter*, 104.

51. Ware, *Still Missing*, 159.

52. Barrington Boardman, *Flappers, Bootleggers, "Typhoid Mary," and the Bomb: An Anecdotal History of the United States from 1923–1945* (New York: Perennial Library, 1988), 16.

53. For a discussion of the image of the flapper in American silent movies, see Sumiko Higashi, *Virgins, Vamps, and Flappers: The American Silent Movie Heroine* (St. Albans, VT: Eden Press Women's Publications, 1978).

54. In contrast to the bubbly, flirtatious image of the flapper, there existed a more mature, almost sinister, female sensuality personified in the movies by the figure of the vamp. See Higashi, *Virgins, Vamps, and Flappers*.

55. Higashi, *Virgins, Vamps, and Flappers*, 169.

56. Boardman, *Flappers, Bootleggers*, 18.

57. Roland Marchand, *Advertising the American Dream: Making Way for Modernity, 1920–1940* (Berkeley: University of California Press, 1985).

58. Fellow Ash Can Cat Pelham Kortheuer noted the event in her diary, commenting that "now we are all bobbed." Hair, always an emotional subject, caused Kortheuer to add that "the barber had wept when Margaret's wavy golden curls were cut off." Quoted in Howard, *Margaret Mead: A Life*, 42.

59. Susan Ware notes how important Earhart's physical appearance was in shaping her popularity. Earhart, in contrast to Mead, was tall and willowy, but like Mead she sported bobbed hair that fit with the then-popular flapper style. Ware, *Still Missing*, 156–61.

60. In contrast to the predominantly WASP student body at DePauw, Mead noted that her classmates at Barnard were more diverse in terms of ethnic background and religion. In addition to Pelham Kortheuer, Mead, and Léonie Adams, the Ash Can Cats included Deborah Kaplan, Viola Corrigan, Louise Rosenblatt, and Mary Ann (Agnes) McCall, known as Bunny. They lived together in a co-op apartment at 616 West 116th Street operated by Barnard College.

61. Nancy Mitford, *Savage Beauty: The Life of Edna St. Vincent Millay* (New York: Random House, 2001), xiii.

62. Mead's biographers have all seized upon this incident as well as Millay's poem as emblematic of the restless spirit of Mead and the Ash Can Cats. For details of this incident, see Howard, *Margaret Mead: A Life*, 71–72 and Mead, *Blackberry Winter*, 133.

63. Manuscript, *Blackberry Winter*, "Life Span," 3, LC.

64. Mead, *Blackberry Winter*, 111.

65. Mead did write that one member of the Ash Can Cats, Anne "Bunny" McCall, lived the life of a flapper. She would report back to them on her activities. Mead, *Blackberry Winter*, 105.

66. Howard, *Margaret Mead: A Life*, 48. The name for the Ash Can Cats came from the students' drama teacher at Barnard, Minor Latham, who reputedly once remarked in her Mississippi drawl, "You girls who sit up all night readin' poetry come to class lookin' like Ash Can Cats." Howard, *Margaret Mead: A Life*, 43.

67. Mead, *Blackberry Winter*, 107–8.

68. Ibid., 108.

69. For more about Mead's lesbian relationships at Barnard see Banner, *Intertwined Lives*, 176, 177–79; Lapsley, *Margaret Mead and Ruth Benedict*, 31, 67–68.

70. Mead, *Blackberry Winter*, 109.

71. Bateson, *With a Daughter's Eye*, 118; Howard, *Margaret Mead: A Life*, 87.

72. See Regna Darnell's biography, *Edward Sapir: Linguist, Anthropologist, Humanist* (Berkeley: University of California Press, 1990), and Howard, *Margaret Mead: A Life*, 74–75.

73. Margaret Mead, ed., *An Anthropologist at Work: Writings of Ruth Benedict* (Boston: Houghton Mifflin, 1959).

74. Howard, *Margaret Mead: A Life*, 66–67.

75. Mead in Jean Houston ms., LC.

76. Mead, *Blackberry Winter*, 129.

77. Mead, ed., *An Anthropologist at Work*; Margaret Mead, *Ruth Benedict* (New York: Columbia University Press, 1974); and Mead, *Blackberry Winter.*

78. Jean Rouch, *Margaret Mead: A Portrait by a Friend*, videocassette, color, sound, 28 minutes (New York: American Museum of Natural History, 1978).

79. Yans-McLaughlin and Berliner, *Margaret Mead: An Observer Observed.*

80. See Bateson, *With a Daughter's Eye*, 119–21; Lapsley, *Margaret Mead and Ruth Benedict*, 124–25n30; Banner, *Intertwined Lives*, 232–33.

81. Clark Wissler, Mead's new boss in the Department of Anthropology at the American Museum of Natural History, had connections with curators at the Bishop Museum, where Mead had an opportunity to spend time with Edward Craighill Handy, a Pacific scholar who helped her start to study the Samoan language and familiarized her with the Bishop Museum's extensive collection of artifacts from Polynesia.

82. Margaret Mead, interview by Lorin Tarr Gill, "To Make Study of 'Flapper' in Primitive State Dr. Margaret Mead Will Visit South Seas to Carry Out Her Research Plan," *Honolulu Star-Bulletin*, August 15, 1925. In Doylestown it was published with the headline "Dr. Mead Explained South Sea Research: The Primitive Flapper." Doylestown, October 22, 1925, Box I-8, LC.

83. Elizabeth Buck, *Paradise Remade: The Politics of Culture and History in Hawaii* (Philadelphia: Temple University Press, 1993).

84. As it turns out, the Musa-shiya shirt ads quickly gained local recognition and an international following: "Comment on those advertisements comes in from every corner of the world. Thousands of them are clipped from the *Star-Bulletin* and sent home by tourists and the twenty thousand soldiers and sailors stationed in the Islands. I don't know how many publications have reprinted them with comment—often editorial—from the *London Times* and various magazines to small country newspapers." *How Musa-Shiya the Shirtmaker Broke into Print*, assisted by George Mellen, 1922, 10. Pacific Archives, University of Hawaii.

85. Mellen, *How Musa-shiya*, 10.

86. Margaret Mead, interview by *New York Sun*, "Says Scientist—Idea Archaic Survival: Has Studied the Flapper in the South Seas," *New York Sun*, 1927, Box Q-33, LC; Samuel Hopkins Adams, *Flaming Youth* (New York: Liveright, 1923).

87. *New York Sun*, 1927, Box Q-33, LC.

88. Beth Buchanan, "Youth Takes the Lead," *New York World Daily Magazine*, 1931. AMNH.

89. E. R. Brand, "An American Princess of the South Seas," 30–34, 1930? Box Q-33, LC.

90. Buchanan, "Youth Takes the Lead."

91. Ibid.

92. Margaret Mead, "Life as a Samoan Girl," in *All True! The Record of Actual Adventures That Have Happened to Ten Women of Today* (New York: Brewer, Warren, and Putnam, 1931), 94–118.

93. Mead, "Life as a Samoan Girl," 94–95.

94. Ibid., 95–96.

95. Ibid., 118.

96. Ibid.

97. Elsie Clews Parsons, born in 1874, occupies that position. See Deacon, *Elsie Clews Parsons*. Parsons paved the way for Mead and her generation of women through her work as a feminist, social activist, and social scientist. But if Parsons helped to invent "modern life" for American women, Mead grabbed the reins Parsons provided and lived that modern life to the fullest.

98. Maureen Molloy, "Margaret Mead, the Samoan Girl, and the Flapper: Geographies of Selfhood in *Coming of Age in Samoa*," in *Reading Benedict/Reading Mead: Feminism, Race, and Imperial Visions*, ed. Dolores Janiewski and Lois W. Banner (Baltimore: Johns Hopkins University Press, 2004), 33–47.

99. Martha Banta, *Imaging American Women: Idea and Ideals in Cultural History* (New York: Columbia University Press, 1987), 91.

100. "Miss Mead to Wed, Keeping Own Name; 'More Convenient,' Explains Daughter of Wharton School Professor," 1923, Box Q-33–4, LC.

101. The series of fifteen stamps also included Notre Dame's famed "Four Horsemen" of college football, the painter Edward Hopper, and Emily Post(!).

102. Text on the back of the Margaret Mead 32-cent, 1920's "Celebrate the Century" Series, United States Postal Service.

Chapter 2
Images of the Mature Mead

1. "Miss Mead to Wed, Keeping Own Name," undated, untitled newspaper clipping, circa August 1923, Box Q-33–4, LC.

2. Margaret Mead to Jane Pawley, in Virginia Yans-McLaughlin and Alan Berliner, *Margaret Mead: An Observer Observed*, videocassette, color, sound, 85 minutes (New York: Filmmakers Library, 1995).

3. Draft manuscript, *Blackberry Winter*, LC.

4. Margaret Mead, *Male and Female: A Study of the Sexes in a Changing World* (New York: William Morrow, 1949).

5. Susan Ware, *Letter to the World: Seven Women Who Shaped the American Century* (New York: W. W. Norton, 1998).

6. Margaret Mead, *Blackberry Winter: My Earlier Years* (New York: William Morrow, 1972), 164.

7. Margaret Mead, "Can Marriage Be for Life?" chap. 17 in *Male and Female: A Study of the Sexes in a Changing World* (New York: HarperCollins/Perennial, 2001), 316–38. Originally published in 1949.

8. Had Bateson been in New York at the time, Mead might also have insisted that he be present at the birth, but he had returned to England to report for war duty.

9. Mary Catherine Bateson, *With a Daughter's Eye: A Memoir of Margaret Mead and Gregory Bateson* (New York: William Morrow, 1984), 28.

10. Mead, *Blackberry Winter*, 253; see also Thomas Maier, *Dr. Spock: An American Life* (New York: Harcourt Brace, 1998), 99.

11. Spock suggested Dr. Claude Heaton, an obstetrician who, it turned out, had an interest in Native American birth practices and was intrigued by Mead and Bateson's observations of childbirth in New Guinea. In order to persuade the nurses at French Hospital in New York City (the only hospital they could find that would allow Spock to be in the delivery room with Heaton) to accede to Mead's requests, he showed the nurses the short films Mead and Bateson had made about the birth of a Iatmul baby. Gregory Bateson and Margaret Mead, *First Days in the Life of a New Guinea Baby*, Character Formation in Different Culture Series, 1951, videocassette, black and white, sound, 15 minutes (New York: Institute for Intercultural Studies, 1989); Mead, *Blackberry Winter*, 255.

12. Mary Catherine Bateson said that Mead wanted Spock as her pediatrician because he had been psychoanalyzed (in Maier, *Dr. Spock*, 99).

13. Benjamin Spock, *The Common Sense Book of Baby and Child Care* (New York: Duell, Sloan, and Pearce, 1946).

14. Bateson, *With a Daughter's Eye*, 33. For details about Mary Catherine's birth, see Jane Howard, *Margaret Mead: A Life* (New York: Simon and Schuster, 1984), 217.

15. Regarding Spock's column for *Redbook*, see Maier, *Dr. Spock*, 320, 362.

16. Howard, *Margaret Mead: A Life*, 228.

17. Virginia Yans-McLaughlin, "Science, Democracy, and Ethics: Mobilizing Culture and Personality for World War II," in *Malinowski, Rivers, Benedict, and Others: Essays on Culture and Personality*, ed. George Stocking Jr. (Madison: University of Wisconsin Press, 1986), 184–217.

18. Howard, *Margaret Mead: A Life*, 221–27.

19. See Thelma Present, *Dear Margaret: Letters from Oak Ridge to Margaret Mead* (Knoxville: Eastern Tennessee Historical Society, 1985).

20. Margaret Mead, *And Keep Your Powder Dry* (New York: William Morrow, 1942.) Reprinted by Berghahn Books, 2000, with an introduction by Hervé Varenne. See also Richard Handler, "American Culture in the World: Margaret Mead's *And Keep Your Powder Dry*," chap. 6 in his *Critics against Culture: Anthropological Observers of Mass Society* (Madison: University of Wisconsin Press, 2005), 141–54.

21. Elizabeth M. Eddy and William L. Partridge, eds., *Applied Anthropology in America* (New York: Columbia University Press, 1987).

22. Chester S. Williams (Office of War Information, British Division) to Margaret Mead, May 8, 1943, Box E-155, LC. Mead accepted the invitation on May 25, 1943, Box E-155, LC.

23. Mead, "The Relationship between American Soldiers and the People of Great Britain." Manuscript, October 24, 1943, Box E-155, LC, and Margaret Mead, *The American Troops and the British Community: An Examination of the Relationship between the American Troops and the British* (London: Hutchinson, 1944). See also Margaret Mead, "A GI View of Britain," *New York Times Magazine*, March 19, 1944, 18–19, 34; Juliet Gardner, "Guys and Dolls," *Guardian Weekly*, February 2, 1992.

24. Juliet Gardner, "Guys and Dolls," 22.

25. For this latter topic Mead indicated that her lecture would focus on "the puritan dogma that the Lord prospers the just man and its American version that if a man is virtuous, industrious and intelligent, he will be successful in this world, and the way this belief combines with the idea of free enterprise." May 31, 1943, Box E-155, LC.

26. Box E-155, LC.

27. Caroline Haslett to Margaret Mead, September 13, 1943, Box E-155, LC.

28. Mead, *Male and Female*, 1949 and 2001.

29. Mead, *Male and Female,* 175, in the 2001 edition.

30. Ibid., 178.

31. *Life* magazine, "Student and Teacher of Human Ways," September 14, 1959.

32. Ibid.

33. Betty Friedan, *The Feminine Mystique*. See Elaine Tyler May, *Homeward Bound: American Families in the Cold War Era* (New York: Basic Books, 1988), 209–17, for letters Friedan received from American women who concurred with her. See also David Horowitz, *Betty Friedan and the Making of the Feminine Mystique: The American Left, the Cold War, and Modern Feminism* (Amherst: University of Massachusetts Press, 1998); Joy Hennessee, *Betty Friedan, Her Life* (New York: Random House, 1999); Daphne Merkin, "Sister Act: Did Betty Friedan Go

Wrong, or Did Feminism?" *New Yorker*, June 14, 1999, 78–84; and Alan Wolfe, "The Mystique of Betty Friedan," *Atlantic Monthly*, September 1999, 98–105.

34. Friedan, *The Feminine Mystique*, 135–36.

35. Friedan remembered seeing Mead and Bateson at a professional conference when she was a graduate student in psychology; they were irreverently referred to there as "God the Mother and Jesus Christ" (Howard, *Margaret Mead: A Life*, 225–26).

36. Friedan, *The Feminine Mystique*, 142.

37. Ibid., 137–38.

38. Ibid., 148.

39. Ibid., 140.

40. Rosalind Rosenberg, *Beyond Separate Spheres: Intellectual Roots of Modern Feminism* (New Haven, CT: Yale University Press, 1982), and Elaine Showalter, *Inventing Herself: Claiming a Feminist Intellectual Heritage* (New York: Scribner, 2001).

41. Eugenia Kaledin, *Mothers and More: American Women in the 1950s* (Boston: Twayne Publishers, 1984), 20, 57.

42. *Life* magazine, 1959.

43. Ibid.

44. Yans-McLaughlin and Berliner, *Margaret Mead: An Observer Observed*.

45. *Life* magazine, 1959.

46. Natalie Angier, *Woman: An Intimate Geography* (New York: Anchor Books, 2000), 238.

47. Margaret Mead, "On Being a Grandmother," *Redbook* magazine, July 1970, 70, 168, 169. Reprinted in Margaret Mead and Rhoda Metraux, *Aspects of the Present* (New York: Morrow, 1980), 140–46.

48. Mead, "On Being a Grandmother"; see also *Blackberry Winter*, 273–84.

49. Mead, "On Being a Grandmother."

50. Yans-McLaughlin and Berliner, *An Observer Observed*.

51. Mead, "On Being a Grandmother."

52. Mary Ellin Barrett, "Margaret Mead: First of the Libbies," *Cosmopolitan*, September 1972, 160–65.

53. Howard, *Margaret Mead: A Life*, 374.

54. In ibid., 377, 378.

55. Mead, "Postscripts," *Chemical and Engineering News*, February 14, 1966.

56. Dr. Christine Gailey in *Margaret Mead: An Observer Observed*. The character Yoda and *Star Wars* are property of Lucasfilm, Ltd.

57. Roy Rappaport, "Desecrating the Holy Woman: Derek Freeman's Attack on Margaret Mead," *American Scholar* (Summer 1986): 313–47.

58. Phyllis Grosskurth, *Margaret Mead* (New York: Penguin, 1988), 76.

59. Allan Bloom, *The Closing of the American Mind: How Higher Education Has Failed Democracy and Impoverished the Souls of Today's Students* (New York: Simon and Schuster, 1987), 369.

60. David Dempsey, "The Mead and Her Message," *New York Times Magazine*, April 26, 1970.

61. Howard, *Margaret Mead: A Life*, 385. See also Marshall Sahlins, "Views of a Culture Heroine," *New York Times Book Review*, August 26, 1984, 20, and Nancy Lutkehaus, "Margaret Mead and the 'Rustling-of-the-Wind-in-the-Palm-Trees' School of Ethnographic Writing," in *Women Writing Culture*, ed. Ruth Behar and Deborah Gordon (Berkeley: University of California Press, 1995), 186–206.

62. The term *gender blending* describes individuals who "indisputably belong to one sex and identify themselves as belonging to the corresponding gender while exhibiting a complex mixture of characteristics from each of the two standard roles." Holly Devor, *Gender Blending: Confronting the Limits of Duality* (Bloomington: Indiana University Press, 1989).

63. See chapter 9.

64. Hilary Lapsley, *Margaret Mead and Ruth Benedict: The Kinship of Women* (Amherst: University of Massachusetts Press, 1999), Lois Banner, *Intertwined Lives: Margaret Mead, Ruth Benedict, and Their Circle* (New York: Knopf, 2003), and Lois Banner, "Mannish Women, Passive Men, and Constitutional Types: Margaret Mead's *Sex and Temperament in Three Primitive Societies* as a Response to Ruth Benedict's *Patterns of Culture*," *Signs* 28, no. 3 (2003): 833–58.

65. *ONE* magazine. I thank Todd White and the ONE Institute in Los Angeles for bringing this quote from Margaret Mead to my attention.

66. Esther Newton, *Margaret Mead Made Me Gay* (Durham, NC: Duke University Press, 2000).

67. Newton, *Margaret Mead*, 1.

68. Ibid.

69. Bloom, *The Closing of the American Mind*, 39.

70. Mead, draft of autobiography, 5/28/72, LC.

71. Mead even cautioned her daughter not to throw away any of her childhood drawings, saying that they might be of value to some researcher in the future (Bateson, *With a Daughter's Eye*). In this book Bateson also explains why she has decided to reveal secrets about her mother's past, in particular, her sexual relationship with Ruth Benedict. She feels that it is important to understand this most intimate relationship of Mead's because of what it reveals about the nature of friendship, love, and support among women (ibid., 119–21).

72. Friedan, quoted in Howard, *Margaret Mead: A Life*, 426.

73. Mead worked closely with a group of psychologists and psychiatrists in New York City who were interested in culture and its effects on personality and

individual psychology. Among them was Erik Erikson, the person most often associated with the introduction of the term *identity* as a psychological concept. See Lawrence Friedman, *Identity's Architect: A Biography of Erik H. Erikson* (New York: Scribner, 1999).

Chapter 3
Mead as Anthropologist: "Sex in the South Seas"

1. N.d., No. 89, Box Q-33–5, LC. This poem was in a series that included "The Social Scientist," "The Historian," and "The Psychoanalyst." Jones, an eminent Americanist scholar and professor of English at Harvard, wrote satirical poetry such as "The Anthropologist" as a hobby. See Peter Brier, *Howard Mumford Jones and the Dynamics of Liberal Humanism* (Columbia: University of Missouri Press, 1994), 160.

2. Mead received her master's degree in psychology in 1924 from Columbia University for her thesis "Intelligence Tests of Italian and American Children." See also Margaret Mead, "Group Intelligence Tests and Linguistic Disability among Italian Children," *School and Society* 25 (April 16, 1927): 465–68. Her research helped prove the cultural bias inherent in the construction of intelligence tests, as those children whose families spoke less English and more Italian in their homes did more poorly on the tests than those children whose parents spoke English at home.

3. See Patricia A. Francis, "Something to Think With: Psychology and the Road to Samoa," unpublished paper, 2001.

4. Mead, *Blackberry Winter: My Earlier Years* (New York: William Morrow, 1972), 111; "Margaret Mead," in *A History of Psychology in Autobiography*, vol. 4, ed. Gardner Lindzey (New York: Prentice-Hall, 1974), 293–326; esp. 295–96.

5. Mead, *Blackberry Winter*, 114.

6. Mead, "Out of the Things I Read," *Redbook* magazine, January 1978, 44; Katherine Pease Routledge, *The Mystery of Easter Island: The Story of an Expedition, by Mrs. Scoresby Routledge* (London: Printed for the author by Hazell, Watson and Viney; sold by Sifton, Praed, 1919).

7. Mead, *Blackberry Winter*, 135.

8. Ibid., 129.

9. Margaret Mead, *Coming of Age in Samoa: A Psychological Study of Primitive Youth for Western Civilization* (New York: William Morrow, 1928; reprinted with a new preface by Margaret Mead, New York: William Morrow, 1961); citations are to the 1961 Morrow edition. Margaret Mead, *Coming of Age in Samoa*, introduction by Mary Pipher (New York: HarperCollins/Perennial, 2001).

Ruth Benedict's *Patterns of Culture* is the most popular anthropology book ever published.

10. These were chapter XIII, "Our Educational Problems in the Light of Samoa Contrasts," and chapter XIV. "Education For Choice."

11. Clifford Geertz coined the term *edificatory ethnography* in Clifford Geertz, *Works and Lives: The Anthropologist as Author* (Stanford, CA: Stanford University Press, 1988), 102–28; esp. 108. According to Geertz, Mead botched her attempts at edificatory ethnography through her tendency for exaggerated self-consciousness, 108.

12. Margaret Mead to William Morrow, January 28, 1928, Box I-2, LC.

13. Margaret Mead, draft of "Abstract of Proposed Concluding Chapter" of *Coming of Age in Samoa*," n.d., Box I-2, LC.

14. Margaret Mead to William Morrow, February 11, 1928, Box I-2, LC.

15. Robert Lowie, Review of *Coming of Age in Samoa*, *American Anthropologist* n.s. 31 (1929): 532–34.

16. *The Nation* (October 17, 1928). Ellis and Malinowski admired each other's work. See Phyllis Grosskurth, *Havelock Ellis, a Biography* (New York: New York University Press, 1985), 380–84.

17. Margaret Mead to Bronislaw Malinowski, August 9, 1928, Box I-2, LC.

18. See Sharon W. Tiffany, "Imagining the South Seas: Margaret Mead's *Coming of Age in Samoa* and the Sexual Politics of Paradise," in *Reading Benedict/Reading Mead: Feminism, Race, and Imperial Vision*, ed. Dolores Janiewski and Lois W. Banner (Baltimore: Johns Hopkins University Press, 2004), 155–79.

19. Mead, *Coming of Age in Samoa*, 12.

20. See Nancy Lutkehaus, "Margaret Mead and the 'Rustling-of-the-Wind-in-the-Palm-Trees School' of Ethnographic Writing," in *Women Writing Culture*, ed. Ruth Behar and Deborah A. Gordon (Berkeley: University of California Press, 1995), 186–206.

21. Herman Melville, *Omoo: A Narrative of Adventures in the South Seas* (New York: Harper, 1847); Herman Melville, *Typee: A Peep at Polynesian Life; During a Four Months' Residence in a Valley of the Marquesas* (New York: Wiley and Putnam, 1846); Robert Louis Stevenson, *In the South Seas* (New York: Scribner's Sons, 1896); Jack London, *The Cruise of the* Snark (1910); Casey Blanton, ed., *Picturing Paradise: Colonial Photography of Samoa, 1875–1925* (Daytona Beach, FL: Daytona Beach Community College, 1995).

22. Frederick O'Brien, *White Shadows in the South Seas* (Garden City, NY: Garden City Publishers, 1919); John Colton and Clemence Randolph, *Rain: A Play in Three Acts*, based on W. Somerset Maugham's "Miss Thompson" (New York: Boni and Liveright, 1923); Robert Flaherty, *Moana: A Story of the South Seas* (Paramount Pictures, 1926).

23. William Morrow to Margaret Mead, January 11, 1929, Box I-2, LC.

24. George Amos Dorsey, *Why We Behave like Human Beings* (New York: Harper and Brothers, 1925).

25. Freda Kirchwey, "This Week: Sex in the South Seas," *The Nation* 127, no. 3303 (1928): 427.

26. Ibid.

27. *Times Literary Supplement*, "Samoan Youth," review of *Coming of Age in Samoa*, June 6, 1929.

28. Henry Neil, *The Book of the Fair* (Chicago, 1904). Whoever saved this letter for Mead while she was in Manus, wrote across the bottom of the note "How's this for a puff?!" Box I-2, LC.

29. Irving Wallace, *The Three Sirens, A Novel* (New York: Simon and Schuster, 1963); James A, Michener, *Return to Paradise* (New York: Random House, 1951).

30. W. A. Brownell to Margaret Mead, February 3, 1930, Box I-2, LC.

31. Mary Austin, Review of *Coming of Age in Samoa*, *Birth Control Review* (June 1929): 165–66.

32. Mary Austin, *The Land of Little Rain* (Boston : Houghton Mifflin, 1903). Also, Melody Graulich and Elizabeth Klimasmith, eds., *Exploring Lost Borders: Critical Essays on Mary Austin* (Reno: University of Nevada Press, 1999).

33. Austin, Review of *Coming of Age in Samoa*.

34. Review of *Coming of Age in Samoa*, *Honolulu Star-Bulletin*.

35. Unsigned review of *Coming of Age in Samoa*, *New York Times*, November 4, 1928.

36. Austin, Review of *Coming of Age in Samoa*.

37. Margaret Mead, *Social Organization in Manua* (Honolulu: Bernice P. Bishop Museum, 1930).

38. In addition to publishing *Growing Up in New Guinea*, Mead also published *Kinship in the Admiralty Islands* (New York: American Museum of Natural History, 1934). In addition to *Sex and Temperament in Three Primitive Societies*, she also published three volumes of ethnographic research about the Mountain Arapesh, one of the three cultures she describes in *Sex and Temperament*. See Paul Roscoe, Introduction to *The Mountain Arapesh*, by Margaret Mead (1938; New Brunswick, NJ: Transaction Publishers, 2002).

39. Margaret Mead, "Civil Government for Samoa," *The Nation* (February 25, 1931): 226–28; Margaret Mead, "Americanization in Samoa," *American Mercury* 16, no. 63 (1929): 264–70.

40. Margaret Mead, "South Sea Hints on Bringing Up Children," *Parents Magazine* 4, no. 9 (1929): 20–22, 49–52.; Mead, "Samoan Children at Work and Play," *Natural History* 28, no. 6 (1928): 26–36; Mead, "Standardized America vs. Romantic South Seas," *Scribner's Magazine* 40, no. 5 (1931): 486–91.

41. William Mitchell, "Communicating Culture: Margaret Mead and the Practice of Popular Anthropology," in *Popularizing Anthropology*, ed. Jeremy MacClancy and Chris McDonaugh (London and New York: Routledge, 1996), 122–34.

42. Ruth Benedict, "The Younger Generation with a Difference," review of *Coming of Age in Samoa*, *New Republic* (November 28, 1928): 50.

43. See Claudia Roth Pierpont, "The Measure of America: How a Rebel Anthropologist Waged War on Racism," *New Yorker*, March 8, 2004, 48–63. For more detailed discussions of the Boasian paradigm of cultural determinism and the role that culture and the social environment play in shaping human behavior, see *A Franz Boas Reader: The Shaping of American Anthropology, 1883–1911*, ed. George W. Stocking Jr. (Chicago: University of Chicago Press, 1974). For more about Boas's anthropology and its relationship to modernity, see Julia E. Liss, "Patterns of Strangeness: Franz Boas, Modernism, and the Origins of Anthropology, in *Prehistories of the Future: The Primitivist Project and the Culture of Modernism*, ed. Elazar Barkan and Ronald Bush (Stanford, CA: Stanford University Press, 1995), 114–32.

44. A. L. Kroeber to Margaret Mead, October 11, 1929, Box I-2, LC.

45. Lowie, Review of *Coming of Age in Samoa*, *American Anthropologist*, 532–34.

46. Ibid.

47. Ibid.

48. Ibid.

49. See, for example, discussions about modernism's fascination with the primitive in Barkan and Bush, eds. *Prehistories of the Future*, and Marianna Torgovnick, *Gone Primitive: Savage Intellects, Modern Lives* (Chicago: University of Chicago Press, 1990).

50. See, for example, James Clifford, "On Ethnographic Surrealism," and other essays in *The Predicament of Culture: Twentieth-Century Ethnography, Literature, and Art* (Cambridge, MA: Harvard University Press, 1988).

51. Peter Jennings and Todd Brewster, *The Century* (New York: Doubleday, 1998), 133.

52. Leach, *Land of Desire*. See also Simon J. Bronner, ed., *Consuming Visions: Accumulation and Display of Goods in America, 1880–1920* (New York: W. W. Norton, 1989).

53. Curtis M. Hinsley, "The World as Marketplace: Commodification of the Exotic at the World's Columbian Exposition, Chicago, 1983," in *Exhibiting Cultures: The Poetics and Politics of Museum Display*, ed. Ivan Karp and Steven D. Lavine (Washington, DC: Smithsonian Institution Press, 1991), 344–66; Robert W. Rydell, *All the World's a Fair: Visions of Empire at American International Expositions, 1876–1916* (Chicago: University of Chicago Press, 1984).

54. For more on the history of the term *culture* and the role anthropologists played in its transformation, see Michael A. Elliott, *The Culture Concept: Writing and Difference in the Age of Realism* (Minneapolis: University of Minnesota Press, 2002); Marc Manganaro, *Culture, 1922: The Emergence of a Concept* (Princeton, NJ: Princeton University Press, 2002); Marc Manganaro, ed., *Modernist Anthropology: From Fieldwork to Text* (Princeton, NJ: Princeton University Press, 1990). For more about Mead's contributions to this discourse, see Richard Handler, *Critics against Culture: Anthropological Observers of Mass Society.* (Madison: University of Wisconsin Press, 2005).

55. Laurence Urdang, *The Timetables of American History* (New York: Simon and Schuster, 1981), 313.

56. "Ten Most Harmful Books of the 19th and 20th Centuries," *Human Events Online*, May 31, 2005, http://www.humaneventsonline.com/article.php?id=7591. *Coming of Age in Samoa* was ranked twenty-first in a list of thirty books that included the Top Ten and Honorable Mentions.

57. See, for example, George E. Marcus and Michael M. J. Fischer, *Anthropology as Cultural Critique: An Experimental Moment in the Human Sciences* (Chicago: University of Chicago Press, 1986), and Thomas Hylland Eriksen, *Engaging Anthropology: The Case for a Public Presence* (Oxford and New York: Berg, 2006).

58. Micaela di Leonardo, *Exotics at Home: Anthropologists, Others, American Modernity* (Chicago: University of Chicago Press, 1998).

59. See Nancy Lutkehaus, "Margaret Mead: Anthropology's Liminal Figure," in *Reading Benedict/Reading Mead*, ed. Janiewski and W. Banner, 193–204. See also P. M. Worsley, "Science or Science Fiction?" *Science and Society* 21 (Spring 1957): 122–34.

60. See Serge Tcherkézoff, *Le mythe occidental de la sexualité polynésienne: Margaret Mead, Derek Freeman et Samoa* (Paris: Presses Universitaires de France, 2001).

61. Roger Sandall, *The Culture Cult: Designer Tribalism and Other Essays* (Boulder, CO: Westview Press, 2001), see esp. 57–67.

62. See Micaela di Leonardo, "The Anthropologist's Dilemma," *Chronicle of Higher Education*, March 19, 1999, B4.

63. See also Torgovnick, *Gone Primitive*; di Leonardo's *Exotics at Home*; and Susan Ware's *Letter to the World: Seven Women Who Shaped the American Century* (New York: W. W. Norton, 1998).

64. Di Leonardo, *Exotics at Home*, 170–83.

65. Ibid.

66. Torgovnick, *Gone Primitive*, 237–38.

67. Ibid.

68. Ware, *Letter to the World*, 93.

69. Margaret Mead, *Coming of Age in Samoa*, 2001 edition.

70. Fa'amotu Uriki to Margaret Mead, 1931, LC. See also Joyce D. Hammond, "Telling a Tale: Margaret Mead's Photographic Portrait of Fa'amotu, a Samoan Tāupou," *Visual Anthropology* 16 (2003): 341–74.

71. Torgovnick, *Gone Primitive*, 238. See also the discussion in chapter 9 of playwright David Williamson's play *Heretic*, in which Williamson suggests that Mead has an affair with a twenty-something Samoan man.

72. Nicholas von Hoffman and Garry B. Trudeau, *Tales from the Margaret Mead Taproom* (Kansas City: Sheed and Ward, 1976).

73. Trudeau and von Hoffman, *Tales from the Margaret Mead Taproom,* back cover.

74. See Talal Asad, ed., *Anthropology and the Colonial Encounter* (New York: Humanities Press, 1973), and Dell Hymes, ed., *Reinventing Anthropology* (New York: Random House, 1969).

75. See also *Anthropology on Trial*, a documentary film in which young Manus Islanders berate Mead for what they felt were inaccurate and biased descriptions Mead wrote about their culture, and Lenora Foerstel and Angela Gilliam, ed., *Confronting the Margaret Mead Legacy: Scholarship, Empire, and the South Pacific* (Philadelphia: Temple University Press, 1992).

76. Esther Newton, *Margaret Mead Made Me Gay* (Durham, NC: Duke University Press, 2000), 1; Elaine Showalter, *Inventing Herself: Claiming a Feminist Intellectual Heritage* (New York: Scribner, 2001); Sharon W. Tiffany, "Flappers in Paradise: Popular Media and the Ethnographic Gaze in Margaret Mead's *Coming of Age in Samoa*." unpublished paper, 2005.

77. Sharon W. Tiffany. "Imagining the South Seas: Thoughts on the Sexual Politics of Paradise in Samoa," *Pacific Studies* 24, nos. 3–4 (2001): 19–49, and "Contesting the Erotic Zone: Margaret Mead's Fieldwork Photographs of Samoa," *Pacific Studies* 28, nos. 3–4 (2005).

78. Sharon W. Tiffany, "Imagining the South Seas: Margaret Mead's *Coming of Age in Samoa* and the Sexual Politics of Paradise," in *Reading Benedict/Reading Mead*, ed. Janiewski and Banner, 155–65, and Sharon W. Tiffany, "Narrative, Voice, and Genre in Margaret Mead's *Coming of Age in Samoa*," special issue, The Gang of Four: Gregory Bateson, Ruth Benedict, Reo Fortune, and Margaret Mead in Multiple Contexts, ed. Gerald Sullivan and Sharon W. Tiffany, *Journal of Pacific Studies*.

79. The American psychologist and educator, G. Stanley Hall, had first described adolescence as a period of storm and stress that he attributed to the physiological changes in the individual at puberty. It was this biologically determined theory of adolescence that Boas had set Mead to investigate with her Samoan research and that her findings reported in *Coming of Age in Samoa* challenged. See G. Stanley Hall, *Adolescence: Its Psychology and Its Relations to Physiology,*

Anthropology, Sociology, Sex, Crime, Religion, and Education (New York: D. Appleton, 1904). For a history of the term *teenager*, see Thomas Hine, *The Rise and Fall of the American Teenager* (New York: Avon Books, 1999). For Hine's comments about Mead and *Coming of Age in Samoa*, see pp. 54–56. See also Jon Savage, *Teen-Age: The Creation of Youth Culture* (New York: Viking, 2007), 224–25, 227.

80. James E. Côté, *Adolescent Storm and Stress: An Evaluation of the Mead-Freeman Controversy* (Hillsdale, NJ: L. Erlbaum Associates, 1994).

81. Louis Menand, *The Metaphysical Club* (New York: Farrar, Straus, and Giroux, 2001), presents an engrossing intellectual history of the development of the ideas of James, Dewey, Peirce, and others during the last decades of the nineteenth century and early twentieth century, and their association with Franz Boas and anthropology.

Chapter 4
Mead as Anthropologist: "To Study Cannibals"

1. Fortune met Mead in New Zealand and they were married in Auckland before continuing on together to Australia and New Guinea. Margaret Mead, *Blackberry Winter: My Earlier Years* (New York: Kodansha, 1995), 162.

2. Since her intended research on animistic thinking in young children could be done in any non-Western, technologically simple society, she left the choice of field location to Reo. He consulted with his advisor, A. R. Radcliffe-Brown, and they chose the Admiralty Islands because no recent ethnological research had been done there. Margaret Mead, *Letters from the Field, 1925–1975* (New York: Harper and Row, 1977), 61.

3. "To Study Cannibals," *Hammonton News*, September 14, 1928, Box I-4, LC.

4. Lucien Lévy-Bruhl, *How Natives Think* (London: G. Allen and Unwin, 1926).

5. Mead, *Blackberry Winter*, 180.

6. Frances Drewry McMullen, "Going Native for Science: Dr. Margaret Mead, Ethnologist, Tells How She Lived in a Grass Hut in the Admiralty Islands and Became a Princess in Samoa to Study the Life of Her Primitive Neighbors," *Women's Journal* (July 1930): 8–9, 31–32.

7. Ibid., 32.

8. Ibid.

9. Ibid.

10. William Morrow to Margaret Mead, June 20, 1928, Box I-4, LC.

11. Margaret Mead, "Melanesian Middlemen," *Natural History Magazine* 30, no. 2 (1930): 115–30.

12. "Tooth Money Panic Rocks South Seas," *New York Times*, November 27, 1929, Box I-4, LC.

13. Associated Press, "Children Smoke at Three," November 27, 1929; Alva Johnston, "Women Studies Smoking Babies of Pacific Isles," *New York Herald Tribune*, Wednesday, November 27, 1929, Box I-4, LC.

14. John Watson and Rosalie Rayner Watson, *Psychological Care of Infant and Child* (New York: W. W. Norton, 1928).

15. Margaret Mead, *Growing Up in New Guinea: A Comparative Study of Primitive Education* (New York: William Morrow, 1930).

16. Ibid., "Just a Puff," 112–13.

17. Ibid. 234–35.

18. Mead, "With Ponkiau, Bopau, and Tchokal," *Blackberry Winter*, 173; Mead, "Carrying Piwen, about 2 years old," *Letters from the Field*, 87.

19. Presumably, Mead was referring to John B. Watson, the founder of behavioral psychology. Alfred Adler, a psychoanalytically oriented psychologist, was especially interested in the areas of child psychology and educational psychology, and Robert S. Woodworth was noted for his functionalist approach to psychology, in contrast to Watson's behaviorist approach.

20. Sociologist William Ogburn had originally met Mead when she took a class from him at Barnard. As he had just published a book about American marriage and family relationships (Ernest R. Groves and William F. Ogburn, *American Marriage and Family Relationships* [New York: Henry Holt, 1928]), Mead would have been eager to have him see the material about the Manus family. Mead had met the sociologist W. I. Thomas when Luther Cressman had invited Thomas to speak at Columbia to the graduate students' Sociology Club, and Thomas had been a dinner guest at their home. He had told the assembled audience that "the family was on its way out." See Luther Cressman, *A Golden Journey: Memoirs of an Archaeologist* (Salt Lake City: University of Utah Press, 1988), 94.

21. Mead was referring to the American psychiatrist William Alanson White. A. A. Brill was an early American disciple of Freud, translator of Freud's work, and proponent of Freudian psychoanalysis.

22. John Dewey, a modern American philosopher, psychologist, and educational reformer, was cofounder of American Pragmatism and a leading representative of the progressive movement in U.S. education during the first half of the twentieth century. From 1904 on he was a professor of philosophy at Columbia University. Much of what Mead wrote about education in *Coming of Age in Samoa* as well as *Growing Up in New Guinea* shows the influence of Dewey's work, such as *Democracy and Education: An Introduction to the Philosophy of Education* (New York: Macmillan, 1916). Alexander Meiklejohn was a humanistic educational reformer. The British philosopher and mathematician Bertrand

Russell was a prominent public intellectual who also experimented with new forms of children's education.

23. Mead, "Melanesian Middlemen."

24. The liberal British economist John Maynard Keynes was noted for his contributions to modern theoretical macroeconomics. R. H. Tawney, an economic historian with socialist leanings, had published *The Acquisitive Society* (1921) and *Religion and the Rise of Capitalism* (1926). James Harvey Robinson propounded a "new history" that chronicled the social, scientific, and intellectual progress of humanity rather than merely political happenings, in *The Humanizing of Knowledge* (New York: Arno Press, 1924).

25. Havelock Ellis was the famous British sexologist. G. V. Hamilton was a pioneer in the study of American sexual life. In 1929, Hamilton had published *A Research in Marriage* (New York: Garland, 1929). Along with Kenneth McGowan he also published a more popular treatment of his research material in *What Is Wrong with Marriage: A Study of Two Hundred Husbands and Wives* (New York: A. and C. Boni, 1929). The author Floyd Dell, coeditor of the left-wing socialist monthly, the *Masses*, had just published *Love in the Machine Age: A Psychological Study of the Transition from Patriarchal Society* (New York: Farrar and Rinehart, 1930). Dr. Katharine Bement Davis published *Factors in the Sex Life of Twenty-Two Hundred Women* (New York: Harper and Brothers, 1929).

26. Although Mead thought Sir Gilbert Murray taught at Oxford, he actually taught classics at Cambridge University. He was also active in the movement to establish a League of Nations. His brother, Sir Hubert Murray, was the administrator of the Territory of Papua from 1908 to 1940.

27. Prior to World War I, the Mandated Territory of New Guinea had been a German colony. After the war Germany lost its colonies and Australia was given control over the Mandated Territory of New Guinea.

28. Hilaire Belloc had just chaired a debate between G. K. Chesterton and Bernard Shaw on politics and the distribution of wealth in society. See G. K. Chesterton, Bernard Shaw, and Hilaire Belloc, *Do We Agree? A Debate between G. K. Chesterton and Bernard Shaw, with Hilaire Belloc in the Chair* (1928; repr., Folcroft, PA: Folcroft Library Editions, 1974). Thus Mead probably thought that Belloc and Chesterton might be interested in her account of the Manus economic system and its emphasis on primitive commercialism.

29. By 1930, the writer Aldous Huxley had published several novels, as had Hemingway. J. B. S. Haldane was a British biologist noted for his work on human population genetics.

30. Margaret Mead to William Morrow, August 13, 1930, Box I-4, LC.

31. Unattributed review of *Growing Up in New Guinea*, *New York Times Book Review*, November 16, 1930.

32. Ibid.

33. C. W. M. Hart, Review of *Growing Up in New Guinea*, *Man* 32 (1932): 146.

34. Ibid.

35. Ibid.

36. Ibid. Hart, an Australian by birth, exhibits his allegiance here to his British training with its emphasis on social structure. See Ian Langham, *The Building of British Social Anthropology: W. H. R. Rivers and His Cambridge Disciples in the Development of Kinship Studies, 1898–1931* (Dordrecht: Reidel Publishing, 1981).

37. Ruth Benedict, undated letter to *Man*, Box I-4, LC.

38. Ibid.

39. Reo Fortune, undated letter to the editor of *Man*, Box I-4, LC.

40. Ibid.

41. A. L. Kroeber, Review of *Growing Up in New Guinea*, *American Anthropologist* n.s. 33 (1931): 248–50.

42. Ibid., 249.

43. Ibid., 250.

44. Margaret Mead, *Kinship in the Admiralty Islands*, Anthropological Papers of the American Museum of Natural History, vol. 34, part 2 (New York: American Museum of Natural History, 1934), 181–358.

45. See Theodore Schwartz, ed., *Socialization as Cultural Communication* (Berkeley: University of California Press, 1976).

46. Margaret Mead, Preface to *From the South Seas: Studies of Adolescence and Sex in Primitive Societies* (New York: William Morrow, 1939): xx–xxi.

47. Ibid.

48. See Margaret Mead, "What I Think I Have Learned about Education, 1923–1973," *Education* 94, no. 4 (1974): 291–97, and Ray McDermott, "America without Margaret Mead: Reworking Gender, Race, Adolescence, and Learning," *Teacher's College Record* (2001).

49. See Mead, *Blackberry Winter*, chap. 14, "The Years between Field Trips," 181–93, for a description of this fieldwork.

50. Wissler gave Mead the summer research assignment as he had received a donation of funds for this specific research from Mrs. Leonard Elmhirst, a wealthy patron of the museum, whose connection with the museum's Department of Anthropology Wissler garnered through his close relationship with anthropologist-benefactress Elsie Clews Parsons. The choice of the Omaha was the result of Ruth Benedict's influence. She found funds to support Reo Fortune should they specifically work among the Omaha where he could investigate their lack of a vision quest, a problem that had vexed Benedict since her own dissertation research on Plains Indians (Mead, *Blackberry Winter*, 189; Mead, *Letters from the Field*, 95).

51. Maureen Molloy, "Disorderly Women and Disordered Culture," unpublished paper. 2005.

52. Mead, *The Changing Culture of an Indian Tribe* (New York: Columbia University Press, 1932), 16.

53. Mead, *Blackberry Winter*, 191.

54. Mead, *Changing Culture*, 3.

55. An article by Mead, "Some Problems of Culture Contact," was included in a classic textbook about the subfield of acculturation: *When Peoples Meet: A Study in Race and Culture Contact*, published in 1942 by the Progressive Education Association. As anthropologist Joan Vincent points out, the textbook was a clear indication of the field's appreciation of the fundamentally political nature of culture contact (Joan Vincent, *Anthropology and Politics: Visions, Traditions, and Trends* [Tucson: University of Arizona Press, 1990], 201).

56. The answer was that among the Omaha membership in religious societies depended upon hereditary right to secret knowledge. Thus, when the Omaha adopted the same convention as their Plains neighbors—that every man was free to seek a vision and claim the power it gave—when individuals who had no such hereditary right to a vision fasted and made claims, they were told that the vision was false. Mead, *Blackberry Winter*, 190–92; Reo Fortune, *Omaha Secret Societies* (New York: Columbia University Press, 1932).

57. Unsigned review of *The Changing Culture of an Indian Tribe*, *The Nation* (January 18, 1933): 72.

58. See chapter 7 for more detail about *New Lives for Old* and the television documentary it inspired, *Margaret Mead's New Guinea Journal*.

59. Alexander Goldenweiser, Review of *The Changing Culture of An Indian Tribe*, *American Anthropologist* n.s. 36 (October 1934): 609.

60. Ibid.

61. C. D. F., Review of *The Changing Culture of an Indian Tribe*, *Man* 33 (1933): 154. The review was most likely written by C. Daryl Forde, who later wrote about the value of "applied anthropology," of which acculturation studies such as Mead's Omaha research was a precursor. See C. Daryl Forde, "Applied Anthropology in Government: British Africa," in *Anthropology Today: An Encyclopedic Inventory*, ed. A. L. Kroeber (Chicago: University of Chicago Press, 1953), 841–65.

62. Vincent, *Anthropology and Politics*, 222.

Chapter 5
Mead as Anthropologist: "To Find Out How Girls Learn to Be Girls"

1. "Sex and Character among Primitive Societies," January 12, 1936.

2. "Dr. Mead to Join Third Expedition," August 18, 1931, Box I-4, LC.

3. "Jungle Expected to Reveal Why Boys Are Boys," *New York Herald Tribune*, August 18, 1931, Box I-4, LC.

4. William Engle, "Going and Getting It for Science: White Woman Studies Ghost-Ruled Savages in Melanesia," *New York World-Telegram*, June 17, 1931, Box I-4, LC.

5. Frances Phillips to Margaret Mead, December 3, 1934, Box I-8, LC.

6. Frances Phillips to Margaret Mead, November 23, 1934, Box I-8, LC. Russell, like Mead and her mentor Boas, was a proponent of a cultural determinist rather than biological determinist theory of human behavior. This similarity would have been an important reason for Mead to seek an endorsement for her book from him.

7. Margaret Mead to Bertrand Russell, December 3, 1934, Box I-8, LC.

8. Bertrand Russell, *Marriage and Morals* (London: George Allen and Unwin, 1929).

9. See Ray Monk, *Bertrand Russell: The Ghost of Madness, 1921–1970* (New York: Free Press, 2000).

10. H. G. Wells, *Experiment in Autobiography: Discoveries and Conclusions of a Very Ordinary Brain (since 1866)* (London: Victor Gollancz, 1934).

11. Frances Phillips to Margaret Mead, December 3, 1934, Box I-8, LC.

12. Margaret Mead to William Morrow, Box I-8, LC.

13. West, "Sex and Character among Primitive Societies."

14. Ruth Benedict, *Patterns of Culture* (Boston: Houghton Mifflin, 1934); West, "Sex and Character among Primitive Societies."

15. West, "Sex and Character among Primitive Societies." When she wrote her review of *Sex and Temperament*, West was not only experiencing a troubled marriage herself, but was also about to publish a novel, *The Thinking Reed,* in which her female characters demonstrated the deleterious effect of men on women, especially on intelligent women who strafe against the confines of the narrow roles they are allowed to play in society. Mead's book, with its argument against the strictures that Western society places on both women and men by its narrow definition of what is appropriate gendered behavior, addressed exactly the issues that West was personally struggling with and professionally critiquing in her writing.

16. West, "Sex and Character among Primitive Societies."

17. Later, in 1949, West wrote a review of Mead's book *Male and Female* in which she said that Mead was "a genius of the prophetic sort." *New York Herald Tribune*, October 30, 1949.

18. See Victoria Glendinning, *Rebecca West, a Life* (New York: Knopf, 1987). Glendinning considers West's life to be "the story of twentieth-century woman . . . both an agent of change and a victim of change." Like Mead, West has also become a heroine to contemporary feminists for her struggle to become a respected journalist and writer.

19. Margaret Mead, Preface to the 1950 edition, *Sex and Temperament in Three Primitive Societies* (New York: William Morrow, 1935; repr., New York: Harper Perennial, 2001).

20. Ibid.

21. Richard Thurnwald, Review of *Sex and Temperament in Three Primitive Societies*, by Margaret Mead, *American Anthropologist* n.s 38, no. 4 (1936): 663–67.

22. Thurnwald, Review of *Sex and Temperament.*

23. Margaret Mead, response to Thurnwald, Box I-8, LC.

24. Mead, *Sex and Temperament* (1935), 280. Betty Friedan, *The Feminine Mystique* (New York: Dell, 1963).

25. Michelle Zimbalist Rosaldo and Louise Lamphere, eds., *Woman, Culture, and Society* (Stanford, CA: Stanford University Press, 1975).

26. Kamala Visweswaran, "Histories of Feminist Ethnography," *Annual Review of Anthropology* 26 (1997): 591–621. Quote from Mead, *Sex and Temperament* (1935), 280.

27. Mead coined the phrase *triangular situation* to describe their predicament. Margaret Mead, *Blackberry Winter: My Earlier Years* (New York: William Morrow, 1972), 216–17.

28. Virginia Yans-McLaughlin and Alan Berliner, *Margaret Mead: An Observer Observed*, videocassette, color, sound, 85 minutes (New York: Filmmakers Library, 1995); Bill Bennett and Janet Bennett, *In a Savage Land*, videocassette, color, sound, 104 minutes (Culver City, CA: Columbia Tristar Home Entertainment, 1999).

29. Bronislaw Malinowski, *The Sexual Life of Savages in North-Western Melanesia*, with an introduction by Annette Weiner (Boston: Beacon Press, 1987). Originally published in 1929, with a preface by Havelock Ellis (London: Routledge and Kegan Paul).

30. While the point is made subtly in Yans-McLaughlin and Berliner's film, it is made more explicit in Lois Banner's biography in which she links Mead and Bateson's infatuation with each other to their mutual discovery that each of them adheres to the free love movement (*Intertwined Lives: Margaret Mead, Ruth Benedict, and Their Circle* [New York: Knopf, 2003], 324, 324n48). She devotes a chapter to the encounter between Mead, Fortune, and Bateson in New Guinea, titled "The 'Squares' on the Sepik" (*Sex and Temperament*, part 1, chap. 11 in *Intertwined Lives*). Psychologist Hilary Lapsley also elaborates upon the emotional conundrums and intellectual dialogues among the three anthropologists in a chapter titled "Points of the Compass" (Chap. 11 in *Margaret Mead and Ruth Benedict: The Kinship of Women* [Amherst: University of Massachusetts Press, 1999]). Both authors chose titles for their chapters that reflect the importance of a theory of temperament that Mead, with the aid of Bateson and to a lesser degree,

of Fortune, was developing that she referred to as "the squares." See also Gerald Sullivan, "The Theory of the Squares" (unpublished paper), and Tony Crook, "Temperamental *Ménage à Trois*: Mead, Bateson, and Fortune and the Trafficking between Social and Analytical Relations in Ethnography," paper presented at the Annual Meetings of the American Anthropological Association, Washington, DC, December 1, 2005.

31. Banner, *Intertwined Lives*, and Lois Banner, "Mannish Women, Passive Men, and Constitutional Types: Margaret Mead's *Sex and Temperament in Three Primitive Societies* as a Response to Ruth Benedict's *Patterns of Culture*," *Signs* 28, no. 3 (2003): 833–58; Lapsley, *Margaret Mead and Ruth Benedict*.

32. Banner, "Mannish Women, Passive Men."

33. Paul Roscoe, "Margaret Mead, Reo Fortune, and Mountain Arapesh Warfare, *American Anthropologist* 105, no. 3 (2003): 481–591.

34. Reo Fortune, "Arapesh Warfare," *American Anthropologist* 41, no. 1 (1939). Other critiques of Mead include Ira Bashkow and Lise Dobrin, "The Anthropologists' Fieldwork as Lived World: Margaret Mead and Reo Fortune among the Mountain Arapesh," *Paideuma* 53 (2007): 79–87, and Lise Dobrin and Ira Bashkow, "The Historical Study of Ethnographic Fieldwork: Margaret Mead and Reo Fortune among the Mountain Arapesh," *History of Anthropology Newsletter* 34, no. 1 (2007): 9–16.

35. Paul B. Roscoe, Introduction to *The Mountain Arapesh*, vol. 1, by Margaret Mead (1938; New Brunswick, NJ: Transaction Publishers, 2002), xxv–xxi. A Big Man is a type of political figure whose authority is based on his ability to achieve support from fellow kinsmen and villagers rather than on hereditary prerogative.

36. See Deborah Gewertz, "The Tchambuli View of Persons: A Critique of Individualism in the Works of Mead and Chodorow," *American Anthropologist* 83, no. 3 (1984): 615–29. See also Frederick Errington and Deborah Gewertz, *Cultural Alternatives and a Feminist Anthropology: An Analysis of Culturally Constructed Gender Interests in Papua New Guinea* (New York: Cambridge University Press, 1987), and Michael Young's new biography of Malinowski, *Malinowski: Odyssey of an Anthropologist, 1884–1920* (New Haven, CT: Yale University Press, 2004).

37. Nancy McDowell, *The Mundugumor: From the Field Notes of Margaret Mead and Reo Fortune* (Washington, DC: Smithsonian Institution Press, 1991).

38. Helen Fisher, Introduction to *Sex and Temperament*, 2001 edition, xx–xxi.

39. See, for example, Paul Roscoe's introduction to a reprint of Mead's *The Mountain Arapesh*, vol. 1, xxv–xxi.

40. Mead had published even more books during that ten-year period if we take into consideration the two technical monographs she wrote about Samoan and Manus social organization and *The Changing Culture of an Indian Tribe*.

41. See, for example, the work of Paul Robinson, *The Modernization of Sex: Havelock Ellis, Alfred Kinsey, William Masters, and Virginia Johnson* (New York: Harper and Row, 1976; repr., Ithaca, NY: Cornell University Press, 1989), and Rosalind Rosenberg, *Changing the Subject: How the Women of Columbia Shaped the Way We Think about Sex and Politics* (New York: Columbia University Press, 2004).

42. Margaret Mead, *From the South Seas: Studies of Adolescence and Sex in Primitive Societies* (New York: William Morrow, 1939).

43. For more about Lawrence Kelso Frank, see Jane Howard, *Margaret Mead: A Life* (New York: Simon and Schuster, 1984), 175–77; Mead, *Blackberry Winter*, 221, 249. See also Lawrence K. Frank, *Society as the Patient: Essays on Culture and Personality* (New Brunswick, NJ: Rutgers University Press, 1948).

44. Arnold Gesell et al., *Infant and Child in the Culture of Today: The Guidance of Development in Home and Nursery School* (New York and London: Harper and Brothers, 1943). For more about the history of child-rearing manuals in America, see Ann Hulbert, *Raising America: Experts, Parents, and a Century of Advice about Children* (New York: Knopf, 2003).

45. Warren I. Sussman, *Culture as History: The Transformation of American Society in the Twentieth Century* (New York: Pantheon, 1984).

46. For more about culture and personality as a subfield, see Philip K. Bock, *Rethinking Psychological Anthropology* (New York: H. H. Freeman, 1988); George Stocking Jr., ed., *Malinowski, Rivers, Benedict, and Others: Essays on Culture and Personality* (Madison: University of Wisconsin Press, 1986); William C. Manson, *The Psychodynamics of Culture: Abram Kardiner and Neo-Freudian Anthropology* (New York: Greenwood Press, 1988). The data Mead gathered about childhood and the family from the non-Western cultures she worked in were of interest to traditional Freudian psychoanalysts such as Karen Horney and Erik Erikson, who used this comparative data, as well as that of other anthropologists, to revise their theories in light of information about the impact of culture on the development of individual personality. See, for example, Susan Quinn, *A Mind of Her Own: The Life of Karen Horney* (Reading, MA: Addison-Wesley, 1988), and Lawrence J. Friedman, *Identity's Architect: A Biography of Erik H. Erikson* (New York: Scribner, 1999).

47. For more about Mead's association with Karl Menninger and the Menninger Foundation, see Lawrence J. Friedman, *Menninger: The Family and the Clinic* (New York: Knopf, 1990). See also Howard, *Margaret Mead: A Life*, 329–32.

48. Geoffrey Gorer, "Development of the Swaddling Hypotheses," in *The Peoples of Great Russia, a Psychological Study*, by Geoffrey Gorer and John Rickman (New York: Berghahn Books, 2001), 135–50. Originally published by Norton Library, 1949. For Mead's discussion, see Margaret Mead, "The Swaddling Hy-

pothesis: Its Reception," *American Anthropologist* 56 (1954): 395–409. For more about Mead, culture and personality, and the swaddling hypothesis, see Bock, *Rethinking Psychological Anthropology*, 41–60, 84–88.

Chapter 6
Mead and the Image of the Anthropologist

1. Clifford, "On Ethnographic Authority," in *The Predicament of Culture: Twentieth-Century Ethnography, Literature, and Art* (Cambridge, MA: Harvard University Press, 1988), 21–54.

2. However, as Micaela di Leonardo points out in *Exotics at Home: Anthropologists, Others, American Modernity* (Chicago: University of Chicago Press, 1998), from its inception American anthropologists have also studied American society.

3. Clifford, "On Ethnographic Authority." See also Eliza McFeeley, *Zuni and the American Imagination* (New York: Hill and Wang, 2001).

4. See, for example, Claudia Roth Pierpont, "The Measure of America: How a Rebel Anthropologist Waged War on Racism," *New Yorker*, March 8, 2004, 48–63. See also "In Focus: A New Boasian Anthropology: Theory for the 21st Century," *American Anthropologist* 106, no. 3 (2004): 433–94.

5. *Time* magazine, 1936.

6. Boas wrote both *The Mind of Primitive Man: A Course of Lectures Delivered before the Lowell Institute, Boston, Massachusetts, and the National University of Mexico, 1910–1911* (New York: Macmillan, 1911) and *Anthropology and Modern Life* (New York: Norton, 1928) for a general readership.

7. For example, Edward Sapir wrote about "The Discipline of Sex," in *American Mercury* 16 (1929): 413–20. See also Regna Darnell, *Edward Sapir: Linguist, Anthropologist, Humanist* (Berkeley: University of California Press, 1990). Thus, anthropologists were included along with other prominent intellectuals of the time in a volume that was to "work towards the advance of intellectual life in America" in order to "do our share in making a real civilization possible." Harold E. Stearns, Preface to *Civilization in the United States: An Inquiry by Thirty Americans*, ed. Harold E. Stearns (New York: Harcourt, Brace, 1922), iii.

8. Stearns, Preface to *Civilization*, iii; Robert H. Lowie, "Science," in *Civilization*, ed. Stearns, 151–62; and Elsie Clews Parsons, "Sex," in *Civilization*, ed. Stearns, 309–18.

9. For more about Ishi, see Theodora Kroeber, *Ishi in Two Worlds: A Biography of the Last Wild Indian in North America* (Berkeley: University of California Press, 1961); Clifford Geertz, "Morality Tale," Review of *Ishi's Brain: In Search of America's Last "Wild" Indian*, by Orin Starn, and *Ishi in Three Centu-*

ries, ed. Karl Kroeber and Clifton Kroeber, *New York Review of Books*, October 7, 2004, 4–6.

10. For more about Kroeber, see Geertz, "Morality Tale." Also, Julian H. Steward, *Alfred Kroeber* (New York: Columbia University Press, 1973), and Robert Brightman, "Jaime de Angulo and Alfred Kroeber: Bohemians and Bourgeois in Berkeley Anthropology," in *Significant Others: Interpersonal and Professional Commitments in Anthropology*, ed. Richard Handler (Madison: University of Wisconsin Press, 2004), 158–95.

11. After beginning his academic career as a sociologist, Luther Cressman became an archaeologist of the Northern Great Basin in the American West and a professor in the Department of Anthropology at the University of Oregon. See Luther Cressman, *A Golden Journey: Memoirs of an Archaeologist* (Salt Lake City: University of Utah Press, 1988). See also Luther Cressman, *Prehistory of the Far West: Homes of Vanished Peoples* (Salt Lake City: University of Utah Press, 1977).

12. Recently, anthropologists have shown a renewed interest in Fortune's work on the Arapesh. See discussion of critiques of Mead's Arapesh material published in *Sex* and *Temperament* in chapter 5, Paul Roscoe, "Margaret Mead, Reo Fortune, and Mountain Arapesh Warfare," *American Anthropologist* 105 no. 3 (2003): 481–591, and Lise Dobrin and Ira Bashkow, " 'Pigs for Dance Songs': Reo Fortune's Empathetic Ethnography of the Arapesh Roads," in *Histories of Anthropology Annual*, vol. 2, ed. R. Darnell and F. Gleach (Lincoln: University of Nebraska Press, 2006), 123–54.

13. Gregory Bateson, *Naven: A Survey of the Problems Suggested by a Composite Picture of the Culture of a New Guinea Tribe Drawn from Three Points of View* (Cambridge: Cambridge University Press, 1936). A younger generation of anthropologists revisited *Naven* in the 1980s and found it to be an early example of the type of experimental ethnographic writing they admired and advocated. See George Marcus, "A Timely Reading of *Naven*: Gregory Bateson as Oracular Essayist," *Representations* 12 (Fall 1985). For more about Bateson, see David Lipset, *Gregory Bateson: The Legacy of a Scientist* (Boston: Beacon Press, 1980), and C. Wilder-Mott and John H. Weakland, eds., *Rigor and Imagination: Essays from the Legacy of Gregory Bateson* (New York: Praeger, 1981). See also Gregory Bateson and Margaret Mead, "For God's Sake, Margaret," *CoEvolution Quarterly* (Spring 1976): 37.

14. The Bateson centennial year was 2004; it was celebrated with a conference at the University of California, Berkeley. Bateson's book *Steps to an Ecology of Mind*, a collection of his essays that range from articles he wrote based on his fieldwork in Bali to ruminations about the importance of play to human learning and his work on dolphin communication, remains in print today. Gregory Bate-

son, *Steps to an Ecology of Mind* (San Francisco: Chandler Press, 1972). See also Wilder-Mott and Weakland, eds. *Rigor and Imagination.*

15. For more on Alice Cunningham Fletcher, see Joan T. Mark, *Four Anthropologists: An American Science in Its Early Years* (New York: Science History Publications, 1980), and Joan T. Mark, *A Stranger in Her Native Land: Alice Fletcher and the American Indians* (Lincoln: University of Nebraska Press, 1988).

16. Fletcher never married. Preferring to live out West rather than on the East Coast, for many years Fletcher and a female companion continued fieldwork among the Pawnee and other Native American groups. She finally settled in Santa Fe and helped to establish the School of American Research there.

17. Barred from the prestigious Anthropological Society of Washington because she was a woman, Stevenson, who wrote and presented scientific papers based on her research at Zuni, started the Women's Anthropological Society in Washington, DC. See McFeeley, *Zuni*, 43–74.

18. McFeeley, *Zuni*, 57.

19. Long an obscure figure in the history of anthropology, feminist anthropologists and historians rediscovered Parsons in the 1980s and 90s. In many ways, Parsons was a precursor of Mead, leading the way as a feminist, anthropologist, and public intellectual. For more on Elsie Clews Parsons's life and career, see Desley Deacon, *Elsie Clews Parsons: Inventing Modern Life* (Chicago: University of Chicago Press, 1997); Louise Lamphere, "Feminist Anthropology: The Legacy of Elsie Clews Parsons," in *Women Writing Culture*, ed. Ruth Behar and Deborah Gordon (Berkeley: University of California Press, 1995), 85–103; Peter H. Hare, *A Woman's Quest for Science* (Buffalo, NY: Prometheus Books, 1985); Rosemary Levy Zumwalt, *Wealth and Rebellion: Elsie Clews Parsons, Anthropologist and Folklorist* (Urbana: University of Illinois Press, 1992); Louis A. Hieb, "Elsie Clews Parsons in the Southwest," in *Hidden Scholars: Women Anthropologists and the Native American Southwest*, ed. Nancy J. Parezo (Albuquerque: University of New Mexico Press, 1993); and Barbara A. Babcock and Nancy J. Parezo, *Daughters of the Desert: Women Anthropologists and the Native American Southwest, 1880–1980* (Albuquerque: University of New Mexico Press, 1988).

20. See Terry Teachout, *The Skeptic: A Life of H. L. Mencken* (New York: HarperCollins, 2002), and Ronald Steel, *Walter Lippmann and the American Century* (Boston: Little, Brown, 1980). Mencken, who did not think much of the social sciences in general, "anointed" Parsons as the only social scientist worth attending to in a long article in his *Prejudices: First Series* (New York: Knopf, 1919), cited in Deacon, *Elsie Clews Parsons*, 232.

21. See Christine Stansell, *American Moderns: Bohemian New York and The Creation of a New Century* (New York: Henry Holt, 2000) for more details about the importance of this group of women. See Deacon, *Elsie Clews Parsons*, 233–

35 for more on Parsons. Parsons, not Mead, first suggested the idea of trial marriage in her 1906 book *The Family.*

22. Although Parsons provided financial support for many of Boas's female graduate students, Mead was not among them. She had the support of her father as well as external grants instead.

23. See Babcock and Parezo, *Daughters of the Desert*, for information about these early female anthropologists and their ethnographic work in the Southwest.

24. Sally Cole's recent biography, *Ruth Landes: A Life in Anthropology* (Lincoln: University of Nebraska Press, 2003), brings Landes's pioneering work on race and gender, especially her book *The City of Women* (New York: Macmillan, 1947), to the attention of a wider audience. But Landes, seven years Mead's junior, never achieved a permanent position as an anthropologist and was marginalized by the profession for her comportment in the field as well as for her theoretical positions.

25. While much has been written about Hurston as a writer, there has been less written about Hurston as an ethnographer. Among the extensive scholarship on Hurston, I have found the following particularly useful: Deborah Gordan "The Politics of Ethnographic Authority: Race and Writing in the Ethnography of Margaret Mead and Zora Neale Hurston," in *Modernist Anthropology: From Fieldwork to Text*, ed. Marc Manganaro (Princeton, NJ: Princeton University Press, 1990); Graciela Hernandez, "Multiple Subjectivities and Strategic Positionality: Zora Neale Hurston's Experimental Ethnographies," in *Women Writing Culture*, ed. Behar and Gordon, 148–65. See also Carla Kaplan, *Zora Neale Hurston: A Life in Letters* (New York: Doubleday, 2002), and Alice Gambrell, *Women Intellectuals, Modernism, and Difference: Transatlantic Culture, 1919–1945* (Cambridge: Cambridge University Press, 1997).

26. Clifford Geertz, *Works and Lives: The Anthropologist as Author* (Stanford, CA: Stanford University Press, 1988), 111.

27. Ruth Benedict, *The Chrysanthemum and the Sword: Patterns of Japanese Culture* (Boston: Houghton Mifflin, 1946). For a discussion of the continuing impact of *The Chrysanthemum and the Sword*, see Joy Henry, "The Chrysanthemum Continues to Flower: Ruth Benedict and Some Perils of Popular Anthropology," in *Popularizing Anthropology*, ed. Jeremy MacClancy and Chris McDonaugh (London and New York: Routledge, 1996), 106–21.

28. Ruth Benedict, *Race, Science, and Politics* (New York: Modern Age, 1940), and Ruth Benedict and Gene Weltfish, "The Races of Mankind," Public Affairs Pamphlet No. 85. New York: Public Affairs Committee. For more on Benedict, see Judith Modell, *Ruth Benedict: Patterns of a Life* (Philadelphia: University of Pennsylvania Press, 1983); Margaret M. Caffrey, *Ruth Benedict: Stranger in This Land* (Austin: University of Texas Press, 1989); Margaret Mead, *Ruth Benedict: A Humanist in Anthropology* (New York: Columbia University Press, 1974), and

Nancy Lutkehaus, Foreword to *Ruth Benedict: A Humanist in Anthropology*, by Mead, xix–xlii. In 1933, Benedict became one of the first women included in the *Biographical Directory of American Men of Science*. *Time* magazine reported the news, as well as the fact that Benedict was "shocked" at the small number of women named in the volume (Ruth Schachter Modell, *Ruth Benedict: Patterns of a Life* [Philadelphia: University of Pennsylvania Press, 1983], 215).

29. Hortense Powdermaker, *Life in Lesu: The Study of a Melanesian Society in New Ireland* (New York: Norton, 1933), and *Hollywood, the Dream Factory: An Anthropologist Looks at the Movie-Makers* (Boston: Little, Brown, 1950). Her best-known book was *Stranger and Friend: The Way of an Anthropologist* (New York: W. W. Norton, 1966), in which she describes her various fieldwork experiences. See also Sydel Silverman, "Hortense Powdermaker," in *Women Anthropologists: A Biographical Dictionary*, ed. Ute Gacs et al. (New York: Greenwood Press, 1988), 291–96, and Jill Cherneff, "The Social Anthropology of Hortense Powdermaker," in *Visionary Observers*, ed. Jill B. R. Cherneff, Eve Hochwald, and Sydel Silverman (Lincoln: University of Nebraska Press, 2006), 119–48.

30. For further discussion of the historical connection between anthropology and Western imperialism, see the collection of essays edited by Talal Asad, *Anthropology and the Colonial Encounter* (New York: Humanities Press, 1973). See also Edward Said, "Representing the Colonized: Anthropology's Interlocutors," *Critical Inquiry* 15, no. 2 (1989): 205–25.

31. I ordered the cartoons from the *New Yorker* before the magazine had put all of its cartoons on CD. All the cartoons I refer to can now be found in Robert Mankoff, ed., *The Complete Cartoons of the* New Yorker (New York: Black Dog and Leventhal Publishers, 2004).

32. For more about the primarily middle- to upper-class readership of the *New Yorker* magazine, see Mary F. Corey, *The World through a Monocle: The* New Yorker *at Midcentury* (Cambridge, MA: Harvard University Press, 1999).

33. In fairness to the cartoonists, however, I should point out that there is another cartoon by Peter Arno (*New Yorker*, May 8, 1954) in which two men, who in all likelihood are anthropologists as they are seated at a table in the midst of a native village, one with paper and pencil in hand, the other holding a camera, in which the younger man is saying to his companion, "There's something I ought to tell you, Dr. Gordon. I think I've fallen in love." The joke reverberates off the fact that all we see in the picture are small, black, naked "native" women carrying bowls and pots on their heads. Who else could this strapping young man have fallen in love with other than one of these kewpie-doll-like figures?

34. Susan Sontag, "The Anthropologist as Hero," in her *Against Interpretation and Other Essays* (New York: Farrar, Straus, and Giroux, 1963), 68–81. Claude Lévi-Strauss, *Tristes tropiques*, trans. John Weightman and Doreen Weightman (New York: Atheneum, 1973), originally published in French as *Tristes tropiques* (Paris: Plon, 1955).

35. Sontag, "The Anthropologist," 74.

36. Ibid., 73, 74.

37. Ibid., 70.

38. Ibid.

39. Beginning with Columbus's "discovery" of the New World, reports generated the creation of "the savage slot." Michel-Rolph Trouillot, "Anthropology and the Savage Slot" in *Recapturing Anthropology: Working in the Present*, edited by Richard G. Fox (Santa Fe, NM: School of American Research Press, 1991), 17–44.

40. Clifford, "On Ethnographic Authority." For the most extended discussion of the establishment of fieldwork as the sine qua non of anthropology, see George W. Stocking Jr., "The Ethnographer's Magic: British Anthropology from Tylor to Malinowski," in *The Ethnographer's Magic and Other Essays in the History of Anthropology* (Madison: University of Wisconsin Press, 1992), 12–59.

41. Roger Sanjek, ed., *Fieldnotes: The Makings of Anthropology* (Ithaca, NY: Cornell University Press, 1990), and Paul Roscoe, Introduction to *The Mountain Arapesh*, by Margaret Mead (New Brunswick, NJ: Transaction Publishers, 2002).

42. Marianna Torgovnick, *Gone Primitive: Savage Intellects, Modern Lives* (Chicago: University of Chicago Press, 1990).

43. Torgovnick, *Gone Primitive*, 241.

44. Di Leonardo, *Exotics at Home*.

45. See, for example, Said, "Representing the Colonized."

46. However, as James Boon points out in his review of Torgovnick's book, there is a substantial difference in the treatment of non-Western cultures by Mead and Malinowski in contrast to authors such as Joseph Conrad and Edgar Rice Burroughs. In the latter cases readers learn very little about the actual lives of indigenous people, while ethnographers at least impart detailed information about them. James A. Boon, "Taking Torgovnick as She Takes Others," in *Verging on Extra-Vagance: Anthropology, History, Religion, Literature, Arts . . . Showbiz* (Princeton, NJ: Princeton University Press, 1999), 221–29. For more on Mead and Malinowski as modernist writers, see Marc Manganaro, ed., *Modernist Anthropology: From Fieldwork to Text* (Princeton, NJ: Princeton University Press, 1990).

Chapter 7
Mead as Scientist

1. Boston: Little, Brown, 1975, 142.

2. Edna Yost, *American Women of Science* (Philadelphia: Lippincott, 1955).

3. Margaret Mead, "Problems of the Atomic Age," *Survey* 85, no. 7 (1949): 385. See also Paul S. Boyer, *By the Bomb's Early Light: American Thought and*

Culture at the Dawn of the Atomic Age (Chapel Hill: University of North Carolina Press, 1994).

4. See Margaret Mead, ed., *Cultural Patterns and Technical Change* (New York: United Nations Educational, Scientific, and Cultural Organization, 1955), and Robert Cassidy, *Margaret Mead: A Voice for the Century* (New York: Universe Books, 1982).

5. Alfred C. Kinsey, Wardell B. Pomeroy, and Clyde E. Martin, *Sexual Behavior in the Human Male* (Philadelphia: W. B. Saunders, 1948).

6. See James H. Jones, *Alfred C. Kinsey: A Public/Private Life* (New York: W. W. Norton, 1997), 567.

7. Bill Condon, *Kinsey*, DVD, color, sound, 118 minutes (Beverly Hills, CA: Twentieth Century Fox, 2005), and T. Coraghessan Boyle, *The Inner Circle* (New York: Viking, 2004).

8. In addition to archival material and Jones's biography of Kinsey, my discussion of Kinsey depends upon Jonathan Gathorne-Hardy's *Sex, the Measure of All Things: A Life of Alfred C. Kinsey* (Bloomington: Indiana University Press, 2000), and Paul Robinson's *The Modernization of Sex: Havelock Ellis, Alfred Kinsey, William Masters, and Virginia Johnson* (New York: Harper and Row, 1976; repr., Ithaca, NY: Cornell University Press, 1989).

9. Jones, *Alfred C. Kinsey*, 567.

10. Kinsey et al., *Sexual Behavior in the Human Male*.

11. Alfred C. Kinsey to Margaret Mead, January 16, 1947, Box K-65, LC.

12. Ibid.

13. I contacted Paul Gebhard and he confirmed that Mead had never been interviewed. Gebhard, an anthropologist, visited the American Museum of Natural History toward the end of 1946 to view some Balinese sculptures she and Bateson had collected on Bali in 1936–37 that represented couples performing coitus in various positions. Paul Gebhard, personal communication, August 2004.

14. Margaret Mead, "An Anthropologist Looks at the Report," in *Problems of Sexual Behavior: Research, Education, Community Education* (New York: American Social Hygiene Association, 1948), 58–69, quotation is on p. 58.

15. Ibid., 58–59.

16. Ibid., 63.

17. Ibid., 62.

18. Ibid., 63.

19. *New York Times*, "Speakers Assail Kinsey on Report: Dr. Eisenbud Charges Biologist with Deep Biases; Dr. Mead with Important Omission," March 31, 1948, Box K-65, LC.

20. Dorothy Bromley, *New York Herald Tribune*, March 31, 1948, Box K-65, LC.

21. Ibid.

22. Mead, "An Anthropologist Looks at the Report," 67.

23. Ibid., 67.

24. Jones, *Alfred C. Kinsey*, 567.

25. Geoffrey Gorer, "A Statistical Study of Sex," Review of *Sexual Behavior in the Human Male*, by Alfred C. Kinsey, Wardell B. Pomeroy, and Clyde E. Martin, *New York Herald Tribune*, February 1, 1948, 4. The interviews, for example, had only been conducted with white males, mostly under the age of forty.

26. Jones, *Alfred C. Kinsey*, 580. Letter from Alfred Kinsey to George W. Corner, March 20, 1948, Kinsey Institute Archives.

27. Jones, *Alfred C. Kinsey*, 580.

28. Quoted in Fred Friendly, *Due to Circumstances beyond Our Control* (New York: Random House, 1967).

29. See, for example, Fredric Wertham, *Seduction of the Innocent* (New York: Rinehart, 1953) on the effects of crime comic books on children.

30. The *Adventure* series aired May 1953 through July 1956. Copies of the series exist in the archives of the American Museum of Natural History as well as at the Museum of Television and Radio in New York and the Paley Center for Media in Los Angeles. Interview with Perry Wolff, New York City, October 12, 1997.

31. See Jane Gregory and Steve Miller, *Science in Public: Communication, Culture, and Credibility* (New York: Plenum Trade, 1998), 39–51, for a discussion of the impact of sputnik as an impetus to the presentation of science in public culture in the United States.

32. Perry Wolff, phone conversation, October 12, 1997, New York City.

33. Ibid.

34. Philip Hamburger, Review of *Adventure*, CBS, *New Yorker*, June 6, 1953, 123–24.

35. *Adventure* series, CBS-AMNH, American Museum of Natural History Film Archives, "Time of Man" program, film no. 27. See also Nina J. Root, ed., *Catalog of the American Museum of Natural History Film Archives* (New York: Garland Publishing, 1987).

36. *Trance and Dance in Bali* was edited from footage Bateson shot in Bali in 1938–39 of a trance performance that he and Mead had commissioned from the Balinese. The film was completed in 1952. *Trance and Dance in Bali*, black and white, 22 minutes, Margaret Mead and Gregory Bateson, Pennsylvania State Audio-Visual Services.

37. As Catherine Russell points out, given how fake the set meant to represent Bali looks, it is not surprising the viewers might question the authenticity of the trance performance as well (*Experimental Ethnography: The Work of Film in the Age of Video* [Durham, NC: Duke University Press, 1999], 199).

38. For more about the Committee for Research on Dementia Praecox that funded Mead and Bateson's Balinese research, see Gerald Sullivan, *Margaret Mead, Gregory Bateson, and Highland Bali: Fieldwork Photographs of Bayung Gedé, 1936–1939* (Chicago: University of Chicago Press, 1999), 193n17.

39. Hamburger, Review of *Adventure*, CBS, 123–24.

40. "Stone Age Culture of New Guinea," in *Catalog of the American Museum of Natural History Film Archives*, ed. Root, 86. This segment did not actually feature Mead's own research in New Guinea. It focused on the 1953–54 expedition ornithologist Ernest Thomas Gilliard had just made to New Guinea. As the footage included images of the Iatmul, the Sepik River people Mead and Bateson had studied in 1938, Mead was asked to comment on Iatmul culture for the program.

41. The Admiralty Islands segment originally aired March 14, 1954. Interview by Charles Collingwood, *Adventure*, CBS, March 14, 1954, 1 videocassette, black and white, sound, 30 minutes, American Museum of Natural History Film Archives, Root, ed., *Catalog of the American Museum of Natural History Film Archives*. The program aired two years before Mead published *New Lives for Old*, her book about her return trip to Manus. The program also preceded two films based on Mead's Manus material, a short documentary titled *New Lives for Old* (Princeton, NJ: Educational Testing Services, 1960), and the television documentary, *Margaret Mead's New Guinea Journal*, produced by the National Educational Television network in 1968, discussed later in this chapter.

42. Mead and Bateson spent two years in Bali between 1936 and 1938. They returned to Bali briefly in 1939 after having spent nine months among the Iatmul in New Guinea.

43. Sullivan, *Margaret Mead, Gregory Bateson, and Highland Bali*, 4–5.

44. See Adrian Vickers, *Bali: A Paradise Created* (Singapore: Periplus Editions, 1989), 118–19. See also James Boon, "Between-the-Wars Bali: Re-Reading the Relics," in *Malinowski, Rivers, Benedict and Others*, ed. George Stocking Jr. (Madison: University of Wisconsin Press, 1986), and James Boon, "Mead's Mediations: Some Semiotics from the Sepik, by Way of Bateson and on to Bali," in *Semiotic Mediation*, ed. E. Mertz and R. Parmentier (New York: Academic Press, 1985), 333–57. For Mead's own description of her time on Bali, see Margaret Mead, "Bali and Iatmul: A Quantum Leap," in *Blackberry Winter: My Earlier Years* (New York: William Morrow, 1972), 223–39.

45. Sullivan, *Margaret Mead, Gregory Bateson, and Highland Bali*, 11.

46. See Sullivan, *Margaret Mead, Gregory Bateson, and Highland Bali* for a detailed discussion of these photographs. See also Ira Jacknis, "Margaret Mead and Gregory Bateson in Bali: Their Use of Photography and Film," *Cultural Anthropology* 3, no. 2 (1988); Andrew Lakoff, "Freezing Time: Margaret Mead's Diagnostic Photography," *Visual Anthropology Review* 12, no. 1 (1996): 1–18; and Russell, *Experimental Ethnography*, 199–206.

47. Margaret Mead and Gregory Bateson, *Balinese Character: A Photographic Analysis* (New York: New York Academy of Sciences, 1942), and Margaret Mead and Frances Cooke Macgregor, *Growth and Culture: A Photographic Study of Balinese Childhood* (New York: G. P. Putnam's Sons).

48. Lakoff, "Freezing Time," 2.

49. Mead did return to Bali with photographer Ken Heyman in 1957 and 1977.

50. The series of films, Studies in Character Formation, was about children and socialization based on the Balinese and Iatmul footage. The films included *First Days in the Life of a New Guinea Baby* (1951), *Karba's First Years* (1952), *Teaching Karba to Dance* (1951), *Bathing Babies in Two Cultures* (1951), and *Childhood Rivalry* (1951). See also Margaret Mead, "Children and Ritual in Bali," in *Childhood in Contemporary Cultures*, ed. Margaret Mead and Martha Wolfenstein (Chicago: University of Chicago Press, 1955), 40–51.

51. The bulk of the footage that went into *Trance and Dance* was filmed at a performance commissioned in honor of Mead's thirty-sixth birthday on December 16, 1937. Mead and Bateson justified their payment for the performances by the fact that Balinese themselves also commissioned these events. See Jacknis, "Margaret Mead and Gregory Bateson in Bali," 167. Another change in the performance was made by the Balinese themselves. They suggested that young women be allowed to perform the trance dance rather than the older women who were the usual performers. See Vickers, *Bali: A Paradise Created*, 123, and Russell, *Experimental Ethnography*, 199–206.

52. For a critique of Mead and Bateson's conclusions about Balinese trance possession, see Luh Ketut Suryani and Gordon D. Jensen, *Trance and Possession in Bali: A Window on Western Multiple Personality, Possession Disorder, and Suicide* (New York: Oxford University Press, 1993).

53. See Jacknis, "Margaret Mead and Gregory Bateson in Bali," 162, and Lakoff, "Freezing Time."

54. See Beatrice B. Whiting and John W. M. Whiting, *Children in Six Cultures: A Psycho-Cultural Analysis* (Cambridge, MA: Harvard University Press, 1975), and L. L. Langness, "Margaret Mead and the Study of Socialization," in *Socialization as Cultural Communication: Development of a Theme in the Work of Margaret Mead*, ed. Theodore Schwartz (Berkeley: University of California Press, 1976), 5–20.

55. See Hildred Geertz, *Images of Power: Balinese Paintings Made for Gregory Bateson and Margaret Mead* (Honolulu: University of Hawaii Press, 1994), and Hildred Geertz and Ida Bagus Made Togog, *Tales from a Charmed Life: A Balinese Painter Reminisces* (Honolulu: University of Hawaii Press, 2005). Togog was one of the Balinese painters whose work most impressed Mead and Bateson.

56. See, for example, Emilie de Brigard, "The History of Ethnographic Film," in *Principles of Visual Anthropology*, ed. Paul Hockings (The Hague: Mouton, 1975), 13–43; Karl G. Heider, *Ethnographic Film* (Austin: University of Texas Press, 1976) 27–30; Bill Nichols, *Representing Reality: Issues and Concepts in Documentary* (Bloomington: Indiana University Press, 1991), 217–19; David McDougall, *Transcultural Cinema* (Princeton, NJ: Princeton University Press, 1998), 66; Jay Ruby, *Picturing Culture* (Chicago: University of Chicago Press, 2000), 8; Anna Grimshaw, *The Ethnographer's Eye: Ways of Seeing in Modern Anthropology* (Cambridge: Cambridge University Press, 2001), 87–88; Alison Griffiths, *Wondrous Difference: Cinema, Anthropology, and Turn-of-the-Century Visual Culture* (New York: Columbia University Press, 2002), xx–xxi; and Russell, *Experimental Ethnography*, 8, 199–206. Even though these scholars are often critical of the "scientism" of Mead's films and photographic analyses, they nonetheless acknowledge the contribution that Mead made to further the use of visual material in the study of culture.

57. "Balinese Dislike the Japs," *New York Sun*, 1942.

58. Ibid. At the time Mead gave her interview the Japanese had landed on several of the islands surrounding Bali, but had not yet occupied the two major islands in Indonesia, Java and Sumatra, both of which lie to the west of Bali. However, soon after Mead made this statement, the Japanese invaded Bali on February 18, 1942, and the Dutch surrendered on March 9, 1942. The irony of Mead's statement about Bali as a balanced society was demonstrated forcefully in 1965–66 when 100,000 Balinese Communist Party members and sympathizers were massacred by fellow Balinese. See Vickers, *Bali: A Paradise Created* (first published by Penguin Books Australia, 1989), and Geoffrey Robinson, *The Dark Side of Paradise: Political Violence in Bali* (Ithaca, NY: Cornell University Press, 1995).

59. *Four Families*, Ian MacNeill, producer; Fali Bilimoria, William Novik, John Buss, et al., directors; 16 mm, black and white, sound, 60 minutes (New York: National Film Board of Canada, 1959).

60. Barry Dornfeld, *Producing Public Television, Producing Public Culture* (Princeton, NJ: Princeton University Press, 1998), 85.

61. Margaret Mead and Craig Gilbert, *Margaret Mead's New Guinea Journal*, 16 mm, color, sound, 75 minutes (Bloomington: Indiana University Audio-Visual Center, 1968); National Education Television advertisement, *Washington Post*, December 4, 1968, Box K-60, LC.

62. In *New Lives for Old*, Mead spells the name of the Manus village where she worked "Peri," but subsequent researchers use the contemporary spelling "Pere." While the film was touted as Mead's final return trip to Manus, she did make two other brief trips to Manus in 1971 and 1975. See Barbara Honeyman Roll, *Stori Bilong Pere: A Genealogical and Photographic Study of Pere Village,*

Manus Province, Papua New Guinea (Monterey, CA: Commercial Press of Monterey, 1982), 11, 14.

63. *New Lives for Old*, Horizons of Science Series, vol. 1, no. 6, 16 mm sound, color, 20 minutes (Princeton, NJ: Educational Testing Service, 1960).

64. Craig Gilbert, in an interview with the author, October 13, 1997, New York City.

65. For more details about this return visit to Manus, see Lola Romanucci-Ross, *Mead's Other Manus: Phenomenology of the Encounter* (South Hadley, MA: Bergin and Garvey, 1985), and "Manus Revisited—Preface 1965," Mead's introduction to the 1966 Laurel paperback edition of *New Lives for Old* (New York: Dell Publishing), 11–15.

66. Gilbert, interview. The story, of course, is a bit more complicated; but the blockbuster notion was the brainchild of Fred Friendly, formerly of CBS. Having recently come to NET, Friendly had convinced the Ford Foundation's head, McGeorge Bundy, to invest a large amount of money in NET so that the struggling station could produce several projects much grander in scope and expense than the typical fare NET had been producing. Gilbert's film received some of this funding.

67. *New Lives for Old* (Princeton, NJ: Educational Testing Service, 1960); Gilbert, interview.

68. Betty Sagir to Margaret Mead, December 3, 1968, Box K-60, LC.

69. Freda Lulinsky to Margaret Mead, December 12, 1968, Box K-60, LC.

70. Mead and Wolfenstein, *Childhood in Contemporary Cultures*; Martha Wolfenstein and Nathan Leites, *Movies: A Psychological Study* (New York: Atheneum, 1950).

71. Martha Wolfenstein, quoted in Goodell, *The Visible Scientists*, 154.

72. Christina Klein, *Cold War Orientalism: Asia in the Middlebrow Imagination, 1945–1961* (Berkeley: University of California Press, 2003), 79–88.

73. William J. Lederer and Eugene Burdick, *The Ugly American* (New York: W. W. Norton, 1958).

74. Thomas W. Russell Jr. to Margaret Mead, November 14, 1968, Box K-60, LC.

75. Margaret Mead, *New Lives for Old: Cultural Transformation—Manus, 1928–1953* (1956; repr., New York: William Morrow, 1975), 167; citations are to the 1975 Morrow edition.

76. Mead writes in detail about the Manus Islanders' reactions to the American troops in *New Lives for Old*. See chap. 7, "The Unforeseeable: The Coming of the American Army."

77. For more about Coca-Cola and its signification of an American way of life to Papua New Guineans, see Robert Foster, *Materializing the Nation: Commodi-*

ties, Consumption, and Media in Papua New Guinea (Bloomington: Indiana University Press, 2002).

78. See also Margaret Caffrey, "The Parable of Manus: Utopian Change, American Influence, and the Worth of Women," in *Reading Benedict/Reading Mead: Feminism, Race, and Imperial Visions*, ed Dolores Janiewski and Lois W. Banner (Baltimore: Johns Hopkins University Press, 2004), 141–52.

79. For a critical perspective on this role, see Lenore Foerstel and Angela Gilliam, eds. *Confronting the Margaret Mead Legacy: Scholarship, Empire, and the South Pacific* (Philadelphia: Temple University Press, 1992).

80. Estelle LuBell to Margaret Mead. December 4, 1968, Box K-60, LC.

81. Joan Mack to Margaret Mead, November 18, 1968, Box K-60, LC.

82. Elizabeth Rodnick (Lubbock, Texas) to Margaret Mead, December 5, 1968. Box K-60, LC.

83. David Riesman to Margaret Mead, December 12, 1968, Box K-60, LC. David Riesman, *The Lonely Crowd: A Study of the Changing American Character* (New Haven, CT: Yale University Press, 1950).

84. *Anthropology on Trial*, written, produced, and directed by Barbara Gullahorn-Holecek. Videocassette, color, black and white, 58 minutes (Boston: WGBH, Nova, 1983).

85. Faye Ginsburg, "Ethnographies on the Airwaves: The Presentation of Anthropology on American, British, Belgian, and Japanese Television," in *Principles of Visual Anthropology*, ed. Hockings, 363–98.

86. Dornfeld, *Producing Public Television, Producing Public Culture.*

87. André Singer and Leslie Woodhead, *Disappearing World: Television and Anthropology* (London: Boxtree in association with Granada Television, 1988), 12, 19. The first program in the Disappearing World series aired in the United Kingdom in 1970.

88. Mead collaborated on projects with other photographers and filmmakers, in particular, Ken Heyman and Paul Byers, She inspired and supported a new generation of ethnographic filmmakers that included Tim Asch, Asen Balicski, and Alison and Marco Jablonko. She was also instrumental in establishing the Ethnographic Film Archives at the Smithsonian Institution.

89. MTV, however, was aware of its predecessor, as it promoted *The Real World* as "the new *American Family.*" Unlike the original *American Family*, however, *The Real World* blurred the boundaries between fiction and documentary by casting individuals who were aspiring performers as its subjects. See Jeffrey Ruoff, *An American Family: A Televised Life* (Minneapolis: University of Minnesota Press, 2002).

90. Margaret Mead, "As Significant as the Invention of Drama or the Novel," *TV Guide*, January 6, 1973, A61–63.

91. Pat Loud, "Some Second Thoughts from *An American Family*," *Los Angeles Times*, March 4, 1973.

92. For Pat Loud's explanation of why her family agreed to be filmed for *An American Family* and the effects the series had on her own life, see Pat Loud with Nora Johnson, *Pat Loud: A Woman's Story* (New York: Coward, McCann and Geoghegan, 1974).

93. Ruoff also cites the proliferation of a new genre of documentary film, the first-person video diary (*An American Family*, 134–37). He also attributes the impact of *An American Family* with contributing to the rethinking of television's representation of family life that began in the 1970s, exploring the family as a site of conflict among couples and generations (ibid., 132).

94. Margaret Mead and Rhoda Metraux, "Image of the Scientist among High-School Students," *Science* (August 30, 1957): 384–90. *Science* magazine is published by the Association for the Advancement of Science.

95. Mead and Metraux, "Image of the Scientist," 237–40. The students assumed that a scientist was a man, but although they were female scientists themselves, Mead and Metraux structured the survey in such a way that they assumed that girls would not be potential scientists but rather only the wives of scientists.

96. C. P. Snow, *The Two Cultures and the Scientific Revolution* (New York: Cambridge University Press, 1959).

97. Deborah Tannen, *You Just Don't Understand: Women and Men in Conversation* (New York: William Morrow, 1990). See also Robin Lakoff, *Language and Woman's Place* (New York: Harper and Row, 1975).

98. Mead believed so strongly in this that she wrote a book about it with Paul Byers, *The Small Conference: An Innovation in Communication* (The Hague and Paris: Mouton, 1968). The book was copiously illustrated with photographs of such events to illustrate the social dynamic this type of group promoted.

99. Margaret Mead, *People and Places* (New York: World Publishing, 1959). This book was reprinted nine times, most recently by Bantam Publishers in 1970, the edition from which the book jacket blurb was taken.

100. For more on the political and intellectual roots of this cold war ideology, see Klein, *Cold War Orientalism*. See also note 77 and the discussion of *Margaret Mead's New Guinea Journal*.

101. Carlotta Hacker, *Women in Profile: Scientists* (New York: Crabtree Publishing, 1998). The other five include Mary Leakey (paleontologist and archaeologist), Chien-shiung Wu (nuclear physicist), Dian Fossey (primatologist), Rachel Carson (marine biologist), and Jocelyn Bell Burnell (astronomer). Anthropologist Ruth Benedict and primatologist Jane Goodall are included among the fourteen shorter profiles in the book.

102. Joan T. Mark, *Margaret Mead: Coming of Age in America*, Oxford Series in Science (New York: Oxford University Press, 1999).

103. Susan Saunders, *Margaret Mead: The World Was Her Family*, Women of Our Time Series (New York: Penguin, 1987).

104. Saunders, *Margaret Mead*.

105. Carol Church Bauer, *Margaret Mead: Student of the Global Village* (Minneapolis: Greenhaven Press, 1976); Mary Bowman-Kruhm, *Margaret Mead: A Biography* (Greenwich, CT: Greenwood Press, 2003); Sam Epstein and Beryl Epstein, *She Never Looked Back: Margaret Mead in Samoa* (New York: Coward, McCann and Geoghegan, 1980); Spencer Johnson, *The Value of Understanding: The Story of Margaret Mead* (La Jolla, CA: Value Communications, 1979).

106. Other examples of this type of book include Edward Rice, *Margaret Mead: A Portrait* (New York: Harper and Row, 1979); Elizabeth Anticaglia, *12 American Women* (Chicago: Nelson-Hall, 1975); Barbara Cady, Jean-Jacques Naudet, and Raymond McGrath, *Icons of the 20th Century: 200 Men and Women Who Have Made a Difference* (Woodstock, NY: Overlook Press, 1998).

107. This latter idea has variously been glossed as humans inhabiting "one [common] world" or "the family of man." The latter phrase refers to the title of a famous photography exhibition held at The Museum of Modern Art in New York City in 1955 that I discuss in more detail in chapter 8. Edward Steichen, *The Family of Man* (New York: The Museum of Modern Art, 1955).

108. Hudson Talbott, *We're Back! A Dinosaur's Story* (New York: Crown Publishers, 1987). Steven Spielberg produced an animated film version of the book that featured the voice of Julia Child—similar in heft and tenor of voice to Mead—as Dr. Bleeb! See *We're Back! A Dinosaur's Story*, directed by Phil Nibbelink and Simon Wells, 1993.

109. Despite her initial reservations about television, Mead eventually embraced it in a similar manner to her mother's initial attitude toward advertising.

110. The term *chautauqua* refers to both events—traveling tent shows that brought musicians, actors, and scholars and intellectuals to talk in small towns across America—and a place in upstate New York. Chautauqua, New York, is home to the Chautauqua Institution, which still serves as a site for public cultural events. Mead was a frequent speaker at the Chautauqua Institution up until her death in 1978. See Jeffrey Simpson, *Chautauqua: An American Utopia* (New York: Harry N. Abrams, 1999).

111. Goodell, *The Visible Scientists*, 141.

Chapter 8
Mead as Public Intellectual and Celebrity

1. Jocelyn Linnekin, "Margaret Mead," in *Thinkers of the 20th Century: A Biographical, Bibliographical, and Critical Dictionary* (Detroit, MI: Gale Research, 1983), 384–86.

2. Rae Goodell, *The Visible Scientists* (Boston: Little, Brown, 1975), 3–6. See also Margaret Mead and Rhoda Metraux's study, "Image of the Scientist among High-School Students: A Pilot Study" for information about high school students' stereotypes of the scientist in the 1950s, in *Science* (August 30, 1957): 384–90.

3. One can see the legacy of Mead's role as a visible scientist in the use that various interest groups make today of her image and her name. See, for example, the Web site cannabisseeds.com, that presents her as a sober scientific voice who spoke out for the legalization of marijuana.

4. For more about the Scientists' Institute for Public Information (SIPI) see Robert Cassidy, *Margaret Mead: A Voice for the Century* (New York: Universe Books, 1982), 132; Jane Howard, *Margaret Mead: A Life* (New York: Simon and Schuster, 1984), 369, 397; and Nancy Lutkehaus, "Margaret Mead, New York, the World," Keynote address, New York Academy of Sciences, New York, October 1, 2001. Mead had been one of the founding members of the organization in 1963.

5. Goodell, *The Visible Scientists*. Other science-celebrities include Jacob Bronowski and Desmond Morris. The late anthropologists Ashley Montagu and Marvin Harris were to some extent heirs of Margaret Mead's slot as a media anthropologist, as are Helen Fisher and Lionel Tiger today.

6. Carol Kaesuk Yoon, "Stephen Jay Gould, 60, Is Dead; Enlivened Evolutionary Theory, *New York Times*, May 21, 2002, A1. Gould taught popular courses on the history of science and biology at Harvard and was the author of over twenty-two books, many of them written for a general reader.

7. Robert Lee Hotz and Elaine Woo, "Stephen Gould, 60; Leading Evolutionary Biologist Was Called 'Latter-Day Darwin," *Los Angeles Times*, May 21, 2002, B10. See also Richard Monastersky, "Revising the Book of Life," *Chronicle of Higher Education*, March 15, 2002, A14–A18.

8. Russell Jacoby, *The Last Intellectuals: American Culture in the Age of Academe* (New York: Basic Books, 1987). See also Richard Posner, *Public Intellectuals: A Study of Decline* (Cambridge, MA: Harvard University Press, 2001); John Michael, *Anxious Intellects: Academic Professionals, Public Intellectuals, and Enlightenment Values* (Durham, NC: Duke University Press, 2000).

9. See Bruce Robbins, ed., *Intellectuals: Academics, Aesthetics, Politics* (Minneapolis: University of Minnesota Press, 1990), and Edward Said, *Representations of the Intellectual: The 1993 Reith Lectures* (New York: Vintage, 1994).

10. The term *academostar* has received much attention in recent years. See David Shumway, "Academostars," *Minnesota Review* n.s. 52–54 (Fall 2001): 175–84.

11. See Said on Jacoby, *Representations of the Intellectual*, 71–73.

12. Jacoby, *The Last Intellectuals*, 17.

13. Ibid.

14. Said, *Representations of the Intellectual*, 65–83.

15. See Dana Polan, "Professors," *Discourse* 6 (Fall 1993): 28–49.

16. Richard Posner, "University as Business," *Atlantic Monthly*, June 2002, 21. See also Jennifer Washburn, *University, Inc.: The Corporate Corruption of American Higher Education* (New York: Basic Books, 2005), and Derek Bok, *Universities in the Marketplace: The Commercialization of Higher Education* (Princeton, NJ: Princeton University Press, 2003).

17. Posner, "University as Business," 21.

18. Martin Jay, "Force Fields: The Academic Woman as Performance Artist," *Salmagundi* (Spring/Summer 1995): 28–34.

19. Said, *Representations of the Intellectual*, 11–13.

20. David Shumway, "The Star System in Literary Studies," *Proceedings of the Modern Language Association* 112 (January 1997): 85–100, quotation p. 86.

21. David Stewart, *The PBS Companion: A History of Public Television* (New York: TV Books, 1999).

22. Margaret Mead to Henry Romeike, Inc., March 13, 1930, LC. See also Susan Ware, *Letter to the World: Seven Women Who Shaped the American Century* (New York: W. W. Norton, 1998), 99.

23. Mary Alden Hopkins to Margaret Mead, December 26, 1930, MM, LC. Also, Ware, *Letter to the World*, 99–100.

24. United States Information Agency, *Reflections: Margaret Mead*, 16 mm, color, sound, 58 minutes (Washington, DC: USIA, 1975).

25. Hope Ridings Miller, "The 10 Outstanding Women of the Modern World," *Washington Post*, February 3, 1943. Miller had been asked to make a list of ten women, but in the end she could only come up with eight. The other women were Dorothy Thompson, a popular political journalist and foreign correspondent; Eve Curie, the daughter of the Nobel Prize–winning physicist, Marie Curie; Sigred Undset, a Norwegian writer who won the Nobel Prize for Literature in 1928; and Louise Boyd, known for her expedition to Greenland.

26. Mead corresponded with Eleanor Roosevelt on several occasions to voice her opinion about various social and political issues. Box C4, C10, C13, LC.

27. Miller, "The 10 Outstanding Women."

28. For example, "They Hitched Their Wagon to a Star," *Mademoiselle* magazine (1941) and "They Proved a Woman's Place Is Where a Job Needs Doing," *Look* magazine, n.d.

29. Terry Davidson to Margaret Mead, February 11, 1959; copy of the *Celebrity Bulletin*, Tuesday, February 10, 1959, Box Q-33-5, LC.

30. The only other nonentertainment personality mentioned besides Mead was the governor of New Jersey, Robert Meyner.

31. *Celebrity Service Bulletin*, New York City, February 10, 1959. Started in 1939, this publication still exists today (www.celebrityservice.com).

32. Terry Davidson to Margaret Mead, February 11, 1959, Box Q-33–5, LC.

33. Ware, *Letter to the World*, 118.

34. Tom Park to Margaret Mead, July 21, 1959, Box Q-33–6, LC.

35. For more about the *Martha Deane Show*, see Susan Ware's biography of the show's original host, Mary Margaret McBride: *It's One O'clock and Here Is Mary Margaret McBride: A Radio Biography* (New York: New York University Press, 2005).

36. Margaret Mead, *Twentieth Century Faith: Hope and Survival* (New York: Harper and Row, 1972).

37. See Erika Doss, ed., *Looking at Life Magazine* (Washington, DC: Smithsonian Institution Press, 2001); Wendy Kozol, *Life's America: Family and Nation in Postwar Photojournalism* (Philadelphia: Temple University Press, 1994); Loudon Wainwright, *The Great American Magazine: An Inside History of* Life (New York: Knopf. 1986).

38. Terry Smith, "Life-Style Modernity: Making Modern America," in *Looking at Life Magazine*, ed. Doss, 23–39, quotation is on p. 36.

39. For more about these goals and how they fit with a middle-class postwar American ideology of containment, see Christina Klein, *Cold War Orientalism: Asia in the Middlebrow Imagination, 1945–1961* (Berkeley: University of California Press, 2003).

40. *Time* magazine memo, CU.

41. For more on the relationship between gossip and celebrity in American culture, see Neal Gabler, *Walter Winchell: Gossip, Power, and the Culture of Celebrity* (New York: Alfred Knopf, 1994), and Gail Collins, *Scorpion Tongues: Gossip, Celebrity, and American Politics* (New York: William Morrow, 1998).

42. Frances Glennon, "Close Up: Student and Teacher of Human Ways," *Life*, September 14, 1959, 143–48.

43. Ibid.

44. Ibid.

45. Ibid.

46. Irene Neves, "Close Up: We Must Learn to See What's Really New," *Life*, August 23, 1968, 30–34.

47. Ibid.

48. Mead specifically addressed the issue of the generation gap in the United States in *Culture and Commitment: A Study of the Generation* Gap (Garden City, NY: Natural History Press, 1970).

49. Neves, "Close Up: We Must Learn to See What's Really New," 30–34.

50. Ken Heyman, in Howard, *Margaret Mead: A Life*, 352. See Ken Heyman and John Durniak, *The Right Picture* (New York: Amphoto, 1986).

51. At the time, Heyman was only twenty-eight; Mead was fifty-six and divorced. Heyman recalls that his mother was concerned that Mead might have designs on her son, but her worries, Heyman acknowledged, were unfounded. See Howard, *Margaret Mead, A Life*, 366. Mead and Heyman continued to collaborate on projects until Mead's death in 1978. Interview with Ken Heyman, New York City, October 15, 1997.

52. Edward Steichen, *The Family of Man* (New York: The Museum of Modern Art, 1955). See also Eric Sandeen, *Picturing an Exhibition:* The Family of Man *and 1950s America* (Albuquerque: University of New Mexico Press, 1995).

53. Margaret Mead and Ken Heyman, *Family* (New York: Macmillan, 1965).

54. Mead also made a film about families for the Canadian Film Board, *Four Families*, an anthropological comparison of families in Japan, India, France, and Canada. *Four Families*, Ian MacNeill, producer; Fali Bilimoria, William Novik, John Buss, et al., directors; 16 mm, black and white, sound, 60 minutes (New York: National Film Board of Canada, 1959).

55. Book-of-the-Month-Club blurb for *Family.*

56. Ibid.

57. Since its inception in 1926, the Book-of-the-Month-Club has been the subject of derision and debate among some intellectuals who criticized the idea of individual choice in reading matter being surrendered to the decisions of a committee, as well as to the commodification of culture that the club represented. For a review of this debate and discussion of the impact that the club has had on American culture, see Janet Radway, "Mail-Order Culture and Its Critics: The Book-of-the-Month Club, Commodification and Consumption, and the Problem of Cultural Authority," in *Cultural Studies*, ed. Lawrence Grossberg, Cary Nelson and Paula Treichler (New York: Routledge, 1992), 512–27.

58. Margaret Mead and Ken Heyman, *World Enough: Rethinking the Future* (Boston: Little, Brown, 1975).

59. Dust jacket blurb for Mead and Heyman, *World Enough*, 1975.

60. Ibid.

61. In fact, Mead felt so protective of the United Nations and was so invested in its success that she tried to get the Australian author, Shirley Hazard, who, after having worked for the UN for ten years, wrote a scathing critique of the corruption and wastefulness of its bureaucracy, to recant what she had written. Hazard's opinion of Mead, after this encounter, was that Mead's egotism was ungovernable and that she was "a woman carried away with ambition and aggression, and pounding her way with brute force." See Howard, *Margaret Mead: A Life*, 405–6.

62. Letter from Andrew Haley of the American Rocket Society to Margaret Mead, February 3, 1959, Box E-46, LC.

63. See Cassidy, *Margaret Mead: A Voice for the Century*, and quote from Alan McGowan in Howard, *Margaret Mead: A Life*, 397.

64. See Elizabeth M. Eddy and William L. Partridge, eds., *Applied Anthropology in America*. (New York: Columbia University Press, 1978). See also Virginia Yans-McLaughlin, "Science, Democracy, and Ethics: Mobilizing Culture and Personality for World War II," in *Malinowski, Rivers, Benedict, and Others: Essays on Culture and Personality*, ed. George Stocking Jr. (Madison: University of Wisconsin Press, 1986), 184–217, and Carleton Mabee, "Margaret Mead and Behavioral Scientists in World War II: Problems in Responsibility, Truth, and Effectiveness, *Journal of the History of the Behavioral Sciences* 21, no. 1 (1987): 3–13.

65. Margaret Mead, ed., *Cultural Patterns and Technical Change* (New York: New American Library, 1955). Originally published by the United Nations Educational, Scientific, and Cultural Organization, 1955.

66. Scholars of women's magazines in the 1950s and 60s have offered a complex and nuanced understanding of this media. *Ladies' Home Journal* carried monthly columns by the former foreign correspondent Dorothy Thompson and former first lady Eleanor Roosevelt, who discussed issues such as the House Committee on Un-American Activities and the FBI's search for communist sympathizers. And both *Good Housekeeping* and the *Ladies' Home Journal* regularly carried articles by well-known writers such as Noble Prize–winning author Pearl Buck and Rebecca West. See Nancy Walker, *Shaping Our Mothers' World: American Women's Magazines* (Jackson: University Press of Mississippi, 2000).

67. Eventually, humorist Judith Viorst and child development specialist Barry Brazelton joined Mead and Spock as regular columnists.

68. The material presented here is from the Columbia University Oral History Project (CU-OHP). Chassler was interviewed for the archives by Barbara Zera on March 1 and April 26, 1982. *Redbook* had started out as a literary magazine that primarily published short stories. However, during the 1940s it began its transformation into a more diverse magazine for "the young adult woman." It still published "good" fiction, but it also included a range of articles that focused on domestic life—how-to articles, articles about home decoration, health, food, marriage, and raising a family.

69. *Redbook*, "Why Young Mother's Feel Trapped," September 1960. Also published as *Why Young Mothers Feel Trapped: A* Redbook *Documentary*, ed. Robert Stein, introduction by Margaret Mead (New York: Trident Press, 1965).

70. CU-OHP, 29.

71. Ibid.

72. For more about Mead's anthropological perspective in her *Redbook* articles, see Robert J. Foster, "Margaret Mead's *Redbook* Project: A Problem in the Sociology of Culture," unpublished paper, 1982, and Paul Bohannon, Review of

A Way of Seeing, by Margaret Mead and Rhoda Metraux, *American Ethnologist* (1980): 198.

73. Eventually, Mead and Metraux shared the authorship of the articles, with Mead often spewing out ideas for a piece and Metraux bringing it to fruition. See Margaret Mead and Rhoda Metraux, *A Way of Seeing* (New York: William Morrow, 1974), and Margaret Mead and Rhoda Metraux, *Aspects of the Present* (New York: William Morrow, 1980).

74. Chassler, CU-OHP, 51.

75. Rhoda Metraux chose to reprint this article in a collection of their *Redbook* pieces published after Mead's death. Margaret Mead and Rhoda Metraux, "Bisexuality: A New Awareness," in *Aspects of the Present*, 269. The article originally appeared as "Bisexuality: What's It All About?" in *Redbook*, January 1975, with Margaret Mead as the only author; references will be to the 1980 Morrow reprint.

76. Mead and Metraux, "Bisexuality," 274.

77. Headline from the *Courier-Post*. This letter from Crary appeared in numerous newspapers across the country.

78. Mildred Rogers Crary, letter to the editor, *Courier-Post* (Camden, New Jersey), April 2, 1971, Box K-66, LC.

79. Joe McGinniss, *The Selling of the President* (1969; reprinted with a new introduction, New York: Penguin, 1988). Both candidates had hired the services of a public relations firm, but McGinniss's book focused on the Nixon campaign simply because the Humphrey campaign managers had refused him access while the Nixon campaign had agreed to have him around ("Introduction," *The Selling of the President*, xix–xx).

80. Crary, letter to the editor, Box K-66, LC.

81. Ibid.

82. Ibid.

83. Al Mattera to Margaret Mead dated Good Friday, 1971 (received April 14, 1971), Box K-66, LC.

84. John Gillerlair to Margaret Mead, April 10, 1971 (received April 28, 1971), Box K-66, LC.

85. Mead wrote to Henry Kissinger at one point to suggest that the government consider using American contractors and Asian labor in place of U.S. troops in Vietnam. Kissinger's response, dated July 12, 1969, acknowledges that her suggestion is "interesting," and he goes on to say that, "As you know we have just announced a 10 percent reduction of American civilian personnel in Vietnam. A troop replacement program is under way." Henry Kissinger to Margaret Mead, July 12, 1969, LC.

86. Quote from anonymous, undated, newspaper article titled "A Clear Image Is Key Asset," Box K-66, LC. Ken Heyman also told me that Mead privately thought there was no way that she would ever be seriously considered as a candi-

date given that she had been married and divorced three times (personal communication, New York City, October 15, 1997).

87. Crary, letter to the editor, Box K-66, LC.

88. Ironically, almost a decade before Mildred Crary initiated her genuinely serious campaign to launch Mead as a presidential candidate, David Cort, a former Time-Life editor and frequent contributor to *The Nation*, wrote an article for *Monocle*, a now defunct magazine started in 1957 by several Yale law school students that specialized in political satire, titled "Margaret Mead for President." In contrast to Crary's letter, Cort's article was a parody of the idea of Mead for president. Cort published his article in 1963, just before Kennedy's assassination and thus before the Republicans had picked their presidential candidate. Cort had great fun putting words in Mead's mouth as to her assessment, in pseudo-Freudian terms, of the childhood experiences of the various potential Republican candidates—Nixon, Goldwater, Nelson Rockefeller, and George Romney.

89. Mead supported the anthropologists because the documents used as evidence against them had been obtained illegally by students who had broken into their offices. For more details about this incident that occurred in 1971, see Eric Wakin, *Anthropology Goes to War: Professional Ethics and Counterinsurgency in Thailand*, Center for Southeast Asian Studies, Monograph No. 7 (Madison: University of Wisconsin Press, 1992).

90. Mead finally received clearance when it was determined that at the time Bateson was employed by the United States' Office of Strategic Services, a fact that initially had been overlooked by the investigators.

91. I obtained access to Mead's FBI records under the government's Freedom of Information act. The Mead Files include the following numbers: HQ-1210014450, HQ-1380002729, HQ-1000386818, HQ-07700288804. I sorted through more than seven hundred pages of government documents kept in Mead's files, much of it repetitious. For more details about Mead's files and the government's investigation of many of Mead's anthropological colleagues, especially from Columbia University, some of whom, such as Gene Weltfish, were subject to intensive interrogation from the FBI, see David Price, *Threatening Anthropology: McCarthyism and the FBI's Surveillance of Activist Anthropologists* (Durham, NC: Duke University Press, 2004).

92. Mead FBI Files.

93. Letter dated October 15, 1953, Mead FBI Files.

94. Mead was employed by the RAND Corporation from 1948 to 1950. The corporation supported part of the study she and others engaged in on the Soviet Union. Mead FBI File, Washington, DC, report, August 4, 1954.

95. Thus, for example, Dr. Carle Gurthe, who had worked with Mead for three years in Washington, DC when they were both employed by the National Research Council, testified that he "knows her to be a woman of marked ability in

her work, of excellent character and reputation, and a truly loyal American." Mead FBI File, Albany, NY, July 26, 1954.

96. Mead FBI File, report dated March 10, 1964.

97. Mead FBI File, report dated November 8, 1962. The peace conference was held September 13–15, 1962.

98. Mead FBI File, copy of letter sent to J. Edgar Hoover, October 29, 1969.

99. *New York Times*, October 28, 1969.

100. James Baldwin and Margaret Mead, *A Rap on Race* (Philadelphia: Lippincott, 1971).

101. This latter event had been proposed by Norman Cousins, then the editor of the serious-minded liberal "middlebrow" publication *Saturday Review.*

102. Donald Tuzin, personal communication, 1997.

103. Nominations for the Nobel Peace Prize can be made by university professors of social science, history, philosophy, law, and theology as well as former Nobel Peace Prize laureates, and it only requires two letters of nomination for someone to be considered as a candidate for the prize. See nobelpeaceprize.org. See also Judith Stiehm, *Champions for Peace: Women Winners of the Nobel Peace Prize* (Lanham, MD: Rowman and Littlefield, 2006).

104. Goodell, *The Visible Scientists*, 154.

105. Wolfenstein, quoted in Goodell, *The Visible Scientists*, 154. See chapter 7 for more discussion of this quote from Wolfenstein. Wolfenstein wrote a psychological analysis of the movies with political scientist Nathan Leites in which they further developed the idea of actors playing themselves in films, *Movies: A Psychological Study* (1950; New York: Atheneum, 1970), 289–92.

106. Wendy Doniger, *The Woman Who Pretended to Be Who She Was: Myths of Self-Imitation* (New York: Oxford University Press, 2005).

107. Goodell, *The Visible Scientists*, 147.

108. Ibid., 153.

109. Ibid., 142.

110. David Dempsey, "The Mead and Her Message," *New York Times Magazine*, April 26, 1970, 23.

Chapter 9
The Posthumous Mead, or Mead, the Public Anthropologist

1. Obituary, *Columbia Alumni Magazine* (Winter 1978): 20–22, quotation is on p. 20.

2. In *The Obituary Book* (New York: Stein and Day, 1971).

3. Although the story may be apocryphal, close to her death Mead was said to have told a nurse that she was dying and the nurse, attempting to comfort her,

said, "Yes, we all will someday." To which Mead replied, "But this is different." Jane Howard, *Margaret Mead: A Life* (New York: Simon and Shuster, 1983).

4. Alden Whitman, "Obituary: Margaret Mead Is Dead of Cancer at 76," *New York Times*, November 16, 1978.

5. Ibid.

6. Elizabeth Peer, "Oracle," 3, "She Spoke Her Mind," 70–73, *Newsweek*, November 27, 1978.

7. Margaret Mead Obituary, *Columbia Alumni Magazine*, 22.

8. "Margaret Mead: Mother to the World," *Time* magazine, 1969.

9. "Margaret Mead: 1901–1978," *Time* magazine, November 27, 1978, 57.

10. Editorial, *New York Times*, November 16, 1978.

11. See Margaret Mead, "A Cruise into the Past—and a Glimpse of the Future," *Redbook*, August 1966, about Constantin Doxiades and Ekistics, his work on human settlements. See also Margaret Mead and Ken Heyman, *World Enough: Rethinking the Future* (Boston: Little, Brown, 1975).

12. Guy Wright, "Thanks to Two Giants," *San Francisco Examiner*, November 22, 1978.

13. Ibid.

14. Ibid.

15. Ibid.

16. Janet Flanner (1982–1978), author of *Paris Was Yesterday, 1925–1939* (New York: Viking Press), 1972.

17. Paul Greenberg, "Two Women," Box S-10, LC.

18. Winthrop Sargeant, "Margaret Mead: It's All Anthropology," *New Yorker*, December 30, 1961. See also Mary F. Corey, *The World through a Monocle:* The New Yorker *at Midcentury* (Cambridge, MA: Harvard University Press, 1999).

19. Greenberg, "Two Women," Box S-10, LC.

20. Greenberg's comparison of Mead's handling of sociological theories to Julia Child's handling of a good slab of meat, besides being inherently humorous, also alludes to the physical heft and no-nonsense purposefulness of these two women.

21. Unattributed editorial, "2 Kinds of Leaders—Making Us Better," Box S-10, LC. Two days after Mead's death, a birthday party was held at the White House in Mickey Mouse's honor, celebrating his screen debut in "Steamboat Willie," on November 18, 1928.

22. Unattributed editorial, "2 Kinds of Leaders—Making Us Better," Box S-10, LC.

23. It is true that once Julia Child began to appear regularly on television, she too began to be known by a broader audience than just those individuals who had purchased *Mastering the Art of French Cooking* and her other cookbooks.

24. Meyer Fortes, "Obituary: Margaret Mead, 1901–1978," *Nature* 278 (March 1979): 289–90.

25. Ibid., 290.

26. British anthropologist Jeremy MacClancy's scathing comments about Mead give further insight into the "Americanness" of her popularity, as he notes that Mead's personal style grated on many British, academics and laymen alike. Jeremy MacClancy, Introduction to Jeremy MacClancy and Chris McDonaugh, eds., *Popularizing Anthropology* (London and New York: Routledge, 1996), 1–57.

27. Edwin McDowell, "New Samoa Book Challenges Margaret Mead's Conclusions," *New York Times*, January 31, 1983.

28. When Freeman wrote his master's thesis about Samoa in 1948, he did not critique Mead's Samoan work. See Paul Shankman, "Virginity and Veracity: Rereading Historical Sources in the Mead-Freeman Controversy," unpublished paper. Shankman has written several articles that critique Freeman's scholarship and support the veracity of much of Mead's work. See Paul Shankman, "The History of Samoan Sexual Conduct and the Mead-Freeman Controversy," *American Anthropologist* 98, no. 33 (1996): 555–67.

29. Derek Freeman, *Margaret Mead and Samoa: The Making and Unmaking of an Anthropological Myth* (Cambridge, MA: Harvard University Press, 1983), xvi.

30. Freeman, *Margaret Mead and Samoa*, xx.

31. See "Bursting the South Seas Bubble: An Anthropologist Attacks Margaret Mead's Research in Samoa," *Time* magazine, February 14, 1983, 68–70; "In Search of the Real Samoa," *Newsweek*, February 14, 1983.

32. Hal Hellman, *Great Feuds in Science: Ten of the Liveliest Disputes Ever* (New York: John Wiley and Sons, 1998), 177–206.

33. "Margaret Mead and Anthropology: An Evaluation," Symposium, Barnard College, New York City, April 8, 1983.

34. See Hiram Caton, "Conversion in Sarawak: Derek Freeman's Awakening to a New Anthropology," http://malinowski.kent.ac.uk/docs/conversion_sarawak.htm, December 5, 2007.

35. "Bursting the South Seas Bubble," *Time* magazine.

36. Ibid.

37. Allan Bloom, *The Closing of the American Mind: How Higher Education Has Failed Democracy and Impoverished the Souls of Today's Students* (New York: Simon and Schuster, 1987), 33.

38. Bloom, *The Closing of the American Mind*, 30.

39. Ibid., 33.

40. For more on the neoconservative critique of liberals, see Barbara Ehrenreich, *Fear of Falling: The Inner Life of the Middle Class* (New York: Harper Perennial, 1990).

41. Edward O. Wilson, *Sociobiology: The New Synthesis* (Cambridge, MA: Belknap Press of Harvard University Press, 1975).

42. Derek Freeman, *Margaret Mead and Samoa*.

43. Given many anthropologists' aversion to Wilson's sociobiology, some were moved to support Mead's Samoan work in order to defend Boasian anthropology and the larger issue, that of the autonomy of culture and its role in determining human behavior. See, for example, George E. Marcus's review of *Margaret Mead and Samoa* by Derek Freeman, "One Man's Mead," *New York Times Book Review*, March 27, 1983, 3; and Marvin Harris's review of Freeman's book, "Margaret and the Giant-Killer: It Doesn't Matter a Whit Who's Right," *The Sciences* 23, no. 4 (1983): 18–21. Others were concerned about the danger the controversy posed to all anthropologists if ethnographic research was seen as suspect.

44. Letter to the editor, *New York Times*, February 1, 1984.

45. Deirdre Carmody, "Speakers at a Symposium Defend the Work of Margaret Mead," *New York Times*, April 9, 1983.

46. James P. Sterba, "New Book on Margaret Mead Dispels Tranquility in Samoa," *Wall Street Journal*, April 14, 1983.

47. Sterba, "New Book on Margaret Mead."

48. Ibid.; Nicholas von Hoffman and Garry B. Trudeau, *Tales from the Margaret Mead Taproom* (Kansas City, MO: Sheed and Ward, 1976).

49. Sterba, "New Book on Margaret Mead."

50. Robert Trumbull, "Samoan Leader Declares: 'Both Anthropologists Are Wrong,' " *New York Times*, May 24, 1983.

51. See Penelope Schoeffel and Malama Meleisea, "Margaret Mead, Derek Freeman, and Samoa: The Making, Unmaking, and Remaking of an Anthropological Myth," *Canberra Anthropology* 6, no. 1 (1983): 58–69; Angela Gilliam, "Symbolic Subordination and the Representation of Power in *Margaret Mead and Samoa*," *Visual Anthropology Review* 9 (Spring 1993): 105–15; Albert Wendt, "Three Faces of Samoa: Mead's, Freeman's, and Wendt's," *Pacific Islands Monthly* 54, no. 4 (1983): 10–14, 69.

52. For more about Freeman's personality disorders, see Hiram Caton, "The Exalted Self: Derek Freeman's Quest for the Perfect Identity," *Identity: An International Journal of History and Research* 5, no. 4 (2005): 359–84, and Peter Monagham, "Archival Analysis: An Australian Historian Puts Margaret Mead's Biggest Detractor on the Psychoanalytic Sofa," *Chronicle of Higher Education*, January 13, 2006, A14.

53. This phrase, used to describe Freeman, appears in the liner notes for David Williamson's play *Heretic*.

54. Williamson wrote the screenplays for the films *Gallipoli* and *The Year of Living Dangerously*.

55. See Adam Kuper, "Coming of Age in Anthropology?" *Nature* (April 6, 1989): 453–55, and Gilliam, "Symbolic Subordination."

56. David Williamson, *Heretic: Based on the Life of Derek Freeman* (Melbourne and New York: Penguin, 1996).

57. While Williamson probed Freeman's libido and the tensions in his marriage for the source of Freeman's animus toward Mead, it is just as likely that it could have been a case of transference and identity with Fortune, Mead's aggrieved second husband. Like Freeman, Fortune was also an anthropologist from New Zealand. After his divorce from Mead, Fortune moved to Cambridge, England, where he lived out a peaceful but undistinguished professional life living with his second wife in a small cottage by the river Cam. Freeman may even have thought that he was avenging Fortune as well as himself in his unyielding and ceaseless attacks on Mead.

58. Derek Freeman, *Margaret Mead and the Heretic: The Making and Unmaking of an Anthropological Myth* (Harmondsworth and New York: Penguin, 1996).

59. Nancy Lutkehaus, "Margaret Mead as Cultural Icon," *American Anthropology Newsletter*, December 1996.

60. David Schneider, "The Coming of a Sage to Samoa," *Natural History* (June 1983): 4–10.

61. John Shaw, "Obituary: Derek Freeman," *New York Times*, August 5, 2001.

62. See, for example, Martin Orens, Paul Shankman, Lenora Foerstel and Angela Gilliam, Lowell Holmes, and Eleanor Leacock.

63. Leon Jaroff, "Margaret Mead," *Time* magazine, March 29, 1999, 183.

64. Motion passed at the 82nd annual meeting of the American Anthropological Association, Chicago, Illinois, in 1983.

65. Von Hoffman and Trudeau, *Tales from the Margaret Mead Taproom*, 97. Von Hoffman writes, "There are supposed to be a bunch of old ladies on the island who claim to be the little girls in Mead's book and who say they just made up every kind of sexy story for the funny *palagi* lady because she dug dirt. Since only Mead knows whom she talked to and she's never revealed the names, the anti-Maggy campaign could be an effort to spruce up the image. On one level, at least, Samoa is the last refuge and bastion of Calvinism." I do not know whether either Freeman or Heimans were aware of von Hoffman and Trudeau's book. However, Freeman did send me a copy of a Doonesbury cartoon that mentioned Margaret Mead that he had in his possession, which he attributed to the late 1960s–early 1970s. Heimans and Freeman were also no doubt familiar with James Sterba's article about American Samoan's reactions to the Mead-Freeman controversy that had been published in the *Wall Street Journal*, April 14, 1983, in which Sterba quoted parts of the above passage from *Tales from the Margaret Mead Taproom*. See note 43 above.

66. "Bursting the South Sea Bubble," *Time* magazine, 70.

67. "Ten Most Harmful Books of the 19th and 20th Centuries," *Human Events Online*, May 31, 2005, http://www.humaneventsonline.com/article.php?id =7591. Similarly, at the end of the twentieth century the Intercollegiate Studies Institute (ISI), another conservative watchdog organization, selected *Coming of Age in Samoa* as the worst book of the century, heading a list of fifty nonfiction titles. The ISI's concern was that the book was still being assigned on college campuses despite the fact that later scholarship proved Mead "to have been lied to by her Samoan informants." Jean Christensen (Associated Press),"Mead's Observations of Samoan Culture Named Worst Nonfiction Book," *Dallas Morning News*, January 21, 2000. For the Intercollegiate Studies Institute's complete list, see http://www.isi.org.

68. *American Anthropologist* published a special issue titled "In Memoriam: Margaret Mead (1901–1978)," *American Anthropologist* 82, no. 2 (1980).

69. Titles of the sessions were "Margaret Mead: Anthropology and the Public Sphere: Historical and Anthropological Perspectives," "New Anthropology for Old: Legacies of Margaret Mead in Oceania," and "The Legacy of Margaret Mead: Founding a Theory of Contemporary Cultures," 2001 Annual Meetings of the American Anthropological Association, Washington, DC.

70. "Margaret Mead: Human Nature and the Power of Culture," Library of Congress, December 2001. Washington, DC, see www.loc.gov/exhibits/mead.

71. See chapter 5.

72. See Paul Roscoe, Introduction to *The Mountain Arapesh*, by Margaret Mead (New Brunswick, NJ: Transaction Press, 2002). See also Nancy McDowell, *The Mundugumor: From the Fieldnotes of Margaret Mead and Reo Fortune* (Washington, DC: Smithsonian Institution Press, 1991).

73. Berghahn Books also reissued a series of Mead's books, Margaret Mead: The Study of Contemporary Western Culture, and Transaction Publishers reissued Mead's *Continuities in Cultural Evolution*, with a new introduction by Stephen Toulmin.

74. *Diane Rehm Show*, "Margaret Mead, to Cherish the Life of the World: 100 Years of Margaret Mead," produced by Nancy Robertson, 2 hours, WAMU and National Public Radio, December 16, 2001.

75. "Change the World," Margaret Mead Centennial Celebration, University of Rochester, March 31, 2001.

76. Ralph Waldo Emerson, *Representative Men*, ed. Pamela Schirmeister (New York: Marsilio, 1995), 13.

77. Emerson, *Representative Men*, 13.

78. Although no other cultural anthropologist has yet to achieve the same degree of celebrity as Mead, in some respects the British primatologist Jane Goodall has replaced Mead in the media slot of "celebrity scientist." Since there are no

longer any so-called primitive people, chimpanzees have become today's "primitives," an endangered species whose way of life must be preserved and studied in their natural habitat before it is too late.

79. Rae Goodell, *The Visible Scientists* (Boston: Little, Brown, 1975), 153.

80. See Marianna Torgovnick's critique of ethnographers in *Gone Primitive: Savage Intellects, Modern Lives* (Chicago: University of Chicago Press, 1990). For discussion of the so-called crisis in representation, see James Clifford and George E. Marcus, eds., *Writing Culture: The Poetics and Politics of Ethnography* (Berkeley: University of California Press, 1986), and James Clifford, *The Predicament of Culture: Twentieth-Century Ethnography, Literature, and Art* (Cambridge, MA: Harvard University Press, 1988).

81. Micaela di Leonardo, "The Anthropologist's Dilemma," *Chronicle of Higher Education*, March 19, 1999, B4.

82. In addition to her own work with WHO and the World Federation for Mental Health, Mead also mentored younger pioneers in this field, anthropologists such as Susan Scrimshaw and Barbara Pillsbury, who went on to work in the fields of public health and anthropology both in the United States and abroad. See Susan C. M. Scrimshaw and Elena Hurtado, *Rapid Assessment Procedures for Nutrition and Primary Health Care: Anthropological Approaches to Improving Programme Effectiveness* (Tokyo: United Nations University; Los Angeles: UCLA Latin American Center Publications, University of California, 1987), and Barbara Pillsbury, *Reaching the Rural Poor: Indigenous Health Practitioners Are There Already* (Washington, DC: U.S. Agency for International Development, 1979).

83. See Susan L. Allen, ed., *Media Anthropology: Informing Global Citizens*, foreword by Mary Catherine Bateson (Westport, CT: Bergin and Garvey, 1994).

84. See, for example, Faye D. Ginsburg, Lila Abu-Lughod, and Brian Larkin, eds., *Media Worlds: Anthropology on New Terrain* (Berkeley: University of California Press, 2002).

85. Elizabeth M. Eddy and William L. Partridge, eds., *Applied Anthropology in America* (New York: Columbia University Press, 1978). See also Virginia Yans-McLaughlin, "Science, Democracy, and Ethics: Mobilizing Culture and Personality for World War II," in *Malinowski, Rivers, Benedict, and Others: Essays on Culture and Personality*, ed. George Stocking Jr. (Madison: University of Wisconsin Press, 1986), 184–217.

86. See, for example, Thomas K. Fitzgerald, ed., *Nutrition and Anthropology in Action* (Assen, the Netherlands: Van Gorcum, 1977).

87. William Beeman, Introduction to *The Study of Culture at a Distance*, edited by Margaret Mead and Rhoda Metraux (Chicago: University of Chicago Press, 1953; repr., New York: Berghahn, 2001), xiv–xxxi.

88. Ray McDermott, "A Century of Margaret Mead," in *Visionary Observers: Anthropological Inquiry and Education*, ed. Jill B. R. Cherneff and Eve Hochwald

(Lincoln: University of Nebraska Press, 2006), 55–86. Also, Wilton S. Dillon, "Margaret Mead," *Prospects: The Quarterly Review of Comparative Education* 31, no. 3 (2001): 447–61.

89. Margaret Mead and Rhoda Metraux, "Image of the Scientist among High-School Students: A Pilot Study," *Science* (August 30, 1957), 384–90. Mead's interest in the impact of technology on human societies began in the 1920s through her friendship with Howard Scott, the founder of the technocrat movement in the United States (see Margaret Mead, *Blackberry Winter: My Earlier Years* [New York: William Morrow, 1972], 185–88, and William E. Akin, *Technocracy and the America Dream*: The Technocrat Movement, 1900–1941 [Berkeley: University of California, 1977]). During the late 1940s and early 1950s Mead participated in a series of conferences and projects initiated by the World Council of Mental Health and UNESCO that were concerned with the impact of Western technology on developing nations. Mead edited the volume *Cultural Patterns and Technical Change* (New York: Mentor Books, for UNESCO, 1955), one of the first collections to consider a set of cross-cultural case studies on the impact of technology in countries such as Greece and Burma.

90. Winthrop Sargeant, "Margaret Mead: It's All Anthropology," *New Yorker*, December 30, 1961.

91. Ken Heyman, interview by author, October 15, 1997, New York City.

92. Virginia Yans-McLaughlin and Alan Berliner, *An Observer Observed: Margaret Mead*, videocassette, color, sound, 85 minutes (New York: Filmmakers Library, 1995).

93. Of course, not all of these links are to Margaret Mead, the anthropologist, although it appears that the majority of them are either about her or about places named for her. This count was as of July 2007.

94. See "Awards: Margaret Mead," The Society for Applied Anthropology, www.sfaa.net/mead/mead.html, for more details about the award.

95. "Working for a Cayuga Return to Their Homeland," a flyer distributed by SHARE (Strengthening Haudenosaunee (Iroquois)-American Relations through Education), a community group based in upstate New York. The flyer ends with the quotation from Margaret Mead, 3. See also www.epa.gov/Region2/library/quotes.htm.

96. Margaret Mead and Muriel Brown, *The Wagon and the Star: A Study of American Community Initiative* (Chicago: Rand McNally, 1966).

97. In *The Wagon and the Star*, Mead and Brown refer to a successful 1950s radio program called *The People Act*, and the book that resulted from it, that Elmore M. McKee, a Yale University chaplain, had initiated with the help of NBC and the Twentieth Century Fund (Elmore M. McKee, *The People Act: Stories of How Americans Are Coming Together to Deal with Their Community Problems* [New York: Harper and Brothers, 1955]). Both the radio program and the book

featured stories about enterprising community projects across the United States. In the wake of World War II and the fear caused by the threat of nuclear annihilation, individuals like McKee and the directors of NBC felt that it was particularly important to trumpet the success of local community projects and their optimistic spirit that individuals still have some control over their immediate lives. Mead and Brown's book, which was distributed at home and abroad by the United States Information Agency, felt that this message was still important a generation later. See Mead and Brown, *The Wagon and the Star*, 71–74.

98. One might also include the ethnographic method since the practice of ethnography—observing people in their cultural milieu, talking with people in their own language, participating in their activities, over an extended period of time—has become a popular research method in many academic and applied fields outside of anthropology.

BIBLIOGRAPHY

Selected Books and Articles by Margaret Mead

The American Character (Harmondsworth and New York: Penguin, 1944). Reprint of *And Keep Your Powder Dry: An Anthropologist Looks at the American Character.* New York: William Morrow, 1942.

"Americanization in Samoa." *American Mercury* 16, no. 63 (1929): 264–70.

An Anthropologist at Work: Writings of Ruth Benedict. Edited by Margaret Mead. Boston: Houghton Mifflin, 1959.

"An Anthropologist Looks at the Report." In *Problems of Sexual Behavior: Research, Education, Community Education*, 58–69. New York: American Social Hygiene Association, 1948. Proceedings of a Symposium on the First Published Report of a Series of Studies of Sex Phenomena by Professor Alfred C. Kinsey, Wardell B. Pomeroy, and Clyde E. Martin.

And Keep Your Powder Dry: An Anthropologist Looks at the American Character. New York: William Morrow, 1942.

"The Application of Anthropological Techniques to Cross-National Communication." Transactions of the New York Academy of Sciences, series 2, vol. 9, no. 4 (1947): 133–52.

"As Significant as the Invention of Drama or the Novel." *TV Guide*, January 6, 1973, A61–63.

"Balinese Dislike the Japs, Says Woman Anthropologist: Dr. Margaret Mead Found No Dark Man Peril in the South Seas—It's Fascism or Democracy as Elsewhere." Interview by the *New York Sun*, 1942.

"Bisexuality: What's It All About?" *Redbook*, January 1975.

Blackberry Winter: My Earlier Years. New York: William Morrow, 1972.

Blackberry Winter: My Earlier Years. With a new introduction by Nancy C. Lutkehaus. New York: Kodansha International, 1995.

The Changing Culture of an Indian Tribe. New York: Columbia University Press, 1932.

"Children and Ritual in Bali." In *Childhood in Contemporary Cultures*, edited by Margaret Mead and Martha Wolfenstein, 40–51. Chicago: University of Chicago Press, 1955.

Childhood in Contemporary Cultures. Edited by Margaret Mead and Martha Wolfenstein. Chicago: University of Chicago Press, 1955.

"Civil Government for Samoa." *The Nation* (February 25, 1931): 226–28.

Coming of Age in Samoa: A Psychological Study of Primitive Youth for Western Civilization. New York: William Morrow, 1928.

Morrow, 1928 (August, September, December), 1929, 1930, 1932.

New York: Random House (Apollo Editions), 1961 (new preface).

New York: Editions for the Armed Services, 1928, 1945.

New York: New American Library/Mentor, 1949.

New York: HarperCollins/Perennial Classics, 2001.

London: [Jonathan] Cape, 1929.

Coming of Age in Samoa: A Psychological Study of Primitive Youth for Western Civilization. Reprinted with introductions by Mary Pipher and by Mary Catherine Bateson. New York: HarperPerennial Classics, 2001.

Continuities in Cultural Evolution. Terry Lectures Series. New Haven, CT: Yale University Press, 1964.

Continuities in Cultural Evolution. With a new introduction by Stephen Toulmin. New Brunswick, NJ: Transaction Publishers, 1999.

"A Cruise into the Past—and a Glimpse of the Future." *Redbook*, August 1966.

Culture and Commitment: A Study of the Generation Gap. Garden City, NY: Natural History Press, 1970.

Cultural Patterns and Technical Change. Edited by Margaret Mead. New York: Mentor Books, for UNESCO, 1955.

"Field Anthropology as a Career for Women" (working paper), LC, I-13. Draft of "Field anthropology as a career for women." P. 8. 1935?

From the South Seas: Studies of Adolescence and Sex in Primitive Societies. New York: William Morrow, 1939.

"Group Intelligence Tests and Linguistic Disability among Italian Children." *School and Society* 25, no. 642 (1927): 465–68.

Growing Up in New Guinea: A Comparative Study of Primitive Education. New York: William Morrow, 1930.

Growing Up in New Guinea: A Comparative Study of Primitive Education. Paperback edition, New York: Mentor, 1953.

"Intelligence Tests of Italian and American Children." Master's thesis, Columbia University, 1925.

"Introduction to the Pelican Edition: Fifteen Years Later." In *Male and Female: A Study of the Sexes in a Changing World*, 11–24. New York: Penguin, 1962.

"Jealousy: Primitive and Civilized." In *Woman's Coming of Age: A Symposium*, edited by Samuel Schmalhausen and V. F. Calverton, 35–48. New York: Liveright, 1931.

Kinship in the Admiralty Islands. Anthropological Papers of the American Museum of Natural History, vol. 34, pt. 2, 181–358. New York: American Museum of Natural History, 1934.

Kinship in the Admiralty Islands. New Brunswick, NJ: Transaction Publishers, 2002.

Letters from the Field, 1925–1975. New York: Harper and Row, 1977.

"Life as a Samoan Girl." In *All True! The Record of Actual Adventures That Have Happened to Ten Women of Today*, 94–118. New York: Brewer, Warren and Putnam, 1931.

Male and Female: A Study of the Sexes in a Changing World. New York: William Morrow, 1949.

Male and Female: A Study of the Sexes in a Changing World. New York: HarperCollins/Perennial, 2001.

"Margaret Mead." In *A History of Psychology in Autobiography*. Vol. 6, edited by Gardner Lindzey, 293–326. Englewood Cliffs, NJ: Prentice-Hall, 1974.

"Melanesian Middlemen." *Natural History Magazine* 30, no. 2 (1930): 115–30.

"The Methodology of Racial Testing: Its Significance for Sociology." *American Journal of Sociology* 31, no. 5 (1926): 657–67.

The Mountain Arapesh. New York: American Museum of Natural History, 1938.

The Mountain Arapesh. With an introduction by Paul Roscoe. New Brunswick, NJ: Transaction Publishers, 2002.

New Lives for Old: Cultural Transformation—Manus, 1928–1953. New York: William Morrow, 1956.

New Lives for Old: Cultural Transformation—Manus, 1928–1953. With a new Preface. New York: Morrow Quill Paperbacks, 1975.

"On Being a Grandmother." *Redbook*, July 1970. Reprinted in *Aspects of the Present*. Margaret Mead and Rhoda Metraux, 140–46. New York: William Morrow, 1980.

People and Places. New York: World Publishing, 1959.

People and Places. Toronto and New York: Bantam, 1970.

"Postscripts." *Chemical and Engineering News*, February 14, 1966.

Ruth Benedict. New York: Columbia University Press, 1974.

"Samoan Children at Work and Play." *Natural History* 28, no. 6 (1928): 26–36.

Science and the Concept of Race. Margaret Mead and Theodosius Dobzhansky. Edited by Ethel Tobach and Robert E. Light. New York: Columbia University Press, 1968.

Sex and Temperament in Three Primitive Societies. New York: William Morrow, 1935.

Sex and Temperament in Three Primitive Societies. New York: New American Library, 1950. With a new Preface by Margaret Mead.

Sex and Temperament in Three Primitive Societies. First Perennial Edition. With an introduction by Helen Fisher. New York: HarperCollins, 2001.

Social Organization in Manu'a. Honolulu: Bernice P. Bishop Museum Bulletin 76, Honolulu, Hawaii, 1930. Reissued 1969.

"Some Problems of Culture Contact." In *When Peoples Meet: A Study in Race and Culture Contact*, edited by Alain LeRoy Locke. New York: Progressive Education Association, 1942.

"South Sea Hints on Bringing Up Children." *Parents Magazine* 4, no. 9 (1929): 20–22, 49–52.

Soviet Attitudes toward Authority: An Interdisciplinary Approach to Problems of Soviet Character. New York: McGraw-Hill, 1951.

"Standardized America vs. Romantic South Seas." *Scribner's Magazine* 40, no. 5 (1931): 486–91.

"Stevenson's Samoa Today." *World Today* 58 (September 1931): 343–50.

Twentieth Century Faith: Hope and Survival. New York: Harper and Row, 1972.

"Visual Culture in a World of Words." In *Principles of Visual Anthropology.* 2nd ed., edited by Paul Hockings, 3–10. Berlin and New York: Mouton de Gruyter, 1995.

The World Ahead: An Anthropologist Anticipates the Future. Edited by Robert B. Textor. New York and Oxford: Berghahn Books, 2005.

World Enough: Rethinking the Future. Boston: Little, Brown, 1975.

General Works

Adams, Samuel Hopkins. *Flaming Youth*. New York: Liveright, 1923.

Akin, William E. *Technocracy and the America Dream: The Technocrat Movement, 1900–1941*. Berkeley: University of California Press, 1977.

All True! The Record of Actual Adventures That Have Happened to Ten Women of Today. New York: Brewer, Warren, and Putnam, 1931.

Allen, Frederick Lewis. *Only Yesterday: An Informal History of the Nineteen-Twenties*. New York: Harper and Brothers, 1931.

Allen, Susan L., ed. *Media Anthropology: Informing Global Citizens*. Foreword by Mary Catherine Bateson. Westport, CT: Bergin and Garvey, 1994.

Angier, Natalie. *Woman: An Intimate Geography.* New York: Anchor Books, 2000.

Anthropology on Trial. Written, produced, and directed by Barbara Gullahorn-Holocek. WGBH-Boston, Nova. Color, black and white, 58 minutes, 1983.

Anticaglia, Elizabeth. *12 American Women*. Chicago: Nelson-Hall, 1975.

Appadurai, Arjun. *Modernity at Large: Cultural Dimensions of Globalization*. Minneapolis: University of Minnesota Press, 1996.

Apted, Michael, director. *Gorillas in the Mist: The Story of Dian Fossey.* Arnold Glimcher and Terrence Clegg, producers. 1988. Videocassette, color, sound, 129 minutes. Universal City, CA: MCA Home Video, 1989.

Asad, Talal, ed. *Anthropology and the Colonial Encounter.* New York: Humanities Press, 1973.

Austin, Mary. *The Land of Little Rain.* Boston: Houghton Mifflin, 1903.

———. Review of *Coming of Age in America*, by Margaret Mead. *Birth Control Review* (June 1929): 165–66.

Babcock, Barbara A., and Nancy J. Parezo. *Daughters of the Desert: Women Anthropologists and the Native American Southwest, 1880–1980.* Albuquerque: University of New Mexico Press, 1988.

Baldwin, James, and Margaret Mead. *A Rap on Race.* Philadelphia: Lippincott, 1971.

Banta, Martha. *Imaging American Women: Idea and Ideals in Cultural History.* New York: Columbia University Press. 1987.

Banner, Lois W. *Intertwined Lives: Margaret Mead, Ruth Benedict, and Their Circle.* New York: Knopf, 2003.

Barkan, Elazar, and Ronald Bush, eds. *Prehistories of the Future: The Primitivist Project and the Culture of Modernism.* Stanford, CA: Stanford University Press, 1995.

Barrett, Mary Ellin. "Margaret Mead: First of the Libbies." *Cosmopolitan*, September 1972, 160–65.

Bateson, Gregory. *Naven: A Survey of the Problems Suggested by a Composite Picture of the Culture of a New Guinea Tribe Drawn from Three Points of View.* Cambridge: Cambridge University Press, 1936.

———. *Steps to an Ecology of Mind: Collected Essays in Anthropology, Psychiatry, Evolution, and Epistemology.* San Francisco: Chandler, 1972.

Bateson, Gregory, and Margaret Mead. *Balinese Character: A Photographic Analysis.* New York: New York Academy of Sciences, 1942.

Bateson, Mary Catherine. *With a Daughter's Eye: A Memoir of Margaret Mead and Gregory Bateson.* New York: William Morrow, 1984.

Baty, S. Paige. *American Monroe: The Making of a Body Politic.* Berkeley: University of California Press, 1995.

Bauer, Carol Church. *Margaret Mead: Student of the Global Village.* Minneapolis: Greenhaven Press, 1976.

Baughman, James L. "Who Reads *Life*? The Circulation of America's Favorite Magazine." In *Looking at Life Magazine*, edited by Erika Doss, 41–51. Washington, DC: Smithsonian Institution Press, 2001.

Beeman, William. Introduction to *The Study of Culture at a Distance.* Edited by Margaret Mead and Rhoda Metraux, xiv-xxxiv. New York: Berghahn, 2001. Originally published by Chicago: University of Chicago Press, 1953.

Bender, Thomas. *New York Intellect: A History of Intellectual Life in New York City, from 1750 to the Beginnings of Our Own Time*. New York: Knopf, 1987.

Benedict, Ruth. *The Chrysanthemum and the Sword: Patterns of Japanese Culture*. Boston: Houghton Mifflin, 1946.

———. *Patterns of Culture*. Boston: Houghton Mifflin, 1934.

———. Review of *Coming of Age in Samoa*, by Margaret Mead. *New Republic* (November 28, 1928): 50.

———. Radio program. Friday, February 28, 1948.

Bennett, Bill, and Jennifer Bennett. *In a Savage Land*. Videocassette, color, sound, 104 minutes. Culver City, CA: Columbia Tristar Home Entertainment, 1999.

Berger, John. *Ways of Seeing*. New York: Viking Press, 1972.

Blanton, Casey, ed. *Picturing Paradise: Colonial Photography of Samoa, 1875–1925*. Daytona Beach, FL: Daytona Beach Community College and the Southeast Museum of Photography, 1995.

Bloom, Allan. *The Closing of the American Mind: How Higher Education Has Failed Democracy and Impoverished the Souls of Today's Students*. New York: Simon and Schuster, 1987.

Blos, Peter. *On Adolescence: A Psychoanalytic Interpretation*. New York: Free Press of Glencoe, 1962.

Boardman, Barrington. *Flappers, Bootleggers, "Typhoid Mary," and the Bomb: An Anecdotal History of the United States from 1923–1945*. New York: Perennial Library, 1988.

Boas, Franz. *Anthropology and Modern Life*. New York: W. W. Norton, 1928.

———. *The Mind of Primitive Man: A Course of Lectures Delivered before the Lowell Institute, Boston, Massachusetts, and the National University of Mexico, 1910–1911*. New York: Macmillan, 1911.

Bock, Philip K. *Rethinking Psychological Anthropology*. New York: H. H. Freeman, 1988.

Bohannan, Paul. Review of Margaret Mead and Rhoda Metraux, *A Way of Seeing*. *American Ethnologist* (1980): 198.

Boon, James. A. "Between-the-Wars Bali: Rereading the Relics." In *Malinowski, Rivers, Benedict, and Others: Essays on Culture and Personality*, edited by George W. Stocking Jr., 218–47. Madison: University of Wisconsin Press, 1986.

———. "Taking Torgovnick as She Takes Others." In *Verging on Extra-Vagance: Anthropology, History, Religion, Literature, Arts . . . Showbiz*, 221–29. Princeton, NJ: Princeton University Press, 1999.

Boone, Joseph. *Libidinal Currents: Sexuality and the Shaping of Modernism*. Chicago: University of Chicago Press, 1998.

Boorstin, Daniel J. *The Image: A Guide to Pseudo-Events in America*. New York: Atheneum, 1985.

Bowman-Kruhm, Mary. *Margaret Mead: A Biography.* Westport, CT: Greenwood Press.

Boyer, Paul. *By the Bomb's Early Light: American Thought and Culture at the Dawn of the Atomic Age.* Chapel Hill: University of North Carolina Press, 1994. Originally published New York: Pantheon, 1985.

Boyle, T. Coraghessan. *The Inner Circle.* New York: Viking, 2004.

Braudy, Leo. *The Frenzy of Renown: Fame and Its History.* New York: Oxford University Press, 1986.

Brier, Peter. *Howard Mumford Jones and the Dynamics of Liberal Humanism.* Columbia: University of Missouri Press, 1994.

Brightman, Robert. "Jaime de Angulo and Alfred Kroeber: Bohemians and Bourgeois in Berkeley Anthropology." In *Significant Others: Interpersonal and Professional Commitments in Anthropology,* edited by Richard Handler, 158–95. Madison: University of Wisconsin Press, 2004.

Brill, A. A. *Freud's Contributions to Psychiatry.* New York: W. W. Norton, 1944.

Bronner, Simon J., ed. *Consuming Visions: Accumulation and Display of Goods in America, 1880–1920.* New York: W. W. Norton, 1989.

Buck, Elizabeth. *Paradise Remade: The Politics of Culture and History in Hawaii.* Philadelphia: Temple University Press, 1993.

Cady, Barbara, Jean-Jacques Naudet, and Raymond McGrath. *Icons of the 20th Century: 200 Men and Women Who Have Made a Difference.* Woodstock, NY: Overlook Press, 1998.

Caffrey, Margaret M. "The Parable of Manus: Utopian Change, American Influence, and the Worth of Women." In *Reading Benedict/Reading Mead: Feminism, Race, and Imperial Visions,* edited by Dolores Janiewski and Lois W. Banner, 141–52. Baltimore: Johns Hopkins University Press, 2004.

———. *Ruth Benedict: Stranger in This Land.* Austin: University of Texas Press, 1989.

Caffrey, Margaret M., and Patricia A. Francis, eds. *To Cherish the Life of the World: Selected Letters of Margaret Mead.* New York: Basic Books, 2006.

Calder-Marshall, Arthur. *The Innocent Eye: The Life of Robert J. Flaherty.* New York: Penguin, 1963.

Carothers, J. Edward, Margaret Mead, Daniel D. McCracken, et al., eds. *To Love or to Perish: The Technological Crisis and the Churches.* New York: Friendship Press, 1972.

Cassidy, Robert. *Margaret Mead: A Voice for the Century.* New York: Universe Books, 1982.

Cherneff, Jill B. R. "The Social Anthropology of Hortense Powdermaker. In *Visionary Observers,* edited by Jill B. R. Cherneff and Eve Hochwald, 119–48. Foreword by Sydel Silverman. Lincoln: University of Nebraska Press, 2006.

Chesterton, G. K., Bernard Shaw, and Hilaire Belloc. *Do We Agree? A Debate between G. K. Chesterton and Bernard Shaw, with Hilaire Belloc in the Chair.* London: C. Palmer; Folcroft, PA: Folcroft Library Editions, 1928. Reprint, Folcroft, PA: Folcroft Library Editions, 1974.

Clifford, James. "On Ethnographic Authority." In *The Predicament of Culture: Twentieth-Century Ethnography, Literature, and Art*, 21–54. Cambridge, MA: Harvard University Press, 1988.

———. *The Predicament of Culture: Twentieth-Century Ethnography, Literature, and Art.* Cambridge, MA: Harvard University Press, 1988.

Clifford, James, and George E. Marcus, eds. *Writing Culture: The Poetics and Politics of Ethnography.* Berkeley: University of California Press, 1986.

Cole, Sally. *Ruth Landes: A Life in Anthropology.* Lincoln: University of Nebraska Press, 2003.

Collins, Gail. *America's Women: Four Hundred Years of Dolls, Drudges, Helpmates, and Heroines.* New York: William Morrow, 2003.

———. *Scorpion Tongues: Gossip, Celebrity, and American Politics.* New York: William Morrow, 1998.

Colton, John, and Clemence Randolph. *Rain: A Play in Three Acts.* Based on W. Somerset Maugham's "Miss Thompson." New York: Liveright, 1923.

Condon, Bill. *Kinsey.* DVD, color, sound, 118 minutes. Beverly Hills, CA: Twentieth Century Fox, 2005.

Corey, Mary F. *The World through a Monocle: The* New Yorker *at Midcentury.* Cambridge, MA: Harvard University Press, 1999.

Cort, David. "Margaret Mead for President." *Monocle* (Summer–Fall 1963): 27–30.

Côté, James E. *Adolescent Storm and Stress: An Evaluation of the Mead-Freeman Controversy.* Hillsdale, NJ: L. Erlbaum Associates, 1994.

Cott, Nancy. *The Grounding of Modern Feminism.* New Haven, CT: Yale University Press, 1987.

Cowley, Malcolm. *Exile's Return: A Literary Odyssey of the 1920s.* New York: Viking Press, 1951.

Cowley, Malcolm, and Robert Cowley. *Fitzgerald and the Jazz Age.* New York: Charles Scribner's Sons, 1966.

Creed, Barbara, and Jeannette Hoorn, eds. *Body Trade: Captivity, Cannibalism, and Colonialism in the Pacific.* New York: Routledge, 2001.

Cressman, Luther. *A Golden Journey: Memoirs of an Archaeologist.* Salt Lake City: University of Utah Press, 1988.

Darnell, Regna. *Edward Sapir: Linguist, Anthropologist, Humanist.* Berkeley: University of California Press, 1990.

Deacon, Desley. *Elsie Clews Parsons: Inventing Modern Life.* Chicago: University of Chicago Press, 1997.

deCordova, Richard. *Picture Personalities: The Emergence of the Star System in America*. Urbana: University of Illinois Press, 1990.

Dempsey, David. "The Mead and Her Message." *New York Times Magazine*, April 26, 1970.

di Leonardo, Micaela. "The Anthropologist's Dilemma." *Chronicle of Higher Education*, March 19, 1999, B4.

———. *Exotics at Home: Anthropologies, Others, American Modernity*. Chicago: University of Chicago Press, 1998.

Dillon, Wilton S. "Margaret Mead." *Prospects: The Quarterly Review of Comparative Education* 31, no. 3 (2001): 447–61.

Doniger, Wendy. *The Woman Who Pretended to Be Who She Was: Myths of Self-Imitation*. New York: Oxford University Press, 2005.

Dornfeld, Barry. *Producing Public Television, Producing Public Culture*. Princeton, NJ: Princeton University Press, 1998.

Dorsey, George Amos. *Why We Behave like Human Beings*. New York: Harper and Brothers, 1925.

Doss, Erika, ed. *Looking at Life Magazine*. Washington, DC: Smithsonian Institution Press, 2001.

Dow, Peter B. *Schoolhouse Politics: Lessons from the Sputnik Era*. Cambridge, MA: Harvard University Press, 1991.

Dower, John W. *War without Mercy: Race and Power in the Pacific War*. New York: Pantheon, 1986.

Dyer, Richard. *Stars*. London: Educational Advisory Service, British Film Institute, 1979.

Eddy, Elizabeth M., and William L. Partridge, eds. *Applied Anthropology in America*. New York: Columbia University Press, 1978.

Edwards, Elizabeth, ed. *Anthropology and Photography, 1860–1920*. New Haven, CT: Yale University Press, 1992.

Ehrenreich, Barbara. *Fear of Falling: The Inner Life of the Middle Class*. New York: Harper Perennial, 1990.

Elliott, Michael A. *The Culture Concept: Writing and Difference in the Age of Realism*. Minneapolis: University of Minnesota Press, 2002.

Ellis, Havelock. *Studies in the Psychology of Sex*. New York: Random House, 1936.

Emerson, Ralph Waldo. *Representative Men, Seven Lectures*. Edited by Pamela Schirmeister. New York: Marsilio, 1995. Originally published 1850.

Eperjesi, John R. *The Imperialist Imaginary: Visions of Asia and the Pacific in American Culture*. Hanover, NH: Dartmouth College Press; University Press of New England, 2004.

Epstein, Sam, and Beryl Epstein. *She Never Looked Back: Margaret Mead in Samoa*. New York: Coward, McCann and Geoghegan, 1980.

Fisher, Helen. *Anatomy of Love: A Natural History of Mating, Marriage, and Why We Stray.* New York: Fawcett Columbine, 1992.

———. "The Anthropologist as Television Subject." In *Media Anthropology: Informing Global Citizens*, ed. Susan L. Allen, 81–89. Westport, CT: Bergin and Garvey, 1994.

———. Introduction to *Male and Female*, by Margaret Mead. New York: HarperCollins Perennial, 2001. Originally published New York: William Morrow, 1949.

———. Introduction to *Sex and Temperament in Three Primitive Societies*, by Margaret Mead. First Perennial Edition. 1963; New York: Harper Collins Publishers, 2001.

———. *The Sex Contract: The Evolution of Human Behavior.* New York: William Morrow, 1982.

Fitzgerald, F. Scott. "Echoes of the Jazz Age." *Scribner's Magazine*, 1931.

———. *Flappers and Philosophers.* New York: Charles Scribner's Sons, 1920.

———. *The Letters of F. Scott Fitzgerald*, edited by Andre Turnbull. New York: Charles Scribner's Sons, 1963.

———. *Tales of the Jazz Age.* New York: Charles Scribner's Sons, 1922.

———. *This Side of Paradise.* New York: Charles Scribner's Sons, 1920.

Flaherty, Frances. "Behind the Scenes with Our Samoan Stars." *Asia: Journal of the American Asiatic Association* 25, no. 9 (1925): 747–53.

Flaherty, Robert. *Moana of the South Seas.* 35 mm, black and white, silent, 7 reels, 90 minutes. United States: Paramount Pictures, 1926.

Forde, C. Daryl. "Applied Anthropology in Government: British Africa." In *Anthropology Today: An Encyclopedic Inventory*, edited by A. L. Kroeber, 841–65. Chicago: University of Chicago Press, 1953.

———. Review of *The Changing Culture of an Indian Tribe*, by Margaret Mead. *Man* 33 (September 1933): 154.

Foerstel, Lenora, and Angela Gilliam, eds. *Confronting the Margaret Mead Legacy: Scholarship, Empire, and the South Pacific.* Philadelphia: Temple University Press, 1992.

Fortes, Meyer. "Obituary: Margaret Mead, 1901–1978." *Nature* 278 (March 1979): 289–90.

Fortune, Reo. *Omaha Secret Societies.* Columbia University Contributions to Anthropology 14. New York: Columbia University Press, 1932.

Foster, Robert. J. "Margaret Mead's *Redbook* Project: A Problem in the Sociology of Culture. Unpublished paper, 1982.

———. *Materializing the Nation: Commodities, Consumption, and Media in Papua New Guinea.* Bloomington: Indiana University Press, 2002.

Foucault, Michel. *The History of Sexuality*, vol. 1, *An Introduction.* New York: Vintage, 1990. Originally published in France, 1976.

Four Families. Ian MacNeill, producer. Fali Bilimoria, William Novik, John Buss, et al., directors. 16 mm, black and white, sound, 60 minutes. New York: National Film Board of Canada, 1959.

Frank, Gelya. "Jews, Multiculturalism, and Boasian Anthropology." *American Anthropologist* 99, no. 4 (1997): 731–45.

Freeman, Derek. *The Fateful Hoaxing of Margaret Mead: A Historical Analysis of Her Samoan Research*. Boulder, CO: Westview Press, 1999.

———. *Margaret Mead and the Heretic: The Making and Unmaking of an Anthropological Myth*. Harmondsworth and New York: Penguin, 1996. Originally published as *Margaret Mead and Samoa: The Making and Unmaking of an Anthropological Myth*. Cambridge, MA: Harvard University Press. 1983.

———. *Margaret Mead and Samoa: The Making and Unmaking of an Anthropological Myth*. Cambridge, MA: Harvard University Press, 1983.

Friedan, Betty. *The Feminine Mystique*. New York: Dell, 1963. Reprint with introduction by Anna Quindlen. New York: W. W. Norton, 2001.

Friedman, Lawrence. *Identity's Architect: A Biography of Erik H. Erikson*. New York: Scribner, 1999.

Friendly, Fred. *Due to Circumstances beyond Our Control*. New York: Random House, 1967.

Gabler, Neal. *Life the Movie: How Entertainment Conquered Reality*. New York: Vintage, 1998.

———. *Winchell: Gossip, Power, and the Culture of Celebrity*. New York: Knopf, 1994.

Gambrell, Alice. *Women Intellectuals, Modernism, and Difference: Transatlantic Culture, 1919–1945*. Cambridge: Cambridge University Press, 1997.

Gamson, Joshua. *Claims to Fame: Celebrity in Contemporary America*. Berkeley: University of California Press, 1994.

Geertz, Clifford. "Morality Tale." Review *of Ishi's Brain: In Search of America's Last "Wild" Indian*, by Orin Starn, and *Ishi in Three Centuries*, edited by Karl Kroeber and Clifton Kroeber. *New York Review of Books*, October 7, 2004, 4–6.

———. *Works and Lives: The Anthropologist as Author*. Stanford, CA: Stanford University Press, 1988.

Geertz, Hildred. *Images of Power: Balinese Paintings Made for Gregory Bateson and Margaret Mead*. Honolulu: University of Hawaii Press. 1994.

Gesell, Arnold, Francis Lillian Ilg, Janet Learned Rodell, and Louise Bates Ames. *Infant and Child in the Culture of Today: The Guidance of Development in Home and Nursery School*. New York and London: Harper and Brothers, 1943.

Gewertz, Deborah. "The Tchambuli View of Persons: A Critique of Individualism in the Works of Mead and Chodorow." *American Anthropologist* 83, no. 3 (1984): 615–29.

Gilbert, Craig, and Margaret Mead. *Margaret Mead's New Guinea Journal.* 16 mm, color, sound, 75 minutes. Bloomington: Indiana University Audio-Visual Center, 1968.

Gill, Lorin Tarr. "To Make Study of 'Flapper' in Primitive State Dr. Margaret Mead Will Visit South Seas to Carry Out Her Research Plan." *Honolulu Star-Bulletin*, August 15, 1925.

Gilliam, Angela. "Symbolic Subordination and the Representation of Power in *Margaret Mead and Samoa*." *Visual Anthropology Review* 9 (Spring 1993): 105–15.

Ginsburg, Faye D. "Ethnographies on the Airwaves: The Presentation of Anthropology on American, British, Belgian, and Japanese Television." In *Principles of Visual Anthropology*, edited by Paul Hockings, 363–98. Berlin and New York: Mouton de Gruyter, 1995.

Ginsburg, Faye D., Lila Abu-Lughod, and Brian Larkin, *Media Worlds: Anthropology on New Terrain*. Berkeley: University of California Press, 2002.

Glendinning, Victoria. *Rebecca West, a Life*. New York: Knopf. 1987.

Glennon, Frances. "Close Up: With Margaret Mead." *Life*, September 14, 1959, 142–48.

Goldenweiser, Alexander. Review of *The Changing Culture of an Indian Tribe*, by Margaret Mead. *American Anthropologist* n.s. 36, no. 4 (1934): 609.

Goldschmidt, W. R., ed., *The Uses of Anthropology*. New York: American Anthropological Association, 1979.

Goodall, Jane. *The Chimpanzee of Gombe: Patterns of Behavior*. Cambridge, MA: Belknap Press of Harvard University Press, 1986.

———. *In the Shadow of Man*. Boston: Houghton Mifflin, 1971.

Goodell, Rae. *The Visible Scientists*. Boston: Little, Brown, 1975.

Gordan, Joan, ed. *Margaret Mead: The Complete Bibliography, 1925–1975*. The Hague: Mouton, 1976.

Gordon, Deborah A. "The Politics of Ethnographic Authority: Race and Writing in the Ethnography of Margaret Mead and Zora Neale Hurston." In *Modernist Anthropology*, edited by Marc Manganaro, 146–62. Princeton, NJ: Princeton University Press, 1990.

Gorer, Geoffrey. "Justification by Numbers: A Commentary on the Kinsey Report." *American Scholar*, 1948, 280–86.

———. "A Statistical Study of Sex." Review of Alfred Kinsey et al., *Sexual Behavior of Men. New York Herald Tribune*, February 1, 1948, 4.

Gould, Stephen Jay. *The Mismeasure of Man*. New York: W. W. Norton, 1981.

Gregory, Jane, and Steve Miller. *Science in Public: Communication, Culture, and Credibility*. New York: Plenum, 1998.

Griffiths, Alison. *Wondrous Difference: Cinema, Anthropology, and Turn-of-the-Century Visual Culture*. New York: Columbia University Press, 2002.

Grimshaw, Anna. *The Ethnographer's Eye: Ways of Seeing in Anthropology.* Cambridge: Cambridge University Press, 2001.

Grinager, Patricia. *Uncommon Lives: My Lifelong Friendship with Margaret Mead.* Boulder, CO: Rowman and Littlefield, 1999.

Grinker, Roy Richard. *In the Arms of Africa: The Life of Colin M. Turnbull.* New York: St. Martin's Press, 2000.

Grosskurth, Phyllis. *Havelock Ellis, a Biography.* New York: New York University Press, 1985.

———. *Margaret Mead.* New York: Penguin, 1988.

Groves, Ernest R., and William F. Ogburn. *American Marriage and Family Relationships.* New York: Henry Holt, 1928.

Guillemin, Jeanne. Introduction to *Kinship in the Admiralty Islands*, by Margaret Mead, ix–xxiv. New Brunswick, NJ: Transaction Publishers, 2002.

Gullahorn-Holocek, Barbara, *Anthropology on Trial.* Videocassette, color, sound, 60 minutes. New York: Time-Life Video, 1983.

Hacker, Carlotta. *Women in Profile: Scientists.* New York: Crabtree Publishing, 1998.

Halberstam, Judith. *Female Masculinity.* Durham, NC: Duke University Press, 1998.

Hall, G. Stanley. *Adolescence: Its Psychology and Its Relations to Physiology, Anthropology, Sociology, Sex, Crime, Religion, and Education.* 2 Vols. New York: D. Appleton, 1904. Vol. 2, reprinted in *American Education: Its Men, Ideas, and Institutions.* New York: Arno Press and the New York Times, 1969.

Hall, Stuart, et al., eds. *Modernity: An Introduction to Modern Societies.* Cambridge, MA: Blackwell, 1996.

Hamburger, Philip. Review of *Adventure.* CBS. *New Yorker,* June 6, 1953, 123–24.

Hamilton, G. V. *A Research in Marriage.* New York: Garland, 1929.

Hamilton, G. V., and Kenneth McGowan. "Physical Disabilities in Wives." In *Sex in Civilization*, edited by V. F. Calverton and S. D. Schmalhausen, 562–79. New York: Macaulay, 1929.

———. *What Is Wrong with Marriage: A Study of Two Hundred Husbands and Wives.* New York: A. and C. Boni, 1929.

Handler, Richard. *Critics against Culture: Anthropological Observers of Mass Society.* Madison: University of Wisconsin Press, 2005.

Haraway, Donna. *Primate Visions: Gender, Race, and Nature in the World of Modern Science.* New York: Routledge, 1989.

Hare, Peter H. *A Woman's Quest for Science.* Buffalo, NY: Prometheus Books, 1985.

Harris, Marvin. "Margaret and the Giant-Killer: It Doesn't Matter a Whit Who's Right." Review of *Sociobiology: A New Synthesis*, by Edward O. Wilson. *The Sciences* 23, no. 4 (1983): 18–21.

Hart, C. W. M. Review of *Growing Up in New Guinea*, by Margaret Mead. *Man* 32 (June 1932): 146.

Hart, C. W. M., and Arnold R. Pilling. *The Tiwi of North Australia*. New York: Holt, Rinehart, and Winston, 1960.

Harvey, David. *The Condition of Postmodernity: An Enquiry into the Origins of Cultural Change*. Cambridge, MA: Blackwell, 1989.

Heilbrun, Carolyn. "Margaret Mead and the Question of Woman's Biography." In *Hamlet's Mother and Other Women*, 25–32. New York: Ballantine, 1990.

Heimans, Frank, director and producer. *Margaret Mead and Samoa*. Videocassette, color, black and white, sound, 51 minutes. New York: Brighton Video and Wombat Film and Video, 1988.

Hellman, Hal. *Great Feuds in Science: Ten of the Liveliest Disputes Ever*. New York: John Wiley and Sons, 1998.

Hennessee, Joy. *Betty Friedan, Her Life*. New York: Random House, 1999.

Hendry, Joy. "The Chrysanthemum Continues to Flower: Ruth Benedict and Some Perils of Popular Anthropology." In *Popularizing Anthropology*, edited by Jeremy MacClancy and Chris McDonaugh, 106–21. London and New York: Routledge, 1996.

Heyman, Ken, and John Durniak. *The Right Picture*. New York: Amphoto, 1986.

Heyman, Ken, and Margaret Mead. *Family*. New York: Macmillan, 1965.

———. *World Enough: Rethinking the Future*. Boston: Little, Brown, 1975.

Hieb, Louis A. "Elsie Clews Parsons in the Southwest." In *Hidden Scholars: Women Anthropologists and the Native American Southwest*, edited by Nancy J. Parezo, 63–75. Albuquerque: University of New Mexico Press, 1993.

Higashi, Sumiko. *Virgins, Vamps, and Flappers: The American Silent Movie Heroine*. St. Albans, VT: Eden Press Women's Publications, 1978.

Hine, Thomas. *The Rise and Fall of the American Teenager*. New York: Bard, 1999.

Hinsley, Curtis M. "The World as Marketplace: Commodification of the Exotic at the World's Columbian Exposition, Chicago, 1983." In *Exhibiting Cultures: The Poetics and Politics of Museum Display*, edited by Ivan Karp and Steven D. Lavine, 344–66. Washington, DC: Smithsonian Institution Press, 1991.

Hobsbawm, Eric J. *The Age of Extremes: A History of the World, 1914–1991*. New York: Pantheon, 1994.

Hockings, Paul, ed. *Principles of Visual Anthropology*. 2nd ed. Berlin and New York: Mouton de Gruyter, 1995.

Holmes, Lowell D. *Quest for the Real Samoa: The Mead/Freeman Controversy and Beyond*. South Hadley, MA: Bergin and Garvey Publishers, 1987.

Horowitz, Daniel. *Betty Friedan and the Making of the Feminine Mystique: The American Left, The Cold War, and Modern Feminism*. Amherst: University of Massachusetts Press, 1998.

Horowitz, Helen. *Campus Life: Undergraduate Cultures from the End of the 18th Century to the Present*. New York: Knopf, 1987.

Howard, Jane. *Margaret Mead: A Life*. New York: Simon and Schuster, 1984.

Hulbert, Ann. *Raising America: Experts, Parents, and a Century of Advice about Children*. New York: Knopf, 2003.

Human Events Online. "Ten Most Harmful Books of the 19th and 20th Centuries." May 31, 2005, http://www.humaneventsonline.com/article.php?id=7591.

Hymes, Dell H., ed. *Reinventing Anthropology*. New York: Random House, 1969.

Jacknis, Ira. "Margaret Mead and Gregory Bateson in Bali: Their Use of Photography and Film." *Cultural Anthropology* 3, no. 2 (1988): 160–77.

Jacoby, Russell. *The Last Intellectuals: American Culture in the Age of Academe*. New York: Basic Books, 1987.

James, William. *The Principles of Psychology*. Volume 1 of *The Works of William James*, edited by Frederick H. Burkhardt. Cambridge, MA: Harvard University Press, 1981.

Janiewski, Dolores, and Lois W. Banner, eds. *Reading Benedict/Reading Mead: Feminism, Race, and Imperial Visions*. Baltimore: Johns Hopkins University Press, 2004.

Jay, Martin. *Downcast Eyes: The Denigration of Vision of Twentieth-Century French Thought*. Berkeley: University of California Press, 1993.

———. "Force Fields: The Academic Woman as Performance Artist." *Salmagundi* (Spring/Summer 1995): 28–34.

Johnson, Dorothy Maloney. "Projections." An interview with Margaret Mead. *Barnard College Alumni Monthly*, April 1934, 11.

Johnson, Spencer. *The Value of Understanding: The Story of Margaret Mead*. La Jolla, CA: Value Communications, 1979.

Jones, Howard Mumford. "The Anthropologist." *Saturday Review*, n.d., 89. LC, Q-33–5.

Jones, James H. *Alfred C. Kinsey: A Public/Private Life*. New York: W. W. Norton, 1997.

Kaledin, Eugenia. *Mothers and More: American Women in the 1950s*. Boston: Twayne Publishers, 1984.

Karp, Ivan, and Steven D. Lavine, eds. *Exhibiting Cultures: The Poetics and Politics of Museum Display*. Washington, DC: Smithsonian Institution Press, 1991.

Kennedy, David M. *Birth Control in America: The Career of Margaret Sanger*. New Haven, CT: Yale University Press, 1970.

Kinsey, Alfred C., Wardell B. Pomeroy, and Clyde E. Martin. *Sexual Behavior in the Human Male*. Philadelphia: W. B. Saunders, 1948.

Kirchwey, Freda. "This Week: Sex in the South Seas." *The Nation* 127, no. 3303 (1928): 427.

Kirk, Malcolm. *Man as Art*. New York: Viking Press, 1981.

Kiste, Robert. "New Political Statuses in American Micronesia." In *Contemporary Pacific Societies: Studies in Development and Change*, edited by Victoria S. Lockwood, 67–80. Upper Saddle River, NJ: Prentice-Hall, 1983.

Knauer, Kelly, ed. *Time 100: Leaders and Revolutionaries, Artists and Entertainers*. New York: Time-Life Books, 1998.

Koestenbaum, Wayne. *Jackie under My Skin: Interpreting an Icon*. New York: Farrar, Straus, and Giroux, 1995.

Kozol, Wendy. *Life's America: Family and Nation in Postwar Photojournalism*. Philadelphia: Temple University Press, 1994.

Kroeber, A. L. Review of *Growing Up in New Guinea*, by Margaret Mead. *American Anthropologist* n.s. 33 (1931): 248–50.

Kroeber, Theodora. *Ishi in Two Worlds: A Biography of the Last Wild Indian in North America*. Berkeley: University of California Press, 1961.

Kuper, Adam. "Coming of Age in Anthropology?" *Nature* (April 6, 1989): 453–55.

Kuznick, Peter J., and James Gilbert, eds. *Rethinking Cold War Culture*. Washington, DC: Smithsonian Institution Press, 2001.

Lakoff, Andrew. "Freezing Time: Margaret Mead's Diagnostic Photography." *Visual Anthropology Review* 12, no. 1 (1996): 1–18.

Lakoff, Robin. *Language and Woman's Place*. New York: Harper and Row, 1975.

Lamphere, Louise. "Feminist Anthropology: The Legacy of Elsie Clews Parsons." In *Women Writing Culture*, edited by Ruth Behar and Deborah Gordon, 85–103. Berkeley: University of California Press, 1995.

Landes, Ruth. *The City of Women*. New York: Macmillan, 1947.

Langham, Ian. *The Building of British Social Anthropology: W. H. R. Rivers and His Cambridge Disciples in the Development of Kinship Studies, 1898–1931*. Dordrecht: Reidel Publishing, 1981.

Lapsley, Hilary. *Margaret Mead and Ruth Benedict: The Kinship of Women*. Amherst: University of Massachusetts Press, 1999.

Leach, William. *Land of Desire: Merchants, Power, and the Rise of a New American Culture*. New York: Pantheon, 1993.

Lears, Jackson. "Beyond Veblen: Rethinking Consumer Culture in America." In *Consuming Visions: Accumulation and Display of Goods in America, 1880–1920*, edited by Simon J. Bronner, 73–98. New York: W. W. Norton, 1989.

Lévi-Strauss, Claude. *Tristes tropiques*. Translated by John Weightman and Doreen Weightman. New York: Atheneum, 1973. Originally published in French as *Tristes tropiques*. Paris: Plon, 1955.

Lévy-Bruhl, Lucien. *How Natives Think*. London: G. Allen and Unwin, 1926.

Lipset, David. *Gregory Bateson: The Legacy of a Scientist*. Boston: Beacon Press, 1980.

Liss, Julia E. "German Culture and German Science in the Bildung of Franz Boas." In Volksgeist *as Method and Ethic*, edited by George W. Stocking Jr., 155–84. Madison: University of Wisconsin Press, 1996.

———. "Patterns of Strangeness: Franz Boas, Modernism, and the Origins of Anthropology." In *Prehistories of the Future: The Primitivist Project and the Culture of Modernism*, edited by Elazar Barkan and Ronald Bush, 114–32. Stanford, CA: Stanford University Press, 1995.

Lodge, David. *Small World: An Academic Romance*. New York: Macmillan, 1984.

Losche, Diane. "The Fate of the Senses in Ethnographic Modernity: The Margaret Mead Hall of Pacific Peoples at the American Museum of Natural History." In *Sensible Objects: Colonialism, Museums, and Material Culture*, edited by Elizabeth Edwards, Chris Gosden, and Ruth B. Phillips, 223–44. New York and Oxford: Berg, 2006.

Loud, Pat, and Nora Johnson. *Pat Loud: A Woman's Story*. New York: Coward, McCann and Geoghegan, 1974.

Lowie, Robert. Review of *Coming of Age in Samoa*, by Margaret Mead. *American Anthropologist* n.s. 31 (1929): 532–34.

Lucas, George. *Star Wars*. 1977. Videocassette, color, sound, 125 minutes. Beverly Hills, CA: Twentieth Century-Fox Film Corporation.

Lurie, Alison. *The Language of Clothes*. New York: Random House, 1981.

Lutkehaus, Nancy C. Foreword to Margaret Mead, *Ruth Benedict: A Humanist in Anthropology*, xix–xlii. New York: Columbia University Press, 2005.

———. Introduction to Margaret Mead, *Blackberry Winter: My Earlier Years*, xi–xx. New York: Kodansha International, 1995.

———. "Man, a Course of Study: Situating Tim Asch's Pedagogy and Ethnographic Film." In *Timothy Asch and Ethnographic Film*, edited by E. D. Lewis, 57–74. London and New York: Routledge, 2004.

———. "Margaret Mead: An American Icon." *Natural History Magazine* (December 2001): 14–15.

———. "Margaret Mead and the 'Rustling-of-the-Wind-in-the-Palm-Trees School' of Ethnographic Writing." In *Women Writing Culture*, edited by Ruth Behar and Deborah A. Gordon, 186–206. Berkeley: University of California Press, 1995.

———. "Margaret Mead: Anthropology's Liminal Figure." In *Reading Benedict/Reading Mead: Feminism, Race, and Imperial Visions*, edited by Dolores Janiewski and Lois W. Banner, 193–204. Baltimore: Johns Hopkins University Press, 2004.

———. "Margaret Mead as Cultural Icon: Anthropology and the Media in American Culture." *Anthropology Newsletter*, 1996.

———. "Margaret Mead as Media Icon." Paper presented at the Annual Meetings of the American Anthropological Association, Washington, DC, November, 1993.

Lutkehaus, Nancy C. "Margaret Mead, New York, the World." Keynote address, "Celebrating the Margaret Mead Centenary." New York Academy of Sciences, New York, October 1, 2001.

Lutkehaus, Nancy C., and Jenny Cool. "Paradigms Lost and Found." In *Collecting Visible Evidence*, edited by Michael Renov and Jane M. Gaines, 116–39. Minneapolis: University of Minnesota Press, 1999.

Mabee, Carleton. "Margaret Mead and Behavioral Scientists in World War II: Problems of Responsibility, Truth, and Effectiveness." *Journal of the History of the Behavioral Sciences* 21, no. 1 (1987): 3–13.

MacClancy, Jeremy. Introduction to *Popularizing Anthropology.* Edited by Jeremy MacClancy and Chris McDonaugh, 1–57. London and New York: Routledge, 1996.

MacClancy, Jeremy, and Chris McDonaugh, eds. *Popularizing Anthropology.* London and New York: Routledge, 1996.

MacDougall, David. *The Corporeal Image: Film, Ethnography, and the Senses.* Princeton, NJ: Princeton University Press, 2006.

———. *Transcultural Cinema.* Edited by Lucien Taylor. Princeton, NJ: Princeton University Press, 1998.

Macgregor, Frances Cooke, and Margaret Mead. *Growth and Culture: A Photographic Study of Balinese Childhood.* Based on photographs by Gregory Bateson. New York: Putnam, 1951.

Maier, Thomas. *Dr. Spock: An American Life.* New York: Harcourt Brace, 1998.

Malinowski, Bronislaw. *Argonauts of the Western Pacific: An Account of Native Enterprise and Adventure in the Archipelagoes of Melanesian New Guinea.* London: G. Routledge; New York: E. P. Dutton, 1922.

———. *The Sexual Life of Savages in North-Western Melanesia: An Ethnographic Account of Courtship, Marriage, and Family Life among the Natives of the Trobriand Islands, British New Guinea.* London: G. Routledge; New York: Halcyon House, 1929.

Manganaro, Marc. *Culture, 1922: The Emergence of a Concept.* Princeton, NJ: Princeton University Press, 2002.

———, ed. *Modernist Anthropology: From Fieldwork to Text.* Princeton, NJ: Princeton University Press, 1990.

Manson, William C. *The Psychodynamics of Culture: Abram Kardiner and Neo-Freudian Anthropology.* New York: Greenwood Press, 1988.

Marchand, Roland. *Advertising the American Dream: Making Way for Modernity, 1920–1940.* Berkeley: University of California Press, 1985.

Marcus, George E. "One Man's Mead." Review of *Margaret Mead and Samoa* by Derek Freeman. *New York Times Book Review,* March 27, 1983, 3.

———. "A Timely Reading of *Naven*: Gregory Bateson as Oracular Essayist." *Representations* 12 (Fall 1985): 66–82.

Marcus, George E., and Michael M. J. Fischer. *Anthropology as Cultural Critique: An Experimental Moment in the Human Sciences*. Chicago: University of Chicago Press, 1986.

Marcus, Jane, ed. *The Young Rebecca West: Writings of Rebecca West, 1911–1917*. New York: Viking, 1982.

Mark, Joan T. *Four Anthropologists: An American Science in Its Early Years*. New York: Science History Publications, 1980.

———. *Margaret Mead: Coming of Age in America*. New York: Oxford University Press, 1999.

———. *A Stranger in her Native Land: Alice Fletcher and the American Indians*. Lincoln: University of Nebraska Press, 1988.

Markey, Kevin. *100 Most Important Women of the 20th Century*. Des Moines, IA: Ladies' Home Journal Books, 1998.

Marks, Percy. *The Plastic Age*. New York: Grosset and Dunlap, 1924.

Marling, Karl Ann. *As Seen on TV: The Visual Culture of Everyday Life in the 1950s*. Cambridge, MA: Harvard University Press, 1994.

May, Elaine Tyler. *Homeward Bound: American Families in the Cold War Era*. New York: Basic Books, 1988.

McDermott, Ray. P. "A Century of Margaret Mead." In *Visionary Observers*, edited by Jill B. R. Cherneff and Eve Hochwald, 55–86. Foreword by Sydel Silverman. Lincoln: University of Nebraska Press, 2006.

McDowell, Nancy. *The Mundugumor: From the Field Notes of Margaret Mead and Reo Fortune*. Washington, DC: Smithsonian Institution Press, 1991.

McFeely, Eliza. *Zuni and the American Imagination*. New York: Hill and Wang, 2001.

McGinniss, Joe. *The Selling of the President*. 1969; New York: Penguin, 1988.

McKee, Elmore M. *The People Act: Stories of How Americans Are Coming Together to Deal with Their Community Problems*. New York: Harper and Brothers, 1955.

McLuhan, Marshall, and Quentin Fiore. *The Medium Is the Massage*. New York: Bantam Books, 1967.

McMullen, Frances Drewry. "Going Native for Science: Dr. Margaret Mead, Ethnologist, Tells How She Lived in a Grass Hut in the Admiralty Islands and Became a Princess in Samoa to Study the Life of Her Primitive Neighbors." *Women's Journal* (July 1930): 8–9, 31–32.

Mead, Edward Sherwood. *Corporation Finance*. New York and London: D. Appleton, 1910.

———. *The Story of Gold*. New York: D. Appleton, 1908.

———. *Trust Finance: A Study of the Genesis, Organization, and Management of Industrial Combinations*. New York: D. Appleton, 1903.

Mead, Edward Sherwood, and Bernhard Ostrolenk. *Harvey Baum: A Study of the Agricultural Revolution*. Philadelphia: University of Pennsylvania Press, 1928.

———. *Voluntary Allotment: Planned Production in American Agriculture*. Philadelphia: University of Pennsylvania Press, 1933.

Mead, Emily Fogg. *The Italian on the Land: A Study in Immigration; Italian Immigration into the South*. Hammonton, NJ: Hammonton Historical Society, 1992.

———. "Italians on the Land: A Study in Immigration." U.S. Bureau Labor Bulletin 14 (May 1907): 473–533.

———. "The Place of Advertising in Business." *Journal of Political Economy* 9, no. 2 (1901): 218–42.

Mead, Margaret, with Gregory Bateson. *First Days in the Life of a New Guinea Baby*. Character Formation in Different Cultures Series. Film, black and white, sound, 15 minutes. New York: New York University Film Library, 1952.

Mead, Margaret, with Gregory Bateson and Jane Belo. *Trance and Dance in Bali*. Character Formation in Different Cultures Series. 16 mm, black and white, sound, 20 minutes. New York: New York University Film Library, 1952.

Mead, Margaret, and Muriel Brown. *The Wagon and the Star: A Study of American Community Initiative*. New York: Rand McNally, 1966.

Mead, Margaret, and Paul Byers. *The Small Conference: An Innovation in Communication*. The Hague and Paris: Mouton, 1968.

Mead, Margaret, and Rhoda Metraux. "Image of the Scientist among High-School Students: A Pilot Study." *Science* (August 30, 1957): 384–90.

Melville, Herman. *Omoo: A Narrative of Adventures in the South Seas*. New York: Harper, 1847.

———. *Typee: A Peep at Polynesian Life; During a Four Months' Residence in a Valley of the Marquesas*. New York: Wiley and Putnam, 1846.

Menand, Louis. *The Metaphysical Club*. New York: Farrar, Straus and Giroux, 2001.

Merkin, Daphne. "Sister Act: Did Betty Friedan Go Wrong, or Did Feminism?" Review of *Betty Friedan and the Making of the Feminine Mystique*, by David Horowitz, and *Betty Friedan, Her Life*, by Joy Hennessee. *New Yorker*, June 14, 1999, 78–84.

Merton, Robert. *The Sociology of Science: Theoretical and Empirical Investigations*. Chicago: University of Chicago Press, 1973.

Michael, John. *Anxious Intellects: Academic Professionals, Public Intellectuals, and Enlightenment Values*. Durham, NC: Duke University Press, 2000.

Milford, Nancy. *Savage Beauty: The Life of Edna St. Vincent Millay*. New York: Random House, 2001.

Mitchell, W. J. Thomas. *Picture Theory: Essays on Verbal and Visual Representation*. Chicago: University of Chicago Press, 1994.

Mitchell, William. "Communicating Culture: Margaret Mead and the Practice of Popular Anthropology." In *Popularizing Anthropology*, edited by Jeremy MacClancy and Chris McDonaugh, 122–34. London and New York: Routledge, 1996.

Modell, Ruth Schachter. *Ruth Benedict: Patterns of a Life*. Philadelphia: University of Pennsylvania Press, 1983.

Molloy, Maureen. "Margaret Mead, the Samoan Girl, and the Flapper: Geographies of Selfhood in *Coming of Age in Samoa*." In *Reading Benedict/Reading Mead: Feminism, Race, and Imperial Visions*, edited by Dolores Janiewski and Lois W. Banner, 33–47. Baltimore: Johns Hopkins University Press, 2004.

———. "Disorderly Women and Disordered Culture," unpublished paper, 2005.

Monk, Ray. *Bertrand Russell: The Ghost of Madness, 1921–1970*. New York: Free Press, 2000.

Morrison, Theodore. *Chautauqua: A Center for Education, Religion, and the Arts in America*. Chicago: University of Chicago Press, 1974.

Mullahy, Patrick. *The Beginnings of Modern American Psychiatry: The Ideas of Harry Stack Sullivan*. Boston: Houghton Mifflin, 1970. Originally published as *Psychoanalysis and Interpersonal Psychiatry*.

Murray, Gilbert. *The League of Nations Movement: Some Recollections of the Early Days*. London: David Davies Memorial Institute of International Studies, 1955.

The Nation. Review of *The Changing Culture of an Indian Tribe*, by Margaret Mead. *The Nation* 136, no. 3524 (1933): 72.

Neil, Henry. *Complete Life of William McKinley and Story of His Assassination: An Authentic and Official Memorial Edition, Containing Every Incident in the Career of the Immortal Statesman, Soldier, Orator, and Patriot*. Chicago: Historical Press, 1901.

Neves, Irene. "Close Up." *Life*, 1967, 30–34.

New Lives for Old. Robert E. Dierbeck, director. Horizons of Science Series, vol. 1, no. 6. 16 mm, color, sound, 20 minutes. Produced in association with the National Science Foundation. Princeton, NJ: Educational Testing Service, 1960.

New York Times Book Review. Review of *Growing Up in New Guinea*, by Margaret Mead, November 16, 1930.

Newton, Esther. *Margaret Mead Made Me Gay*. Durham, NC: Duke University Press, 2000.

Nichols, Bill. *Blurred Boundaries: Questions of Meaning in Contemporary Culture*. Bloomington: Indiana University Press, 1994.

Nordstrom, Alison Devine. "Photography of Samoa: Production, Dissemination, and Use." In *Picturing Paradise: Colonial Photography of Samoa, 1875–1925*, edited by Casey Blanton, 11–40. Daytona Beach, FL: Daytona Beach Community College and the Southeast Museum of Photography, 1995.

O'Brien, Frederick. *Atolls of the Sun*. New York: Century, 1922.

———. *Mystic Isles of the South Seas*. New York: Century, 1921.

———. *White Shadows in the South Seas*. Garden City, NY: Garden City Publishing, 1919.

O'Brien, Lucy. *Expedition: Treasures from 125 Years of Discovery*. New York: American Museum of Natural History, 1995.

Ogburn, William Fielding. *Social Change with Respect to Culture and Original Nature*. New York: Viking Press, 1922.

O'Hanlon, Michael, and Robert L. Welsch, eds. *Hunting the Gatherers: Ethnographic Collectors, Agents, and Agency in Melanesia, 1870s-1930s*. New York: Berghahn, 2000.

Parkinson, Richard. *Thirty Years in the South Seas: Land and People, Customs and Traditions in the Bismarck Archipelago and on the German Solomon Islands*. Edited by B. Ankermann. Translated by John Dennison. Translation edited by J. Peter White. Honolulu: University of Hawaii Press, 1999. Originally published in German as *Dreißig Jahre in der Südsee: Land und Leute, Sitten und Gebräuche im Bismarckarchipel und auf den deutschen Salomoinseln* (Stuttgart: Strecker and Schröder, 1907).

Parsons, Elsie Clews. *The Family: An Ethnographical and Historical Outline with Descriptive Notes, Planned as a Text-Book for the Use of College Lecturers and of Directors of Home-Reading Clubs*. New York and London: G. P. Putnam's Sons, 1906.

———. *Fear and Conventionality*. New York and London: G. P. Putnam's Sons, 1914.

———. *The Old-Fashioned Woman: Primitive Fancies about the Sex*. New York and London: G. P. Putnam's Sons, 1913.

———. "Sex." In *Civilization in the United States: An Inquiry by Thirty Americans*, ed. Harold E. Stearns, 309–18. New York: Harcourt, Brace, 1922.

———. *Social Freedom: A Study of the Conflicts between Social Classifications and Personality*. New York and London: G. P. Putnam's Sons, 1915.

Peck, Ann. *Margaret Mead, Taking Note*. Odyssey Series, edited by Michael Ambrosino. Videocassette, color, sound, 60 minutes. Boston: Public Broadcasting Associates, 1981.

Peer, Elizabeth. "Oracle" and "She Spoke Her Mind." *Newsweek*, November 27, 1978, 3, 70–73.

Pierpont, Claudia Roth. "The Measure of America: How a Rebel Anthropologist Waged War on Racism." *New Yorker*, March 8, 2004, 48–63.

Pillsbury, Barbara. *Reaching the Rural Poor: Indigenous Health Practitioners Are There Already*. Washington, DC: U.S. Agency for International Development, 1979.

Pipher, Mary. Introduction to *Coming of Age in Samoa: A Psychological Study of Primitive Youth for Western Civilization*. New York: Perennial Classics, 2001. Reprint of New York: William Morrow, 1930.

———. *Reviving Ophelia: Saving the Selves of Adolescent Girls*. New York: Putnam, 1994.

Posner, Richard. *Public Intellectuals: A Study of Decline*. Cambridge, MA: Harvard University Press, 2001.

———. "University as Business." *Atlantic Monthly*, June 2002, 4.

Postman, Neil. *Amusing Ourselves to Death: Public Discourse in the Age of Show Business*. New York: Penguin, 1985.

Powdermaker, Hortense. *Hollywood, the Dream Factory: An Anthropologist Looks at the Movie-Makers*. Boston: Little, Brown, 1950.

———. *Life in Lesu: The Study of a Melanesian Society in New Ireland*. New York: W. W. Norton, 1933.

———. *Stranger and Friend: The Way of an Anthropologist*. New York: W. W. Norton, 1966.

Present, Thelma. *Dear Margaret: Letters from Oak Ridge to Margaret Mead*. Knoxville: Eastern Tennessee Historical Society, 1985.

Price, David. *Threatening Anthropology: McCarthyism and the FBI's Surveillance of Activist Anthropologists*. Durham, NC: Duke University Press, 2004.

Rappaport, Roy. "Desecrating the Holy Woman: Derek Freeman's Attack on Margaret Mead." *American Scholar* (Summer 1986): 313–47.

Ray, Gordon N. *H. G. Wells and Rebecca West*. New Haven, CT: Yale University Press, 1974.

Renov, Michael, *Theorizing Documentary*. New York: Routledge, 1993.

Renov, Michael, and Jane M. Gaines, eds. *Collecting Visible Evidence*. Minneapolis: University of Minnesota Press, 1999.

Reynolds, Michael. "Hemingway as Icon." In *Picturing Hemingway*, edited by Frederick Voss, 1–9. Washington, DC: Smithsonian National Portrait Gallery; New Haven, CT: Yale University Press, 1999.

Rhodes, Richard. "Father of the Sexual Revolution: A New Biography of the Man Who Studied Sex the Same Way He Studied Insects." Review of *Alfred C. Kinsey: A Public/Private Life*, by James H. Jones. *New York Times Book Review*, November 2, 1997, 10–11.

Rice, Edward. *Margaret Mead: A Portrait*. New York: Harper and Row, 1979.

Riesman, David. *The Lonely Crowd: A Study of the Changing American Character*. Garden City, NY: Doubleday, 1953.

Robbins, Bruce, ed. *Intellectuals: Academics, Aesthetics, Politics*. Minneapolis: University of Minnesota Press, 1990.

Robinson, Geoffrey. *The Dark Side of Paradise: Political Violence in Bali*. Ithaca, NY: Cornell University Press, 1995.

Robinson, Paul. *The Modernization of Sex: Havelock Ellis, Alfred Kinsey, William Masters, and Virginia Johnson*. New York: Harper and Row, 1976. Reprint, Ithaca, NY: Cornell University Press, 1989.

Rochberg-Halton, Eugene. "Life, Literature, and Sociology in Turn-of-the-Century Chicago." In *Consuming Visions: Accumulation and Display of Goods in America, 1880–1920*, edited by Simon J. Bronner, 311–38. New York: W. W. Norton, 1989.

Rogin, Michael Paul. *Ronald Reagan, The Movie and Other Episodes in Political Demonology*. Berkeley: University of California Press, 1987.

Rollyson, Carl E. *Rebecca West: A Life*. New York: Scribners, 1996.

Rollyson, Carl E., and Lisa Olson Paddock. *Susan Sontag: The Making of an Icon*. New York: W. W. Norton, 2000.

Romano, Marc. *Crossword: One Man's Journey into America's Crossword Obsession*. New York: Broadway Books, 2005.

Romanucci-Ross, Lola. *Mead's Other Manus: Phenomenology of the Encounter*. South Hadley, MA: Bergin and Garvey Publishers, 1985.

Root, Nina J., ed. *Catalog of the American Museum of Natural History Film Archives*. New York: Garland Publishing, 1987.

Rosaldo, Michelle Zimbalist, and Louise Lamphere, eds. *Woman, Culture, and Society*. Stanford, CA: Stanford University Press, 1975.

Roscoe, Paul. Introduction to *The Mountain Arapesh*, by Margaret Mead. New Brunswick, NJ: Transaction Publishers, 2002.

———. "Margaret Mead, Reo Fortune, and Mountain Arapesh Warfare." *American Anthropologist* 105, no. 3 (2003): 581–91.

Rosenberg, Rosalind. *Beyond Separate Spheres: Intellectual Roots of Modern Feminism*. New Haven, CT: Yale University Press, 1982.

———. *Changing the Subject: How the Women of Columbia Shaped the Way We Think about Sex and Politics*. New York: Columbia University Press, 2004.

Routledge, Katherine Pease. *The Mystery of Easter Island: The Story of an Expedition, by Mrs. Scoresby Routledge*. London: Printed for the author by Hazell, Watson and Viney; sold by Sifton, Praed, 1919.

Rouch, Jean, director. *Margaret Mead: A Portrait by a Friend*. Videocassette, color, sound, 28 minutes. New York: American Museum of Natural History, 1978.

Ruoff, Jeffrey. *An American Family: A Televised Life*. Minneapolis: University of Minnesota Press, 2002.

Russell, Bertrand. *Marriage and Morals*. London: George Allen and Unwin, 1929.

Russell, Catherine. *Experimental Ethnography*. Durham, NC: Duke University Press, 1999.

Rydell, Robert W. *All the World's a Fair: Visions of Empire at American International Expositions, 1876–1916*. Chicago: University of Chicago Press, 1984.

Sahlins, Marshall D. "Poor Man, Rich Man, Big-Man, Chief: Political Types in Melanesia and Polynesia." *Comparative Studies in Society and History* 5 (1963): 285–303.

———. *The Use and Abuse of Biology: An Anthropological Critique of Sociobiology.* Ann Arbor: University of Michigan Press, 1976.

Said, Edward, "Representing the Colonized: Anthropology's Interlocutors." *Critical Inquiry* 15, no. 2 (1989): 205–25.

———. *Representations of Intellectuals: The 1993 Reith Lectures.* New York: Vintage, 1994.

Sandall, Roger. *The Culture Cult: Designer Tribalism and Other Essays.* Boulder, CO: Westview Press, 2001.

Sandeen, Eric. *Picturing an Exhibition:* The Family of Man *and 1950s America.* Albuquerque: University of New Mexico Press, 1995.

Sargeant, Winthrop. "Margaret Mead: It's All Anthropology." *New Yorker*, December 30, 1961, 31–34, 36–38, 40–42, 44.

Saunders, Susan. *Margaret Mead: The World Was Her Family.* New York: Penguin, 1987.

Savage, William W., Jr., *Comic Books and America, 1945–1954.* Norman: University of Oklahoma Press, 1990.

Schickel, Richard. *Intimate Strangers: The Culture of Celebrity.* Garden City, NY: Doubleday, 1985.

Schiebinger, Londa. *Has Feminism Changed Science?* Cambridge, MA: Harvard University Press, 1999.

Schneider, David. "The Coming of a Sage to Samoa." *Natural History* (June 1983): 4–10.

Schultz, James R. *The Romance of Small-Town Chautauquas.* Columbia: University of Missouri Press, 2002.

Schwartz, Ted, ed. *Socialization as Cultural Communication: Development of a Theme in the Work of Margaret Mead.* Berkeley: University of California Press. 1976.

Scott, Bonnie Kime. *Refiguring Modernism*, vol. 1, *The Women of 1928.* Bloomington: Indiana University Press, 1995.

Scott, Bonnie Kime, and Mary Lynn Broe, eds. *The Gender of Modernism: A Critical Anthology.* Bloomington: Indiana University Press, 1990.

Scrimshaw, Susan C. M., and Elena Hurtado. *Rapid Assessment Procedures for Nutrition and Primary Health Care: Anthropological Approaches to Improving Programme Effectiveness.* Tokyo: United Nations University; Los Angeles: UCLA Latin American Center Publications, University of California, 1987.

Shankman, Paul. "The History of Samoan Sexual Conduct and the Mead-Freeman Controversy." *American Anthropologist* 98, no. 3 (1996): 555–67.

Shankman, Paul. "Virginity and Veracity: Rereading Historical Sources in the Mead-Freeman Controversy." Unpublished paper presented at the annual meetings of the Association for Social Anthropology in Oceania, Kauai, Hawaii, 2005.

Sheehy, Gail. "She Was a Mentor to Us All." *Newsday*, November 19, 1978.

Showalter, Elaine. *Inventing Herself: Claiming a Feminist Intellectual Heritage*. New York: Scribner, 2001.

Shumway, David. "Academostars." *Minnesota Review* n.s. 52–54 (Fall 2001): 175–84.

———. "The Star System in Literary Studies." *Proceedings of the Modern Language Association* 112 (January 1997): 85–100.

Silver, Brenda R. *Virginia Woolf Icon*. Chicago: University of Chicago Press, 1999.

Silverman, Sydel. "Hortense Powdermaker." In *Women Anthropologists: A Biographical Dictionary*, edited by Ute Gacs et al., 291–96. New York: Greenwood Press, 1988.

Simpson, Jeffrey. *Chautauqua: An American Utopia*. New York: Harry N. Abrams, 1999.

Singer, André, and Leslie Woodhead. *Disappearing World: Television and Anthropology*. London: Boxtree in association with Granada Television, 1988.

Smith, Terry. "Life-Style Modernity: Making Modern America." In *Looking at Life Magazine*, edited by Erika Doss, 25–39. Washington, DC: Smithsonian Institution Press, 2001.

———. *Making the Modern: Industry, Art, and Design in America*. Chicago: University of Chicago Press, 1993.

Snow, C. P. *The Two Cultures and the Scientific Revolution*. New York: Cambridge University Press, 1959.

Sontag, Susan. "The Anthropologist as Hero." In *Against Interpretation and Other Essays*, 68–81. New York: Farrar, Straus, and Giroux, 1963.

Speare, Dorothy. *Dancers in the Dark*. New York: George H. Doran, 1922.

Spigel, Lynn. *Make Room for TV: Television and the Family Ideal in Postwar America*. Chicago: University of Chicago Press, 1992.

Spock, Benjamin. *The Common Sense Book of Baby and Child Care*. New York: Duell, Sloan, and Pearce, 1946.

Stansell, Christine. *American Moderns: Bohemian New York and the Creation of a New Century*. New York: Metropolitan Books, 2000.

Stearns, Harold E., ed. *Civilization in the United States: An Inquiry by Thirty Americans*. New York: Harcourt, Brace, 1922.

Steel, Ronald. *In Love with Night: The American Romance with Robert Kennedy*. New York: Simon and Schuster, 2000.

———. *Walter Lippmann and the American Century*. Boston: Little, Brown, 1980.

Steichen, Edward. *The Family of Man*. New York: The Museum of Modern Art, 1955.

Stein, Robert, ed. *Why Young Mothers Feel Trapped: A* Redbook *Documentary*. Introduction by Margaret Mead. New York: Trident Press, 1965.

Stevenson, Robert Louis. *A Footnote to History: Eight Years of Trouble in Samoa*. London: Cassell, 1892.

———. *In the South Seas: Being an Account of Experiences and Observations in the Marquesas, Tuamotus, and Gilbert Islands in the Course of Two Cruises on the Yacht "Casco" (1888) and the Schooner "Equator" (1889)*. New York: Charles Scribner's Sons, 1896; London: William Heinemann, 1924.

———. *Island Nights' Entertainments: Consisting of The Beach of Falesa, The Bottle Imp, The Isle of Voices*. London: Cassell, 1893.

———. *Vailima Letters: Being Correspondence Addressed by Robert Louis Stevenson to Sidney Colvin, November 1890–October 1894*. London: Methuen, 1895.

Steward, Julian H. *Alfred Kroeber*. New York: Columbia University Press, 1973.

Stewart, David. *The PBS Companion: A History of Public Television*. New York: TV Books, 1999.

Stocking, George W., Jr. "The Ethnographer's Magic: British Anthropology from Tylor to Malinowski." In *The Ethnographer's Magic and Other Essays in the History of Anthropology*. Madison: University of Wisconsin Press, 1992.

———. *Race, Culture, and Evolution: Essays in the History of Anthropology*. New York: Free Press, 1968.

———. *Romantic Motives: Essays on Anthropological Sensibility*. History of Anthropology, vol. 6. Madison: University of Wisconsin Press. 1989.

Stocking, George W., Jr., ed. *A Franz Boas Reader: The Shaping of American Anthropology, 1883–1911*. Chicago: University of Chicago Press, 1974.

———. *Malinowski, Rivers, Benedict, and Others: Essays on Culture and Personality*. Madison: University of Wisconsin Press, 1986.

Sturken, Marita, and Lisa Cartwright. *Practices of Looking: An Introduction to Visual Culture*. New York: Oxford University Press, 2001.

Sullivan, Gerald. *Margaret Mead, Gregory Bateson, and Highland Bali: Fieldwork Photographs of Bayung Gedé, 1936–1939*. Chicago: University of Chicago Press, 1999.

Sussman, Warren. *Culture as History: The Transformation of American Society in the Twentieth Century*. Washington, DC: Smithsonian Institution Press. 2003.

Talbott, Hudson. *We're Back! A Dinosaur's Story*. New York: Crown Publishers, 1987.

Tannen, Deborah. *You Just Don't Understand: Women and Men in Conversation*. New York: William Morrow, 1990.

Tcherkézoff, Serge. *Le mythe occidental de la sexualité polynésienne: Margaret Mead, Derek Freeman et Samoa*. Paris: Presses Universitaires de France, 2001.

Teachout, Terry. *The Skeptic: A Life of H. L. Mencken*. New York: HarperCollins, 2002.

Textor, Robert B. Introduction to *The World Ahead: An Anthropologist Anticipates the Future*, by Margaret Mead, 2–34. The Study of Contemporary Western Cultures, vol. 6. New York and Oxford: Berghahn.

Thurnwald, Richard. Review *of Sex and Temperament in Three Primitive Societies*, by Margaret Mead. *American Anthropologist* n.s. 38, no. 4 (1936): 663–67.

Tiffany, Sharon W. "Contesting the Erotic Zone: Margaret Mead's Fieldwork Photographs of Samoa." Special Issue: Reflections on Pacific Ethnography in the Margaret Mead Centennial, 2001. Edited by Sharon W. Tiffany. *Journal of Pacific Studies* 28, nos. 3/4 (2005): 19–45.

———. "Imagining the South Seas: Margaret Mead's *Coming of Age in Samoa* and the Sexual Politics of Paradise." In *Reading Benedict/Reading Mead: Feminism, Race, and Imperial Visions*, edited by Dolores Janiewski and Lois W. Banner, 155–65. Baltimore: Johns Hopkins University Press, 2004.

———. "Narrative, Voice, and Genre in Margaret Mead's *Coming of Age in Samoa*." Special Issue: The Gang of Four: Gregory Bateson, Ruth Benedict, Reo Fortune, and Margaret Mead in Multiple Contexts. Edited by Gerald Sullivan and Sharon W. Tiffany. *Journal of Pacific Studies*, 2005.

Time. Great People of the 20th Century. New York: Time Books, 1996.

Torgovnick, Marianna. *Gone Primitive: Savage Intellects, Modern Lives*. Chicago: University of Chicago Press, 1990.

Toulmin, Stephen. Introduction to *Continuities in Cultural Evolution*, by Margaret Mead, xi–xxiv. New Brunswick, NJ and London: Transaction Publishers, 1999.

Toumey, Christopher P. *Conjuring Science: Scientific Symbols and Cultural Meaning in American Life*. New Brunswick, NJ: Rutgers University Press, 1996.

Traweek, Sharon. *Beam Times and Lifetimes: The World of High Energy Physicists*. Cambridge, MA: Harvard University Press, 1988.

Trilling, Lionel. "The Kinsey Report." In *An Analysis of the Kinsey Reports on Sexual Behavior in the Human Male and Female*, edited by Donald Porter Geddes, 213–29. New York: Mentor Book; *New American Library*, 1954.

Trouillot, Michel-Rolph. "Anthropology and the Savage Slot: The Poetics and Politics of Otherness." In *Recapturing Anthropology: Working in the Present*, edited by Richard G. Fox, 17–44. Santa Fe, NM: School of American Research Press, 1991.

United States Information Agency. *Reflections: Margaret Mead*. 16 mm, color, sound, 58 minutes. Washington, DC: USIA, 1975.

Urdang, Laurence. *The Timetables of American History.* New York: Simon and Schuster, 1981.

Van Dyke, W. S. *White Shadows in the South Seas*. 1927. Videocassette. Black and white, sound, 85 minutes. Cosmopolitan Productions, 1990.

Van Tilburg, Jo Anne. *Among Stone Giants: The Life of Katherine Routledge and her Remarkable Expedition to Easter Island*. New York: Scribner, 2003.

Vincent, Joan. *Anthropology and Politics: Visions, Traditions, and Trends*. Tucson: University of Arizona Press, 1990.

Visweswaran, Kamala. "Histories of Feminist Ethnography." *Annual Review of Anthropology* 26 (1997): 591–621.

Von Hoffman, Nicholas, and Garry B. Trudeau. *Tales from the Margaret Mead Taproom*. Kansas City, MO: Sheed and Ward, 1976.

Wakin, Eric. *Anthropology Goes to War: Professional Ethics and Counterinsurgency in Thailand*. Madison: University of Wisconsin, Center for Southeast Asian Studies, 1992.

Walker, Nancy A. *Shaping Our Mothers' World: American Women's Magazines*. Jackson: University Press of Mississippi, 2000.

Wallace, Irving. *The Three Sirens, a Novel*. New York: Simon and Schuster, 1963.

Ware, Susan. *It's One O'Clock and Here Is Mary Margaret McBride: A Radio Biography*. New York: New York University Press, 2005.

———. *Letter to the World: Seven Women Who Shaped the American Century*. New York: W. W. Norton, 1998.

———. *Still Missing: Amelia Earhart and the Search for Modern Feminism*. New York: W. W. Norton, 1993.

Wells, H. G. *Experiment in Autobiography: Discoveries and Conclusions of a Very Ordinary Brain (since 1866)*. London: Victor Gollancz, 1934.

Welsch, Robert Lewis, ed. *An American Anthropologist in Melanesia: A. B. Lewis and the Joseph N. Field South Pacific Expedition, 1909–1913*. Honolulu: University of Hawaii Press, 1998.

Wendt, Albert. "Three Faces of Samoa: Mead's, Freeman's and Wendt's." *Pacific Islands Monthly* 54, no. 4 (1983): 10–14, 69.

Wertham, Fredric. *Seduction of the Innocent*. New York: Rinehart, 1954.

West, Anthony. *H. G. Wells, Aspects of a Life*. New York: Random House, 1984.

West, Rebecca. *Black Lamb and Grey Falcon: A Journey through Yugoslavia*. New York: Viking Press, 1941.

———. "Sex and Character among Primitive Societies." Review of *Sex and Temperament in Three Primitive Societies*, by Margaret Mead. *Sunday Times*, January 12, 1936.

White, Geoffrey M., and Lamont Lindstrom. *The Pacific Theater: Island Representations of World War II*. Honolulu: University of Hawaii Press, 1989.

Whiting, Beatrice B., and John W. M. Whiting. *Children in Six Cultures: A Psycho-Cultural Analysis*. Cambridge, MA: Harvard University Press, 1975.

Whitman, Alden. *The Obituary Book*. New York: Stein and Day, 1971.

Wilder-Mott. C., and John H. Weakland, eds. *Rigor and Imagination: Essays from the Legacy of Gregory Bateson*. New York: Praeger, 1981.

Williams, Vernon, Jr. *Rethinking Race: Franz Boas and His Contemporaries*. Lexington: University Press of Kentucky, 1996.

Williamson, David. *Heretic: Based on the Life of Derek Freeman*. Melbourne and New York: Penguin, 1996.

Wills, Garry. *John Wayne: The Politics of Celebrity*. London and Boston: Faber and Faber, 1997.

Wilson, Edward O. *Sociobiology: The New Synthesis*. Cambridge, MA: Belknap Press of Harvard University Press, 1975.

Wilson, Rob, and Arif Dirlik, eds. *Asia/Pacific as Space of Cultural Production*. Durham, NC: Duke University Press, 1995.

Wolfe, Alan. "The Mystique of Betty Friedan." Review of *Betty Friedan and the Making of the Feminine Mystique*, by David Horowitz, and *Betty Friedan, Her Life*, by Joy Hennessee. *Atlantic Monthly*, September 1999, 98–105.

Wolfenstein, Martha, and Nathan Leites. *Movies: A Psychological Study*. New York: Atheneum, 1950.

Worth, Sol. "Margaret Mead and the Shift from 'Visual Anthropology' to the 'Anthropology of Visual Communication.' " In *Studying Visual Communication*, edited by and introduction by Larry P. Gross, 185–99. Philadelphia: University of Pennsylvania Press, 1981.

Yans, Virginia. "On the Political Anatomy of Mead-Bashing, or Rethinking Margaret Mead," in *Reading Benedict/Reading Mead*, edited by Dolores Janiewski and Lois W. Banner, 229–48. Baltimore: Johns Hopkins University Press, 2004.

Yans-McLaughlin, Virginia. "Science, Democracy, and Ethics: Mobilizing Culture and Personality for World War II." In *Malinowski, Rivers, Benedict, and Others: Essays on Culture and Personality*, edited by George Stocking Jr., 184–207. Madison: University of Wisconsin Press, 1986.

Yans-McLaughlin, Virginia, and Alan Berliner. *Margaret Mead: An Observer Observed*. Videocassette, color, sound, 85 minutes. New York: Filmmakers Library, 1995.

Yost, Edna. *American Women of Science*. Rev. ed. Philadelphia and New York: Frederick A. Stokes, 1955.

Young, Michael. *Malinowski: Odyssey of an Anthropologist, 1884–1920*. New Haven, CT: Yale University Press, 2004.

Young, Virginia Heyer. *Ruth Benedict: Beyond Relativity, beyond Pattern*. Lincoln: University of Nebraska Press, 2005.

Zumwalt, Rosemary Levy. *Wealth and Rebellion: Elsie Clews Parsons, Anthropologist and Folklorist*. Urbana: University of Illinois Press, 1992.

INDEX

Note: Page numbers in **bold** indicate illustrations